DICTIONARY OF PAINTING

Dictionary of Painting

BY

MARTIN L. WOLF

With an Introduction

By ERIC PARTRIDGE

PHILOSOPHICAL LIBRARY
NEW YORK

15 East 40th Street, New York

Printed in the United States of America

INTRODUCTION

By Eric Partridge

Many years ago I coined an epigram which has, often defaced, been coming back to me ever since, usually as "of unknown origin." It goes: *The world contains far too many people who have nothing to say—and persist in saying it.* That is a charge which nobody will ever be able to make against this book.

Yet I have a very grave charge to make. Against myself, for having failed to think of the idea. This is decidedly a book I shall constantly use in my lexicographical and other philological work. Still, I shouldn't, after all, complain, for I have providentially been spared the trouble of inciting some publisher to gather a team of experts and of urging him to get on with the job before some other fellow beat him to it. Instead of writing this introduction—an introduction similar to one that I should endeavor to write for some dear friend and, incidentally, extremely able man at his profession or his trade—I should be writing to the Philosophical Library and thanking them for performing a memorable public service and for doing me, personally, such a good turn.

To employ an idiom popularized by Mr. Evelyn Waugh, I feel that there is something "blush-making" in my writing at all about Dictionary of Painting. Don't get me wrong! Although adult and indeed mature, this dictionary contains nothing that would bring a blush to the most maidenly cheek *(Où sont les joues d'antan?)*; yet one hesitates to write intimately about a happy marriage. That is what we have here. A marriage, consummated and fruitful, between imagination and scholarship.

Since, as the old proverb has it, "there goes more to

marriage than four bare legs in a bed," and since what causes marriage to endure is neither passion nor ecstasy but friendship and sympathy, I should like to state what, in this DICTIONARY OF PAINTING, constitutes the true marriage I rejoice to find in it.

Exceedingly few marriages are made in heaven. This is one of the few. The vernal impulses haloing the courtship, the impact of the idea upon the collaborators, were happy; the union as it has existed, the work of the contributors in cooperation with Mr. Wolf and the publisher, has been no less happy; the fruit of the marriage, this book which has resulted, is a lusty yet most attractive child.

But no simile should be worked to death; no metaphor continued to the point of tedium.

Many of the thousands of terms listed in this compendious and comprehensive work do, naturally, appear in such dictionaries as *Webster's New International,* and the big *Oxford English Dictionary*. But here they are defined with an objectivity and an accuracy and a pertinence that are invaluable. Then there are numerous terms that one will find only in specialist volumes; volumes of which the general—even the art-educated—reader has not heard.

Nor will the intelligent layman be subjected to the humiliating experience of being "dazzled with science" and "blinded with learning." One of the beauties of this DICTIONARY OF PAINTING is that all the technical terms inevitably employed are defined within the book. The scholar, the librarian, the curator; the research worker; the practicing artist and the operative artisan; they, too, will be grateful for this DICTIONARY OF PAINTING for it will spare them much wastage of shoe-leather, many fares to this library or that museum or the other art gallery, and innumerable headaches.

I can hardly speak more fairly than that. Nor could I speak more truthfully.

DICTIONARY OF PAINTING

A

ABSORPTION—In *printing,* a term referring to the capacity of a given grade of *paper* to take up and retain *ink* or coloring matter.

ABSTRACTION—In *art,* a design which is non-representational in purpose, is more or less geometric, and which presumes to have at least decorative beauty while possibly having *cultural* meaning and association. It may be derived from *natural* forms, geometric forms, or be entirely the product of *esthetic* ingenuity, invention and imagination, with no reference whatever to nature; it is generally more popular in *painting* than in *sculpture.* In the hands of Picasso, the name became *semi-abstraction,* and after 1910 it was successively called *purism, synchromism, orphism, futurism, dadaism,* and *surrealism* (qq.v.). It is when *abstraction* is carried completely beyond any reference to reality that confusion and lack of communication (and therefore *criticism*) will result.

ABSTRACTION, CREATION GROUP—A group of geometric-abstract *painters* and *sculptors* founded in Paris in the early 1930's led by Piet Mondrian and including Jean Helion. See *geometric style* and *abstraction.*

ABSTRACTIONISM—A term little used in modern *art* language; synonymous with the doctrine of *abstraction.*

ACADEMICISM—As applied to *art* creation and appreciation, in a *classical* period or one in which art is means to an end other than *esthetic,* the term is used as one of approval. It connotes the force of romantic *tradition,* stressing formal relationships rather than vital *expression.*

ACADEMY BOARD—A piece of pasteboard about 1/8th inch thick, having a pale *gray* or *white* ground of lead *pigment* mixed with *oil,* and with various other ingredients. The name probably came from its wide use in *art* schools, where it furnished a cheaper support of *painting* than wooden *panels* or stretched *canvas.* Also known as *canvas board.*

ACADEMY FIGURE—In *painting* and *sculpture,* (1) a reproduced human figure somewhat smaller than one-half life size; (2) a human figure shown in any conventional pose, with importance placed on the artist's ability to compose suitable background and other incidental effects apart from the central figure; (3) a living human *model* so posed as to emphasize the action of the muscles.

ACAROID—A natural *resin* (q.v.) extracted from the XANTHORRHEA tree of Australia; used extensively in the *sizing* of *paper,* manufacture of *wax,* and as a *surface film* applied to *sculpture* and *paintings.* Known also as *accroides gum.*

ACCESSORIES—In painting, a term referring to any objects, figures, etc., not belonging to the principal subject of the picture, but added solely to furnish background.

ACCIDENTAL—In *painting,* a chance effect occurring when *luminous* rays fall on certain objects, by which they are brought into stronger light than otherwise possible, and their *shadows* are consequently of greater *intensity.*

ACCOMMODATION—A correctional process undergone by some artists, designed to adjust the eye for vision at various distances. Monocular *accommodation* adjusts the lens of one eye; binocular, of both eyes.

ACCROIDES GUM—A variety of natural *resin* having a number of uses in the *arts;* known also as *acaroid* (q.v.).

ACETONE—A substance used as a *solvent* for *painters' varnishes,* particularly those derived from *plastics* and synthetic *resins.* It possesses the unusual quality of being miscible with water, *oils,* and most other solvents.

ACHILLES—The leading warrior of the Greek tribal expeditionary force in the siege of Troy. His exploits were a favorite subject of Greek *vase painters* and *gem cutters.* In post-classical *sculpture* he was represented by Thorvaldsen, Dannecker, Bissen, Herter, and Westmacott.

ACID BATH—A term in *etching;* see *biting.*

ACID BLAST—A technique of *etching* line and *half-tone* plates by forcing sprays of acid against the face of the *plate,* instead of simply immersing it in an *acid bath* (see *biting*). This method produces sharper lines and greater depth of etching.

ACINACES—A weapon in the form of a short straight *dagger,* apparently local to the old Medes and Persians, used for direct stabbing rather than for slashing. It is believed to have been worn on the right side, but perhaps only when a longer weapon was carried at the left. Authorities have recognized the *acinaces* in the dagger shown in *sculptures* at Persepolis, and also that shown in the Mithra sacrificial groups.

ACROLITH—In *sculpture,* a *statue* made of two or more materials. The trunk of the person *represented* is generally of *wood,* and the extremities of *stone.* The wooden portion is sometimes covered with drapery or *metal.*

ACROPODIUM—In *sculpture,* any elevated *pedestal* bearing a *statue,* esp. if raised from the substructure on supports of feet; the *plinth* of a statue or other *work* of *art,* if resting on feet. The *acropodium* often forms part of the statue itself.

ACROTERIUM—In *sculpture* and *architecture,* the decorative *statues* or *abstract* designs (e.g., *palmetto*) placed on *pedestal* blocks over the three angles of the *pediment* of a Greek *temple.* On 6th century B.C. structures they were made of *terra cotta;* later examples were invariably of *marble.* From Greek AKROTERION, topmost part.

ACTAEON—A Greek hunter who was slain by *Artemis* when he saw her bathing. The subject became one of great *artistic* interest, and was treated by 5th century (B.C.) *vase* painters of Athens, notably the PAN PAINTER. In modern sculpture, the Manship group in the New York Metropolitan Museum is a spirited *representation* of the scene.

ACTION—In *painting,* a general term applied to the movement of activity of persons or objects within the scene represented.

ADA GROUP—A 9th century *art* school of the *Carolingian*

epoch, emphasizing *decoration* and *illustration* of the famous *Evangeliars* of the period. Named after the Abess Ada who, in about 804, supervised the making of the magnificent *Evangeliar* now in the city library at Trier.

ADJUSTABLE RULER—In *drawing,* a type of ruler which can be bent to any curve desired, holding fast to the position while *pen* or *pencil lines* are drawn; made of *metal,* it forms perfect curves and cannot break in normal use. Not to be confused with the *slide rule,* a rigid device.

ADONIS—The Asiatic lover of *Aphrodite,* slain by a wild boar and mourned bitterly by goddess of love. The myth personifies the death of all the world's vegetation. In *sculpture,* Adonis has been portrayed by Rossi de Vries, Canova and Thornvaldsen.

ADORATION—In *art* and *archæology,* (1) any scene or *representation* depicting the adoration of the infant Jesus by the magi or the shepherds; (2) a representation of the worship of an ancient divinity, of the deified dead, or of a king or emperor (Latin, *adoratio*). Such representations are common in Greek *vase-paintings* and funerary *sculptures* and in Roman *reliefs* and *medals.* The ancient *adoration* is usually characterized by the gesture of raising the right hand with the thumb laid across the index finger.

ADRIANOPLE RED—An *intense* scarlet red *color,* better known as *Turkey red* (q.v.)

ADULTERANT—A term in *painting;* see *extender.*

ADVANCING COLOR—The term denoting a *color* giving the *illusion* of nearness to the receptor. *Red-orange* is one of the *warm colors* (q.v.), and as such it *advances* and reduces the apparent distance from the spectator.

AEGICRANES—In ancient *sculpture,* name given to the *carved* heads of rams and goats, esp. those used as decorative and *symbolic* elements at the *altars* of Greek and Roman *temples.*

AEGINETAN ART—During the 50 years preceding the conquest of Aegina by Athens (457 B.C.), that island was a famed *art* center, its *culture* reaching its zenith with the building of the *Aphaia temple* (500 to 480 B.C.). The work was distinguished by skillful grouping of human figures in *pedimental* decoration, and by lithe, nervously energetic *sculptural* forms. The marbles, depicting scenes from the Trojan War, were discovered in 1811, and constitute one of the finest groups of ancient Greek sculpture extant. They are now at the Glyptothek, Munich.

AEGIS—The name for the defensive *shield* of *Zeus* and the cloak of *Athena.* In Greek *vase* painting and *sculpture,* Athena was generally represented wearing a breast-covering of this kind, decorated with a *Gorgon's head* in the center and serpents on the border.

AERIAL PERSPECTIVE—the term applied to the effects of distance upon the *color* and clarity of objects. The air, especially when hazy, causes far-off objects to appear *bluer, grayer,* less distinct in edges, and with less contrast of light and *shade* than if seen nearby. Beginners tend to ignore such effects, and *paint* the distance of a *picture* too much like the *foreground.* Compare with *linear perspective* (q.v.). See also *illusionism.*

AERUGO—(1) An artificial *bluish-green color* used as a *pigment,* better known as *verdigris* (q.v.). Any substance having the nature of or resembling verdigris is said to be *æruginous.* (2) Copper rust, esp. green copper adhering to old *bronzes.*

AERY—A term frequently used in *art criticism* to denote an ethereal, visionary *quality* in a work.

AFRICAN BRECCIA—A term in *sculpture;* see *mischio marble.*

AGALMA—The Greek word for a piece of *sculpture* of any kind. The meaning was extended through common usage to include a *painting,* especially a *portrait.*

AGARIC—One of the sources of *Chinese ink* and fine black *dye.* It is a species of boletus or fungus which grows in dunghills, and the coloring matter is derived by addition of iron salts.

AGNI—The Vedic god of fire; the most important of Vedic gods, represented entirely in the *color red,* and pictured in *art* as having two heads, each containing a split tongue. The Vedic *language* is closely related to classical Sanskrit, the extinct, *ancient,* literary language of India.

AIRBRUSH—A device used for the mechanical spraying of *paints* and other coloring materials, retouches, *varnishes, surface films,* etc., but employed esp. by *commercial artists* in the creating of designs to be reproduced by the *half-tone* process. Available in a wide variety of sizes and forms, it is generally operated by compressed air forced through a needle point that has been charged with color, etc.; the spray may be regulated to produce numerous *gradations* and effects. Often referred to as *spray gun.*

AIR-DRIED PAPER—A variety of *paper* used in the *arts.* It is dried rapidly while in a continuous web by passing over revolving fans which release superheated air. This is usually done after the surface *sizing* has been applied.

AJAX—A Greek hero in the Trojan War, famous for his great strength and tragic suicide. Canova, the great Italian *sculptor,* included him among his portrayals of historical and mythological subjects.

AKROTERION—See *acroterium.*

ALABASTER—*Marble*-like *gypsum,* usually white, sometimes veined with *red*dish-*brown.* Worked with the same tools used on marble, harder types are employed for the *sculpture* of large figures. The softer variety, pure white and semi-*transparent,* is used in the making of smaller ornamental objects, e.g., *vases,* lamps, *pedestals,* etc.

ALA DE MOSCA—In *sculpture,* a fine variety of *granite* or very hard rock found chiefly in Peru.

A LA GRECQUE—A French term used in referring to any work of *art* done in the Greek style; any object having the character of Greek art, due to strong Grecian influence.

À LA MODE—Pertaining to the current style or trend, particularly with reference to *painting* and to *fashions* in clothes.

ALBANI STONE—In *sculpture* and *architecture,* a prized variety of volcanic rock employed extensively by the Romans prior to the use of *marble;* it is the *peperino* (q.v.) of the Italians.

ALBUM PAINTINGS—A *fad* in the early part of the 20th century prevailed upon many artists to create *paintings* and *graphic prints* in small size, so that they could be mounted in albums. Also known, at the time, as *picture album paintings.* Many excellent and famous *miniature* works of *art* came about in this brief and unusual period, some of which are prized *museum* pieces.

ALCOHOL–As either the pure spirit, or as a distillate of vegetable waste (particularly *wood*) it has a limited use in *art* as a solvent for *resins* and as a general cleaning agent. It is added to some picture *varnishes* as a *fixative* for *drawings.* Its use in the field of art is widening, as new purposes for its fine dissolving properties and volatility are discovered.

ALEMBIC–A *glass* vessel frequently found in the *studios* of 15th century *painters,* the neck of which was bent downward for purposes of distillation. Leonardo da Vinci mentions it many times in his notes as a device he found valuable in the distilling of *turpentine.*

ALEXANDRIA BLUE–In *painting* and *archæology,* the name given to the famous bright blue *pigment* used on wall paintings by the ancient Egyptians. Analysis establishes that it was composed of the silicates of copper and lime. Similar to *Egyptian blue* (q.v.).

ALEXANDRIAN SCULPTURE– Term applied to the excellent representations of ALEXANDER THE GREAT, King of Macedon (356 to 323 B.C.). The court *sculptor* was Lysippus, who succeeded best in portraying Alexander's 'masculine and leonine appearance.' Several *busts* now extant are copies or adaptations of the work of Lysippus, notably the Azara bust in the Louvre and one in the British Museum. More trustworthy representations are perhaps those on Macedonian coins of the period itself. The *sarcophagus* of *Alexander* (q.v.) is probably the most beautiful existing example of the 4th century B.C. *relief sculpture.*

ALEXJEJEVITE–A fine variety of *resin* found only in the Kaluga province of Russia, prized by 18th century Russian artists for its *stability* when used as a *surface film* on *oil paintings* and *statuary.*

ALIZARIN—One of the coloring materials in the *pigment madder;* isolated and synthesized in 1868, it has since replaced the natural *color* of the madder root. It is a deep *crimson* and varies somewhat in *hue* according to manufacture. It is one of the *lake* pigments, being a soluble *dye* precipitated on a base. Like all lake colors, it is highly *transparent.* In its reaction to *light* it is more *stable* than the *natural* madder. A product of *coal-tar,* it is known also as *Turkey red.* See *madder.*

ALKYD RESIN—In *sculpture* and *painting,* a type of *surface film* (q.v.) fast replacing the age-old *drying oils.* Its rapid-drying quality renders it an excellent addition to *varnish* and *enamel;* used also as a *furniture* finish.

ALLA PRIMA—In *painting,* the process of laying on each *pigment* completely at once, i.e., a single application of the pigments rather than several in layers.

ALLEGORY—In *art,* the use of *images* to represent *abstract* concepts and their relations. Proper allegorical use of images is to present them "to stand for" and "instead of" rather than to illustrate or to confirm. Historically, *allegory* is an invention of the ancient Greeks, originating when Greek rationalism began to interpret the ancient mythological figures as embodiments of philosophical truths. It was so firmly established, and so well-received, that subsequent attempts to dislodge it from *art* and *literature,* however strong, failed.

ALMAGRA—In *painting,* a deep red variety of *ochre* originally from Andalusia, Spain, strikingly similar to *Indian red.* Used as a *pigment,* and as an ingredient of the *rouge* used by the *lapidary.*

ALSBACHITE—In *sculpture,* a variegated type of *granite-porphyry* containing large *mica* crystals and red-rose *garnets.*

ALTARPIECE—A decorated screen, *panel,* or series of panels, fixed or movable, placed upon or to the rear of an *altar,* usually *enriched* with *paintings* or *sculpture* in *relief.* While thought to belong to the Christian Church alone, many are found in the wall *carvings* and painted banners at the *shrines* of Buddhist and related faiths. Few are found to have existed prior to the 11th century, the oldest known being that of *San Marco,* Venice, made in the 11th century and subsequently restored. See *triptych* and *polytych.* An *altarpiece* is often referred to as a *retable.* See *iconostasis.*

ALTOGETHER—In *painting* and *sculpture,* the informal term of the *studio* describing the state of complete nudity in which the *model* is posing; usually as 'in the *altogether.*'

ALTO-RELIEVO—*High relief;* a *technique* of *sculpturing* in which the figures stand out in high prominence against the background. As a rule, more than half of the outline of the figure is projected from the background, in measure of depth. See *relief.*

ALUMINA—For *oil painting,* a *glazing* agent when mixed with *lake colors.* Chemically, aluminium oxide, Al_2O_3. Also, the principal constituent of many varieties of *porcelain, pottery, bricks* and *tiles.*

ALUMINUM—In *painting,* sheets of *aluminum* have been used as *panel* supports, mainly in the practice of *restoration.* It is a relatively modern *metal* in any general use, large-scale production having emerged early in the 20th century. As a leaf or powder mixed with a suitable *medium,* it has been applied to the backs and edges of panels as a protective coating. Used in *printing* process of reproduction; see *aluminum powder.*

ALUMINUM POWDER—In *painting,* a powdered form of *aluminum* used in the manufacture of *paints* and *varnishes;* known also as *flake aluminum.*

AMALTHEA—A cornucopia, or horn of plenty, so-called from the name of the goat which suckled *Zeus,* from whose horn flowed whatever the possessor wished. It is *represented* frequently in *painting* and *sculpture.*

AMASSETTE—In ancient and medieval *painting,* a knife-like instrument or scraper made of animal horn, used for piling paint on the *grinding slab* prior to pulverizing with the *muller.* Its use appears to have waned after the mid-16th century.

AMATEUR— One who studies and practices an *art,* e.g., *music, painting, sculpture,* etc., for interest and pleasure, and not as a profession. The training of an *amateur* is generally not thorough, although many notable exceptions are (and have been) known. Nevertheless, the ability of an *amateur* extends far beyond the stage of mere passive appreciation. Those who have an intimate knowledge of the art but do not pursue it professionally are more properly termed *cognoscenti*. Equivalent to the Italian *amatore* or *dilettante,* and to the German *dilettant*.

AMATITO—A fine red *pigment* prepared from *hematite*. Although its 'bite' rendered it popular in *fresco* work at one time, it has since fallen into disfavor.

AMBER—A *yellow* solid mineral having a glassy *luster*. Fine varieties are used in the making of *ornamental* objects and in the fashioning of small trinkets. Dissolved in *linseed oil,* it makes a strong and durable *varnish* of the type used by the 19th century coachmakers. The name is also applied generally to its deep yellow-*brown* color ranging to *red*dish-brown. Originally extracted from a variety of *pine* now extinct, it is a form of *fossil resin* today. Little used because of its high price and scarcity, a successful substitute is *copal gum* (q.v.) Appears to have been used first as a varnish by Jan Van Eyck, Flemish artist.

AMINOFORM—A white crystalline substance used as a hardening agent in the *resins* employed as *surface films* or coatings over *paintings* and *statuary*.

AMMONIA—In *oil painting,* a substance frequently used for general or destructive cleaning, valued because of its alkaline character, usually as ammonium hydroxide. In one form or another, it was an ingredient of cleaning agents for oil paintings since the *Renaissance*.

AMOR—*Cupid*. See *amorino*.

AMORINO—An infant *cupid;* common in Italian 16th century *sculpture* and *painting*.

AMYL ACETATE—A substance widely used in the *arts* as a solvent for *synthetic resins* which are growing in popularity as *surface film* materials for *oil paintings,* pieces of *sculpture,* and other works of art requiring *coating*. It is distinguished by its sweet, penetrating odor which gives it the common name, *banana oil*.

AMYL FORMATE—A colorless liquid having a variety of applications in the *arts.* Miscible with *oils,* it is a valued ingredient in the manufacture of *surface films* and coatings for *paintings* and pieces of *sculpture.* Used also in the making of *celluloid* substitutes and as a *paint* solvent.

ANAGLYPTA—In *sculpture,* a general term applied to any type of chiseling or *carving* executed in *relief;* anything wrought in *low relief.*

ANAGLYPTOGRAPH—A device for producing *drawings* or *etchings* on a flat surface, but having the appearance of *relief* work; also, any *engraving* made by this *technique.* The *art* or process itself is known as *anaglyptography.*

ANALOGOUS COLORS—In *painting,* the term applied to certain groups of *colors* so closely related in their *shadings* and *gradations* that they can be mistaken for each other. Prominent among them is the series *blue,* blue-green, and *green.*

ANALYTICAL CUBISM—A critical term applied to *cubism* (q.v.).

ANAMORPHOSIS— A method of *drawing* which results in a distorted *image* of the object represented when it is viewed directly or nearly so, but a natural image when it is viewed from a certain point, is reflected by a curved mirror, or is seen through a polyhedron. The direct view is totally lacking in *perspective.*

ANCIENT—Of a time long past, particularly before the demise of the Western Roman Empire in 476 A.D.; dating from a remote period or having great age. The period in *art* and history immediately preceding the *Middle Ages* (q.v.). See also *antique.*

ANDROSPHINX—In Egyptian *archæology* and *sculpture,* a variety of *sphinx* having the head of a man, as distinguished from the *criosphinx* which has the head of a goat, and the *hieracosphinx,* the hawk-headed type.

ANGLE WORM LINES—In Chinese *art,* a *painting* technique employed in the representation of garments in portraiture, making use of a *vertical brush* full of heavy *ink.* The brush point is started in the direction opposite to the course of the stroke, and the termination is similarly handled with a return movement intended to give the desired finish to the edges.

ANGULAR PERSPECTIVE DRAWING—See *two-point drawing.*

ANILINE COLORS— The term applied to the numerous *colors* produced from coal-tar processes; e.g., *aniline violet* (q.v.).

ANILINE RED—An *intense,* brilliant red-violet *color,* better known on the artist's *palette* as *magenta* (q.v.).

ANILINE VIOLET—A *reddish violet* dye, famed as the first organic *dye* to be manufactured synthetically.

ANIMAL BLACK—A carbon *pigment* used in *painting* and *drawing,* prepared by a process of destructive distillation of degreased animal bones. Known also as *animal charcoal* and *bone black.*

ANTAEUS—In Greek mythology, frequently represented in *art,* a giant of invincible strength as long as he remained close to his mother, *Ge* (earth). He was overcome by Heracles, who tore him from the earth and crushed him in the air. *Heracles* is also the famed *Hercules* of mythology.

ANTIC WORK—In *art* generally, any composition consisting of fantastic *figures* of men, animals, foliage and flowers, all incongruously combined or run together; any fantastic, *grotesque,* or fanciful figure. The term is applied to certain ancient *sculptures* etc., and to such figures as Raphael's *arabesques;* in *architecture,* to figures of *griffins, sphinxes, centaurs,* etc., introduced as ornamental features.

ANTIMONY PIGMENTS—The best known, historically, is *Naples yellow,* its *color* running from an *orange* to a pale, almost *green-yellow.* As a glaze in ceramics, it has been found in the ruins of Babylonia and Assyria; Egyptian *glass* of the 19th dynasty is known to have contained this lead antimoniate. A few modern *paints* are derived from it. One is antimony oxide, a *white pigment* used industrially, but not introduced to the artist's *palette.* See *massicot* and *Naples yellow.*

ANTIQUE— (1) *Ancient;* old; of actual antiquity. In this sense, the term refers to the ages of flourishing *art* in

Greece and Rome, preceding the *Middle Ages* (q.v.), known as the period of *classical antiquity.* (2) Any object of great age; specifically, a term applied to the remains of ancient art, as *vases, paintings, statues,* pieces of *furniture,* and the like. The word has been corrupted to mean any object of art currently out of style.

ANTIQUE YELLOW—A term in *sculpture;* see *giallo antico.*

ANTIQUITY—See *antique.*

ANTWERP BLUE—The first *blue* pigment made synthetically on a large scale, better known as *Prussian blue* (q.v.).

ANTWERP SCHOOL—An *art* school at Antwerp developed between 1480 and 1505 by a group of *painters* who came from Cologne, Westphalia, the lower Rhine, and Bruges. It succeeded Bruges as the center of Flemish *art,* Among the artists who practiced there were Massys, Mabuse, Patinir, Bles, Breughel, Moro, Rubens, Van Dyck, Snyders, Seghers, and many others.

ANUBIS—In Egyptian archæology, a god entrusted with the care of those entombed, conducting their spirits outward. Represented in the *arts,* esp. *painting* and *sculpture,* as a human with the head of a jackal, holding a staff in his left hand. With a view toward bringing him as close to the dead as possible, the *carvings,* etc., were most frequently executed on the *tombs* containing the *mummies.*

APHAIA—See *Aeginetan Art.*

APHRODITE—The Greek and Roman goddess of love and beauty; in Latin, *Venus.* She was the favorite subject of Greek *sculptors* and *vase* painters; *represented* in the various *visual arts* by such creators as Botticelli, Bellini, Raphael, Correggio, Giorgione, Rubens, Sansovino, Maillol, and Manship, among numerous others, often accompanied by her son, *Eros* (Cupid). See *Adonis.*

APIS—In Egyptian *archæology,* the name given to any one of the embalmed bodies of bulls discovered in the Apis cemetery, belonging to the period from the Late Empire until the Ptolemies. *Apis* was the *bull-god* of the Egyptians, represented in *paintings* as black wth distinctive white markings, worshipped as the body of the god Ptah. When a bull-god died it was buried with elaborate *ceremonies.*

APOLLO—One of the most important of Greek and Roman gods, the divinity of light and healing, *music,* athletics, and prophecy. He was a famous subject of Greek artists, who *represented* him either as a vigorous young athlete or in more *lyric* fashion as a graceful musician, leader of muses. Among the artists portraying him were Praxiteles, Raphael, Giorgione, Sansovino, Bernini, Thorvaldsen, Flaxman, Michelangelo, Barye, Rodin, and Bourdelle. *Apollo's* chief *attributes* were the *lyre, bow,* and *laurel wreath.*

APOLLONIAN AND DIONYSIAN—A distinction made by Nietzsche between the two methods of artistic self-revelation in nature, *Apollonian* being the *art* world of dreams, and *Dionysian,* that of drunkenness; or, reality on the one hand and chaos on the other. Accordingly, the human artist is to be regarded as an imitator of the two, and may produce either type. Only the tragedian, however, combines the two. Nietzsche regarded *sculpture, epic poetry,* and *painting* as *Apollonian arts,* and *music, dramatics, lyric poetry,* and *dancing* as *Dionysian.* Set forth in great detail in Nietzsche's THE BIRTH OF TRAGEDY.

APOTHEOSIS—The act of divine glorification, or deification, elevating man to the status of immortal. Introduced into *art* by the Romans in connection with emperor worship; revived in 16th century Italy and in 17th century France as a metaphorical celebration of the absolute prince. Spread from France throughout Europe.

APOTROPAIC EYES—In Greek *art,* a human eye with lids and eyebrow painted on art objects, especially *vases* and prows of ships, to ward off evil spirits. See *Gorgon's head.*

APOTROPAIC IMAGERY—Any *abstract* or representational configuration designed to ward off evil influences and frighten ghosts away. Often takes the form of human and animal faces, particularly their staring eyes (relation to hypnotism). The entire practice, universal in all primitive *art,* is based on the assumption that an *image* has the power of the thing it *represents,* and that demons are best defeated by their own likenesses. In Greek art, the eye alone was used for this purpose. See *apotropaic eyes.*

APOXYOMENOS—From the Greek, meaning to "scrape off." The name of a *statue* in the Vatican, presumed to be a copy of the famous piece of work by the Greek *sculptor* Lyssipus, representing a young athlete in the process of scraping himself with a *xystris,* or *strigil,* after a gladitorial contest. This statue is often used as an example to illustrate the change of style in *sculpture* at the beginning of the *Hellenistic* epoch.

APPUIE-MAIN—In *painting,* a lightweight rod of *wood,* about four feet long, held in the *palette* hand of the artist in the execution of fine work. A soft *leather*-covered ball at one end is placed against the *easel* or the picture itself, and on it the painter rests his working hand. See *mahlstick.*

APRISMO—An anti-foreign, pro-Indian social movement founded by Torre of Peru early in the 1920's. It exerted a strong influence on the *art* and *literature* of the predominantly Indian countries of So. America, chiefly Bolivia, Ecuador and Peru. (Fr. APRA—ALIANZA POPULAR REVOLUCIONARIA AMERICANA.)

APSARAS—In Hindu mythology, a divine water nymph, or dancer of the heaven of Indra. Frequently *represented* in *art,* showing the nymph dancing at a stream or waterfall. Loosely, any representation of an angel in *painting* or *sculpture.*

AQUA FORTIS—The colorless, highly corrosive liquid known chemically as nitric acid (HNO^3) ; used extensively in the *arts* for dissolving metals, esp. in *etching* as the *mordant* in the *biting* operation.

AQUARELLE—In *painting,* the term applied to a *water-color* work, esp. one whose colors exhibit a high degree of *transparency.*

AQUARESIN—A substance having a wide variety of uses in the *arts.* Odorless, non-drying, and water-white, it is a viscious liquid employed successfully to prevent the caking of *pigments* while in water suspension (important in

Chinese *painting,* most colors being kept under water until used). It is also a prized ingredient in *glues, gums* and *resins,* functioning as a plasticizer, and is important in the manufacture of *lake* pigments. Chemically it is a glycol bori-borate, *aquaresin* being a trade name.

AQUATINT—In *plate-etching,* an intaglio process of *biting tones,* instead of lines, into the plate, thereby producing rich, deep, velvety, dark tones, as well as delicate transparent *tints.* In this process, as distinguished from the usual methods of etching, the *ground* placed on the *plate* to protect it from the acid does not cover the plate completely. Instead, a *resin*ous dust covers specified areas only, by settling on them. Rarely used by itself, *aquatint* is often combined with *soft ground etching, drypoint, pen process,* and other *intaglio* media.

AQUATINT MEZZOTINT—In *etching,* a *plate* prepared by the *biting* of a solid *tone* of *aquatint.* The *design* is subjected to the action of a *scraper* and a *burnisher,* employing the mezzotint method, the result being quite similar to a *mezzotint.*

AQUATINT PEN PROCESS—A method of making *aquatints* having the *quality* of a *pen* or *brush line.* See *pen process.*

ARABESQUE—In *painting* and *sculpture, mural* or surface *decoration* in *color* or *low relief* composed of flowing lines and *patterns* of flowers, leaves, branches and *scroll*work fancifully intertwined. The term is not of Arabic origin, but was inherited by *Renaissance* artists from Greco-Roman work found in abundance and high *quality* on the walls of numerous *Pompeiian* villas. *Arabesque* is extended in common usage to include any decorative work of capricious nature, containing arbitrarily intertwined foilage, tendrils, flowers and scrollwork, and in addition, there may be introduced, into the same work, human figures, birds, beasts, fishes, reptiles, insects, and bits of fantastic edifices. This is also known as the *grottesque* (not *grotesque)* system of decoration. Today, any fantastic work based on flowing lines may be called *Arabesque.* Moorish and Arabic art work is known as *mauresque.*

ARALU—In Babylonian mythology, the gloomy abode of the dead, frequently represented in *paintings* characterized by dark *colors* showing frightening caves and misshapen animals. Each cave was entered through a hole in the earth guarded by seven doors, all persons gaining entrance at death, none ever returning. They led a semi-conscious existence and lived on dust, and could give oracles to people on earth, hence the alternate name *Shualu* (signifying 'to ask'), which appears as *Sheol* in the OLD TESTAMENT. Referred to also under the names *Ekur* and *Kigallu.*

ARAPAHO—That tribe comprising many of the Plains Indians of the mid-west United States which attained the highest *culture* in the *arts.* At their climax in the 19th century, they produced an amazingly fine grade of *pottery, weaving* and basketry, in addition to bead and feather work, *weapon-carving* and *painting.* See *gross ventre.*

ARCHAIC—A term of frequent misapplication in the *arts.* The *archaic* is not simply the quality of rudeness or of being *primitive,* but rather a rudeness and imperfection of embryonic character, implying the promise of future advance. Work that is merely barbarous is not properly *archaic.* In an art of sufficient force to have any development the *archaic* survives the first rude attempts of a people to arrive at graphic representation, and exhibits a manifest sincerity and striving to attain truth, until finally the *archaic* quality disappears little by little as truth is reached in the great art schools, such as those of Greece and of the *Renaissance painters,* or until art sinks into lifeless conventionalism before reaching truth, as in the *sculpture* of Egypt and Mesopotamia.

ARCHAIC GREEK—Greek *sculpture* from its beginning in the 6th century B.C. up to about 480 B.C., termed *archaic* because of the sculptors' technical inexperience, and because of the influence of Asia Minor and Egypt. Unable to portray the human form realistically, and because they were novices in the mastery of their limited tools, their work was considered poor. Nevertheless, they exhibited a keen delight in elements of formal *designs,* and fresh, buoyant vitality in their pioneer experiments in representing human and animal forms. Examples of this "free" sculpture are reminiscent of Egyptian work in their rigidity of pose, the figures standing without any twist of the body to disturb the perfect median symmetry, and the torso muscles patterned in regular geometric *design*. Winsomeness and charm characterized facial expression, but there was no strength, detail, or attraction.

ARCHAISTIC GREEK—A reaction in favor of simplicity and formality of design in 6th century Greece, following the period of sensuous, realistic and dramatic Hellenistic *sculpture*. The *statues* emerged with severely stylized faces and drapery (see *archaic Greek*). The resemblance to archaic was only superficial; the garments were mechanically similar, but hard and dry, lacking the subtlety of finish which early Greek sculptors lovingly worked out with their *emery stones*. The faces were monotonously regular, with poor eye and mouth work. The result was an arid antiquarianism. See *archaic Greek*.

ARCHITECTURAL SCULPTURE—In the greatest periods of *architecture* and *sculpture*, the two *arts* have worked in intimate association with each other, sculpture indicating the social and historical purposes of buildings, helping to suggest functional relationships, and enriching the surface; architecture giving its sister art increased dignity and power by virtue of the alliance. Such cooperation is natural, for both arts use similar materials and organize them into three-dimensional *designs*. To be successful, however, it demands the closest sympathy, understanding and collaboration between *architect* and *sculptor*, both adapting themselves to the demands of physical surroundings, function, and *esthetic* construction.

ARES—The Greek and Roman god of war, known best by the Latin name, *Mars*. Popular in *classical literature* and *art*, some famous *statues* represent him clad in armor and usually seated in a nonchalant pose, as on the *Parthenon frieze* and in the LUDOVISI *Ares*. In post-classical *sculpture* he has been done by Coustou II, Thorvaldsen, and Dannecker. Iannelli's *Mars* on the Adler Planetarium, Chicago, realizes best of all the sterner quality of the god of war.

ARGILLA—Decomposed *granite* rock used in the making of the finest *porcelains* in the world. Better known as *kaolin,* it is used also as a *ground* material for *painters* and *sculptors,* and as a wash over *clay* walls in the Far East. In recent times it has been employed successfully in the making of the *zinc* and *titanium oxide* pigments, in wall-paper *printing,* in the making of *resin* emulsion *paints,* and in the production of certain *inks.*

ARGILLITES—*Carvings* of animate and inanimate forms by the Indians of western Canada, first appearing in 1820. Although produced chiefly for sale to the whites, these carvings are impresive both in *sculptural design* and vitality of *expression.*

ARGIVE SCHOOL—A school of Greek *sculpture* at Argos, famous for its athletic tradition and canon of masculine proportions. Earliest examples are the 6th century B.C. twin *kouroi* at Delphia, signed by Polymedes (or Agamedes) ; these are figures of robust youths standing stiffly in a symmetrically frontal position (see *archaistic Greek*) . The greatest *Argive sculptor* was Polyclitus (450-420 B.C.) whose bronze *statues* of athletes were made according to his own system of ideal proportion known as the *canon.*

ARIADNE—The Cretan princess who made it possible for *Theseus* to slay the Minotaur and escape from the labyrinth. While going to Athens, he deserted her on the island of Naxos, where she was comforted by *Dionysus.* The scene is best known in *art* by the *paintings* of Titian and Tintoretto, *representing* Dionysus blithely approaching to console the forlorn *Ariadne.*

ARISTION—A *stele* in the National Museum, Athens, dating about 510 B.C., representing a warrior standing in *profile. Archaic Greek* in rigid pose and *patterned* detail, it has the crispness and clarity of *design* characteristic of its period. Traces of the original *color* remain—*red* on the background and *blue* on the *cuirass.* See *archaic Greek* and *stele.*

ARMATURE—A skeleton or framework upon which *sculpture* may be modeled. In small works it is usually made of stiff wire; for heavy pieces, wire mesh, iron pipe, etc., can be used with success. Any frame of metal or *wood* serving as the support for the *clay* of a *statue* while the sculptor models it. Many *armatures* are prepared commercially, and are available in the form of animals or human figures in various positions, ready for application of the clay.

ARMENIAN BLUE—A fine *pigment* used by the ancients. Although its precise composition is unknown, most authorities believe it to have been a product of native *ultramarine.*

ARMENIAN BOLE—A variety of *clay* formerly obtainable only in Armenia, but more recently available in various parts of Europe. It is *pink* in *color,* soft and unctuous to the touch, and has been used as a *pigment* in many *techniques.*

ARM PALETTE—A variety of *palette* having the customary *thumb hole,* with the added feature of a large cut-out allowing it to be supported by the arms. Balance is believed better, and it relieves the thumb-stain. The burden may be shared by combined arm and thumb support.

ARRICCIO—In *fresco painting,* the term applied to the first rough coat of *plaster* used in the making of the *ground.* It is the thickest and coarsest layer used.

ART—The skill, *technique,* or manipulation which is organized and communicable, and is *culturally* transmitted. It is the means by which the creating *artist,* through his work, is united with a receptive audience. Practical or applied arts are distinguished from the *fine arts* (*dance, drama, poetry, architecture, painting, sculpture, music*) which have in common the extension of human experience through the sharing of imagination and feeling. *Art* is distinct from games, ritual, etc., by virtue of its *esthetic* objectives.

ART CRITICISM—Basically, a judgment of the *esthetic* value of a work of *art* in accordance with some standard or criterion of esthetic acceptance, or in accordance with some logical method of reaching an esthetic evaluation. In another sense, *art criticism* is equated with the personal expression of the critic's appreciation of, or reaction to, a work of art. This latter is often called *expressionistic* or *impressionistic criticism.*

ART D'AVANT-GARDE—A phrase loosely descriptive of various French movements (e.g., *Futurism, Imagism* and *Surrealism*) between 1910 and 1930, reacting violently against conventional *techniques* and materials in the *arts,* and searching for the new (French, "Art of the Vanguard.") See *bohemian.*

ARTEMIS—Same as the Latin *Diana,* the sister of *Apollo,* virgin huntress, protector of maidens and matrons, and goddess of the moon. Her *attributes* were the bow, deer, hound, and crescent moon. In *art* she has been *represented* as a sturdy, athletic young woman engaged in the hunt. As such, she appears in Greek and Roman *sculpture,* and later sculptors, including Goujon, St. Gaudens, Huntington, Miles, and Manship continued the tradition. Excellent *oil paintings* of *Artemis* were executed by Coreggio and Boucher. See *Actaeon.*

ARTIST—One who is skilled in the practice of a *fine art* in which *creative activity* is acompanied by originality, *imagination* and *esthetic* judgment. Differs from *artisan* in point of creativeness.

ARTIST'S MODEL—See *model.*

ART NOUVEU—A style of *art* which flourished between 1890 and 1905 in France, Belgium, Germany and Austria, and more or less sporadically in England, Spain, Italy, and the U.S.A. The name is accidental, having come from the fact that the art dealer (S. Bing) who carried examples of the work called his gallery *Art Nouveau.* The style was given many local names; in France it was *yachting style;* in Germany, *Jugendstil;* in Italy, *stile liberty.* In Belgium, the art was associated with a group called *Les XXs,* and later, *La Libre Esthetique;* in Vienna its proponents were called the *Sezzessionists.* The movement found its expression in *architecture, painting, sculpture,* the *graphic arts, furniture, stained glass, textiles, silver ceramics,* and *jewelry.* Its leaders sought to break with old traditions; their watchwords were spontaneity, *naturalism,* simplicity, and good craftsmanship. Specifically, they urged the use of new materials (*cement,* iron, steel, and *glass*) in construction, with all work characterized by a *motif* of frankness. Many great artists, including Whistler, Thayer, and Abbey emerged from this school.

ART RESTORATION—See *restoration.*

ARUNDEL MARBLES—The famous group of ancient Greek *sculptures* and inscriptions collected by Thomas Howard, 2nd Earl of Arundel, in the 17th century, presented to the *Ashmolean Museum* of Oxford University. Included is the priceless *Parian Chronicle,* an inscription recording events in Greek history.

ASHANTI—An artistic Negro tribe on the African Gold Coast, famed for the making of small *brass* weights used in measuring *gold* dust. These weights, which are miniature *sculptures* translated into permanent material through the *lost wax process,* are given many different and curious forms, illustrating *proverbs* and folk tales. This *art* reached its highest development in the 17th century. The *Ashanti* also made some excellent *wood carvings* in the form of ornate stools and maternity fetishes, along with other fine sculptures in brass.

ASHCAN SCHOOLS—In *painting,* the contemptuous name applied to a movement originating in Philadelphia in the early 20th century. The group, started by a number of well-known American artists (including Sloane, Luks, and Schinn) sought to perpetuate the local scenes of their endeavors on *canvas,* never wandering far from home in search of a subject.

ASHMOLEAN MUSEUM—A *museum* that is a part of Oxford University, containing one of the largest and most valuable collections of ancient Greek *sculpture* in the world. Included is the famous group of *Arundel Marbles,* one item of which is the priceless *Parian Chronicle.*

ASH ULTRAMARINE—In *painting,* a *pigment* consisting of the residue of *lapis lazuli* (q.v.) after removal of the *ultramarine.* It *resembles the ultramarine,* but has a *tinge* of *red* and appears to have been diluted with white. *Ash ultramarine.* It resembles the *ultramarine,* but has a *tinge* for flesh and sky work.

ASPHALTUM—In *painting,* one of the oldest known *pigments.* A tarry compound, it was an important item in the Egyptian process of *mummification.* It is a neutral *brown,* and since it is essentially a liquid it dissolves to some extent in the *oil medium.* As a glazing material, it was much favored for this reason, and because of its warm, *neutral tone.* As an oil *paint,* however, it never becomes thoroughly dry and it is always subject to further softening from heat. It tends to *crawl* and flow like tar in a heavy *film* and has been the cause of much of the breaking and *crackling* found in dark passages of oil paintings since the 17th century, the period of its greatest use. In *printing,* it is used in many photo-mechanical *engraving* processes. In *etching,* it is used in *stopping out* or covering certain parts of the *plate* in order to prevent the acid from *biting* at those points. Known also as *bitumen;* see *mummy pigment* and *mummification.*

ASSYRIAN ART—One of the later branches of Mesopotamian *art,* flourishing between 750 and 612 B.C., parallel to the later Babylonian. Its most characteristic manifestation is found in the lavish wall *sculptures* executed in *low relief.* In its first period it displayed great vigor and truth in its interpretation of nature, esp. in the presentation of animal forms; it later suffered a decline from which it never recovered. Its human figures never have the life and force of its animals, but are heavy and conventional. It is marked by unusual minuteness of detail, with ornaments, texture of *fabrics,* etc., being carefully rendered. In *metalwork* of all kinds, the Assyrian craftsmen took high rank, and they excelled also in *gem engraving.*

ASYMMETRY—Asymmetry in *art* does not mean simply lack *of symmetry,* and it is not, therefore, the negating antonym of symmetry. It means that a symmetrical arrangement is specifically avoided for certain artistic reasons. Each artist has his own concept of perfection, and to many, *asymmetry* is the ideal. The definition, then, is not "wanting in symmetry," but rather "having no symmetry," or posessing no plane, line or point as a center of duality. See *opposition, contrapposto* (in *sculpture*) and *facial asymmetry*.

ATELIER—An artist's *studio;* a workshop.

ATHENA—(Latin *Minerva*) The goddess of administration, sagacity, warfare, statesmanship, and of the women's *arts,* especially *weaving*. She was the patron goddess and *eponymous* heroine of Athens, her *attributes* including the owl, *aegis,* olive, and suit of armor. She was often pictured on Greek *vases* fighting the giants or sponsoring *Theseus,* the hero of Athens. In *sculpture* she was usually *represented* as a warrior. The most famous *statue* depicting her was Phidias' great *chryselephantine* figure in the *Parthenon.* Phydias' *Lemnian Athena* was of a more gracious type. Roman *Minervas* were colder in character. In later European and American sculpture she was represented by Cellini Sansovino, Permoser, Thorvaldsen, and Sheldon.

ATLAS—One of the Titans, whose duty it was to bear the world on his shoulders. The most famous *classical* illustration is a *metope* at Olympia, which pictures him offering the apple of the Hesperides to *Heracles.* In modern *art* he is shown on the cover of almost every book of maps (or *atlas,* from his name), and he has been represented by Lee Lawrie in a mammoth *bronze statue* at Radio City, New York.

ATMOSPHERIC—In *painting and water-color* work, a term applied to such *colors* as sky-blue and *azure* which give an impression of air and open space.

AUREOLE—A *halo* or soft, misted light emanating from or surrounding a sacred figure, indicating divine *attribute.* Also known as *shekinah.* It is not to be confused with the *halo* or *nimbus,* which surrounds only the head of the figure with light. The *aureole* surrounds the entire figure. When oval-shaped, it is known as a *mandorla.* In post-medieval *art* the *aureole* is comparatively rare, although it was used widely in religious *art* prior to that time. Sometimes referred to as *gloriole.*

AUREOLIN—In *oil painting,* a *pigment* of fine *yellow* color made from *cobalt.* Belongs to the large group known as *yellow pigments;* see also *cobalt pigments.*

AUTOMATISM—In *art,* the principle of creation without the interference of thought, practiced, e.g., by Gertrude Stein. As a theory, a *mechanistic* transformation of the concept of the divine afflatus as the source of *inspiration.* It constitutes a deliberately sought method of procedure in *surrealism* (q.v.). Practically (esp. in surrealist *painting),* it is the unfettered stroke of *brush* or *pencil,* with no direction, will, or control exercised by the conscious mind.

AXE CUTS—In Chinese *painting,* a brush stroke technique giving the effect of the incisions made by a small axe. The *brush* is dragged sideward, producing a wide ragged stroke; used chiefly to represent faulted angular rocks in *landscape* work. Each ridge is outlined in black. Compare with *hogback* (Q.V.).

AXONOMETRIC PROJECTION—A geometrical *drawing* the purpose of which is to show an object in three dimensions. The plan is set up in true *representation,* turned to a convenient angle, with verticals projecting from it to scale. In this process, all dimensions on a horizontal plane and all verticals are in precise proportion. However, diagonals and curves on a vertical plane are somewhat distorted. See *isometric projection.*

AYR STONE—In *sculpture,* a very fine-grained stone valued for its *marble*-polishing qualities; gives an excellent surface to *metalwork* as well. Known also as *Scotch stone* and *water of ayr.*

AZURE—A fine *pigment* of *blue,* known also as *smalt,* best described as the *color* of the clear sky; the *hue* of *lapis lazuli.* It is actually a form of *glass,* colored with oxide of *cobalt* and ground to an impalpable powder. Well-suited for *painting* upon *porcelain* and for the manufacture of blue glass.

AZURITE—Common among the *blue pigments* of the *Middle Ages* and the *Renaissance,* this is now available only as a pure mineral. The blue *stone* was ground and purified, but retained something of its crystalline *character.* Because of the extensive labor required in its preparation, it went out of use when artificially prepared blues were devised. See *malachite* and *shih ch'ing.*

B

BA—In ancient Egyptian religion and *art,* (1) the soul, which could return to the body so long as the body had not been destroyed; hence the great care taken in *mummification* and the use of the *canopic jars;* (2) the name of the sacred goat worshipped at Mendes, frequently found in *archaeological sculpture* and *painting.*

BABA YAGA—In Slavonic *mythology,* a supernatural female hag represented in *literature* and *painting* as a fiend who devours or petrifies her victims, rides aloft in a mortar urged on with a pestle, and sweeps away all traces of her flight with a broom.

BABUL GUM—A whitish substance in powder or *amorphous* form, used chiefly as an ingredient in *surface films* and coatings applied to *paintings* and *statuary;* employed also in the making of *inks,* in *textile printing,* and as a substitute for *arabic gum.*

BABYLONIAN ART—A subdivision of *Mesopotamian Art,* flourishing prior to the *Assyrian,* and reaching the heights of its artistry in the 9th century B.C. Its *architecture,* like that of Assyria, featured the sundried brick, and was characterized by thick walls and massive forms, necessitated by the *friable* quality of this material. Since *stone* was scarce, the chief form of decoration was *painting* on *plaster* surfaces for interiors, with brilliantly *enameled tiles* sometimes forming huge exterior ornamentation. *Sculpture* was scanty, but the *art* of the *lapidary* produced engraved *gems* and *seals* of considerable merit; *pottery, metalwork* and textile *fabrics* likewise attained remarkable perfection.

BACCHANALS—The ecstatic dancing women who attended *Dionysus,* the Greek vegetation god. Their worship was a favorite subject of many Greek *sculptors* and *vase* painters. In neo-Attic *reliefs* the representation was popular, as it was on *Arretine pottery,* giving *artists* the opportunity to create groups of lovely dancers swinging about in joyous abandon. Titian and Tintoretto used the *theme* in their *paintings* of Dionysus discovering the deserted *Ariadne* on the island of Naxos. These dancing women were also known as *Bacchantes.*

BACCHANTES—See *Bacchanals.*

BACCHUS—See *Dionysus.*

BACK-PAINTING—A technique of applying *varnish* colors to *mezzotint* prints that have been affixed to *glass* in such manner as to give the effect that they were *painted* directly on the glass.

BALANCE—Originally, as applied to *art,* a rather broad, vague term denoting some kind of coordination between parts. In *criticism,* the word indicates that proper respect has been paid to all the elements used, all aspects having received due attention. A work is *unbalanced* when some parts manifest false emphasis. This distortion may involve a sacrifice of *form* to *meaning* or vice versa. See *proportion.*

BALSAM—*Varnish* material, a few varieties of which come under this heading, including *Copaiba varnish* (frequently an ingredient in varnish mixtures), *Canada balsam, Venice turpentine,* and *Strasbourg turpentine.* Generally, *balsam* is the *resinous* exudate from coniferous trees. The volatile *oils* (as *turpentine*) are derived from it by distillation, and the residue is a crude *resin.* See *oleoresin* and *Chinese varnish.*

BAMBOCCIADE—In Italian *art,* any painting representing a *grotesque* scene from common or rustic life. Sometimes spelled *bambochade.*

BAMBOO—An East Indian plant of the *reed* variety, often growing to heights exceeding 100 feet in sectional, jointed parts. In Chinese *art,* it is used in making the paper ground for *painting* and *calligraphy* (see *chih* and *hsuan chih*) and as a handle for the artist's *brush* (see *pi*). Most *mahlsticks* (q.v.) are made of *bamboo,* because of the light weight required.

BAMBOO LINE—In Chinese *painting,* a brush stroke technique similar to the *liu yeh miao,* but with the center portions wider and rounder, and the taper proportionately longer. The *brush* is slanted in the manner of the side *brush technique,* to make use of the side of the tip. See *liu yeh miao.*

BAMIYAN BUDDHA—In *archaeology,* name given to an enormous *statue* of Buddha, 130 feet in height, *carved* into a cliff of solid *breccia,* almost *in the round.* Showing excellent proportion and *linear* work, it is believed to have been executed by *ancient tribes* who fled persecution in India and settled in Afghanistan, in the desert regions beyond Khyber Pass, site of this great piece of *sculpture.*

BANANA OIL—The sweet oil of *amyl acetate,* used widely as a solvent for *resins* in the making of *varnish* and other *surface films* for *sculpture* and *oil paintings;* see *amyl acetate.*

BANDEROLE—In *architecture,* a *sculptured band* or *course,* often bearing an inscription. Used extensively during the *Renaissance.* Also spelled *banderol* and *bannerol.*

BANDING WHEEL—In *sculpture* and *ceramics,* a variety of turntable, the topmost surface of which is marked by concentric circles regularly spaced from center to outer edge. A *clay* object is placed on the *banding wheel* which is spun, and the hands or tools are used to impress or incise lines around the object. Not synonymous with *gentleman* (q.v.) which is used chiefly in the original shaping of the object. The *banding wheel* is also used in the *painting* of circular lines or bands on *ware.*

BANNEROL—A term in *sculpture* and *architecture;* see *banderole.*

BARDIGLIO—In *sculpture,* a fine variety of *marble* found at Montalto, on the southern borders of Tuscany.

BAREN—In the production of Japanese *wood-block prints,* a circular pad made of a braided mat covered with a *bamboo* sheath, used to transfer the *image* by pressure and circular motion from block to *paper.* See *wood-block print.*

BARIUM YELLOW—An artificial pale *green pigment,* also known as *lemon yellow.* It is rather weak in *color* and somewhat *translucent,* but has the advantage of being among the most *stable* of *yellow* coloring materials. It was developed in the early 19th century, and has been a popular *medium* since. See *lemon yellow.*

BAROQUE—The *art* and *architecture* style prevailing from about 1600 to 1720. The name derives from the Portuguese "barroco," meaning an irregularly shaped pearl, but the term was actually one of ridicule, interpreted as peculiar, and over-ornate. If the *Rococo* Period is included (it was really the last phase of *Baroque*) then *Baroque* ended in 1760. During this period, *sculpture, painting, architecture, furniture,* and household *decoration* took on a lavish extravagance of *design.* First efforts to break away from the severe *classic* styles were too radical, resulting in broken *contours,* ungainly heaviness, and meaningless exaggeration. Churches, temples, *façades,* etc., remained basically the same, as did the ornamental parts, such as the *columns, pilasters, cartouches,* etc. But optical and sensorial effects were heightened. Proportions grew in height and heaviness, rich curves and staggering *embellishment* overflowed, and unending adornment abounded. Michelangelo, with gentle elegance, led the movement. Sculpture found similar change, as did painting. Rich *concave* and *convex* treatment of *marble,* lavish fountains, draperies and *colors,* and great dramatization of composition characterized the *visual arts.* While there is much to be said pro and con, considerable of the early ridicule was converted to praise, and *Baroque* stands as a milestone in the progress of the arts.

BARREL SHAPE—In *ceramics, sculpture, architecture,* and any other applicable art, any object greater in height than in breadth, *bulbous* in the center, and tapering equally toward each end.

BARYTA WATER—In *fresco* work, a *lime-wash* with which a *plaster* wall is saturated prior to the application of the fresco *pigments.* See *fresco secco.*

BASALT—A variety of *stone* possessing a splintery *fracture,* used extensively in the *sculpture* of the ancient Egyptians, many specimens of which are in a fine state of preservation today. Used as the medium in the making of many *obelisks* and *tombs.* The famous *Moabite stone* (q.v.) is made of *basalt.* The stone itself is a form of volcanic rock, dark and compact, containing a quantity of feldspar and iron.

BAS-RELIEF—*Low relief;* a mode of *sculpturing* with the figures almost flat; sculpture in which the raised portions stand out but little from the background. In *alto-relievo* or *high relief,* the figures project boldly and strongly from the background; in *demi-relief* (*half relief*) they are afforded a medium prominence; in *bas relief* the projection is less than half the real proportion. Known also as *basso-relievo* and *sculpture painting.*

BASSO-RELIEVO—A mode of *sculpturing* with the figures almost flat, better known as *bas-relief* (q.v.).

BATTLE PIECE—Any work of *art,* whether it be executed in *sculpture, painting, architecture, porcelain,* etc., representing a battle. An extremely popular subject, particularly to those *artists* possessing *ability* to accomplish fine detail.

BAUHAUS—An important *art* movement of the early 20th century growing out of Walter Gropius' reorganization of the Weimar Art School, 1914. Gropius set up the school in Dessau, designed the buildings himself, and gave the organization the formal title *Staatliches Bauhaus.* It served as a laboratory for the standardization of all arts and *handcrafts,* and a number of *architects, painters, sculptors, photographers,* and other craftsmen worked together under the guidance of such leaders as Oskar Schlemmer, Herbert Bayer, Moholy-Nagy, Joseph Albers, Paul Klee, and Marcel Breuer in a form of 'community spirit.' The cooperative endeavors led to the discovery of new *techniques,* based on the principle of 'learning by doing.' The primary purpose of the school was to close the gap between the *fine arts* and industry, thereby establishing a more secure position for the artist in the machine age.

BEAN OIL—A natural, pale yellow oil having a wide variety of uses in the *arts;* better known as *soya bean oil* (q.v.).

BEAUX ARTS ECOLE—A famous school of the *fine arts,*

founded by endowment in Paris in 1648, and exercising strong influence on contemporary and subsequent schools and movements.

BEESWAX—Now widely used as a *modeling* and *coating* substance, this *wax* was also employed as a painting *medium*. Among pictures in which it served the latter purpose, the so-called *Fayum mummy paintings* (early Christian Egypt) are prominent. Unwieldy, except perhaps in full tropical sunlight, it has the great advantage of *stability*.. Used also in the making of adhesive, cements, transparent *paper*, and in various *engraving processes*. See *wax*.

BELGIAN MARBLE—See *rance*.

BENI—A color peculiar to Japan, designated as rose-*red*. It was used extensively on early Japanese *prints*. See *beni-zurie*.

BENIE—Early Japanese *wood-block prints* in which single *coloring* was added by hand to a *black* and *white* impression. The names derives from the predominating color, a rose-*red pigment* known as *beni* (q.v.).

BENI-ZURIE—Japanese *wood-block prints* in which rose-*red* (*beni*) was prominent. The *colors* in *beni-zurie* were printed, whereas the earlier *benie* (q.v.) was colored by hand.

BENZENE—A colorless liquid with an unusually high *refractive index*, dangerously inflammable and possessing a characteristic odor. A product of the fractional distillation of petroleum, it is used as a *paint* and *varnish* remover, a solvent, and an ingredient in certain paints. Chemically, C_6H_6.

BENZOIN—A dark gum or *resin* from trees native to Siam and Sumatra, added to *varnishes* and *lacquers* to render them less brittle. It is mentioned in various *manuscripts* of *medieval* origin.

BERLIN-BLUE—The first *blue pigment* made synthetically on a large scale. Although first made in Berlin (early 18th century), it is better known as *Prussian blue* (q.v.)

BERMELLON—In *painting*, (1) a fine vermilion *pigment*

originating in Spain; (2) an earthy variety of *cinnabar* having a *vermilion* hue.

BERYL BLUE—In Chinese *painting,* a famous pale blue mineral *pigment* obtained from the first stratum of the *azurite* stone when it is rubbed down in water. Known natively as *san ch'ing,* it is used chiefly for the painting of garments in figure studies. See *shih ch'ing.*

BESTION—A rare term sometimes employed to designate any fantastic or *grotesque* representations in *carving* or *sculpture;* popular during periods of florid design, the works generally set forth *legendary* animals and highly complicated foliate arrangements.

BIAS—In *art,* an intellectual pre-*judgment* of the validity of forthcoming *compositions, paintings,* etc., involving knowledge of subject, information concerning the *artist* or composer, and supported by involuntary *emotional* factors.

BIEDERMEIER—A phase of German *art,* popular from 1830 to 1860, characterized by sober orderliness and simple pleasure which, in *furniture* and *interior decoration,* transformed the *Empire Style* into one of simple usefulness. In *paintings* and *sculpture,* it was a mild reaction to the *Romantic* period, replacing the religious, historical, and symbolic *themes* with scenes from everyday life among the peasants and middle class. Human, animal, and plant nature were *represented* with loving care and simplicity, describing with virtue those who were content with the simple pleasures; this *theme* was particularly strong in *furniture.* The movement grew out of a 19th century demand for local designing and materials, and although French and English sources continued to furnish the patterns (in ornamentation, curves, and *gilding* processes), no imported wood was used. The term derives from PAPA BIEDERMEIER, a character in magazine *literature* of the time.

BIMORPHIC ART—In *painting,* a type of *abstraction* (q.v.) in which organic forms prevail. The term originated with *archaeologists* who employed it to describe certain designs executed on small stones by men of the *paleolithic* period. Also spelled *biomorphic.*

BINDER—In *painting,* a cohesive *liquid* added to *paint* for the purpose of having it unite the ingredients. *Linseed oil* and *poppy-seed oil* are widely used in the paints employed in oil painting, as *binders.* A *binder* is not to be confused with a *thinner,* as *turpentine.* Also known as *binding medium.* See *paint.*

BINDING MEDIUM—See *binder.*

BIRD'S EYE—In *sculpture,* a name given to several species of *marble* in which the markings assume the appearance of the eye of a bird.

BISTRE—A tarry, *asphaltum*-like residue from the soot of burned *resinous wood,* the *color* ranging from *orange-yellow* to *brown-black.* Unlike asphaltum, it can be used with water-soluble media, though it is comparatively *unstable.* Used largely for *drawing* since the 14th century, it is still sold by *artists'* colormen for use in *water-colors,* to which it is added as is *Chinese ink.* Derives from the wood soot of the *beech.* Used in 14th century Italian book illustrations, and by Rembrandt in his *wash drawings.*

BITING—In *etching,* the key process of transferring the *design* to *the plate.* A metal plate (usually *copper*) is covered completely with a type of *wax* impermeable to the acid intended to be used. The etcher then incises his *design* through the *wax* and into the metal, using a *burin, stylus, graver,* or other instrument, and places the plate in acid. The acid "bites" through the metal at those points that had the wax removed by incision, thus rendering permanent the *pattern.* The parts having wax are unaffected by the corrosive. See *aquatint* and *line etching.* See also *stopping out* and *acid blast.*

BITUMEN—One of the oldest substances known in the *arts,* used in *mummification, painting, glazing, printing* and *etching.* Properly known as *asphaltum* (q.v.).

BLACK AND GOLD MARBLE—In *sculpture,* a variety of dense black *limestone* veined with *gold,* properly known as porto marble (q.v.).

BLACK BELGIAN—A term in *sculpture;* see *Noir Belge.*

BLACK-BOY GUM—A natural *resinous* product obtained from the Australian XANTHORRHEA tree, used extensively in the *sizing* of *paper* and manufacture of numerous *waxes.* Employed also a *surface film* or protective coating over *paintings* and *statuary.*

BLACK EARTH—In *painting,* a variety of coal that is pounded fine and used in *fresco* work.

BLACK JAPAN—In *painting,* a fine grade of *lacquer* consisting of *asphaltum* (q.v.) dissolved in *linseed oil* and thinned with *turpentine.*

BLANC D'ARGENT—A series of *pigments* having wide use in the *arts* as fine coloring matter. The various pigments within the group differ from each other principally in the quantity of lead oxide they contain.

BLANC FIXE—A fine white *pigment* used extensively in *paints;* it is a heavy white powder, soluble in water, requiring the application of a *surface film* after conpletion of the *art* work. Chemically, it is a precipitated barium sulphate; known also as *permanent white* and *terra ponderosa* to artists' colormen. Used successfully in the making of *photographic* paper.

BLAUE REITER—A Russo-German *art* movement of the early 20th century, co-founded by Burliuk, Kandinsky, Javlensky and Marc. Known also as the *Blue Riders,* the group developed and intensified the *color* discoveries of the *fauves* (q.v.) into a new plastic language of line and color without the use of *natural* objects. Kandinsky is credited with having created the first pure *abstract* painting (1911).

BLEEDING—In *painting,* the *pigments* are said to *bleed* when the coloring matter from either the *ground* or an undercoat works itself up into the succeeding coats and imparts to them a certain amount of the color of the *underpainting* or *imprimatura.*

BLENDER—In *painting,* a *brush* of large size used to smooth and soften *oil-paint coatings.* Usually made of badger hair, it is fairly long, round in shape, and flat at one end. This allows it to be tapped over the wet paint, as well as drawn over it with the customary stroke. Used from the 15th century to the present, it is now made with the tufted hair set into a bone base and covers about a five inch width to the stroke; used also for the staining of *glass.*

BLENDING—In *painting,* the method of merging two *pigments* so that their *colors intermingle;* the fusion of colors or *tones* into one grand overall *pattern* experienced as a whole.

BLISTERING—In *painting,* the formation of bubbles on the surface of the paint film, usually caused by moisture behind the layer of *paint* or the *surface film.*

BLOOM—In *painting, sculpture,* and allied *arts,* the clouded finish sometimes occurring as a defect on *varnished* surfaces; similar in general appearance to the clouded surface of a plum or grape. Known also as *chill* and *blooming.*

BLOOMING—The cloudy white film occurring on the *varnished* surface of *paintings,* pieces of *sculpture,* etc; induced chiefly by moisture in the atmosphere. Known also as *bloom* and *chill* (qq.v.).

BLOTTESQUE—A term applied generally to any work of *art* coarsely made, or representing the subject in coarse fashion. Also, any object having blots.

BLUE BICE—A *blue pigment,* similar to *azurite.* Same as *blue verditer* (q.v.).

BLUE-BLACK—In *painting* and *drawing,* a name often given to the famed *ivory black* (q.v.) because of its perceptible bluish *hue;* also, any well-burnt and levigated variety of *charcoal* prepared by a technique of trapped combustion.

BLUE FRIT—A famous blue color found in the *wall paintings* of ancient Egypt and Mesopotamia, possessing a remarkable degree of *stability;* known commonly as *Egyptian blue* (q.v.).

BLUE LAKE—In *painting,* a blue *pigment* similar to *Antwerp blue* (q.v.).

BLUE RIDERS—A Russo-German *art* movement of the early 20th century; furthered the *color* ideas of the *fauves* (q.v.) in representing *line* and color work without the use of objects found in nature. Properly known as *Blaue Reiter* (q.v.).

BLUE ROSE—A Russian *art* group formed just prior to the 1905 revolution, seeking to escape in mysticism and dreams from the oppressive rule of Nicholas II. In *impressionistic* technique, the imaginative adherents depicted weird and fantastic subject matter, specializing in misty *landscapes* overcast with gloomy *blue shadows* and haunted by strange demons. Often highly colorful, the chief works appear to have been Oriental in feeling. Leading *artists* of the movement were Serov (called the 'Russian Degas'), Levitan, and Vrubel.

BLUE VERDITER—In *oil painting,* an artificial copper carbonate often referred to as *blue bice*. It is a *pigment* of rich *blue,* chemically similar to *azurite,* originating in the early *Middle Ages*. Though now rare, it is still available.

BLUNT BRUSH— In Chinese *painting,* a brush stroke technique of free style in which, e.g., one zig-zag stroke may serve for all the wrinkles of a sleeve, ordinarily represented by several separate strokes. A blunt brush is used, and it travels in the manner of a ricocheting object. This is the typical style of MA YUAN and LIANG K'AI.

BOASTING-CHISEL—In *sculpture,* a flat chisel with a two-inch edge, used in the first rough shaping of the stone.

BODHISATTVA—In the *painting* of India, any one of the sacred Buddhist figures who are believed to refuse heavenly blessedness in order to spare others from misery; often portrayed in the throes of physical suffering.

BODIED LINSEED OIL—In *painting,* a variety of *linseed oil* that has been thickened by blowing or by heat treating, thus increasing the 'body' or consistency. It is obtainable in many degrees of viscosity.

BODY-COLOR—In *painting,* any *pigment* possessing a high degree of substance and *hiding power*. In *water-color* painting, works are said to be executed in *body-colors* when, as distinguished from the more common practice of employing *transparent* tints, and washes, the pigments are mixed with white and thus rendered *opaque*. Any opaque pigment as distinguished from a transparent finishing paint; any color possessing 'body.'

BODY STAIN—In *ceramic* and *sculpture,* any one of the many *pigments* used for producing a uniform color throughout a *clay body;* the technique is employed by mixing the color with the *moist clay* or dry powder clay before shaping. Not to be confused with colors or *glaze* used as a surface decoration only.

BOHEMIAN—The happy-go-lucky *artist* or *art* student; leader of revolts against bourgeois conventionality, or living in happy disregard of such concerns. See *art d'avant-garde.*

BOISSEREAN COLLECTION—Name given to the famous Bavarian collection of early specimens of German *art* in all of its phases, amassed by the brothers Sulpiz and Melchior Boisseree and sold to the king of Bavaria in 1836.

BOITE—A valise-like affair carried by some *artists* to prospective customers. It contains an intricately-contrived arrangement of rods and hooks upon which numerous of the artist's previous works may be displayed as 'samples' of his work, *style* and *palette.* Some painters have *half-tone* reproductions made of previously-executed works for this display.

BOLE—The *inert* or *pigment* material laid as a *ground* for *gold leaf.* The word is an ancient one, and in modern *gilding* the term *gold size* is more frequently used. Having no fixed color, *bole* may be *green, white,* or dull *red,* the last being the most popular. A *bole* must be *amorphous,* providing a smooth foundation for the leaf. In construction it is almost identical with *kaolin,* and is softer and more unctuous than *ochre.* It is available today under the names *gilder's red clay* and *red burnish.*

BOLOGNESE SCHOOL—A 15th century school of *painting,* founded in Bologna by Marco Zoppo, and stressing Roman lines, patterns, and styles. It gave way toward the end of the 16th century to the new *School of Bologna* founded by the Carraccis.

BONE BLACK—A *pigment* used in *drawing* and *painting,* being one of a series of many *black* carbon pigments; made by charring animal bones in a closed vessel. It is believed by many artists that the so-called *ivory black* is nothing more than *bone black,* made in the same manner, but given a more glamorous name. Known also as *bone char* and *animal black.*

BOOK OF HOURS—The name applied to *illuminated* prayer books of the *Middle Ages,* for use by persons of high civil and ecclesiastical rank. The scenes represented in many of these works were painted by the Limbourg brothers, and are considered the peak of *miniature painting* of the Middle Ages.

BOSS—In *sculpture,* a general term applied to any projecting mass intended to be afterward cut or *carved.*

BOSSING—In *sculpture,* the technique of so finishing a large work that elevations appear at certain points on the surface, intended to enhance the effects of light and shadow; appears to have originated with Rodin (1840-1917), who instituted the practice of *hollowing* (q.v.) at the same time.

BOTTEGA—The *artists'* workshop prior to the abolition of the guilds at the turn of the 19th century. A cooperative enterprise based upon common need for livelihood and the master's responsibility for the welfare of his associates. In many cases it was a family project, inherited by successive generations. Also, any shop; the *studio* of an Italian artist; an *atelier.*

BOUCHARDE—In *sculpture,* a tool with which the finished surface of *marble* is roughened for decorative purposes. It is in the nature of a hammer, with the striking parts arranged in rows of teeth. Known also as *bushhammer.*

BOUGARD—In *architecture* and *sculpture,* a fine grade of dark gray mottled stone with yellow, brown and pink in streaks and clouds; originates in Germany. Also referred to as *bougard marble.*

BOUNDARY PAINTING—In Chinese *art,* the term applied to any *painting* or *drawing* having formal, ruled or measured outlines. Known natively as *chieh hua,* the technique is employed chiefly in *architectural* representations.

BOWENITE—In *sculpture,* an unusually hard, massive, apple green or greenish-white variety of *serpentine* (q.v.).

BOYCHUK SCHOOL—A Ukrainian *art* movement of the 20th century, named for its founder, Mykhailo Boychuk. Combining *Byzantine* tradition with the modernistic trends, the group turned out *paintings* bearing a striking similarity to those of Diego Rivera in *style* and *meaning.* Followers of the school were bitterly opposed and even persecuted in the Soviet Union as 'nationalistic deviators.' Prominent among its members were Padalka, Muzyka, Kryzhanivsky, and Pavlenko.

BRAZIL WAX—An ingredient of fine *lacquers, varnishes, enamels,* and clear *surface films,* obtained from the Brazilian palm where it occurs as a deposit on the leaves; distinguished by its hardness and high melting point, it is successfully used as a substitute for *beeswax* (q.v.).

BREADTH—(1) A term in *painting criticism* applied to the effect growing out of the treatment of a subject in which sharp detail, harmony of color, and satisfactory *chiaroscuro* are all subordinated individually by interweaving them with each other for purposes of simplicity. When detail can be expressed without the sacrifice of *breadth* or simplicity, the effect is referred to as *finish.* Thus, a painting possessing both *breadth* and *finish* is simple, though clear and sharp. See *finish.* (2) Any *art* object is thus characterized when its details are so massed as to give the effect of fine unity in combination with vast or *colossal* sizes. Does not necessarily refer to width standing alone, but requires unity in addition thereto. *Sculptors* recognize a well-executed *chryselephantine* (q.v.) as a good example of art in *breadth.*

BRECCIA MARBLE—In *sculpture,* the general name given to any *marble* made up of angular fragments.

BRECHE AFRICAINE—A term in *sculpture;* see *mischio marble.*

BREMEN BLUE—In *painting,* a blue *pigment* made by precipitating nitrate of copper with lime (see *Alexandria blue*). Used chiefly for *fresco* painting, it is highly *stable* and retains its color even under artificial light. Used widely in the 19th century, it is now rare, though still available at some *art* supply sources.

BRICK RED—In *painting* and *water-color,* a dark orange-red color resembling that of the common brick, popular on the *palette,* esp. in sunset work.

BRIGHT—In *art* generally, a term describing colors that

are *vivid* and *intense,* as *orange* or sunflower *yellow;* a term in art *criticism* applied to such vividness (e.g., an artist uses a *bright* palette), as contrasted with 'dull' and 'dark.'

BRINGING UP—In *painting,* the popular term applied to the technique of brightening the dull spots in a picture by use of *retouch varnish* or *retouch colors;* also used where colors have been so absorbed or 'dried in' as to lose their original high *value.*

BRISTOL BOARD—A variety of fine *drawing* board made in many qualities and thicknesses, usually of smooth finish; used extensively for drawing and *printing.* So-called because first made at Bristol, England, it is required as the *ground* for *sketches,* diagrams, etc., in submitting applications to the U. S. Patent Office. Can be used on either side, and is also suitable for *charcoal, airbrush, line drawings, pastels, tempera,* and *water-color.*

BROCATELLE MARBLE—In *sculpture,* a fine grade of *marble* quarried in the French Pyrenees. The body of the stone is fine-grained, compact, and of light yellow color traversed by vari-colored veins and dull red blotches. Known in Italy as *brocatello,* the name derives from a coarse type of *tapestry*-like material which it resembles in general appearance. The term is loosely applied to any *brecciated* or variegated marble.

BROKEN COLOR—In *painting,* the impression of airiness and space created by the interspersing of one *color* with another by means of short strokes.

BROKEN REED—In Chinese *painting,* a brush stroke technique creating lines resembling split and sharply-broken reeds. The lines are long, stiff, sporadically angular, and rather coarse, showing sudden changes of direction; made with a pointed *brush* used in zig-zag fashion.

BRONZE—In *metalwork,* an *alloy* whose origin in the *arts* is lost in *antiquity.* Modern varieties include *speculum metal* (67% *copper,* 33% tin); *coinage bronze* (95% copper, 4% tin, 1% *zinc*); *bronze* itself, or *gunmetal* (90% copper, 10% tin).

BROWN—A dark, earthy *color, tinged* with a *red*dish or *yellow*ish *hue.* See *ochre.*

BROWN PINK—A *water-color,* being one of the several *lakes* of *yellow* or *green*ish *hue.* It is made by precipitating vegetable juices on a *white* earth product, such as *alumina* or *chalk.*

BRUGES SCHOOL—A 14th and 15th century school of *art* that grew out of the *medieval tradition* at Bruges. Its accomplishments are evident in the works of Hubert and Jan Van Eyck, Gheeraert David, Hans Memlinc, Peter Christus, and others, whose creations are often referred to as *Flemish* primitive art. See *Flemish style.*

BRUSH—The chief tool of the *painter,* it has not changed appreciably in the entire history of this *art.* With the exception of a special type used in Egypt (a reed macerated at one end to separate the *fibers*) *brushes* have always been of animal hair tied into a tuft and set into a handle. Modern painters' *brushes* are in two general types: bristle, or coarse hair, usually that of the pig; and fine hair, made of sable, or so-called 'camel hair.' Fine hair *brushes* are made from the tail hair of the Asiatic mink (*kolinsky*), native of northestern Russia, the *color* being a *red*dish *yellow.* This is considered the finest of all hair brushes. 'Camel hair' actually comes from squirrel, and the best of these is also found in Russia and Siberia, the color being red, *gray,* or *black.* The Chinese *brush* used in *painting* and *calligraphy* is made of goat or wolf hair, bunched-up and affixed to the end of a *bamboo* tube; the *fibers* are so graded as to give the *brush* a fine point. See *pi.*

BRUSH STROKE—See *hitsui.*

BRUSH WASHER—A simple, effective device used for cleaning the colors out of *brushes.* Consists of a coil spring having loose sections, suspended crosswise over a container, supported by vertical braces extending to the bottom of the container. The brush handles are placed between the coils with the painting ends suspended into the cleaning fluid in the container; the important aspect of the arrangement is that the hair of the brushes does not touch the bottom, keeping it from twisting and bending, and preserving the points. Also effective is the home-made system of drilling a small hole in a brush handle, inserting a nail, straightened hairpin, paper clip, etc., and placing the nail or wire across the top of a glass, can, etc., suspending the brush in the cleaning fluid therein.

BUCKLING—In *oil painting,* the term applied to any *surface film* upon which *blisters* are forming or have formed; extended by usage to include a *ground* in similar state.

BUCKTHORN LAKES—In *painting,* a series of famous yellow *lake colors,* better known as *Persian lakes* (q.v.).

BUNJIN-GA—A modern Japanese school of *painting,* fostering the Chinese style.

BURIN—In *engraving* (q.v.), a sharp tool, usually of *copper,* with which the lines of the *design* are drawn on a metal *plate.* The *ridge* of metal turned up as the *burin* is pushed forward is polished down to leave a smooth surface except for the cut lines which receive the *ink* and produce the *print.* Similar to *stylus, drypoint,* and *graver* (qq.v.). The term is also applied to the *style* or manner of the engraver's artistry, e.g., soft *burin,* brilliant *burin,* etc.

BURMITE—A *fossil resin* resembling *amber,* but considerably tougher and harder; the name derives from the fact that it occurs only in Upper Burma. Among other uses, it is employed as a valued ingredient in *surface films* for the protection of *paintings* and *statuary.*

BURNISHER—In *etching,* a smooth, highly-polished, round piece of steel, used for reducing shadings that are too dark, and for removing scratches. Not synonymous with the etcher's *scraper.* See *drypoint.* The variety of *burnisher* used in *pewter*-work (known also as *brunissoir*) is frequently made of *agate,* silex or *bloodstone.*

BURNT PLATE OIL—A material used for thinning the body of *etching* ink that does not flow readily.

BURNT SIENNA—An *earth color,* similar to *ochre,* but finer in *grain* and more *translucent.* *Raw sienna* (q.v.) resembles *yellow ochre;* when burnt, it becomes a warm, *red*dish *brown.* Both are used as a *glazing* to *tone* or soften *paintings;* both belong to the group known as the *iron pigments* (q.v.). The unique fiery *tint* produced by the roasting is *transparent* when brushed out. Also spelled *siena.*

BURR—In an *engraving* or *drypoint,* the rough or torn edge or ridge made on the metal *plate* by the cutting action of the *stylus* or *graver.* In some instances (as in drypoint) the *burr* is not ground off or removed, since it has the effect of beautifying the finished *print.* In engravings, however, the *burr* is removed with a scraper so that the lines will be sharp and clean.

BUSSHI—In Japanese *sculpture,* a *carver* whose subject is Buddha exclusively, rendering *images* in various positions and dress.

BUST—In *sculpture,* the head and shoulders of a human done completely in the *round* or in *relief, deep* or shallow; may be accomplished in *stone, metal, wood,* or in any other material, the word alluding principally to the portion of the body represented.

BUST PEG—In *sculpture,* a wooden device in the shape of an inverted *T,* upon the upright portion of which the materials may be modeled in the making of a *bust;* it subsequently remains as the inner foundation of the finished work.

BUTSU—In Japanese *painting,* the term applied generally to any picture representing Buddha.

BUTTERFLY—In *sculpture, a wooden device in X*-shape, attached to the *armature* to further assure that the plastic substance to be used will not fall away, sag, or bulge.

BYOBU—An elaborate Japanese folding screen of six *panels,* on which the greatest Oriental masters lavished their *painting* skill. Rare collectors' items today.

BYZANTINE ART—Developed in the 6th century A.D., the *painting* pursued a course of continued attraction through the centuries. It combines Greek or Oriental ingredients in *style, technique,* and thought processes, the Greek influence being evident in the almost mathematical precision of layout, and the Oriental in the rich *color* harmonies. It is an *art* of great distinction, power and tenacity. Like

Egyptian, it is an art of formulas used for calculated, and not academic, purposes. There is very little *sculpture* in *marble,* the principal *media* having been *mosaic, frescoes* of high color, *miniature* and *panel* paintings, *icons, ivories, enamels, jewels, textiles* and objects of utility. See *Salian art.*

C

CABINET DRAWING—An *oblique* drawing (q.v.) with all measurements on the oblique axis reduced one-half to overcome its distorted appearance. Any angle may be used for the oblique axis of a *cabinet drawing,* though angles of 45 degrees or 30 degrees are preferred. See also *isometric drawing.*

CADMIUM PIGMENTS—A range of *colors* from pale *yellow* to deep *red,* all deriving from the element *cadmium.* All are of comparatively recent origin, going back to the mid-19th century. They change slightly under strong heat, but in normal temperatures are quite *stable* and *fast* to light. Some artists have found that *cadmiums* will injure other colors when mixed with them. See *yellow pigments.*

CAEN STONE—In *sculpture,* a light, cream-colored variety of limestone used largely in carved *architectural* and *relief* work. Name derives from the fact that it is quarried chiefly in Caen, Normandy.

CALCAR—In Mexican *art,* a general term referring to excellence of technique in the executing of tracings or *drawings.* As *calco:* the tracing of a previously-executed drawing or *painting* on *paper or cloth.*

CALCINED MAGNESIA—A white powder of varying weight, used in the making of *paints* and *varnishes,* cements and other adhesives, fine *lacquers,* and artificial *stone,* brick and plaster tiles; employed also as a substitute for *platinum.* Chemically it is magnesium oxide, MgO.

CALCIUM CARBONATE—A white powder, occurring as colorless crystals or in an *amorphous* state, used in the making of fine *pigments,* as an ingredient in *ceramics,* and in the manufacture of *glass, enamels,* and building *stones.*

CALCOGRAPHY—The *art* of *drawing* with *chalk* or *pastel.*

CALCUTTA OIL—The finest quality of *linseed oil,* used as a *siccative* and *hardening* agent in *oil paints.* See *linseed oil.*

CALEDONIA BROWN—In *painting,* a fine *pigment* of orange russet-brown color; it is a native *earth color* of England, prized by *artists* who work in *oils.*

CALENDAR—A series of emblematic *pictures* of the months, a common *motive* of decoration during the *Middle Ages* in *sculpture, painted glass, earthenware tiles,* and the like. For each month the sign of the *zodiac* is represented, with one or more persons shown engaged in labors or sports characteristic of the month. An excellent example is found on the portal of the 13th century Amiens Cathedral.

CALIPERS—A device used to measure the diameters of curved figures and objects, and to compare distances and sizes. It gives the appearance of *compasses* with a small scale attached above the two pivoted points. Sometimes spelled *callipers.*

CALKING—The copying of a *picture* or *design* by means of tracing; three techniques are (1) rubbing the back of the design with a *pencil, chalk* or *crayon,* and tracing over its lines with a hard point, causing the coating on the back to make an impression on a sheet of *paper* or other material placed beneath; (2) same as the above (1), but instead of coating the back of the design with a *painting medium,* interposing a piece of transfer-paper between it and the surface which is to receive the copy; (3) tracing the design directly upon a piece of transparent paper, oiled *linen,* or the like, fixed over it. Known also as *caulking, cocking,* and *cogging.* See *tracing paper.*

CALLIGRAPHIC ETCHING—A process of *etching* in which the *design* is made with a *pen* and *ink* on a clean *copper* plate. When dry, the *plate* is covered with a thin *varnish* or etching *ground,* smoked, and then soaked in water to soften the ink, which can then be removed along with the varnish by gentle rubbing, leaving the design to be etched in the customary manner.

CALLIGRAPHY—The *art* of fine *writing* in the making of

a product; elegant penmanship as an art or profession, distinguished from writing only by its excellent *quality*. Pursued as a great art in China. In old Persia, *calligraphy* was a greater art than *painting* and was found primarily in copies of or extracts from the QUR'AN. Not so profound as the Chinese, wherein each character was both beautiful and *symbolic*, the Persian had an *abstract* quality of *beauty* giving the effect of a perfect mathematical equation or an exceedingly *melodic measure*. The Chinese used various types of *grounds* for the execution of this work, esp. *paper* and *silk*, prepared and sized for that purpose. See *hsüan chih, yü pan hsüan, fan hs üan, and tz'ü ch'ing.*

CALLIOPE—In Greek *mythology*, one of the nine famous daughters of Zeus and Mnemosyne, considered the chief *Muse;* she was associated with *epic poetry* and science generally. Frequently represented in the *arts* (esp. *painting* and *sculpture*), she is shown holding a *pen* and a scroll of *parchment* as her *attributes*. See *Muse*.

CALLIPYGA—In the *esthetic* of ancient Greece, the term applied to a female representation (often in *painting* or *sculpture*) exhibiting an artistically beautiful posterior; any female figure, alive or in image, having greatest accent of attractiveness at the buttocks. Derives from the Greek *calli*, beautiful and *pygos*, rump. Also spelled *kallipygos*, it was the name of a famous *statue* of *Aphrodite* (*Venus*) befitting the definition.

CAMAIEU—In *painting*, the term applied generally to any picture executed in *monochrome* (q.v.).

CAMPAN MARBLE—In *sculpture*, a fine pale yellow to yellowish-green stone, *mottled* with white. A dark green variety containing red blotches is known as *campam rouge*.

CANADA BALSAM—One of the *balsams* used directly in the *arts*, as an ingredient in painters' *varnishes*. It is an exudate from coniferous trees, derived by distillation. A crude *resin* remains as residue. Used in *photography* for slide mountings and to cement *lens* elements together. See *balsam, oleoresin*, and *tracing paper*.

CANDELILLA WAX—A hard variety of *wax,* brown and *brittle,* used as an ingredient in the making of *lacquers, varnishes* and *surface* films. Used chiefly where a high *gloss* is desired. Derives from the botanical PEDILANTHUS PAVINIA of Mexico, and is used successfully as a substitute for *beeswax* and *montan wax.* It serves as a painting *pigment* to a certain extent, and may have been the wax ingredient of the famous *mummy portraits* of *Fayum.*

CANDLENUT OIL—An ingredient of *paints* and *varnishes* deriving from the botanical ALEURITES MOLUCCANA. A highly controversial substance among artists, some use it extensively while many claim it will harm the finished *painting.* It is somewhat similar in *viscosity, consistency,* and purpose to *tung oil* (q.v.).

CANEPHORA—In Greek *sculpture,* a female figure with a basket on the head, the basket usually containing religious objects. Not to be confused with *caryatid.*

CANNES MARBLE—A term in *sculpture;* see *griotte marble.*

CANON—In *sculpture,* a Greek system of ideal human proportion, particularly of *kouroi* (youths) in athletic contests. This system was devised by Polyclitus (450-420 B.C.) who was the greatest *sculptor* at the famous *Argive School.*

CANTON ENAMEL—A variety of *surface enamel* (q.v.) in which the *ground* is usually plain white, yellow, or light blue, and is decorated with *enamel paintings* in many colors, representing conventional flowers, *scrolls,* etc. *Vases, incense burners,* etc., are made of it, and it was one of the most successful Chinese artistic industries at the close of the 19th century.

CANVAS—The common *support* for *painting* since *ancient* times. Applied today to any *fabric* support made up for use with *oil paint. Linen* with a thin ground was painted in *tempera* as early as the 12th Egyptian dynasty, and probably much earlier. The change to oil painting and large-scale work has widened its use, the change-over coming during the *Renaissance.* For the most part, *artists' canvas* was linen in plain cloth *weave,* though *twill* has been in evidence since the 16th century. Recent developments in the field have produced *canvas* in *cotton* and in *glass* cloth. As made ready for the market, artists' *canvas* is prepared with a ground of complicated construction, the upper *coatings* including oil with *white* or colored *pigments* and inert materials. By tightening a piece of raw *canvas* on *stretchers,* the weave acquires a variegated design of irregularity that will enhance the final result in any type of paintings.

CANVAS BOARD—Same as *academy board* (q.v.).

CANVAS PLIERS—An instrument similar to an ordinary pair of pliers, having deeply-toothed gripping edges. Used for pulling or stretching painters' *canvases* tightly around the rigid under-frames supporting them. Known also as *stretching pincers, canvas stretchers, pulling pliers,* etc.

CANVAS SKETCHING PIN—A small device consisting of two to four joined washers through all of which a double-pointed pin is inserted, extending out of both sides. Used for keeping damp *sketches, drawings, canvases,* etc., apart while carrying; also allows for 'stack-drying' where space is a problem.

CAPE IVORY—A soft variety of *ivory* used widely in *carving*; the color varies from pure white to an off-white or grayish tint, it takes a high polish, and does not *fracture* under the sculptor's tools.

CAPPADOCIA—Name given to a group of ancient *fresco* paintings excavated from *tombs* under the churches of the Cappadocian province of Asia. Rich in color, the faces represented on the hundreds of stonebased pictures appear Oriental. Coupled with the religious scenes thereon (Christ, the Virgin, and various saints in BIBLICAL incidents), authorities date these excellent works of *art* to the 7th and 8th centuries.

CAPPAGH BROWN—In *painting,* a fine *pigment* used by *artists* who work in *oils,* made from a species of bog-earth containing manganese, found near Cappagh in Ireland.

CAPUT MORTUUM—In *oil painting,* one of the *iron pigments* (q.v.) having a purplish *tinge,* better known as *Indian red* (q.v.).

CARBON BLACK—A fine black *pigment* obtained when natural gas is burned with insufficient air for combustion; the liberated carbon is collected on a metallic surface. Used in *printing ink, paints* and enamels; also an ingredient in the making of *crayons,* glazed *paper,* black *leather,* and *Chinese* and *India inks.* Known also as *gas black* and *channel black.*

CARDIGLIO MARBLE—In *sculpture,* a gray, clouded variety of *marble* used principally for ornamental purposes. Obtained almost exclusively from the Island of Corsica.

CARICATURE—In *drawing,* a process of characterization which over-emphasizes the individuality of a person. A drawing or description of a person in which the *artist* selects and accentuates unusual features to the point of grotesqueness, often with the intent to ridicule the subject. Although the practice was popular among ancient Greeks and Romans, the word appears to have been first used by Sir. Thos. Brown in the mid-17th century.

CARMINE—A fine red *pigment* used in *painting,* deriving from the dried bodies of Mexican insects. Better known as *cochineal* (q.v.).

CARNATION—In *art criticism,* esp. that devoted to *oil painting,* a term (now rare) applied to the *natural* or flesh-colored *tints* in any *picture.* See *natural.*

CARNAUBA WAX—A hard *wax* derived from the Brazilian palm where it occurs as a deposit on the leaves. It is *yellowish* in color and is distinguished by its hardness and high melting point. It is a frequent ingredient of wax mixtures designed to obtain a high *gloss.* Often used successfully as a substitute for *beeswax* (q.v.), it is employed also in the making of *varnishes, surface films, enamels* and *lacquers.* See *wax.*

CAROLINGIAN ART—Starting about 800 A.D., as a delayed reaction to the fine innovations in *Carolingian architecture* this art placed emphasis upon *miniature painting* in its many famous schools including that of *Godescale.* In *sculpture,* the *ivory carvings* have become renowned for their excellence. Starting about 900, elegance and lavishness comparable to that of the later *Baroque* (q.v.) period predominated in sculpture and *painting.* Sometimes spelled *Carlovingian.*

CARRARA MARBLE—A *marble* quarried in Luna, Italy, popular since Caesar for *sculpture* because of ready availability at cheap cost. Due to its *texture* of very small crystals, it lacks *luminous* quality, and its dull *white color* is not suitable for expressing delicate modulations or sensuous *values.* The prevailing colors are white to bluish, or white with blue veins. Within the same group is a finer grade of true *statuary* marble occurring at Carrara, Italy.

CARTHAME—A fine red coloring substance made from the dried petals of CARTHAMUS TINCTORIUS, the same plant that produces the fine *siccative* known as *safflower oil* (q.v.). The *dye* is orange when extracted, but deepens to heavy red with chemical treatment. Used in Egypt since antiquity as a dye, as a *pigment* base, and as an ingredient in *kohl* and other cosmetics. Known as a *safflower.*

CARTOCCIO—In Italian *art,* a small plate affixed to the *painting, carving,* or other work of art, inscribed with the name of the artist, or of the work, or both.

CARTOON—In *art,* a full-scale *drawing* on *paper,* to be used as a *model* for *easel paintings, mural* paintings, *tapestries, stained-glass, mosaics,* etc. The *cartoon* may be copied, or may be transferred to *plaster* or *canvas* by tracing, *pouncing,* or by cutting out and placing behind the *wool,* as in the case of tapestry. The practice of preparing accurate *cartoons* in *chiaroscuro* was general in the *Renaissance.*

CARVING—In *art,* (1) to cut or fashion *wood, stone, ivory, marble,* or other material into a particular form, or to *decorate* an existing object by cutting or *engraving* figures, *designs,* etc.; to make or shape by cutting, as to *carve* an *image* out of the chosen *medium,* aided by a chisel, *graver,* or other instrument; (2) *n.* any piece of decorative work, artistically designed, and cut or incised in any substance; ornamental *sculpture,* as distinguished from heavier, more pretentious work known generally as *statuary.*

CARYATID—In *architecture,* a draped female figure serving as a *column,* so-called after the dancing women of the town of CARYAE. The earliest examples in Greece are found at

Delphi, where two figures in *Ionic costume* support the *entablature* of the *porch* of the *Cnidian Treasury* (about 550 B.C.). The most famous *caryatids* are the six on the south porch of the *Erechtheum,* at Athens. These stalwart figures, subtly varied in pose and in the folds of their garments, with thick masses of hair to strengthen the weak neck element, bear the weight of the enatblature with serene dignity. Three *caryatids,* set back to back, served to support the tripod surmounting an *acanthus* column at Delphi. The device was used infrequently thereafter. The male version is known as *atlante,* or *telemon.*

CASEIN—Used as a *painting medium,* and also as an adhesive for joining the *wood* of painters' *panels.* It is prepared by adding hydrochloric acid to heated skimmed milk. This throws the curd of the milk out of suspension and, when dry, it forms a workable dry powder. Also used in the manufacture of *erinoid, lactoid,* and other *plastic* materials. It is rapidly growing in popularity as a *tempera* mixture, giving a firm, dull finish in true *matte* (q.v.) fashion. Originally found difficult to handle and control, modern chemistry creates *stable,* brilliant colors of *casein* with wide versatility in techniques. Nevertheless, certain precautions must still be taken. *Casein* paint used without added *medium* shows considerable 'suction' to *oil* paint used over it, unless first isolated by *retouch varnish;* oil absorbed into the *casein* layer spreads out as an unsightly discoloration. Also, *casein* colors cannot remain on the brush or in the pan overnight, since it becomes insoluble upon drying. When fairly fresh, it can be removed from equipment and brushes with soap and lukewarm water.

CAST—To *carve* a *design* in *stone* or *metal,* fill the form with a substance having hardening *qualities* and remove the substance after solidification takes place. The material thus removed is found to bear the *pattern* of the *mold* from which it was taken. The most common substance used in *casting* is *gypsum,* or *plaster of Paris* (qq.v.). See also *mold.*

CAST—In *color,* the tendency of one *hue* toward another, sometimes forming a third, e.g., the pale *yellow* of sulphur has a *greenish cast,* creating *chartreuse.* The basic ground of a color, distinguishing it from others of an apparently similar *shade.*

CASTING PLASTER—In *sculpture,* a variety of milk-white *plaster* prepared especially for *castings* and *carvings;* possesses unusual durability, and is found suitable for making *molds* of any modeled object. See *cast.*

CASTUNG—A variety of *oil* compounded with *resin* and used in the making of *surface films* for *paintings* and *sculpture;* employed also as an ingredient of certain *inks* and *plastic* products. Chemically it is a processed oil obtained from a breakdown of castor oil, *castung* being a trade name.

CATTLE HAIR—In Chinese *painting,* a brush stroke technique employing short, fine lines, the effect of which is suggested by the name. Frequently used in executing the smooth roundness of *igneous* rocks in *landscape* work.

CAULKING—In *drawing,* any one of the techniques employed in the copying of a *picture* or *design* by means of *tracing.* See *calking.*

CAUTERIUM—A metal spatula with a rounded end, mentioned as a tool in the history of ancient *painting.* It was evidently used with melted *wax* and may have been responsible for the conformation in the group of *mummy* paintings known as the *Fayum portraits.*

CAVE PAINTINGS—In *archaeology* and *painting,* a general term applied to all artistic representations and *symbols* executed upon the inside walls of caves in Europe and India. The paintings (usually human and animal figures) were invariably set down in *earth colors.* While most are found to be crude and *primitive* (many pre-date the Stone Age), there is an occasional art work of striking beauty and craftsmanship, as the bull group on the wall of Altamira Cave, Spain.

CAVO-RELIEVO—In *sculpture,* an obsolete term formerly applied to the technique now known as *hollow relief* (q.v.).

CELLOSOLVE—A colorless liquid used widely as a solvent for artists' *resins* and *gums,* esp. those employed in the making of *surface films;* used also in the *leather industry,* and in the *dyeing* and *printing* of *textiles. Chemically* it is ethylene glycol mono-ethyl ether, *cellosolve* being a trade name.

CELLULOID—Occasionally used as a *film* material or *varnish;* associated with the various *cellulose* products that have come into the *paint* trades in comparatively recent times.

CELURE—In *sculpture* and *architecture,* any *carved* work in *relief;* any sculptured decoration for the walls and/or ceiling of a room; a *canopy.*

CEMENT—A *burned* and ground *lime* compound, *natural* or *artificial.* In the *arts,* the word has broader meaning, used as a synonym for "adhesive," and relating to any kind of *film* material which will join parts of objects together. As a lime compound, it is used as a *support* for *wall painting* and a joining agent for blocks, *bricks,* etc.

CENOTAPH—In funerary *sculpture* and *architecture,* an empty *tomb,* frequently ornate, commemorating a person whose body is interred elsewhere. Sometimes erected in memory of a group.

CENTAUR—In Greek *mythology,* a combative and amorous horseman, the favorite subject of many *artists* and *sculptors* through the centuries. His picturesque exploits and interesting physical structure attracted top-level *representations,* starting with 8th cent. B.C. *art* in which he was regarded as a human being in front, with the body and hind legs of a horse. By the 6th cent., the *centaur* was shown as a man to the waist only. Bourdelle's THE DYING CENTAUR is considered one of the finest sculptural achievements ever executed.

CENTER OF INTEREST—The dominant center which gains attention through *color,* while other details are subserviant to it. The focal point of interest in a *painting* on display.

CERBERUS—In Greek *art* or mythology, the three-headed dog guarding the entrance to Hades. However, certain ancient *paintings* represent *Cerberus* with as many as fifty heads.

CERESIN WAX—Occasionally used as a surface *coating* on *paintings, sculpture,* and other objects of *art.* It is harder and whiter than paraffln, melts at a point above 65 degrees Centigrade, and has a smooth and unctuous consistency.

Used successfully as a substitute for *beeswax* (q.v.). See also *film.*

CEREOGRAPHY—A method of *painting* which employs *wax* as a *binder.* The wax is heated with hot irons to render the *colors* fluid and to fix them. The technique was employed by the ancient Romans who inscribed wax tablets with a *stylus.* See *encaustic painting.*

CERULEAN BLUE—A *bright,* faintly *greenish blue pigment,* available *to artists since* 1860, but known prior to that time. It is a *stable,* fine-*grained,* inert pigment, synthetically prepared. It possesses *brilliance,* good *luminosity,* and high strength in *grinding;* it is one of the *cobalts.*

CESTRUM—Like the cauterium (q.v.) this was an *ancient* tool of the *painter* and probably of other workers in the *arts.* It is mentioned in Pliny, and from its description appears to have been a pointed instrument used with *wax.* It may have been used in the making of the famous *Fayum mummy portraits.*

CEYLON IVORY—A white to pink-tinted variety of *ivory* used widely in *carving.* It responds to a high polish, cuts easily and does not *fracture* under the carver's tools.

CHALDEAN ART—The earliest development of Accadian or *Mesopotamian art,* from which the later art of *Babylon* and *Assyria* was directly derived.. Though still imperfectly known, this *culture* clearly contains the essence of all the later developments from it, including the substructural mounds, fine *enamels,* terraced *temples* of brick, exquisitely engraved *gems,* and the use of bright *colors.* The stone *sculptures* that have been found, esp. those excavated from 1877 to 1881 from the mound of Tello in southern Chaldea, exhibit a much less conventional idea of the human form, and much more artistic promise, than was fulfilled in this branch of art by the Babylonian and Assyrian sculptors. The height of the culture appears to have been reached in the vicinity of 1450 B.C.

CHALK—In modern use, an ingredient in *grounds,* for *painting;* in old Europe it was used widely at the time when *panel* paintings with white *gesso* were popular. Mixed with *white lead, linseed oil,* and other materials, it is a regular

18500

ingredient in many of the substances used in preparing the ground to receive the *oils*. See *whiting*.

CHALKING—In *painting*, a phenomenon of coatings manifest by loose powder coming from the *surface film* itself, at or just below the surface.

CHAR—A black carbon *pigment* of good covering value, used in *painting* and *drawing*. Prepared by a process of destructive distillation of degreased animal bones in an iron retort.

CHARCOAL—The carbon made from roasting pieces of *wood* in a closed vessel. This has been an accepted drawing and *coloring* material from prehistoric times. As thin sticks made from close-*grained* wood like *willow* or *beech*, it is a standard *drawing* instrument. When pulverized, it provides a *pigment* of *black* in common use. *Charcoal* possesses unusually high absorption qualities, rendering it valuable in numerous industrial fields. *Engravers* and *artists* use it to polish zinc and *copper plates*. See *yung hsiu*.

CHARCOAL DRAWING—A freehand *drawing* or *design* made with charcoal sticks or *pencils*, usually on a special *paper*, e.g., *charcoal paper*.

CHARCOAL PAPER—In *drawing*, a soft variety of *paper* having a rough finish, used as a *ground* for *illustrations* made with *charcoal crayon* or *pencil*. Durable and very white, it usually has a high rag content and is frequently used for *watercolor* and *pastel* work as well. It is available in a variety of sizes, most often in pad form.

CHARTREUSE—In *color*, a clear, light *green* with a *yellowish tinge*. See *cast*.

CHASSIS—In *painting*, a *frame* upon which the *canvas* is stretched.

CHÂSSIS—In *sculpture*, (1) the modeling stand with revolving top upon which a *wax* model or *armature* (q.v.) may be placed. See also *gentleman*. (2) A type of *pantograph* used to duplicate a piece of sculpture in *plaster*, allowing for enlargement, reduction, or re-creation in the same size as the original.

CHEF-D'OEUVRE—French term applied to any object or accomplishment deemed a *masterpiece*.

CHÊ HUANG—In Chinese *painting*, an *ochre yellow* pigment having the color of muskmelon, made through a mixture of *t'êng huang* and *chê shih* (qq.v.). It is used for painting late autumn trees, mid-mountain level spots, and pathways through grass.

CHEMIGRAPHY—In *engraving* and *etching,* the term applied to any process of mechanical engraving depending on the action of chemical.

CHÊ MO—In Chinese *painting,* an *ochre*-colored *ink* used for rock and mountain work; prepared by mixing *chê shih* (q.v.) with ink.

CHÉNG—In Chinese *art,* a *painting* on *silk* or other fabric, loosely backed with cloth or with borders sewn on, and usually folded when not on actual display. The subjects are invariably Buddhistic and the pictures are hung in *temples* during specified *ceremonies.* The paintings found at TUN HUANG were this type; the general style and technique can be found in Tibetan art of more recent times. *Chêng* is not to be confused with the *scroll paintings,* or *chüan chou.*

CH'ENG HSIN—In Chinese *painting,* a fine, thin, smooth variety of *paper* of superior quality, used as a *ground.* Exceedingly popular with the best artists of the SUNG and YÜAN periods. See *chih.*

CHÊNG PI—In Chinese *painting,* a technique in which the *brush* is held and used in a vertical position with respect to the *ground,* in the manner of writing. Used chiefly for *dotting* (see *tien*) and for some forms of shading. Known to Western artists as *upright brush technique.*

CHERRY—A bright *red color, yellow*ish-red in *hue,* having a very small quantity of *blue in the mixture;* it is of high *saturation* and low *brilliance,* and is *somewhat* bluer than *claret.*

CHERRY GUM—An ingredient of some *paints,* adding considerable *transparency* to any color. Deriving from various fruit trees (esp. cherry, plum, and apricot), it gives a brilliant, *glossy* effect when mixed with an egg or *casein* emulsion. Practically obsolete since the mid-19th century, chiefly because of its tendency to crack and chip.

CHÊ SHIH—In Chinese *painting,* a variety of *umber* prepared from an iron oxide known as limonite, the color resembling hyacinth *red* or almost terra cotta. One of the most popular and commonly used of all Oriental *pigments,* it is available now in prepared form with the *glue* already added; used extensively in flower and *landscape* painting.

CHIAO MO—Chinese *painting,* dense black *ink,* applied with the *brush* fairly dry, although not quite as dry as in the *dry brush* (q.v.) technique. Used chiefly for adding touches to a picture to accentuate planes and *contours.*

CHIAROSCURO—A term referring to the manner in which a *painter* handles atmospheric effects, creating the *illusion* that his subjects are surrounded by space, and standing "free." The word itself means "light and dark," a sister word to *pianoforte,* meaning "soft and loud." It originally dealt only with *woodcuts,* the finished picture displaying a pleasant *tone* of contrasting *lights* and *shades.*

CHIAROSCURO EFFECT—Differential *shadings* in an inkblot *design* or work of *graphic art.*

CHIDORI—In Japanese *art* and *weaving,* a bird scene; often associated with waves, as a bird and wave *pattern.*

CHIEH HUA—In Chinese *painting,* the term describing any picture having ruled or measured outlines; used principally in *architectural* representation, it is known to Western artists as *boundary painting.*

CH'IEN CHIANG—In Chinese *painting,* a light purplish-red *pigment* somewhat similar to but darker than *tan chê* q.v.) ; used primarily in *ink* painting.

CH'IEN FÊN—In Chinese *painting,* the equivalent of *white lead* as used in the West. It is rubbed up and preserved under water; when wanted, a small quantity is taken out and mixed with *glue.* Although used for the painting of practically all subjects, it has a tendency to darken. See *k'o fên.*

CHIH—The general term for *paper* used in Chinese *painting;* has been made of rice straw, *hemp,* certain reeds, mulberry, *bamboo,* and other substances. Typically white, all of the types had a fine *pattern* of parallel *mold* marks. Bamboo is said to have been the best for use as painting *ground.* See *ch'eng hsing, hsüan chih,* and *ping hsüeh.*

CHIH HUA—In Chinese *art,* the technique of using finger

tips and fingernails in place of or in addition to the *brush* in executing a *drawing*. Originating during the T'ANG DYNASTY, the process is known to Western artists as *finger drawing* (q.v.).

CHILL—A clouded appearance occurring as a defect on the *varnished* surface of an *oil painting*, piece of *sculpture*, etc.; resembles the powdery or frosted surface of a plum or grape. Known also as *bloom* and *blooming*.

CHILUCA—In *sculpture*, a variety of *porphyry* found in Mexico, used in the making of ornamental objects.

CHIMERA—In any *visual art*, a *representation* of a monster, made up of parts of various animals. Also spelled *chimaera*. See *sphinx*.

CHINA STONE—In *sculpture* and *ceramics*, a variety of semi-decomposed *granite* having nearly the same composition as *China clay*, but harder and receptive to *carving* and inscribing.

CHINA-WOOD OIL—A yellow *drying oil* of natural, origin finding increased uses in the *arts*. Better known as *tung oil* (q.v.).

CHINESE ART—One of the oldest, strongest and most highly developed branches of Oriental *art*. Chinese *architecture* makes extensive use of *bamboo*, and its forms and methods of construction, even in *brick* and *stone*, are largely influenced by this material. Roofs are usually *tiled*, and have a characteristic hollow dip, as if copied from the form of a tent; when rectangular, the lower corners are sharply turned up, esp. in the many-tiered roofs of *temples* and *towers*. The tiles are often *glazed* in various colors, and the walls are frequently encrusted with *porcelain* and *marble* slabs. A peculiarity is found in the fact that construction starts with the roof, which is supported on posts, and the walls are then built beneath it. *Drawing* and *painting* are of great delicacy, but show no knowledge of *perspective*. Higher merit is found in the *decorative arts*. Small *bronzes* and *carvings* in wood are of great technical excellence, and porcelain-making is unsurpassed. The Chinese are fond of the *grotesque*, as observed in their wide use of *dragon* and kindred fantastic creations.

CHINESE BLUE—The first *blue pigment* made synthetically on a large scale (Berlin, early 18th century), better known as *Prussian blue* (q.v.).

CHINESE INK—A carbon-black *pigment,* usually *lampblack* (q.v.), combined with *glue* as a *medium.* In the Far East it is made in the form of small sticks which, in use, are rubbed with water on a *stone* slab, dissolving the glue and carrying the black pigment in suspension. This was used extensively as a writing and *drawing* material in the West during the *Middle Ages* and the *Renaissance.* It is highly volatile, and is indelible to moisture and erasure. Known widely as *India Ink,* it is also made from *agaric* (q.v.). Frequently added to *water-colors* as a modifier. See *mo.*

CHINESE INSECT WAX—A pale-colored *wax,* fibrous and *opaque,* used in the *arts* for *modeling,* as an ingredient of *surface films,* and as a *painting* medium in various periods. Prepared by a complicated process after deriving the raw deposit of the Asiatic COCCUS CERIFERUS. Employed for many of the purposes to which *beeswax* (q.v.) is put, its greatest use is still in the Orient. It is believed by many that the famous *Mayum mummy portraits* were executed in *Chinese insect wax.* Not synonymous with *insect wax* (q.v.).

CHINESE PENCIL—In *etching,* an instrument in *brush* form having strong, sharp bristles, strongly resistant to the action of acid; used for stirring up the acid during the *biting* (q.v.) process. The *Chinese pencil* has recently replaced the age-old technique of agitating the acid with a feather.

CHINESE VARNISH—A *turpentine*-like substance of *greenish-yellow,* belonging to the *balsam* group. In thin layers it quick-dries into smooth, shining *lac.* Its use in China for *lacquering* and *varnishing* surfaces, alone or in combination with *colors,* goes back to antiquity.

CHINESE YELLOW—In *painting,* a fine *yellow* pigment used extensively in *ancient* and *medieval* art, identified on many *illuminated manuscripts.* Known also as *orpiment,* and *king's yellow* (qq.v.).

CH'ING LÜ—In Chinese *painting,* a *landscape* in *blue* and *green,* distiguished by the fact that large areas of mineral blue (see *shih ch'ing*) and green are used. Works of this type are always *kung pi* (featured by meticulous attention to detail). See also *shih lü* and *Watteau blue.*

CHINKINBORI—A Japanese *lacquer* process employed when shallow *engravings* are traced with *gold.* The *technique* was derived from the Chinese.

CHIOS SCHOOL—One of the most productive and influential schools of *sculpture* in the history of *art.* Located on the island of *Chios* in the 6th century B.C., it dealt mainly with the art of facial expression, and characteristic faces possessed oval contours, thin eyes, and engaging smiles. Melas and Achermos were adherents of the school, and *Chios* is credited with having invented the soldering of iron which allowed for the making of *relief designs* in *metal.* Known also as *Chiot school.*

CHIP CARVING—A type of *relief* decoration executed in wood, characterized by numerous small, vari-shaped incisions rather than lines of any appreciable length. Usually filled with *tesserae, enamel,* or other colored *inlay* material; *hydro-plastic* (q.v.) can be used successfully, simplifying the operation. The original *carving* is usually accomplished by using a *relief carving knife* (q.v.).

CHIRIJI—In Japanese *painting,* a substance used to create a mottled effect. It was accomplished by sprinkling *gold* dust into plain black *lacquer.*

CHISEL CUT TECHNIQUE—In Chinese *painting,* a brush stroke technique creating the appearance of a series of chisel cuts. There is unvarying evenness of thickness throughout the length of each line, with sharp angles closely giving the effect of stiffness. Executed in *vertical* brush style, with heavy *ink*-dipping allowing for long lines.

CHISEL DRAFT—In *sculpture,* the marked and prepared edge of a stone, serving as a guide in cutting the rest.

CHONDRIN—A *transparent* substance made of cartilaginous tissue, chief use in the *arts* is as an ingredient of *size,* used as a *binding* agent and often applied under *paint* and *distemper* to prevent absorption. See *size.*

CHOU—In Chinese *painting,* the rod or spindle at the bottom of a *chüan chou* or *scroll painting,* upon which it is rolled when not in use. This cylindrical rod is knobbed at either end (see *chou shou*).

CHOU SHOU—In Chinese *painting,* the ornamented ends of the rod (*chou*) upon which a *scroll painting* is rolled. The embellishment may consist of tassels, carved *bulbous* shapes, *mosaic* work of *ivory* or *jade, etc.* See *chüan chou.*

CHROMA—In *painting* and *water-color,* the term applied to a concentrated *saturation* by one outstanding color, untainted by *gray* or *white;* color *intensity;* the degree of departure from *black* or white. In color *pigments* it is the quality distinguishing an intense color from one not so intense; e.g., bright *red, vermilion,* flaming *scarlet, emerald green,* and other light colors possess high *chroma.*

CHROMATITES—In *painting,* a general term applied to all *paints, pigments,* and coloring matter deriving from mineral sources.

CHROME PIGMENTS—Synthetically prepared *artists' colors,* the most important being the *yellow,* which can vary from a pale *tint* of *greenish hue* to *orange.* The green, popular commercially, is made by mixing the yellow with *Prussian blue. Chrome red* completes the list. These *pigments* are crystalline and not entirely permanent to light.

CHROME RED— One of the *chrome pigments* (q.v.), not substantially *stable* to light; a basic lead chromate used largely as a *painting pigment.*

CHROME YELLOW—One of the *chrome pigments* (q.v.); a lead chromate used chiefly as a *pigment* in *oil painting.*

CHRYSELEPHANTINE—Any one of the great cult *statues* in 5th century B.C. Greek *temples,* made of *ivory* and *gold.* Notable among them were the *Asklepios* by Calamis, the *Dionsyus* by Alcamenes, and the *Zeus at Olympia* and *Athena in the Parthenon* by Phidias. The technique appears to have come from the Orient. In the Egyptian *tomb* of *Tutankhamen* there are *statuettes* in which the flesh is ivory and the hair and drapery gold. Similar examples have been found in Mesopotamia and Crete. The Greeks made their *chryselephantines* on a tremendous scale. *Athena* was forty feet high, the drapery of riveted gold plates and the flesh of ivory. The seated *Zeus* was nearly as high.

CHRYSOCOLLA—An ancient *coloring* compound of mineral origin, somewhat similar to *malachite* although of a deeper blue while preserving the characteristic green. When pulverized, it retains its green character sufficiently to be used as a water-soluble *pigment,* although heat will cause a blackening despite its otherwise *stable* features. It is not available as an artist's color today; however, it has been identified on *wall paintings* of Chinese Turkestan and on the *tombs* of Egypt's XII DYNASTY.

CHRYSOTILE—A fibrous form of *serpentine* (q.v.).

CHŬAN—In Chinese *painting,* the term for *silk,* but only in the sense of its use as a *ground* in this *art.* Both *paper* and silk are used as painting grounds, the choice depending only on the preference of the artist. Silk lends itself better to the bright mineral *colors,* while the freer *impressionistic* styles, as well as all forms of *calligraphy,* are more effective on paper. See also *hua chüan.*

CHŬAN CHOU—In Chinese *art,* rolled *paintings* or *scrolls* of all types, as distinguished from *murals, albums,* screens, *fans,* etc. It is the most common form of painting in China. Historians assert that the portability of scrolls allows for their safety in fire, war, removal to another dwelling, etc., not possible in the case of *wall paintings* and murals. The rod upon which the painting is rolled is the *chou,* incorporated into the mounting at the bottom of the picture. See also *hêng fu, kua fu,* and *p'ing chang.*

CH'UAN SHÊN JÊN WU—In Chinese *painting,* a general term applied to portraiture as a class or subject, rather than to any individual picture. Not as broad in scope as *jên wu* (q.v.), although more comprehensive than *hsiang.*

CHŪBAN—A Japanese *wood-block print* of medium size in vertical arrangement.

CHUI YING—In Chinese *art,* the 'model' from which an *artist* works in painting the features of a deceased person, consisting of a verbal description from a close relative. Employed when there is no previous *portrait* or *photograph* of the deceased, and where it is not possible to copy the actual corpse. The *painting* executed under such circumstances is known as *ying hsiang.*

CH'UN HUA—In Chinese *painting,* the term applied to any picture that is essentially erotic in subject matter. Despite the high station involved, *hsing lê t'u* (q.v.) paintings often fell within this classification.

CHURI—In Oriental *ivory-carving,* a device used to cut the medium into the rough shape generally desired prior to the actual carving. One variety of *churi* has a smooth, sharp edge for cutting; another has a toothed edge for sawing.

CHURINGA—Prominent forms of Australian aboriginal *art,* combining *music* and *design* in sacred *wood* or *stone carvings.* See *tjurunga.*

CHU SHA—In Chinese *painting,* a prized *pigment* of *vermilion* color; mineral in origin, it derives from *cinnabar* (q.v.). The stones from which it is taken are described as softer than the blue *(shih ch'ing)* and green *(shih lü)*, and those found in the shape of arrowheads are preferred. The name applies to the heavier, or lower stratum taken from the mineral in emulsion, the first skimming known as *piao chu.* Used chiefly in painting maple leaves, temple and palace ornaments, and the bright railings of terraces.

CILERY—In *sculpture* and *architecture,* the ornamental *carving* frequently found at the head of a *column* or *pillar;* a *volute;* any sculptured work in relief. Also spelled *cillery.*

CINCEL— A *primitive* tool in the nature of a stone chisel, used by the Indians of So. America in their *carvings* and inscriptions.

CINNABAR—Natural *red* sulphide of mercury, related to artificial *vermilion.* It is an ore, somewhat duller than the synthetic product. Though known to ancient *artists,* it was probably confused with artificial *red lead.* Pliny speaks of *cinnabar* as *minium,* and the latter term became associated ultimately with the lead *pigment..* See *chu sha.*

CINQUECENTO—An Italian *art* period which, though indicating the 16th century by its name, extended roughly from the 14th through 16th centuries. The term designates a style rather than a period, stressing strong individualism. *Baroque* (q.v.) elaboration and great attention to mass and detail. This was true in *architecture* as well as in *painting* and *sculpture.* Bremante and da Vinci are considered *cinquecento artists.*

CIPOLINO—In *sculpture,* a white crystalline *limestone* traversed by veins of greenish *mica;* a favorite Italian marble.

CIPPUS—In Roman *antiquity,* a post or pillar of *wood* or *stone* used as a mark or monument; specifically, any such monument marking a grave or a sacred place. The *cippus* was either cylindrical or square, and sometimes had a *base* and *capital* with *sculptured* ornamentation. Many *cippi* bear the inscription *S.T.T.L.* (SIT TIBI TERRA LEVIS, *May the earth be light to thee*) ; but many other forms of inscription appear.

CIRE PERDUE—A *technique* of casting *bronze statues* and other forms. After the original figure is *modeled* in *wax* over a core, the wax flows out of the space between the core and the *mold* when melted by the hot metal, which runs into its place, taking upon itself the shape of the mold. The famous 12th century Gloucester candlestick, now in the Victoria and Albert Museum, is of pale *bronze,* cast by the *cire perdue* process. It depicts forty monsters in grotesque attitudes, struggling with nine humans, all in remarkable detail. Known also as *lost wax process.* See *Ashanti.*

CLARET—A *color, red* in *hue,* having high *saturation* and low *brilliance;* in the *gradations* of red, it falls at a point slightly less *blue* than *cerise.*

CLASSICAL—Based upon the accurate subdivision of data into classes or categories, and to that extent systematic and scientific. In accord with accepted tastes and *traditions,* as distinguished from *novelty,* radicalism and change. Basically, founded on Greek and Roman *arts.*

CLASSICISM—Generally, the *style* of *arts* as produced by the ancient Greeks and Romans, stressing impeccable correctness, simplicity, and unostentatious elegance. Any school or movement pursuing the stylistic influence of Greece or Rome is a school, etc., of *classicism.*

CLAY—Now basically the working material of the *sculptor, clay* varies widely in composition and in its uses in the *arts.* It is the substance of *pottery* and *terra cotta* (dehydration occurring on *burning*), and when *colored;* has furnished *pigments* for *painters.* Its *attributes* are smoothness, fine *texture,* and its *unctuous* quality when mixed with water. The oldest of all *plastering* materials, it has endured remarkably as a painting *support,* and its *plasticity* has rendered it valuable as a *ceramics* material since *primitive* times.

CLAY ROCK—A popular item of equipment in the studios of sculptors and makers of *ceramics,* consisting simply of a large-sized container made of *clay,* having a heavy cover of the same material. Used for the storing of clay in either moist or dry form, keeping it clean and plastic; usually accommodates 15 pounds of *moist clay* for each gallon of capacity.

CLAY ENAMEL—In *ceramics* and *sculpture,* a synthetic material prepared in a wide range of colors, used for decorating *pottery, plaster casts,* etc. Featured by its ease of use, it is simply applied with a *brush;* it then dries to a hard, enamel *luster.*

CLAY-STONE PORPHYRY—An old and somewhat indefinite name for those varieties of *porphyry* whose naturally fine groundmass is more or less *kaolin*-ized so as to be soft and earthy, suggesting hardened *clay.*

CLICHE—In *etching* and *engraving,* any stereotype *plate* created for pictorial or word reproduction.

CLINCHFIELD—A variety of *China clay* product, used as an extender in *paint* and *enamel.* Chemically, it is a form of aluminum silicate, *clinchfield* being a trade name.

CLIO—In Greek mythology, one of the nine famous daughters of Zeus and Mnemosyne. She was the *Muse* of history and heroic exploits, and like her sister, *Calliope,* was represented in the *arts* with *pen* and *parchment* as her *attributes.*

CLOUD BAND—In *painting,* a ribbonlike *theme* of conventionalized cloud forms.

CLOY—In *sculpture* and *ceramics,* the term applied to any *clay*-like substance that is not *natural* clay; any plastic *cement* mixture, or material of workable *plasticity.*

COAL-TAR—A thick viscous substance resulting from the distillation of coal, it is the basis of thousands of various compounds. Among the numerous products are fine *dyes,* building compounds, *alizarin* (q.v.), paving materials, painting *pigments,* etc.

COATING—A term in *painting* and *sculpture;* see *film* and *surface film.*

COBALT BLUE—Chief among the *cobalt pigments* (q.v.), this *blue* possesses an unusually high degree of *luminosity* and tends strongly toward the group known as the *cyanic colors.* Known also as *Hungary blue, Leithner's blue,* and *Parish blue.*

COBALT GLASS—In *painting,* a pulverized *pigment* prepared by fusing cobalt-*glance* (previously roasted) with sand and potash. When powdered finely it is the well-known *smalt* (q.v.).

COBALT PIGMENTS—Important additions to the *artist's palette* in the early 19th century included *cobalt blue,* discovered in 1802. It is fine in grain, bright in *color,* and unusally *stable.* Earlier blues, notably that which appeared in *ceramic glazes,* were known as smalt. A *green* made with *cobalt* is as stable as the blue, but has less strength as a color. *Cobalt violet* is *red*dish, *weak* in *tinting power,* and rather *transparent. Cobalt yellow,* known as *aureolin,* has fairly good strength as a color, and moderate hiding power. Blue is by far the finest *cobalt* color. See *yellow pigments.*

COCHINEAL—One of the many *pigments* made from *dyes.* This, also known as *carmine lake* and *crimson lake,* is made from the dried bodies of an insect which lives on cactus plants in Mexico and Central and South America. The dye is extracted and precipitated to form a pigment. On different bases, it produces *tints* from *scarlet* to *purple.* It is not *stable* to light, though its *fugitive* or fading character is less evident when it is used with an *oil medium.* See *lac.*

COELANAGLYPHIC—In *sculpture,* a term relating to any variety of *hollow relief* (q.v.).

COGGING—In *drawing,* any one of the three principal techniques employed in the copying of a *picture* or *design* by means of *tracing.* See *calking.*

COIL METHOD—One of the three techniques employed in the *sculpture* which uses the *medium* of *terra cotta* (q.v.). Platters and *vases* made by this method consist of cylindrical strips of *clay* having the thickness of an ordinary pencil, made by rolling the clay on a flat surface with both hands. The elongated strip is then wound up to create the desired shape. Compare with *slab system* and *shaping method* (qq.v.).

COLCOTHAR—An *iron pigment* having a *purple tinge.* Better known as *Indian red* (q.v.).

COLD FOREST—In Chinese *art,* the term applied to a popular type of *painting* showing trees without leaves; known natively as *han lin.*

COLLAGE—The designation of certain *pictures* or other visual arrangements usually in the *surrealist* class, sometimes *dadaist.* These are made, entirely or in part, of pasted pieces of paper, newspaper, wallpaper, *chromos,* illustrations, *photographs,* and other textured and figured material, assembled in a manner totally incongruous with ordinary experience. When the elements consist entirely of photographs or parts thereof, the resulting combination is known as *photomontage,* and the *artist,* a *photomonteur.*

COLOPHONY—An ingredient in *wax-resin* mixtures for impregnating *wood,* and used for the re-lining of old *paintings* on *canvas.* It now enjoys little use as a *resin* ingredient in painters' *varnishes.* It forms a brittle *film,* easily discolored by exposure or by dampness, and is easily scarred by friction, although its *qualities* are improved when it is mixed with *oils.* It is the 'rosin' used on the *bows* of the *violin* family to enable the horsehair to grip the *strings;* name derives from Colophon, region in Asia Minor producing the best quality.

COLOR—In *painting,* (1) the general effect of all the *hues* entering into the composition of a *picture;* (2) an effect of *brilliance* combined with *harmony:* said either of a work in different *colors,* or of a work in *monochrome,* or of an *engraving;* e.g., the picture has no *color;* the engraving is rich with *color;* (3) that which is used for *coloring; paint;* a *pigment or dye.*

COLOR AQUATINT—An *aquatint* using more than one *color,* produced in either of two ways: (1) Printing from one *plate,* on which all the colored *inks* have been applied, or (2) Multiple plate printing, in which each color is applied to a separate plate.

COLOR CONTRAST—In *photography,* a property by which the form of an object can be recognized by its variation in *color,* whether or not the *brightness* is equal in all parts of the object.

COLOR DESIGN—The *art* of organizing *color* in a total *esthetic* form wherein the detalis are so arranged as to emphasize orderliness in variation, repetition, contrast, etc., among color traits.

COLORED AQUATINT—A *monochrome print* tinted with *water colors* after *printing.* The *hues* may be added by aid of a *stencil,* thus bringing the finished product into the *aquarelle* classification.

COLOR GLOW—The presence of *luminosity* where there is also a specifically defined figure in the work of *art,* usually a *painting.*

COLORING STRENGTH—In *painting* and *water-color,* a term applied to the relative strength of various *pigments* when used in coloring a light *ground.*

COLOR MILL—A device consisting of rotating cylinders operated mechanically, used to grind the mixture of *pigment* and *oil* or water into a brushable *paint.* This discovery replaced the *ancient* method of making pigments by hand with the use of the *grinding slab, muller,* and *slice* (qq.v.). See also *porphyry.*

COLOR PYRAMID—Titchener's graphic representation of the manner in which *primary colors* combine to form the 32,820 individual elements of visual *sensation* (1897). At the four sides are *red, green, blue,* and *yellow; black* at the bottom, *white* at the top.

COLOR RETOUCHING—See *retouch varnish.*

COLOR VALUE—The amount of light and dark in a *color.* The greater the amount of light, the higher its *value,* with lower *values* prevailing as the quantity of light diminishes.

COLOR VISION—White light, as daylight, consists of a mixture of wave-motions varying in length. Any object reflecting all of these will appear *white;* some objects will absorb some of the radiations they receive, reflecting the others. Thus, an object absorbing all light except the radiations corresponding to *green,* will appear green because it reflects those radiations, holding to itself the others. In the cases of *color* observed by transmitted light, as in colored glass, the glass absorbs all the radiations except those which are visible, passing through. No object possesses color in darkness; black is not a color, since it absorbs all the rays of the white light without breaking them. See *primary colors.*

COLOR ZONES—In *color* study, the term describing the areas of differential with respect to the sensitivity of various parts of the *retina* to different colors. See *campimeter.*

COLOSSAL—In *sculpture,* the term applied to any *statue* in which the figures are larger than *heroic* (q.v.).

COLOSSUS OF RHODES—One of the *seven wonders of the world,* it was an immense *statue* (over 150 feet high) built to commemorate the successful defense of Rhodes against Demetrius Poliorcetes (304 B.C.). It is said to have been made from the engines of war abandoned by Demetrius, and took 12 years of work before completion. Chares of Lindus was the *sculptor.*

COMMON SERPENTINE—In *sculpture,* a type of *marble*-like rock occurring in winding, irregular veins (hence, the name), belonging to the general *serpentine* (q.v.) family. Usually *green* or greenish-*red* in color, it is frequently *mottled,* streaked or spotted. Takes a good polish and responds well to sharp cutting.

COMPASSES—An instrument employed in describing circles. This drafting tool has a long history of utility in the *studio* of the *painter* and of other workers in the *arts.* In its simplest form, it was known from earliest *classical* times, *sketches* of it having been found among the notes of Leonardo da Vinci. It is a V-shaped device, one leg of which is pointed for imbedding into the *drawing* surface, and the other equipped to hold pencil, crayon, etc., which renders a circumference about the point. It is adjustable. See also *calipers* and *dividers.*

COMPATIBILITY—In *painting* and *watercolor,* the ability of *colors* to exist together in one picture without clash or other harmful reaction.

COMPLEMENTARY COLORS—Two *colors* which, when properly mixed, will result in a *grayish-white,* or *achromatic* color. It has been demonstrated that every color has a *complementary*; *red* is *complementary* to *blue-green,* etc.

COMPOSITION—The putting together and organizing of *components* in a work of *art,* or a product of such organization. The manner in which inner experience is brought into being through a *technique,* artfully and skillfully, the result being a symbol of the creator's expression. *Composition* appears in all of the *fine arts.*

CONCAVE RELIEF—A term in *sculpture*; see *hollow relief.*

CONCEPTUAL COLOR—The *artist's* use of *color* to bring out the *meaning,* rather than to reproduce exactly the colors of the objects in the actual scene. *Perspective, lights,* and *shadows* involve the use of this procedure by the *painter.*

CONFLUENT COLORS—A term describing any series of *colors* in one *painting* or other *work of art,* so selected and applied that they gradually pass into each other without any marked division.

CONFUSED DOTS—In Chinese *painting,* a variety of brush stroke technique of the *tien* (q.v.) class, giving the effect of small ovals; applied with the side of the tip of the brush, light and dark together. Used chiefly for *dotting* rocks and leaves in *landscape* work.

CONNOISSEUR—In *art,* one who has a trained, discriminating *judgment* of what is rare or choice, developed by the combination of historical knowledge of the art in question, practical understanding of its characteristics, and sound acumen in *esthetic criticism. Connoisseurship* may be described as the ideal goal of the historian of any art.

CONSERVATIVE—In *art,* a person who clings to the status quo, opposing all but inconsequential changes, on the assumption that anything new is likely to be worse.

CONSISTENCY—As applied to *paints* and *surface films,* the relative firmness, body, limpidity, or resistance to agitation or deformation that characterizes any coating material when in bulk.

CONSTRUCTIVISM—A Russian-French *geometric-abstract* movement in *painting* and *sculpture* founded by Naum Gabo and Antoine Pevsner in 1920 and flourishing during the ensuing decade. The movement attracted such *artists* as Lissitzky, Moholy-Nagy, Tatlin, and Rodchenko. It absorbed and assumed the principles of *Tatlinism* (q.v.), which came into being in 1916.

CONTOUR—In *drawing* or *sculpture,* the outline of a figure or body; the line that bounds.

CONTRAPPOSTO—In *sculpture* of the *baroque* period, the principle of balancing the body in *opposition*; e.g., the left arm and right leg being features, rather than left arm and left leg. Static version of the principle of *opposition* (q.v.). A popular form of *contrapposto* among sculptors is an arrangement of the torso in such manner that the shoulders face in a different direction from the hips. See also *Praxiteles curve.*

CONVERSATION PIECE — A type of *genre painting* in which a group of human figures is *represented.*

COOL COLORS—In *painting* and *water-color,* the term applied to certain *hues* of *blue* and others approaching blue, e.g., blue-*green* and blue-*violet*; any *color* in which blue, green or violet predominates. Compare with *warm colors* (q.v.).

COPAIBA VARNISH—One of the *balsams* used directly in the *arts,* as an ingredient in painters' *varnishes.* It is the exudate from coniferous trees, and the volatile oil is derived by distillation with a crude *resin* remaining as residue. See *oleoresin* and *balsam.*

COPAL GUM—In the *arts,* a hard, *lustrous,* transparent *resinous* substance prized for its use as a *surface film* over *oil paintings* and *sculpture.* Citron colored, it is dissolved in *linseed oil* and diluted with *turpentine,* forming an excellent *varnish* which, when carefully applied and slowly dried, is remarkably hard and durable, and responsive to a high polish. Often used as a substitute for the scarce, high-priced amber (q.v.). Known also as *animé,* it is collected from living trees or is dug from the ground as a fossil. Numerous varieties fall within the general classification.

CONTOUR—In *drawing* or *sculpture,* the outline of a figure or body; the line that bounds.

COPING—In *sculpture,* the process of trimming the edge of a slab of *marble.* Industrially, the *coping machine* (a carborundum wheel) cuts and trims marble slabs for use as base boards, tiles, etc.

COPPER—An elementary *metal* used widely in the *arts,* particularly those connected with *etching* and *engraving* wherein *copper* is used as the principal *medium* for *plates.* Its *green* salts are employed as *pigments* for the *palette,* offering an excellent *artistic* and practical *hue* to *painting.* Also, the principal ingredient in the making of *bronze* (q.v.).

COPPER ETCHING—In *etching,* (1) a technique of producing fine pictures, the *plate* being etched with acid instead of *engraved* with a tool. The entire plate is covered with a *ground* resembling *varnish,* and the lines of the *drawing* or *design* are scratched through the ground, after which the acid is poured over and the lines eaten or bitten down to various depths; see *biting.* (2) Any *line drawing* reproduced on *copper* instead of zinc; the softer effect in direct *printing,* as obtained in this manner, appears to warrant application of the term.

COPPER POINT—A *drawing* instrument developed from the ancient *stylus* (q.v.); used chiefly in Western *art.* As in the case of all metal points *(see silver point)* it requires an abrasive *ground* in order to create an effective line.

COQUINA—In *architecture* and *sculpture,* a coarse-grained, porous, friable variety of *limestone,* made up chiefly of fragments of shells of living or recently extinct species of mollusks and of coral, cemented together strongly as a firm rock.

CORBIE SCHOOL—A 9th century *art* group of the *Carolingian* epoch, emphasizing *decoration* and *illustration* of the famous *Evangeliars* of the period.

CORDATE—In the *arts* generally any object, *pattern,* etc., that is heart-shaped.

CORINTHIAN BRONZE—In *metalwork,* a famous *alloy* produced at Corinth, noted in antiquity (esp. among the Romans) for its excellent quality and the artistic character and technical perfection of the *works of art* made from it. Erroneously referred to as *Corinthian brass,* a term used *colloquially* to denote excessive impudence or assurance.

CORNISH STONE—In *sculpture* and *ceramics,* the term referring to *China stone* or *kaolin* (qq.v.).

COROPLAST—In Greek *antiquity,* the name applied to any *sculptor* who employed *terra-cotta* as his *medium.* The principal product of this *art* was the *figurine.*

CORPSE PAINTING—In Chinese *art,* a ceremonial *portrait,* usually painted posthumously with regard to the subject. It may be executed with the actual corpse as the model, or from a previous portrait, *photograph,* or verbal description furnished by a close relative of the deceased; the last is known as *chui ying.* It is interesting to note that photographs are replacing *corpse paintings* in modern China; by 1950 the original practice was almost obsolete.

CORRECT DRAWING—A term used by *artists* to denote specific information or instruction in connection with freehand *drawing.*

COSMATI—Families of *marble* workers, *sculptors* and *mosaic*ists who flourished in and around Rome from the late 12th to the early 14th century. The word derives from the fact that the names COSMAS and COSMATUS appeared in several of these families. The *Cosmati* provoked an *artistic* revival, equipping many of the older churches with *pavements, chancels, ambos, altars, ciboria, cathedras, sepulchres* and *porticos* of a refined and elegant character. That the artists took pride in their work is evident from the inscriptions with their names, rarely lacking.

COSMETIC BISMUTH—A white powder of crystalline structure, used as a *pigment* in the making of artists' *paints* and *varnishes*. Known also as *pearl white*, it has been used successfully as a pigment in artificial *pearls*.

COSMORAMA—A view or series of views of the world; specifically, a type of exhibition formerly held, showing a number of *drawings, paintings,* or *photographs* of cities, buildings, landscapes, and the like, so arranged that they were reflected from mirrors, the reflections being observed through a *lens*.

COUNTER RELIEF—A Russian type of *sculptural relief* having volume and planes of contrasting materials. Invented by Tatlin, whose most famous work (the model for the Third International) consisted of a huge *spiral* built in the form of a cube, *pyramid,* and cylinder, these forms designed to rotate according to the day, month and year of the calendar. Never erected, the *model* was later destroyed. See *constructivism* and *Tatlinism*.

COWRIE—In the *arts*, a fine, *resinous gum* used as a *surface film* over *paintings* and *sculpture*; prized for its remarkable hardness and durability. Derived from the botanical *kauri pine*, it is known also as *kauri gum*.

CRACKING—A term in *painting*; see *crackle*.

CRACKLE—In *oil paintings*, cracks extending through the picture itself to the *support* behind it, causing a definite series of interruptions in the portrayal. Often caused by a non-drying *pigment*, as *asphaltum*. In *pottery*, the numerous "age cracks" often observed, particularly in Oriental pieces. Forgers sometimes produce fine *crackle* to create an appearance of age. This is done by *varnishing* the *paint* before it is completely dry. Still others actually paint *crackle* over the surface of the painted imitation; the closest inspection with a good glass is required to detect such a forgery. See *crazing.*

CRADLE—A 19th century device used in repairing and restoring damaged *paintings* on *wood.* It consisted of a system of strips attached to the reverse of the wood *panel,* which held the painting without warping for an extended period of time. Thus securely braced, the work on the face of the painting could be started by the *artist.* The *value* of the cradle has long been questioned, and it is little used today, having given way to the *technique* of *parquetage de champ* (q.v.).

CRADLING—The *technique* employing the use of the *cradle* (q.v.) in *art restoration.*

CRAQUELE'—In *oil painting,* same as *crackle* (q.v.).

CRAYON—Any small stick made for *drawing.* It usually designates a combination of *pigments* or *dyes* in a *medium* of *wax,* formed into a thin, cylindrical shape. A few *crayons* contain water-soluble *dyes,* and one type of *crayon* has been made by cooking *charcoal* in *linseed oil.* As tools for the draftsman, they are said to have come into use in the 16th century, and are found in many drawings of that time. See *intaglio crayon aquatint.*

CRAZING—A type of *paint* failure consisting of minute interlacing cracks on the surface of a finish, caused by unequal contraction while drying.

CREACIONISMO—In *art,* a post-modernist *esthetic* movement in Spain and Spanish America in the 1920's, holding that it is the function of the *artist* to *create,* and that his material is to be found in the realm of experience that is beyond reason; akin to *ultraism* (q.v.).

CREMNITZ WHITE—A series of *pigments* having wide use in the *arts,* chiefly as fine coloring matter. The various pigments within the group differ from each other principally in the amount of lead oxide they contain. Known also as *kremnitz white* and *crems white.*

CREVÉ—In *etching,* a condition prevailing when the acid has widened and broken down the areas between lines, piercing the uncut portions of the *ground.* The *plate* will then print a *gray,* faint impression. If recognized, this condition can be corrected with a *scraper.* See *line etching.*

CRIBBLE—In the *arts* generally, to cover with small punctures or dots, as in *engraving* or otherwise decorating *wood* or *metal.*

CRIMSON—A term in *painting;* see *cochineal.*

CRIMSON LAKE—In oil *paintings,* an excellent *carmine*-colored *lake* which may vary to *scarlet* or *purple* according to the base used with the *pigment.* Better known as *cochineal* (q.v.).

CROSS-HATCHING—In *cartography, drawing* and *engraving,* a shading made by parallel lines crossing over each other; used chiefly to indicate *relief* in terrain. See *section lines.*

CRUCIFIX—A *representation* of Christ on the cross; loosely, a *cross* used as a Christian *symbol,* always the sacred sign of the followers of Christ. The *crucifix* came into general use after the 6th century, showing Christ robed, and representations at the time were chiefly Oriental. In the west, the realistic presentation became normal and universal starting in the 9th century.

CUBISM—An important movement in modern French *painting,* and to a lesser degree, in *sculpture,* begun by Picasso and Braque in 1907, and expanding shortly thereafter into a significant international *art* development. The name derives from the fact that the art is semi-*abstract* and comparatively geometric, reducing *natural* forms to their fundamental shapes. Said Cezanne, "You must see in nature the cylinder, the sphere, and the cone." A later phase (1913) stressed the use of *collage* (q.v.), and this was followed by a period in which two-dimensionalism and high *coloring* prevailed. This style was continued by Picasso until 1925, when he began to introduce psychic meanings and *surrealist* (q.v.) elements into his *cubist* work, and by Braque in a purer and less phychic form until the 1930's. Known also (esp. by critics) as *analytical cubism.*

CURSOR—A *drawing* instrument consisting of a *transparent* slide device with a fine hair-line; used widely in the making of good slide-rules.

CUT—A *relief engraving* of any kind, original or *electrotype*; also, the printed impression thereof. The term survives from the times when all engravings used with type forms were *woodcuts*; it is not properly applied to *plates* made by modern engraving techniques.

CUT-OFF—In *sculpture* and *masonry,* the term for the direction along which the granite must be channeled. Channeling is required because granite does not split. Known commonly among quarrymen as *hard way*.

CYANIC COLORS—In *art,* the *blue hues* that are dark, and therefore low in *value,* usually shading toward *black*; e.g., *cyanine blue,* the *color* between blue-*green* and blue.

CYSTOGEN—A white crystalline substance used as a hardening agent in the *resins* employed as *surface films* or coatings over *paintings* and *statuary.*

D

DABBER—(1) A pad used by *engravers, etchers,* etc., to apply *ink* or *color* in even distribution. (2) In *painting,* a large round *brush,* usually of camel hair, used in smudge and *stencil* work.

DADAISM—A movement in *painting, sculpture* and *literature* which began officially in Zurich in 1916. Its philosophy involved a complete nihilism, *satirical* disillusionment, violent protest, disgust with and ridicule of civilization, *iconoclastic* destruction, programmatic disorder, systematic *demoralization,* and a glorification of the irrational or anti-rational, and anti-*esthetic,* and the amoral. Generally considered to be a revolt against the "senseless holocaust" that was World War I. Frequently found release in *collage* (q.v.), employing violent humor and devastating irony. Tristan Tzara was prominent in the origin of the movement which developed (1924) into *surrealism* (q.v.). Compare with *Tatlinism.*

DAI—In Japanese *sculpture,* any ornate *pedestal* or stand. See also *daiza.*

DAI-BON—A Japanese *wood-block* stressing *contour* lines, better known as *key-block* (q.v.).

DAIBUTSU—In Japanese *sculpture,* a general term applied to any large *image* of Buddha, such as those found in Nara and Kamakura. The latter city (see *Kamakurabori*) was famous for its *lacquered wood carvings.*

DAIZA—In Japanese *sculpture,* a *pedestal* especially made as the resting place for a *carved* figure, often bearing a *design* similar to that of the piece of sculpture. The *dai* (q.v.), although a pedestal, need not be used as such a base.

DAMMAR—A favorite among the *resins* used in *varnish*

making. Exuding from Malay trees, it is pale in *color,* has a good *luster,* and adheres well. The fact that it dissolves in *turpentine* renders it highly valuable as a varnish ingredient. Used widely as a protective *film* in the *restoration* of *oil paintings,* and as an ingredient in *printing ink.* See *resin.*

DANCE OF DEATH—A symbolic *dance* of 14th century Germany in which a figure representing death, accompanied by a number of typical followers, danced with other figures representing the living; its purpose was to remind the living of the power and presence of death. During the reign of Henry IV, the dance became a popular subject of British *paintings, tapestries, reliefs,* etc., and a processional *dance of death* was painted around the *cloisters* of old St. Paul's.

DATE PIT TECHNIQUE—In Chinese *painting,* a brush stroke technique creating a line resembling a series of date pits; actually, it is nothing more than a series of connected *tien* (q.v.) which are fine at the ends and thick in the middle, not quite as pointed as *liu yeh miao* (q.v.). Executed with the fine point of a large brush.

DAUB—A sticky application, as of mud or *plaster.* Also, the process of coating or smearing with such a substance.

DAVEY'S GRAY—In *painting,* a color prepared from *clay* or slate, used as a *pigment;* so called after Henry Davey, its discoverer in England. It is semi-transparent and highly *stable,* used chiefly in mixture with other colors to reduce the tones, thereby yielding shades clearer than those produced by the addition of black.

DAY OF THE DEAD—In Russia, the one day in each year set aside as an anniversary in memory of all of the country's dead; observed since the earliest days of the nation's history, and particularly strong during the *Druzhina Period.* Frequently represented in 11th and 12th cent. *painting,* showing the grief of the multitudes alleviated by the antics of professional buffoons retained for that purpose.

DEAD CLAY—In *ceramics* and *sculpture,* the term applied to *clay* (or any other plastic modeling substance) that has become lifeless or unresponsive, usually because of prior exposure to moisture. *Dead stone* is a term employed in describing the softer varieties of the sculptor's medium into which air and water have infiltrated. Usually identified by the dull thud it emits when struck with a steel hammer, as contrasted with the sharp 'clink' of the harder stones.

DEAD COLORING—In *painting,* the preparatory picture, lacking warmth and richness, over which the finishing colors and details are added to give life and expression to the completed work.

DEAD DIPPING—In *metalwork,* a technique by which a dead, dull or matte surface is imparted to *brass, bronze,* or other metal. Usually accomplished by dipping the metal into an acid for a controlled period.

DEATH MASK—A *cast* of the facial features of a newly-deceased person. Advanced to a highly developed *art* among the Romans and Egyptians, the former using a thin *gold* plate. Modern death masks are made of *plaster of Paris.*

DEATH PORTRAITURE—A term in Chinese *art;* see *corpse painting.*

DECADENCE—In *art,* the process or the result of the process of *esthetic* decay by which artistic accomplishment and *culture* traits generally lose their force, and the achievements dissolve into small and diversified units. It is, in essence, a cultural *demoralization.*

DECORATION—A mode of *art* composition, creative or added, in which the details are arranged in such a way as to please the spectator through visual experience, especially through such sensory *qualities* as *line, color, rhythm,* etc. Although chiefly applied to the *visual arts,* the word is frequently extended to *music* and *literature.* It may be simple, as in a solid color or *tone* of a *bell,* or can be developed as a *theme* in complex *pattern* or *design.* As a rule, *decoration* is purely *ornamental,* having no utilitarian purpose.

DEEP—In *painting,* a term employed by *artists* and critics to denote a *color* which, though possessing *intense* depth, shows no presence of *black.* Example: *ultramarine blue.*

DEEP DISTANCE—In *painting,* the Chinese term applied

to a view across and beyond mountain peaks, through to additional mountains behind; the principle of reiteration or the piling of peak upon peak. In this technique, the *colors* are dull and obscure, and the figures fine and small. The inclusion of clouds assists in furnishing the *illusion* of distance. Compare with *high distance* and *level distance* (qq.v.).

DEEP RELIEF—See *high relief.*

DEESIS—In Russian *art,* the term applied to a *painting* or other representation of Christ accompanied by the Madonna and John the Baptist. Frequently found in the central row of the 14th century *iconostasis* (q.v.), the other four rows being devoted to various saints, other holy figures, and feasts. Also spelled *deisus.*

DEMETER—Greek goddess of the earth and harvest, known in Latin as *Ceres.* Her *attributes* were ears of grain, poppies, a cornucopia, and a pig. In mythology she is best known for her sad quest after the abduction of her daughter *Persephone (Proserpina)* by Pluto, the story personifying the death of vegetation. The most famous *statue* of her in *ancient* times was the 4th century (B.C.) DEMETER of Cnidus, a seated *classical* figure.

DEMI-RELIEF—A *technique* of *sculpturing* in which the raised figures stand out in medium prominence against the flat background. Also known as *half relief.* See *relief.*

DEMORALIZATION—In *art,* the disintegration of a previously progressive or standardized scale of artistic values. A state in which solidarity gives way to individualism of ends, and the entire structure is threatened with swift decay. See *decadence* and *dadaism.*

DERBY RED—In *painting,* a *pigment* of brilliant, *vermilion*-like red, properly known as *victoria red* (q.v.).

DESICCATION—Drying or dehydration, as applied to *paintings, surface films, varnishes, oils,* etc.; removal of moisture, esp. with a drying agent. See *siccative* and *dryer.*

DESIGN—Generally, the combination of the features or details of a *painting,* building, or any other object; the basic *pattern* or device of any work of art; some frame-work to a completed work, usually *ornamental* rather than useful, as the geometric or pictorial addition to *pottery,* the *tracery* in *architecture,* the *bead* in *molding,* etc. The arrangement of *color, light* or line in painting, the *motif* in *music,* etc; occasionally, the pattern or *metrical scheme* of a *poem,* esp. in *free verse.* The application of *esthetic* principle to any creative effort.

DE STIJL—A geometric-*abstract* movement in the *visual arts* and *architecture,* characterized by rectangles and primary colors, founded in Holland in 1917 and lasting until 1931. The movement had a strong influence on industrial and *commercial art.*

DETAIL DRAWING—A *drawing* displaying every minute detail pertaining to the construction of every part of an object or assembly; includes specifications of materials, dimensions, changes, part numbers, finish, quantities, and other information relative to the construction of the object, thus affording a complete advance picture.

DETAIL SECTION—In *drawing* and *cartography,* a view of part of the whole, shown at some convenient location on the paper, entirely separate and removed from the regular projected view. The *detail section* is set forth by a cutting plane line. In order to clarify the construction or situation or small details, this section is frequently drawn to a larger scale than that of the over-all picture of which it is a part, and in which it is indicated again in the scale of the drawing proper.

DEVIL'S FACE—In Chinese *painting,* a brush stroke technique employed to give the effect of a much-wrinkled surface, e.g., the bark of an old tree. The style is irregular, and is occasionally used for special effects of extreme roughness, in addition to its normal use in *landscape* work.

DIMORPHITE—An orange-yellow mineral having an arsenic base, obtained as a volcanic product. It is closely related to, and used as a substitute for *orpiment* (q.v.).

DIONYSIAN—The 'chaotic' half of the *Apollonian* and *Dionysian* division of *art* as propounded by Nietzsche in THE BIRTH OF TRAGEDY. See *Apollonian* and *Dionysian.*

DIONYSUS—A tremendous 5th century B.C. Greek *chryselephantine* cult *statue* by Alcamenes, constructed of *ivory* and *gold.* The subject himself was the Greek god of vegetation who rescued the abandoned *Ariadne* from the island of Naxos. His attendants, the *Bacchanals* or dancing girls, were often represented in the *arts. Dionysus* is better known by the name of *Bacchus,* fabled in art and *literature.* See *chryselephantine;* also *Bacchanals.*

DIORITE—General name given to a group of mineral stones used in *carving;* known commonly by its original name, *greenstone* (q.v.).

DIPPER—In *painting* (esp. medieval), a small cup or vessel attached to the artist's *palette,* containing the diluent or *thinner.* Used through the *Renaissance* period, it fell into disuse thereafter, but has been revived in modern *studios.*

DIPTYCH—In *painting* and *drawing,* two *panels* generally designed as a single composition, the hinge allowing for opening and closing. Used widely in connection with the making and exhibiting of Japanese *prints.* The *triptych* and *polyptych* were usually reserved for sacred work, the *paneled* results functioning as *altarpieces.* The term is also applied to the Roman two-hinged writing tablet. The Japanese *diptych* is known as *nimai tsuzuki.* See *iconostasis.*

DISCOBOLOS—In *sculpture,* the *disc thrower,* a famous *statue* by Myron of Eleutheria representing an athlete about to throw the disc. It is famed for the excellent transitory movement of the body. Probably made about 450 B.C.

DISPOSABLE PALETTE—A modern type of *palette* consisting of numerous layers of processed sheets, requiring only the peeling of the top layer used in a painting project. Eliminates the necessity for scraping, washing, etc., and prevents the possibility of new *pigments* being influenced by the old. *Thumbhole* is cut through all the layers at a common point. Some varieties have as many as 100 sheets, and are quite light in weight despite the thickness. See also *palette.*

DISTEMPER—A method of *painting* which employs an egg *emulsion* as a *binding medium.* It is made with egg-yolk, *size,* or the egg-white. A pure *distemper,* as distinguished from *tempera* (q.v.) makes use of *size* only. The term is loosely applied to any paint made with a glutinous medium for use on *murals* or *wall paintings,* or large scene paintings.

DISTEMPER COLORS—A term applied to *colors* ground in water to a creamy consistency. A *sizing* of *glue* or egg-white is added, to make them adhere to the surface to which they are applied; used generally for decorating plastered walls and ceilings, they are frequently referred to as *fresco colors.*

DIVIDED SLANT—In *painting,* a flat *ceramic* tray having oblong cut-outs for mixed colors or for the original mixing ingredients. Generally available in three or six such compartments to the tray. See *well slab* and *nest saucers.*

DIVIDERS—In *drawing,* an instrument similar in appearance to the *compasses* except that both legs are equipped with points. It is used to transfer measurements to drawings, and to divide lines into equal parts.

DIVIDING BRASS—In *sculpture, a* variety of *brass* prepared in thin sheets or strips, used in separating the *cast* or *mold* from the carved *model* after hardening. Found to be as effective as the various chemical *mold separators* applied prior to addition of the *moist plaster.*

DIVINE MADMAN—Name given to Michelangelo (Michael Angelo Buonarroti), famous Italian *sculptor painter, architect* and *poet* (1475-1564); so-called because of his habit of secluding himself when meditating upon any large project.

DIVISION ON COLOR—In *painting,* the *technique* of *juxtaposing* small quantities or strokes of pure *color* directly upon the *canvas* for the eye to mix at a distance, rather than undertake preliminary mixing upon the *palette.* The principle was first employed by 12th century *glass*workers, and was perfected by the French *Impressionists.*

DOMINANT COLOR—In *painting, watercolor, ceramics,* etc., the key *color,* prevailing over all others, in a *picture,* scene or *design.*

DOROPHOROS—In *sculpture,* the famous *statue* of a spear-bearer, made in the 5th century B.C. by the Greek *sculptor*

Polyclitus. Its stalwart form embodies his ideal sense of proportions for the male body. There are several *marble* copies of this *bronze* figure, the best of which is now in the Naples Museum. See *Argive School.*

DOSA—A *painting* material used chiefly by *artists* of Japan; consists of a *size* (q.v.) made of *glue* and alum.

DOTTING—In Chinese *painting,* a technique by which small dots of *color* or *ink* are added to a *landscape* picture for the purpose of emphasis or better definition of planes or *contours.* On rocks, mountains, trees, etc., *dotting* may be interpreted as moss, grass, etc.

DOUBLE END TOOL—In *ceramics* and *sculpture,* any one of the numerous instruments used for shaping or modeling *clay* or other workable substance. Usually consists of a wooden handle in the center, from each end of which extends a heavy wire in loop, point, square, angular, or other shape. The working ends are ferruled to the handle. Compare with *plaster tool* (q.v.).

DOUBLE IMAGE—A popular device in *primitive* and *surrealistic art;* any *image* that allows two irreconcilable interpretations simultaneously, e.g., a cloud appearing also as a human face, or a mountain appearing as a recumbent lion. Used in art as an element of playful surprise as well as of the weird, combining the humorous and the uncanny.

DOUBLE LEAVES—In Chinese *painting,* the term applied to a *brush* stroke technique by which leaves are given the appearance of existing in pairs. Five or six straight or curved strokes are arranged in a fan downward, superimposed in color in similar pattern. Although the strokes are actually a form of *tien* (q.v.), the effect nevertheless shows double outlines of leaves.

DOUBLE SPLIT COMPLEMENTARIES—In *painting,* two neighboring *colors* of one *primary,* combined with two neighboring colors of another.

DRAFTING PAPER—In *drawing,* a fine, white or cream, hard-surfaced *paper* of good erasure quality, upon which drawings are made; usually *sized.*

DRAGGING—In *painting,* the technique of applying a *brush*

charged with thick, *opaque* color heavily but quickly over the picture.

DRAGON—A mythological animal with the features of many animals in combination, including deer horns, ox ears, serpentine body, tiger paws and hawk talons. Popular in Chinese *art,* it was the Taoist *symbol* of vitality. The *dragon* is depicted in *heraldry* as having four legs and wings, a long barbed tail (usually knotted), and a body protected by scales. In any form, the *dragon* has been a symbolic subject in the arts since ancient times. Hebrew tradition made it the source of evil in the world, and Christianity carried forward the same idea. As a menace to mankind, *dragons* were especially feared during the *Middle Ages,* and popular saints or heroes (e.g., St. George) were reputed to have slain these legendary monsters. Widely represented in *painting* and *sculpture,* shown in a variety of physical form and composition.

DRAGON'S BLOOD—In *painting,* a purplish-red substance used as a *stain* in *varnishes;* the extracted color can be used as a *dye* or *lake pigment.* Though known to *medieval* painters of *manuscript illuminations,* it is no longer listed as an artist's color. It is known to have been used as an ingredient of the *varnishes* made by early 18th century Italian *violin* makers.

DRAWING—The *art* of representing or delineating an idea, *emotion* or object by the use of *color,* line, or *tone;* a mode of *expression* making use of *symbols* or *literary* ideas; in a strict sense, the most direct means of expressing *beauty* of form, usually accomplished through the use of outlines or tones. Generally limited to pictorial *representation* executed in *crayon, pen* or *pencil,* frequently without reference to color.

DRAWING PENCILS—Drawing pencils are graded from 6B (softest) through 5B, 4B, 3B, 2B, B, HB (medium soft), F, H (medium hard), 2H, 3H, 4H, 5H, 6H, 7H, 8H, to 9H (extremely hard). Grades 4H and 6H are generally used for the drawing of lines, while F, H, and 2H are preferred for *lettering* and *sketching.* See *graphite.*

DRIER—See *dryer.*

DRIVEN STAKE—In Chinese *painting,* a variety of brush stroke creating the effect of a stake jutting up from the ground. A blunt *brush* is brought down firmly to produce a vigorous dot, from which the straight line is extended vertically.

DROLERY—In Gothic *art,* the playful use of freely-invented *scenes* or figures to give attraction to the empty parts of *architecture, furniture,* or books. Usually *satiric* or paradoxical, often bordering upon the uncanny and demoniac. It takes the form of (1) scenes featuring bizarre, imaginary creatures; (2) animal fables; (3) reversal of real life parts, e.g., animal hunting the hunter; (4) jocular description of everyday activities. Also spelled *drollery.*

DROP BLACK—A black carbon *pigment* used in *drawing* and *painting.* Prepared through a process of destructive distillation of degreased animal bones in an iron retort. Though possessing little *opacity* or *hiding power,* it is usually *stable,* and is used successfully in all techniques.

DROPOUT—In *etching, a half-tone* in which the areas of high light print *white* instead of *gray* because the fine dots have been etched away. Known also as *half-tone, high light.*

DRY BRUSH—In Chinese *art,* a *painting* technique in which the *ink* is used sparingly with a minimum of moisture in the *brush;* known natively as *kan pi* (q.v.).

DRYER—In *oil painting,* a chemical added to the *paint* to hasten drying. Those in common use include *litharge* (q.v.), manganese, and *cobalt* oxide. Not synonymous with *drying oils* (q.v.), but added to the *paint* after the drying *oil* has been *blended* into the paint. Also used in *inks* and *varnishes* for the same purpose; often spelled *drier.* See *siccative* and *desiccation.*

DRYING OILS—All *oils* used in *painting* come under this heading. Popular among them are *linseed oil, walnut oil,* and *poppy-seed oil* (qq.v.) More recently, though with little effect upon the above staples, such *drying oils* as *soya bean, tung, sunflower, hempseed,* have been offered on the commercial market. *Drying oils* were used in medicine and in the *crafts* as early as the 8th century, in *varnish* and *resin.* By the 12th century, they enjoyed wide use as painting *mediums.* See *oils.*

DRYPOINT—In *etching,* an *intaglio* process resulting in a velvety richness of the proof. It is the simplest of all intaglio methods, requiring only a bare *plate,* a steel point, a *scraper,* an oil stone, a *burnisher,* and some *ink.* The beauty of the finished product is due not to the groove which is cut into the surface, but to the *burr* or *ridge* thrown up along the edge of the incision by the passage of the tool. It is the burr that catches and holds the ink on the surface of the plate during the action of *wiping.* No acid is used in cutting the plate, and this art is closer to *engraving* than it is to etching. *Drypoint* has a tremendous range in line strength, far exceeding anything produced by etching. It is extremely fragile, however, the usual *edition* being limited to about thirty *prints.* If the plate is faced with chromium-steel, a great number of proofs can be pulled without injuring the delicate burr, showing no noticeable change in the proofs. The term is also applied to any sharp needle on a handle used in cutting the fine lines in this process.

DULL—In *painting* and *water-color,* a term applied to a certain *gray* or neutral quality present in some *colors,* e.g., in dusty pink.

DUMONT BLUE—A term in *painting;* see *smalt.*

DURA-EUROPOS—The city of *Euphrates;* in ruins since 265 A.D. Excavation from 1932 to date, interrupted only by World War II, brought to light monuments of Parthian, Hellenistic, and early Christian *art,* remnants of a *synagogue,* and well-preserved *frescoes.* The latter, *painted* between 245 and 256 A.D. are significant for their *iconography.* Excellent *wall-paintings* were discovered in the Jewish *catacombs.*

DÜRERESQUE—In the manner or *style* of Albert Dürer, the most famous *artist* of *Renaissance* Germany (1471-1528), noted for the perfection of his *drawing* and the facility with which he delineated character and passion; e.g. *Düreresque* detail. Albert Dürer was a *painter, sculptor, engraver* and *architect,* but his fame is most widely spread through his admirable engravings, both on *wood* and on *copper,* which far surpassed anything that had been produced in that branch of *art* in his day, and provided free scope for his remarkable confidence and delicacy of hand. One of the greatest merits of his work lies in the *harmony* of *composition* characterizing even his most complicated designs. The detail in his early work, though always rendered with almost unparalleled truth, is somewhat profuse and labored, and often sacrifices beauty to exactness; but toward the close of his career he sought to attain repose and simplicity of manner and subject.

DUREX—A variety of *synthetic resin,* soluble in oil, with a rapid-drying quality rendering it valuable as in ingredient in *varnishes, printing inks,* and *paints.* Used also as a bond between metal and *lacquer.* Chemically, it is a phenolic and terpene compound, *durex* being a trade name.

DÜSSELDORF SCHOOL—The type of *painting* associated with the Düsseldorf Academy of Art which flourished in the 1840's. Peter von Cornelius and William von Schadow were its leading exponents.

DUTCH PINK—One of the several *lakes* of *yellow* or *greenish color,* used in *water-color* work. It is made by precipitating vegetable juices on a *white* earth product, such as *alumina* or *chalk.* It is highly *fugitive,* and will generally produce *unstable* colors in mixture, as in *green lake* (q.v.).

DUTCH SCHOOL—In *painting,* the name given to the 17th century works by Holland artists featuring faultless drawing, arrangement and color, and great detail in the texture of garments; particular precision characterized the representations of hair of the head, the beard, and the skin. Leading painters of the 'school' were Cuyp (1605-1691, animal work); Hobbema (1638-1709, tree foliage); Franz Hals (1584-1666, unsurpassed in *portrait work*); Rembrandt (1607-1669, one of the greatest artists of all time); and Weenix (1640-1719, famous for still life).

DUTCH WHITE—A fine white *pigment* made of a mixture of *white* lead and *permanent white.*

DYE—A *coloring* matter, distinct from a *pigment* in that it can be used in resolution as a *stain* (q.v.), whereas the pigment is relatively granular, the color being contained in fixed or definite particles which are suspended in a *medium.* Until recently, *dyes* were of *natural* origin, e.g., *madder* and *indigo* (qq.v.). The development of coal-tar as a source of dyestuffs has introduced innumerable *hues* of high *tinting* strength. While used chiefly as a coloring for *fabrics,* some varieties have been precipitated on a mineral base and used as *painters'* pigments.

DYSMIMIA—Impairment of the ability to imitate gestures and strike postures. Particularly damaging to living *art models.*

E

EARLY RENAISSANCE—See *Renaissance.*

EARTH COLOR—Any *colored* mineral used as a *painter's pigment.* The group includes the *iron pigments* (q.v.), *umber, sienna, ochre,* and *green earth.* Care must be exercised in washing all natural soluble matter from the *earth colors* prior to their use on the *palette.*

EASEL—Any *frame* built to hold a *painting* during the time when it is being made. Usually a three-legged structure, with the two forward legs holding the painting, the third standing backward as a brace. Complex *designs* have been developed, e.g., the *studio easel* with screw adjustments for both height and the angle of the painting. *Sketching easels* which fold up into compact units are made for *landscape artists,* and various small *table easels* are available. The *easel* goes back to remote *antiquity,* having been shown in *relief* on a *tomb* of the Old Kingdom of Egypt.

ECCE HOMO—(Lat. of Joh. 19:5, Behold, the Man) The title of numerous *paintings* of the suffering Christ (see *Man of Sorrow*).

ECCENTRIC CUTTER—In the *carving* of *ivory,* a small instrument resembling a drill-stock, moved by a bow. The cutting point can be fixed at different distances from the center by means of a groove or screw. Name derives from the fact that it is usually employed to produce *grotesque* or eccentric figures.

ÉCHOPPE—A needle used by the earliest *etchers,* the point of which is cut at a *bevel,* enabling them to make a line that swells and tapers, imitating the *engraving* process.

ECLECTICISM—Term applied to the style of those artists who compose their works by using the identifying characteristics of other artists without being capable of harmonizing the various 'adopted' peculiarities into a unified whole.

ECORCHÉ—In *sculpture,* an anatomical figure or *mannikin* showing the muscles.

ECTYPE—In any *visual art,* a copy of the *artist's* original.

ECTYPOGRAPHY—An *etching* technique in which the lines are left in *relief* upon the *plate* instead of being incised or otherwise depressed into it.

EFFIGY—A *sculptured* likeness, as on a *sepulchral* monument. See *wax sculpture.*

EGGSHELL—A term applied to a surface that is somewhat lacking in *gloss* or *luster,* although not approaching the state of *matte.*

EGG TEMPERA—The yolk of an egg which constituted the *medium* in *painting* prior to the introduction of *drying oils* (q.v.). The *pigments* were ground in water, with enough egg yolk added to serve as a *binding* medium. Being oily, it was relatively impervious to water when dry, and the survival of many paintings from the *Middle Ages* gives testimony of its favorable *qualities.* For *panel* paintings and *illuminated manuscripts,* the white of the egg was more often used. See *tempera.*

EGYPTIAN ART—A comprehensive term embracing the *architecture, sculpture* and *painting* of ancient Egypt, one of the most important of the great artistic developments of the world. The earliest known Egyptian sculptures, not less than 6,000 years old, exhibit superior technical skill, and surpass by far in *naturalness* the more conventional works which succeeded them. The best Egyptian works of all periods possess striking individuality as well as refinement, and many of the vast number of *portrait statues* and *reliefs* exhibit remarkable differences in class, employment, ethnology, etc. Many are *colossal* in size, the great SPHINX OF GIZEH being the oldest as well as the largest work of sculpture known. Egyptian painting is strictly *illumination* (q.v.), as the colors are laid on flat, without *shading* or *gradation,* within a definite outline. The *drawing* is typically of great beauty, the outlines being firm, accurate and graceful. In *gem*-cutting and *jewelry,* in *enamel,* in *terra-*

cotta, and *glass,* in the *carving* of *wood* and *ivory,* in *metal-working,* and in the industrial arts generally. Egyptian *artists* and *artisans* displayed great taste and skill, and were able by the diffusion of material prosperity to devise and perfect their products and *works of art* in endless diversity.

EGYPTIAN BLUE—A *bright,* rather pale *blue color* found in *wall paintings* of Egypt through *classical* times, closely related to the blue *glaze* of Egyptian *pottery.* Though the ancient method of manufacture is not known, a synthetic *pigment* closely resembling it has been produced under the name *Pompeian blue* (q.v.). The basic element of the color appears to be *copper,* the source of the famous blue and green *porcelain* of *mummy beading.* It is probably the most *stable* of all colors, with many specimens well over 3000 years old showing little or no deterioration. Some authorities state it was used as early as the IV DYNASTY (3050 B.C.), and it has appeared in numerous paintings executed from 2000 B.C. to 600 A.D., after which the secret appears to have been lost. Known also as *frit, blue frit,* and *Pompeian blue.*

EIRENE—In Greek mythology, the goddess of peace, frequently represented in *sculpture* and *painting.*

E-KOTOBA—A Japanese *scroll painting* which includes both painting and text. See *e-maki.*

EKUR—A term in ancient Babylonian *art* and mythology; see *Aralu.*

ELECTRUM—An *alloy* of *gold* and *silver,* natural pale-yel*low* in *color,* used in finely-detailed *sculpture* and *carving.* Sometimes *cast* in *molds.*

ELEMENT—In *painting,* the term applied to the base (i.e., *cobalt, copper, zinc,* etc.) of an *artist's pigment.*

ELEMI—A sticky, *resin*ous material, having the viscosity of *balsam,* used in the *arts* as an addition to *varnishes.* It has also been included in *wax* combinations for the relining of *pictures.* Known also as *gum elemi.*

ELEUSINIAN MARBLE—An exquisite *black marble* used in fine *friezes* of the 3rd, 4th and 5th centuries B.C.

ELEVATION—Any *drawing* made in *projection* on a vertical plane.

ELFENBEINSCHWARTZ—In *painting* and *drawing,* a fine black *pigment* made by charring chips of *ivory;* commonly known as *ivory black* (q.v.).

ELGIN MARBLES—A part of the *frieze* executed by Phidias in the construction of the famous *Parthenon* (5th century B.C.), now in the British Museum. So called because the collection was brought to England between 1801 and 1803 by the Earl of Elgin, who sold it to the British government in 1816 for $175,000.

E-MAKI—A Japanese *scroll painting,* differing from the *e-kotoba* in that it need not necessarily contain a text.

E-MAKIMONO—A Japanese rolled horizontal *scroll* containing a *picture;* differs from the *makimono* in that the latter may contain text alone, not illustrated.

EMAUZY—A famous literary *art* center, picture gallery, and *printing* office of Prague, located in a Benedictine *monastery* founded by Emperor Charles VI for Slavonic monks in 1346. During the Nazi occupation its abbot, Arnost Vykoukal, was tortured and killed at Dachau concentration camp. The monastery was partly destroyed during World War II, but the art activities were resumed thereafter.

EMBOSSED—Generally, having a raised *design* in the same material, without coloring or *appliqué.* The term applies to any substance so woven, stamped or impressed; a form of *relief* (q.v.).

EMERALD GREEN—*Bright* in *color,* and rather *bluish-green,* often confused with *viridian* (q.v.). It is a distinct *pigment,* identical with the insecticide *Paris green* which also carries that name. Although fairly permanent in an *oil* or *varnish medium,* it can be blackened by sulphurous pigments; is poisonous, and dangerous to handle. Varying somewhat in chemical composition according to the manufacturing process employed, it is invariably produced on a base of aceto-arsenite of copper. Known also as *mitis green, Schweinfurt green, Veronese green, Paris green, vert cendre, verde ceniza,* and *mineral green.* See *Scheele green.*

EMERY—A fine polishing agent for *gems, marble, metal,* etc., consisting of finely pulverized *corundum* (q.v.) In its most common use it is affixed to hand or power wheels for speed and uniformity of pressure during the griding and/or polishing operation. Ancient Greek *sculptors* used the *emery stone* for finishing the details of their *statuary* work. See *archaistic Greek.*

EMULSION—A *painting medium* in which drops of one kind of liquid are suspended in another liquid with which the former does not form a *stable* mixture. The most common in the history of *art* is the yolk of an egg, the natural emulsifying property of which keeps the two elements (the egg oil, and the watery, albuminous mixture) in a stable suspension. Other *emulsions* are made by mixing *gums* or *glues* with *oils* and *varnishes.* The use of *emulsions* explain much of the fine *character* of late *Renaissance* oil painting, and they were important in the making of oil *paint* through the 17th and 18th centuries.

ENAMEL—In *painting,* a term used by *artists* to describe a *finish* of rather strong reflecting power, approaching the highest degree of *gloss* or *luster.* Although applied most frequently to *paint* materials, the term is loosely extended to all surfaces, as in *sculpture, ceramics,* etc. See *gloss.*

ENAMEL METHOD—One of the two principal techniques in *glass-painting* (q.v.).

ENAMEL PAINTING—The technique of *painting* in *vitrifiable colors,* esp. upon a surface of *porcelain, glass* or *metal,* the work being subsequently *fired* in a *muffle* or *kiln.*

ENAMEL PAPER—A variety of *paper* having a high *gloss* imparted as a coating by means of heat and pressure. The coating itself is fine *China clay,* ground into powder and pressed into the paper through rollers. Used in *half-tone* and other *engraving* work. Known also as *coated paper.*

ENCAUSTIC PAINTING—An ancient method of *easel* and *mural painting* which employed *pigments* mixed with *beeswax* with or without modifying ingredients (e.g., *oils* or *resins*). The *paints* were applied with the aid of heat, but the term (which implies a strong "burning in" of the *colors*) is not synonymous with any of the molten wax processes which used the *cauterium* and *cestrum* (qq.v.). *Encaustic* was the principal painting method used during the entire *classical* period. It became obsolete during the 9th century, and although the *medium* is permanent and has desirable *textural* and optical *qualities,* it is difficult to control. 19th and 20th century revivals have been isolated and sporadic. The term is applied to any variety of painting executed upon a wax *ground;* known also as *cerography,* it is believed to have been the technique employed in the famous *Fayum mummy portraits.* Some excellent modern examples of the technique have been created by George Sklär, American artist.

ENGLISH RED—A *color* prized by artists for its remarkable *stability;* a deep *shade* of *red,* it is better known as *Venetian red* (q.v.). It occurs in nature as a red iron oxide, and belongs to the group known as *iron pigments.*

ENGLISH WHITE—A substance used in *gilding,* and as an adulterant in the making of *lake colors;* commonly known as *whiting* (q.v.).

ENGRAVER'S METAL—An *alloy* of tin, antimony and lead, mounted on a block similar to an electroplate, on which an *engraving* can readily be cut; used for *color plates,* tinted backgrounds, etc.

ENGRAVING—The process of incising lines on a *plate* with a *graver* or *burin* to produce *intaglio* prints having precise, angular beauty. Since it is simpler to make straight cuts than curved ones with the burin, many parallel straight lines and hatchings are characteristic of this process. When the *design* is composed predominantly of short lines and little dots, it is called *stipple engraving* (q.v.). Generally, the *art* or technique of creating letters or designs on *wood, metal* or other substance by cutting or *etching* (as above), for the purpose of subsequent printing or stamping of the pattern or picture on paper or other material. Also, any impression made from such a plate.

EPHESIAN ARTEMIS—An ancient Asiatic divinity whose worship was adopted by Ionian Greeks. She was a personification of the fruitfulness of nature, and was quite distinct from the Greek goddess deriving from *Diana,* though likened to her by the Ephesians because of some resemblance of *attributes.* In a *statue* now at the Museo Nazionale,

Naples, she is represented wearing a mural *crown* and with many breasts, and with the lower part of her body cased, like a *mummy,* in a sheath bearing mystical figures.

EPIGONE—In *art,* a general term denoting the successors and imitators of an age or era. From Greek, born afterward.

ERATO—In Greek mythology, one of the nine famous daughters of Zeus and Mnemosyne. She was the *Muse* or goddess of *erotic poetry,* geometry, and *pantomime,* and was frequently represented in *painting* and *sculpture* with a large stringed instrument and a crown of roses as her *attributes.* Her name was given to the gloomy underground cavern through which the passage to Hades was accomplished. See *Muse.*

ÊR CH'ING—In Chinese *painting,* the medium *blue* mineral *pigment* obtained from the middle layer of the *azurite* stone when it is rubbed down in water. It is used chiefly in painting the hills and rocks of *ch'ing lü* (*landscapes*). Known also as *Watteau blue;* see *shih ch'ing.*

EROS—In Greek mythology, the god of love; youngest of all the gods; counterpart of the Roman *Cupid.* Frequently represented in the *arts,* a famous *statue* of *Eros* stands in Piccadilly Circus as one of the best-known landmarks in London. See *Aphrodite.*

ESNAFS—In Slavonic *art,* the guilds of the craftsmen, corresponding to the medieval guilds of the West, except that each member was required to execute a *masterpiece* (also known as *esnafs*) prior to advancement. The collective groups were governed by *londja* (from the Italian *loggia*) composed of all recognized masters who met annually under the chairmanship of the chief master, known as the *ustabashi,* to consider the works submitted by the applicants for advancement.

ESPARTO—A type of grass used in the manufacture of *paper,* esp. in England. Its fibers are strong and flexible, and it is easily reduced to a *pulp.* The resulting paper is often used as a *support* in *painting.*

ESQUISSE—A first or thumbnail *sketch* of any *illustration,* layout, *design,* etc.

ESTER GUMS—A series of hard *synthetic resins* having varied uses in the *arts*. It is an excellent substitute for *copal, dammar,* and *kauri gums* in the making of *enamels, paints* and *lacquers,* and in combination with *tung oil* it creates a fine waterproof *varnish* used as a *surface* over *oil paintings* and *sculpture.*

ETCHING—An "eating away" *technique,* with acid used in the process. In *print* making the term includes not only the *plates* subjected to the *biting,* but to the *proofs* made from such plates. In a general way, the term includes the following *intaglio* processes: *line etching, soft ground, pen process, stylotint,* and other types of bitten graphic work. The heart of the entire *etching* art is found in the *biting* (q.v.) operation.

ETCHING GROUND—The acid-resisting coating applied to a *plate;* better known as *ground* (q.v.).

ETCHING NEEDLE—A steel point used for making the *drawing* on a *grounded plate* for a line *etching* (q.v.) See also *stylus, drypoint, graver, burin.*

ETCHING PAPER—Specially made *paper,* soft, and with a minimum of *size,* for printing *etchings.*

ETCHING PRESS—A *printing* press for pulling *proofs* or impressions on *paper* from *intaglio designs* on metal *plates.*

ETRUSCAN ART—The objects evidencing the *culture* of the Etruscan civilization which centered in Tuscany on the west coast of Italy and thrived from 700 to 100 B.C. *Architecture* is represented by *tombs* and rock formations, stressing narrow, intimate spaces hollowed into large mounds, adorned with Oriental gods and monsters in exquisite granulation. Its *jewelry* had a *rhythmic* alternation of *light* and shade on gleaming *metal.* Greek influence was apparent in the *roofed porches* and broad *cella* abounding with *terra cotta* images, although the Etruscan work lacked the discipline and logic of the Greek models. In *painting,* Greek Hellenistic prototypes of *sculptural* forms and richly graded *palette* were reduced to flat outline *drawings* with strong *contours* and expressive outlines. However, this work can scarcely be distinguished from the poorer products of the Roman republic. Though contributing little to the history of art, the Etruscans' *decorative pattern, strong color,* and voluminous masses express a passionate art vitality which appeals strongly to many modern critics.

EVANGELIAR—An *illustrated manuscript* containing all four Gospels in unabridged *form. Evangeliars* have become of great artistic importance, because of their exquisitely *ornamented* letters, illustrated texts, and ingenious physical structure. See *Ada group.*

EXHIBITION—In *museum* terminology, a temporary display of *art* objects based on a central *theme.* Many museums arrange varied programs of *exhibition,* with changes at regular intervals. In a broader sense, the word refers to the display of objects of art in a museum's permanent collection. Art *exhibitions* are also held in schools, colleges, *galleries* of art dealers, clubs, theatres, and other institutions, public and private, with the objects displayed often offered for sale.

EXTENDER—Generally, any inert, *translucent* substance, colorless or white, added to *pigments* to *diffuse* or dilute the colors, and to increase and improve the wearing qualities thereof. When an *extender* is added to a *paint* in such quantity that it reduces the *tinting* power, it is known as an *adulterant.*

EZO—In Japanese *art,* the term applied generally to any *portrait painting.*

F

FABRIC PAINTING—A term in Chinese art; see *chêng.*

FACIAL ANGLE—Angle formed by the crossing of the axis of the face with the axis of the skull. Frequently set down by *painters* in preliminary *sketch* work. See also *prognathous.*

FACIAL ASYMMETRY—The state of imbalance between expressions and morphology of the right and left halves of the human face; a subject of study by *painters* and *sculptors.* See also *prognathous.*

FALSE BITING—In *etching,* a *tone* bitten on a *plate* without intention of the artist. Usually caused by a defective *ground.* See *biting* and *line etching.*

FAN—In *art,* a device consisting of a series of ribs joined at the hub by a handle; made of *paper,* leaves, cloth, feathers, thin *wood,* etc., this broad portion was often the *ground* for excellent *drawing* or *painting work,* especially those of China and Japan.. See *sensu, uchiwa,* and *shan mien.*

FAN BRUSH—In *oil painting,* a type of *brush* consisting of a thin range of soft animal hair (usually sable or bristle) arranged in *fan*-shape, bunched at the ferrule. Used chiefly for unusual finishing techniques, as in the representation of fine grass, hair, etc.

FANG—In Chinese *art* (esp. *painting*), to copy, usually implying a free or interpretive copy. When the term is found on an Oriental *colophon,* it is intended in the sense of 'after' or 'in the style of.' This practice is not frowned upon, since it exhibits the acceptance of a standard by others who hold it in high regard. Compare with *lin pên;* see also *k'uan.*

FAN HSÜAN—In Chinese *art,* a variety of *sized* paper used as a *ground* in *painting* and *calligraphy.* See *chih.*

FAN PAINTING—A technique of *painting,* using the *silk* or *satin* of an Oriental *fan* as the *ground.* For this purpose *watercolors* have been used with striking success, and they acquire satisfactory results on *canvas* and other materials as well.

FAUVES—A French group expressing dissatisfaction with the *post-impressionists* because of their refusal to inject personal emotions and inspirational factors into their works of creative *art.* See *post-impressionism.*

FAYUM—A district in Egypt where, during the early Christian era, the *wax* painting process reached artistic heights. The famous *mummy portraits,* representing the greatest accomplishments in wax *medium pigments* were executed here. See *wax* and *Chinese insect wax.*

FEI PO—In Chinese *painting,* a technique in which the hairs of the brush are permitted to separate so that a stroke is not solid black, but broken by streaks of untouched *ground;* appears almost three dimensional. Known to Western artists as *flying white.*

FÊNG-HUANG—In Chinese *art* and mythology, the bird of good omen. It appears in many fine *paintings* and *sensus* as a long-tailed, pheasanttype of bird, commonly called the *phoenix.* Scientifically it is known as Rheinart's *ocellated argus.* Equivalent in Japan is the *hoo bird.*

FÊN LIN—In Chinese *art,* copying by tracing and transferring. The *painting* is traced in outline, and then the tracing paper is reversed and the outline retraced in white. The paper is placed white side down on a new piece of *silk* or *paper* and rubbed with a damp cloth, transferring the white outline to the new *ground.*

FÊN PÊN—In Chinese *painting,* any draft, preliminary *sketch, study* or *cartoon* (qq.v.).

FÊN SU GÊN WU—In Chinese *art,* the use of earthly or everyday subject matter in painting, as distinguished from the lasting subject matters of God, religion, immortality, etc. Known in western art as *genre painting.*

FIERCE DEITIES—In Tibetian *art,* the name given to a certain group of three gods frequently represented in *painting* and *sculpture,* generally life-size to *heroic* in scale. The central figure sits astride a donkey and carries a skull-headed staff, while the two lesser gods, one having the head of a sea monster and the other lion-headed, are on foot. The particularly menacing features of all the three are intended to frighten evil-doers and re-establish them on the path to *nirvana.*

FIGURE—(1) Generally, the visible or tangible form of anything; the shape of the outline or exterior surface; *form;* shape; fashion; as a beautiful female *figure;* the *grotesque figure* of a *satyr; the figure* of the earth, etc. (2) The artificial *representation* of a form, as in *sculpture, drawing* or *painting, embroidery,* etc.; esp., the human body represented by *art* of any kind.

FIGURE AND GROUND—In *sculpture* and *architecture,* the term denoting the tendency of one part of a configuration to stand out clearly, as in *relief,* and the rest to form a background.

FIGURINE—A small group of figures or a single figure, executed in *clay, porcelain,* or other vitreous substance, often decorated in *gold* or *colors.* Many excellent examples are extant, some showing exquisite detail in garment lines, lacework, etc. See also *Tanagra figurines.*

FILIGREE—A type of decorative work in *gold* and *silver* wrought delicately in the manner of thin threads or grains, or of both intermixed; any *sculptured* work executed in delicate *patterns.* The term is becoming a derogatory one, referring to any object so fanciful, ornate, or light in structure as to render it perishable or of little use functionally. Going beyond *metalwork* through usage, the word extends in the same general meaning to *carving, tracery, printing,* etc.

FILM—In *art,* a general term applied to any outer *coating* material which may be used on a *picture,* a piece of *sculpture,* or any work of art. It includes *oils, varnishes, waxes,* and other substances capable of forming a thin surface, *transparent* and reasonably permanent. A *thinner* is occasionally used, to render the substance more suitable for application as a *film*. Many of the *resins*, esp. *vinyl resins*, are found to be excellent *film materials*. See *thinner*.

FILM INTEGRITY—In *painting*, a term somewhat related to *stability* (q.v.). The serviceability of *paint* may be described by (1) the general appearance of the coating: discoloration by dust, loss of *gloss*, fading of color, ability to hide, *chalking*, and the type of vision obtainable at six feet; (2) the *film integrity: cracking, slitting, crazing*, flaking, and scaling of the *surface* film, or discontinuities therein that lay bare the *ground* or undercoat.

FILM LINE CUTTER—An instrument used for incising through the film in *silk screen* work, *stencil* cutting, *line drawings*, etc. Cuts out the lines and peels the film in the same stroke. Usually made of highly-sharpened steel, it is known also as *line cutter*.

FILMOGENS—In *painting* and *sculpture*, a general term applied to all types of coatings of *surface films* used as protective coverings after completion of a work; e.g., *resins, varnishes, linseed oil*, etc.

FINE ARTS ACADEMY—A school or center of learning in which the subjects taught are limited to *drawing, painting, architecture, sculpture*, and other *fine arts* of vision or space. See *academy*.

FINGER DRAWING—A *drawing technique* developed by the Chinese as *chih hua*. Limited to pictorial work, the drawing is made by dipping the finger or fingernail into paste or liquid *color*ing matter and producing the *picture* without the aid of a *brush*. An analogy might be drawn between this method and painting with a *palette knife* in *impasto* style. Some of the earlier artists employing this technique used the finger work in addition to the brush. Originated during T'ANG DYNASTY.

FINISH—In *painting*, the term applied to a work that is generally simple in over-all effect, yet possesses the clarity of detail required in some varieties of subjects for proper interpretation and evaluation. See *breadth*.

FINISHING TOUCH—The name of the writer or *artist* along with brief information concerning the book or *paint-*

ing; usually found at the end or corner of the work. See *colophon.*

FIOR DI PERSICOR—In *sculpture,* a fine type of white *marble* with veins and clouds of purple or red; occurs chiefly in Albania.

FIRE MARBLE—A term in *sculpture;* see *lumachelle.*

FIXATIVE—A liquid used by artists to bind the loose particles on *charcoal, pastel* or *crayon* pictures, preventing them from rubbing off. Since it functions as a weak but complete operation in one application, it is neither necessary nor desirable to use an impervious *film* such as *varnish,* etc., as employed in *oil* and *tempera* paintings. Frequently sprayed through an atomizer. Sometimes spelled *fixatif.*

FLAKE ALUMINUM—In *painting,* a powdered form of *aluminum* used in the manufacture of paints and *varnishes*; known also as *aluminum powder.*

FLAKE WHITE—The most popular *white pigment* in the entire history of the *painting art*; better known as *white lead* (q.v.).

FLAT—A term used by artists to describe a surface finish (usually of *paint*) that possesses little or no *gloss* or *luster,* although not quite as non-reflecting as *matte.* See *gloss.*

FLAVINE LAKE—In *painting* and *water-color,* a series of yellow *lake colors* best known as *quercitron lake* (q.v.).

FLAX—The soft, silky *fiber,* two or three inches long, which comes from the inside of the bark of the flax plant. There are more than a hundred species of this plant, the fiber of which can be made into the sheerest *linen,* the most exquisitive *lace,* or the heaviest rope. It is easily *dyed* and is readily bleached into *white.* Most of the *canvas* used in *oil painting* derives from *flax.* See *linen* and *linseed oil.*

FLEMISH STYLE—A style of *art* essentially different from the *Italian style* in that the emphasis was on literal *representation* in strict accordance with *realism,* while the Italian gave importance to the plastic effect of *form* and *color.* The term is *applied* generally to the style of *painting* developed in Flanders between the 14th and 17th centuries. See *Italianizers.*

FLESH COLOR—The average *shade* of the skin of a Caucasian; low *saturation* of *red-yellow color,* high in *brilliance.*

FLESH OCHRE—In *painting,* a *pigment* having the color of Caucasian skin, the tint deriving from the presence of various iron oxides. As in the case of all natural *ochres,* it has a high degree of *hiding power,* and it is thoroughly reliable in *stability.* However, when mixed with *lake colors,* it will usually decompose and destroy them; the same result is found when *flesh ochre* is mixed with certain other *organic colors.*

FLOURISHING FOREST—In Chinese *art,* the term applied to any *painting* of a forest showing the trees in a state of thick foliage, as distinguished from the *cold forest* technique or style, showing them leafless. Known natively as *mao lin.*

FLOWER BLUE—In Chinese *painting, a blue pigment* resembling *indigo,* known natively as *hua ch'ing.* Used widely as an undercoat, or applied to the back of a painting to give depth to the subject as well as to prevent the fabric from cracking when rolled up. See *t'ou ch'ing.*

FLOWERS OF ZINC—A term in *painting*; see *zinc oxide.*

FLUORESCENCE—(1) The characteristic glow observed in some objects under *ultra violet* light. This behavior is useful in detecting repairs, *restorations,* forged sections, etc., on *paintings* and other *art* objects. (2) A property of some *transparent* substances by which incident rays of light are emitted in colors different from their own and from those of the *fluorescent body.* See *repainted wreck.*

FLYING WHITE—In Chinese *art,* a *painting* technique in which the hairs of the *brush* are allowed to separate so that a stroke is not solid black, but broken by streaks of untouched *ground;* the strokes appear almost three dimensional. Primarily a technique of writing, its use in painting is limited exclusively to drawing the *bamboo.* Known natively as *fei po.*

FOREGROUND—In *art,* that part of a scene in a *painting, bas relief, mosaic* picture, etc., which is closest to, and directly in front of, the viewer. See *aerial perspective.*

FORESHORTENING—The apparent diminution of intervening spaces because they are observed from an acute angle; e.g., in a view down a railroad track, the rails seem to converge to a vanishing point on the horizon while the successive telegraph poles appear to become progressively smaller and closer together as they recede in the distance. See *illusionism* and *perspective.* Beginners often ignore these effects and *paint* the distance of a *picture* too much like the *foreground.*

FOREST MARBLE—In *sculpture,* a form of *limestone* which, when cut along certain planes, shows a dark coloring matter so distributed throughout as to be imitative of woodlands and forests; known also as *landscape marble,* esp. when polished representations add the suggestion of rivers and open country.

FORGERIES—In painting.

FORMIN—A white crystalline substance used as a hardening agent in the type of *resins* employed as *surface films* or coatings over *paintings* and *statuary.*

FORM LACQUER—In *sculpture* and *ceramics,* a thin variety of *varnish* or *lacquer* used as a coating over the *relief* or *intaglio* parts of a *mold,* to prevent the *plastic* substance from adhering thereto after *casting.* If not extremely thin, it will blur the fine lines and edges of the original *model* from which the reproductions are *cast.*

FORMOSA MARBLE—In *sculpture,* a prized variety of *marble* having a characteristic white to dark gray color sporadically *mottled* and blotched with pale yellow and deep red; occurs cliefly in Germany.

FORTIFICATION MARBLE—In *sculpture,* a variety of *limestone* which, when highly polished or seen along certain planes, shows its veins and blotches in forms suggesting forts, walls, towers, and the like; the markings are caused by infiltration of iron oxide. See also *forest marble.*

FOSSIL RESIN—A pale *yellow-brown* substance better known in the arts as *amber* (q.v.).

FOSSIL WAX—A natural substance having the consistency of *wax,* used as a *surface film* or coating over *paintings* and *statuary.* It is yellow-brown to green or black in color, and is *translucent* in its pure state. Used also as a substitute for *beeswax* and *carnauba* (qq.v.) in all of their uses in the *arts.*

FOUNDING—The general term applied to the *art* of melting and *casting.*

FRACTIONAL CONCEPT—A belief, in early and *primitive* art *forms,* that the *perspective* of an object of *art* brought a visual *picture* of many component parts, and not of one entity. Thus, each line of a *design* had meaning to an extent greater than that of the combination as a whole. See *memory picture.*

FRAME—An object constructed of *wood, metal,* or other material, forming an enclosure or border around a work of *art* such as a *painting, relief* or stretched *tapestry,* etc. It provides a neat or *ornamental* finish around the work, isolates it from its surroundings or harmonizes it with them, serves as a means of protection, and often as the means of attaching the work in its appointed place. Also, the non-ornamental *chassis* upon which a *canvas* is stretched. The term is often extended to include *easel* (q.v.).

FRANKFORT BLACK—A fine black *pigment,* the active coloring agent of which is carbon. It is made from the yeast of spent wine (carbon is found in the 'tartar'), and an excellent blue-black hue is obtained when mixed with any good white pigment. Although somewhat low in *opacity* and *hiding power,* it possesses an unusually high degree of *stability,* and is suited to practically all techniques.

FREESTONE—In *sculpture* any stone that may be cut freely in any direction without a tendency to split; an important feature in the sculptor's medium. This quality exists because the stone has no grain.

FRENCH ULTRAMARINE BLUE—An important *blue pigment* added to the artist's *palette* in 1814 when ancient *ultramarine* was produced from *lapis lazuli* (q.v.). Though identical in chemical composition, the *artificial* pigment is far more *intense* in *color* and much finer in particle size. It has a more *purplish tinge* than the *natural,* but is equally *stable,* being unaffected by *light,* temperature, or alkali.

FRESCO—In *art,* the *technique* of *painting* on a *support* of freshly spread moist *plaster.* The *pigments* are mixed with water, thus incorporating themselves chemically with the plaster. The term is also applied to any painting or *mural* so executed. See *arriccio* and *fresco secco.*

FRESCO COLORS—See *distemper colors.*

FRESCO SECCO—A *mural painting* method of *ancient* origin; specifically, the process of painting with *fresco* pigments ground in *glue* and applied to a finished *plaster* wall saturated with *baryta water.* The term has been inaccurately applied to designate any *painting* which imitates or approximates the effects of true *fresco* by painting on a dry wall with *pigments* ground in an aqueous binding *medium,* such as *tempera;* 14th century writers applied the name to any dried fresco painting. *Fresco secco* paintings are similar in visual effect to true fresco, but lack much of its *brilliance,* clarity, durability, and manipulative *quality.*

FRESH GREEN—In Chinese *painting,* a prized *green* pigment popular in *landscape work,* prepared from *ts'ao lü.* Known natively as *nên lü,* its color is that of *celadon.*

FRIABLE—Any substance which is easily crumbled is said to possess the physical characteristic of *friability.* See *plasticizer.*

FRISKET PAPER—A type of *transparent,* gummed *paper* prepared in strips or rolls. Used for affixing *ledger bond, bristol board,* or other *drawing* or *water-color* ground *to* the *drawing board* while the *work of art* is being rendered; removes without scarring the *ground* or picture. Likewise employed in *stencil* cutting, *airbrush* work, and *retouching.* Known also as *frisket tape* and *frisket mask,* it is often produced ungummed, in which case it is bound with a variety of frisket *cement.*

FRIT—A famous *blue pigment* found in the *wall paintings* of Egypt and Mesopotamia, possesing a degree of *stability* that is probably unequaled in the history of art. Some specimens more than 3000 years old show no apparent fading, discoloration, or other defects. Popularly known as *Egyptian blue* (q.v.).

FROTTAGE—A *technique* employed esp. by *surrealists,* resulting in the transference of the superficial topography of an object, e.g., weathered *wood* or *stone,* leaves, sacking material, a spool of thread, etc., to another surface. A piece of *paper,* for example, placed on a rough or irregular surface, is rubbed with *pencil, paint,* etc., and an approximate *image* of the peaks and valleys results. The image is likewise known as *frottage,* deriving from the French, 'rubbing.'

FUCHSIN—Or *fuchsine;* an *intense* red-violet color of high *brilliance,* better known on the artist's *palette* as *magenta* (q.v.).

FUDE—In Japanese *art,* any *brush* used for *painting, drawing* or *writing.*

FUGITIVE COLORS—In *painting,* those *colors* which have a tendency to fade, sooner or later, because of the *instability* of the base. Dampness, heat, and other elements often hasten the *fugitive* activity of a color. See *stable* and *magenta.*

FULL COLOR—In *oil painting,* the quality of great purity, strength and *intensity* of *color.*

FULLER'S EARTH—In *ceramics* and *fresco* work, a gray or off-white substance having the same properties as fine *clay,* but possessing the added feature of remarkable absorption and retention of all *oil colors* deriving from animal and vegetable sources.

FUNDAMENTAL COLORS—Name given to the seven *colors,* making up the *spectrum:* violet, indigo, blue, green, yellow, orange and red.

FURFURAL—A colorless liquid which becomes pale *amber* in color upon exposure to light and/or air. Used as a solvent in the manufacture of artists' *lacquers, resins,* and *varnishes.* Chemically, it is pyromucic aldehyde or furfuranecarboxylic aldehyde, C_4H_3OCHO. The *tinge* of amber is often desired as a softening device when *furfural* is applied over an *oil painting* as a *surface film* (q.v.).

FUSMA—An *opaque,* movable room-*partition,* upon which Japanese *artists* lavish their best pictorial efforts. The *painting* itself is known as *fusuma* (q.v.).

FUSUMA—The actual *painting* appearing on a *fusma* (q.v.), or Japanese portable *partition.*

FUTURISM—An Italian school of *painting, sculpture* and *literature* flourishing from 1911 to 1915, endeavoring to portray the essence of *movement* without the thing that moves. It encouraged total abandonment of *traditional* usage, and attempted to reconstruct *art* and life on the basis of the revolutionary, dynamic, mechanical future. Interwoven somewhat with *simultaneism* (q.v.).

G

GAINE—In *sculpture,* the lower part of a figure of which the head alone (occasionally extending to the bust) is *carved* to represent nature; the remaining portion presents the appearance of a sheath closely enveloping the body, and is consequently broader at the shoulders than at the feet. Sometimes the feet are shown at the bottom of the *gaine,* while above them the solid lines of the squared or circular sheath continue up to the chest or head. A simple comparison can be made to the mermaid. Found most frequently in *Archaic Greek* and Egyptian *architectural* sculpture.

GAKU—In Japanese *art,* a *panel-painting* mounted and enclosed in a *frame;* any frame picture. Known also as *gakumen.*

GAKUMEN—In Japanese *art,* any *framed picture.* See *gaku.*

GALLIPOT—In *oil painting,* the small *porcelain* vessel clipped or otherwise fastened to the *palette* of the artist, in which the favored diluent or *thinner* was contained. Now obsolete, the metal or glass *dipper* (q.v.) appears to have replaced it.

GAMBOGE—In *painting,* a bright *yellow* substance used in the *color* enhancement of fine *paints;* obtained from the solidified *gum-resin* of the botanical GARCINIA HANBURII. Used for many centuries as a *pigment* in the Orient, its qualities came to the attention of the early Flemish oil painters who used it extensively. When pulverized in oil it is fairly *stable;* however, it fades rapidly in sunlight when employed as a *water-color.* In some *illuminated manuscripts* many centuries old, *gamboge* has lasted unusually well where treated with a *surface film.* Used also in *varnishes* and *lacquers.*

GANGUE—A term in *painting;* see *mineral gray.*

GANOSIS—In *sculpture,* a process of toning down the glare of *marble.*

GANYMEDE—In Greek *mythology,* the cup-bearer of *Zeus* and of the Olympian gods, originally a beautiful Trojan youth, transferred to Olympus and made immortal (according to Homer, by the gods; according to others, by an eagle representing Zeus, or by Zeus himself in the form of an eagle). Frequently represented in the *arts,* the most famous *statue* extant is GANYMEDE AND THE EAGLE in the Museo Nazionale, Naples.

GARANCE BRUN ROUGE—In *painting,* a *lake color* of warm brown *hue,* made from the *madder* root. It is not as transparent as the *alizarin* madders, which yield more permanent *pigments.* Known also as *madder brown* and *garanza roja parda.*

GATHER—In the making of *stained glass,* a small amount of molten *glass* affixed to the end of the blow-pipe. This *gather* of clear glass is then dipped into another color of glass and the bubble is blown. The colored glass forms a film around the clear glass bubble, forming *flashed glass.* The *gather,* or clear glass, is used in the mixture to prevent such *colors* as *red* and *blue* from appearing too dark for use in *stained* glass windows. Colored glass is occasionally given further treatment with hydrofluoric acid, producing glass having varying degrees of *intensity,* known as *shaded glass.* Likewise, two colors are sometimes stirred together slightly prior to the blowing process, resulting in intentionally *streaked glass.* See *stained glass.*

GAUFFRAGE—Any variety of *intaglio* or *relief printing* without color.

GEAT—The hole in a *mold* through which the metal is poured in *casting.*

GELVA RESINS—A series of neutral, water-white *resins* used in the making of fine *lacquers, surface films* for *painting* and *statuary,* and various adhesives. Chemically they are polyvinyl acetate products, *gelva* being a trade name.

GENERAL COLOR—In *painting,* the effect in combination of all the *hues* or *tones* appearing in one *picture.*

GENRE PAINTING—In Oriental *art,* the term applies to subjects "of the passing world" or everyday life, as distinguished from the grand style of immortality, God or religion in subject matter. Known in Chinese art as *fên su gên wu.* In *photography,* the term has similar application, i.e., pictures of everyday incidents; human interest pictures that tell a story; pictures illustrative of common life.

GENRE TRADITION—A tradition of *painting* in the *Flemish* school that portrays the rustic life. It was an integral feature of Flemish *art* almost from the inception of this great and influential school. Among the artists who worked in this *tradition* were Adriaen Brower, Pieter Breughel, Jerome Bosch, and many others. There is association of meaning between *genre tradition* and *genre painting,* esp. with regard to subject matter.

GENTLEMAN—In *sculpture* and *metalwork,* a rotating iron table upon which the object is placed prior to final forming. As the table is spun, a tool or other shaping agent is pressed against the object, forcing it to assume the desired form. See also *chassis.*

GERANIUM LAKE—One of the most *brilliant* red colors known, made by precipitating *eosine* on an aluminum base. Despite its unusual *hue,* its popularity is limited because of its tendency to fade rapidly in direct sunlight; failing in *stability,* it is used chiefly where even moderate permanency is not required. The *coal-tar* ingredients recently used in producing *geranium lake* have rendered it considerably more stable, but many artists have not yet been won over to the new product. Known also as *laque géranium* and *lacca geranio.*

GESSO—A mixture of *chalk* or *whiting,* and *glue,* applied thickly as a *ground* for *painting,* or as a *decorative* coating for the application of *carved* or *gilded* figures. Used principally in old Northern Europe, it took a smooth polish, and gave unusual *brilliance* to the *pigment* applied over it. The term is also applied to the actual *plaster*-glue layers affixed to *panels* to provide the smooth ground for the pigment. See *chalk.*

GESSO PANEL—A painting *ground* with a *gesso* layer previously applied, often treated on both sides. Available at most art supply sources, it is ready for use with *oils, watercolor, pastel, gouache,* or *tempera.*

GHENT SCHOOL—An important 15th century *art* school pursuing *miniature painting* exclusively. Located in Ghent, it boasted such famous families of miniaturists as the Bininks and the Horenbauts. The school also produced the vigorous *realist* Hugo van der Gos.

GIALLO ANTICO—In *sculpture,* a yellow *marble* favored by the ancient Greeks and Romans; literally, *antique yellow.* Occurs chiefly in Algeria.

GIALLO INDIANO—In *painting,* a deep, translucent, orange-yellow *pigment* of moderate *stability,* commonly known as *Indian yellow* (q.v.).

GIROUETTE—An artistically *carved* or *sculptured* weather vane.

GIS—In Mexican *art,* a general term having reference to any type of *pencil, chalk* or *crayon;* any *writing* or *drawing* device in stick form, requiring no dipping.

GLANCE—A term used to designated a high *gloss* or *luster* on various mineral substances; e.g., silver *glance,* bronze *glance,* etc.

GLASS OF COBALT—In *painting,* a variety of *pigment* commonly known as *cobalt glass* (q.v.).

GLASS-PAINTER—One who produces colored designs on or in *glass* by either of the two techniques set forth in *glass-painting* (q.v.).

GLASS-PAINTING—The *art* technique of producing designs in color on or in glass. Known also as *glass-staining,* there are two methods widely employed: (1) the *enamel method,* consisting of applying *paint* colors to the glass which are later burned into it; (2) the *mosaic method,* by which a design is formed of separate pieces of stained or colored glass previously prepared, braced and supported by a frame-work of lead; the famous medieval windows of the 13th century (thus far defying duplication) were made by the latter process. A third method used is a combination of both. See *stained glass.* The term is also applied to a comparatively modern technique of painting in China by which *pigments* are brushed directly on sheets of glass. The finished work is backed and framed, and equipped with a hook-like device affixed to the glass so that the painting may be hung.

GLASS-STAINING—See *glass-painting.*

GLAZING—In *painting,* the application of a thin coating of *raw* or *burnt sienna* over a painted surface in order to soften or *tone* down the effect of the *colors* previously affixed. In addition to the siennas, any other *translucent* colors-in-oil such as *umber* or *Van Dyke brown* (qq.v.), thinned with flatting oil, may be used to obtain the antique decorative effect. This technique is employed most frequently on *wall paintings.*

GLORY—In *painting,* a term applied to a scene representing heaven opened. Forcefully exhibited in many of Michelangelo's paintings on the ceiling of the Sistine Chapel (1508-1512), e.g., CREATION OF ADAM, etc.

GLOSS—A term applied to any *bright* or *lustrous* finish on a smooth surface of *metal, porcelain, marble,* etc.; the property of a surface by which it reflects light specularly. Artists use the terms *high, enamel,* or *mirror* to indicate an unusually high degree of *gloss* or *luster;* they use *semi-gloss, eggshell,* and *flat* to denote decreasing degrees of *gloss* in the order given. See *luster.*

GLUE—An *adhesive* employed for joining purposes, used also as a binding *medium* in *paints.* Through the Far East this is still the traditional *vehicle* in *tempera painting.* It is prepared from a wide variety of organic materials such as bones, skins and intestines of animals and fish. See *size.*

GLYCERIN—A pale *yellow* or colorless clear liquid having a vast number of uses in the *arts.* Employed in the making of artists' *resins* and *gums,* the finishing of *leather,* as a softener in *glues* and other adhesives, in *plastics* and *plasticizers,* in *textile* processing, and in the manufacture of *inks.* Known also as *glycerol, glycol alcohol,* and *propenyl alcohol.* Chemically, $C_3H_5(OH)_3$.

GLYPHIC ART—That branch of the *arts* which concerns

itself principally with *modeling* and *carving* in *plastic* material; plastic *sculpture.*

GOFUN—A white *chalk* wash often used as a *ground* by Japanese *painters.*

GOLD—A bright-*yellow,* rather soft metal, extremely *malleable* and *ductile.* Does not corrode, and cannot be attacked by most acids. Occurs freely, and when hardened with *silver* or *copper,* is used in *jewelry, coinage,* and dentistry. Some of its compounds are used in *photography.* Many of its uses in the *arts* are lost in antiquity, and numerous of the finest examples of *gilding, sculpture, painting, inlay, carving,* etc., of ancient *cultures* have *gold* as a *medium.* It is one of the heaviest substances known.

GOLD LEAF—The most *malleable* of all metals, *gold* can be beaten into sheets or leaves 254,000 thicknesses to the inch. Although apparently the color of true gold, it actually transmits *green* light, as shown when a leaf is held to the light. The ancient Egyptians hammered out *gold leaf* between pieces of ox intestines, and the Greeks and Romans used *parchment.* This process is still used, no other method having been invented to supersede the hand-beating. The beaten leaves are laid in books, the paper of which is rubbed with *chalk* to prevent the leaf from sticking to it. Used in *gilding, lettering, restoration* work, etc.

GOLD POINT—Now little used as a *drawing* instrument, there is some record to establish that a wire or point of *gold,* like that of *silver,* drawn over a slightly abrasive *ground,* has been employed in the *arts.* It is said to impart a somewhat warmer *tint* than the line made by silver.

GORGON'S HEAD—In Greek art, the face of the terrible, ugly Gorgon with exaggeratedly large features, wide open eyes, broad nose, grinning mouth, and *spiral* curls, sometimes surrounded by curling snakes. Represented frequently in *painting* and *sculpture,* it has *apotropaic* significance.

GOUACHE—A type of *painting* made with *opaque watercolors.* A pliable adhesive is usually added to the *binder* to give the surface a soft sheen and to retard the drying of the *paint*. Known also as *gouache-drawing*. See *water-color*.

GOUGE—In *sculpture,* a chisel-like tool having a curved cutting edge, used for the incising of *stone*. Employed also to cut holes, channels or grooves in *wood,* and to cut out forms from *leather, paper,* etc.

GRADATION—In *painting,* a gradual passing in *color* from one *tint* or *shade* to another. Known also as *shading,* there are frequently hundreds of different *gradations* of one color found in proceeding from the darkest to the lightest shade.

GRANITE—A grained rock, famed for its hardness and firmness. Usually composed of orthoclase and quartz in combination with another mineral, such as mica. Used widely in fine building and in monument work.

GRAPHIC ART—A term originally covering all *forms* of representation on flat surfaces, as *engraving, drawing* and *painting*. Recent usage, however, removes it from painting generally and applies it to the fields of *printing, lithography, etching, wood-block work,* and allied *arts,* all of which are characterized by substantially flat surfaces, as distinguished from *high relief, sculpture,* and *architecture,* along with *music, literature,* etc.

GRAPHIC GRANITE—In *sculpture,* a variety of binary *granite* deriving its name from the fact that its cross-sectional markings bear a resemblance to Hebrew and *cuneiform* inscriptions.

GRAPHITE—A mineral having little use in the *arts* until employed in the making of *pencils* and *crayons*. Its *gray color* and greasy *texture* caused confusion with lead in early times, and the modern *graphite* pencil is still called "lead pencil." Though easily abraded, it is entirely permanent and, because of its texture, can be used on soft *paper*. It is widely distributed as a *natural* mineral, but has also been made synthetically since 1891. Known also as *blacklead* and *plumbago*. The pencil itself is a *medium* of wide popularity in the arts. See also *drawing pencils*.

GRATICULATION—The method of breaking down a *picture* or *pattern* into *graph*-like squares for the purpose of simplifying reproduction. The size of the squares, constant in each project, depends on the proportions of the original, and the need for detail.

GRAVER—In *engraving* (q.v.), a sharp, triangular, chisel-like tool, usually of *copper,* with which the lines of the *design* are drawn on a metal *plate.* The edge of metal, turned up as the tool is pushed forward, is polished off to leave a smooth surface except for the *graven* lines, which receive the *ink* and produce the *print.* Similar to a *stylus* and *drypoint* (qq.v.). See also *multiple graver.*

GRAY CAMEO-PAINTING—A technique of *glass* painting in which the markings and shadings are extremely delicate, producing an all-over effect of light-gray *monochrome.*

GRAYISH—Lacking purity of *color;* having no definite *hue; neutral.*

GREASY—One of the classification of *luster* (q.v.).

GREEN—The *color* of plants, grass, foliage, etc., when growing; any *pigment* of *green* color; the color composed of *blue* and *yellow* which, when mixed in various proportions, result in different *shades* of the basic *green.*

GREEN CINNABAR—In *painting,* a *pigment* of deep green, made by subjecting the oxides of *cobalt* and *zinc* to a *firing* process.

GREEN EARTH—The most popular of the *green pigments* used by *painters* of the *Middle Ages* and the *Renaissance.* It was known long before that time, having been found on *wall paintings* of *classical* times. Its *hues* range from *gray*-green to *yellow*-green. Though its *tint*ing strength is slight, it is unusually *stable,* and with thorough grinding it provides a smooth, workable pigment. Belonging to the group known as the *iron pigments* (q.v.), it is also known as *terre-verte.* Chemically it is glauconite, found in the cavities of certain eruptive rocks of the amygdaloid class.

GREEN IVORY—One of the most highly prized varieties of *ivory,* employed chiefly for *carving.* Commonly known as *Pangani* (q.v.)

GREEN LAKE—In *painting,* a green *lake* color made up of various ingredients, differing according to the beliefs and experience of the individual colorman. A *green lake* of rather good *stability* can be made by an admixture of *zinc yellow* and *Prussian blue.* Those varieties produced by using *Dutch pink, Italian pink,* or any of the other *fugitive* organic yellows in combination with Prussian blue are not generally trusted by artists, since experience has shown that they will fade in direct sunlight within a few hours. Known also as *Gruenerlack.*

GREEN MARBLE—In *sculpture,* popular name for *serpentine* (q.v.).

GREEN MINERAL—A *green pigment* famous through the centuries, properly known as *malachite* (qv.).

GREEN SMALT—Term applied to the *cobalt green color,* prized for its *stable* qualities, although its strength is relatively weak. See *cobalt pigments.*

GREENSTONE—A mineral found principally in the South Pacific islands. *Nephrite,* one of the varieties of *greenstone,* was used widely in the making of tools for *Maori carving* (q.v.). Known also as *diorite,* it consists chiefly of feldspar and hornblende in beautiful crystalline structure, sometimes speckled with *mica.*

GRIGIO DI PAYNE—A term in *painting;* see *payne's gray.*

GRINDING—The technique of crushing *pigment* substances to render them mixable for use on the artist's *palette,* each color receiving the maximum *grinding* consistent with its properties and needs; the process also produces the greatest *brilliance* any color is capable of rendering, with caution exercised to make certain that the process is not too severe. Fine *grinding* prevents colors from separating after mixing or thinning; also brings about maximum *transparency* while preserving *stability.*

GRINDING SLAB—Any *stone* on which *paint* is hand-ground, traditionally *granite* or *porphyry.* It was about 12 inches across, and the *pigment* was worked on it with a smaller stone, fitting the hand, known as a *muller.* It probably grew from the prehistoric means of grinding grain, and examples of its use are found in the earliest records of the *art* of *painting.* It is now exceedingly rare, having been replaced by the *color mill* (q.v.). See also *slice* and *grinding.*

GRIOTTE MARBLE—In *sculpture,* a *French* marble of prized red color, often variegated with small dashes of purple, and spots or streaks of white. Known also as *Cannes marble.*

GRISAILLE—An effect of *light* and shade produced in *printed enamel,* acquired by covering the background with *opaque white* and then modulating it to produce the desired *gradations.* The term is also applied to any *decorative painting* in *gray monochrome.*

GRIS DE PAYNE—One of the finest *gray pigments* on the artist's *palette,* commonly known as *payne's gray.*

GROS VENTRE—A tribe of the mid-western Plains Indians of the United States, approaching in artistic accomplishment the fine work produced by the *Arapaho* tribe. Their efforts were directed mainly to bead and feather work, basketry, *pottery, carving, weaving* and *painting.* See *Arapaho.*

GROTESQUE—The term applied to an *ornament,* either *painted* or *sculptured,* consisting of fantastically shaped human beings, animals, and fabulous beings. Frequently found in Greek and Roman palaces, *grotesques* were revived in the late 15th century in Italian *decoration.* Ornamental *engravers* took up the style, which was not in contrast with, but rather connected to the *arabesque* or *grottesque* (q.v.), with which *grotesque* is still not considered synonymous.

GROTTESQUE—In *painting* and *relief work,* a style characterized by intertwined leaves, flowers, foliage, and *scrollwork* in fantastic *design;* commonly known as *arabesque.* Not to be confused with *grotesque,* although in recent years the terms have been merging.

GROUND—In *etching,* the acid-resistant coating on a *plate;* must be a substance that will be impervious to the *biting* action in the *acid bath,* allowing only the incised lines to be attacked thereby. When unevenly spread, or otherwise defective, a *false biting* (q.v.) may occur. See *biting.*

GROUND—In *painting,* the preparation laid over the support, providing a smooth, even-*textured,* even-*toned* surface to receive the *design.* The most popular through the centuries was a mixture of *chalk* or *whiting* and *glue,* known as *gesso* (q.v.). This was applied to the *wooden panels* that were the chief painting *supports* in the *Middle Ages,* prior to the use of *canvas.* Gesso was subsequently replaced by *oil grounds.* The term is loosely applied to any material or surface (e.g., *canvas, panel, porcelain,* etc.) upon which a *picture* is rendered. See *medium.*

GROUNDING—In *sculpture,* the process of polishing *marble* with a fine abrasive.

GROUT—(1) A term applied to the chips, powder, and all waste pieces remaining after a piece of *sculpture* has been executed in stone. (2) A variety of thin *mortar* poured into the interstices between stones and *bricks.* (3) A type of *cement* or *plaster* into which pebbles or small stones have been mixed for strength and for ornamentation, esp. when used as a wall coating.

GRUENERLACK—A term in *painting;* see *green lake.*

GUACHE—See *gouache.*

GUAI-A-PHENE—A substance of a *resinous* nature, used in the making of artists' *paints, varnishes, inks,* etc. Chemically it is a mixture of phenols derived from resinous *pine* wood, *guai-a-phene* being a trade name.

GUIGNET GREEN—In *painting,* a brilliant *chrome*-green *pigment* named for the discoverer of the process by which it is made. The basic ingredients are calcined boracic acid and potassium bichromate alternately treated with hot and cold water. This transparent color is one of the finest and most valuable on the *palette,* having good tinting strength. depth of *hue,* and a remarkably high degree of *stability.* Known also as *Pannetiers green.*

GUIMET—In *painting,* the term applied generally to any variety of *ultramarine blue* that has been artificially prepared.

GUM—Any of the various *ground* and *surface film* preparations used in *painting,* having a base of *resin* or other tenacious and *stable* substance. Among the *gums* that have found use in the *arts* are *sandarac, gamboge, elemi* (qq.v.).

GUM ELEMI—A *resious* substance used in *varnish,* better

known as *elemi* (q.v.).

GUM WATER—Any one of a number of simple mixtures used as a binding agent for *water-colors;* employed also for the 'pointing' of *brushes.*

GUPTA PERIOD—In the *arts* of India, one of the great epochs of that country's civilization. Flourishing from 320 to 600 A.D., it developed an exquisite and talented *culture* marked by the unparalleled magnificence and dusty splendor of the imperial courts and a rich flowering of all the arts, including *painting, sculpture, literature,* and *music.* Prominent among the examples extant are the great *wall-paintings* covering the perpendicular areas of the rock-cut Buddhist *sanctuaries* at Ajanta.

GURI—A Japanese *lacquer* technique. Successive layers of various *colored* lacquers are applied, and then *carved* through in a V-shape to show the striated colors as a *pattern.*

GYPSUM—Better known as *plaster of Paris,* a substance *molded* and *carved* since *ancient* times. Pulverized, it served as the inert material of *grounds;* the gesso in *paintings* on *supports* of *wooden panels.* Most *gypsum* used in the *arts* is first burned, and it sets rapidly to a firm *plaster* when again combined with water. Generally *stable,* and slightly soluble in water, it is the most common of all *casting* materials. Known also as *terra alba* and *mineral white.*

H

HAARLEM SCHOOL—A Dutch school of *art* centering in Haarlem; its chief characteristic was the truthful representation of garden backgrounds in *painting,* first introduced by Dierick Bouts. This school was a foreunner of painting schools and movements that were to flourish in great number in Holland in the 17th century.

HALF RELIEF—A *technique* in *sculpture* in which the raised portions emerge in medium prominence against the background. Also known as *demi-relief.* See *relief.*

HALF-SECTIONAL DRAWING—In *drawing,* a view executed in sectional fashion providing a scene which shows the internal and external features of an object.

HALF-TONE, HIGH LIGHT—In *etching,* a *half-tone* in which the *highlight* areas print white instead of gray because the fine dots have been etched away; known also as *dropout.*

HALF-TONE, SILHOUETTE—In *etching,* a *half-tone* in which the principal object in the *picture* stands alone, the background having been etched away.

HALF-TONE- SQUARE FINISH—In *etching,* a *half-tone* in which the background is trimmed to a definite shape by the *engraver;* though usually rectangular in shape, it may be oval or circular.

HALF-TONE, VIGNETTE—In *etching,* a *half-tone* in which the background gradually fades away to an imperceptible edge. If the fading effect extends to all edges of the *picture,* it is a *true vignette;* if it applies to part of the picture only and the balance of the background is entirely removed, it is an *outline vignette.*

HALMSTADGRUPPEN—Scandinavian school of young *painters* led by Halland, developing *expression* and *technique* along *surrealist* lines. Many of the group, including Stellan Morner, Axel Olson, Sven Jonson, and Waldemar Lorentzon, gained wide recognition in Stockholm.

HANDLE—The short projection on an *artist's* work-board, used for ease of grip. Used as an appurtenant to the *palette* in Europe since the early *Renaissance.* See also *thumbhole.*

HANDLING—In *painting,* a general term applied to the method employed by an *artist* in using the materials. In some instances it refers merely to manipulation; in others, to the finished work itself, as the '*handling of a subject.*'

HAND-WIPED PRINT—A term in etching; see *wiping.*

HAN DYNASTY—A period in Chinese *history* (206 B.C. to 220 A.D.) rich in the development of the *arts. Painting* reached remarkable heights of line and *color* (see *malachite*), *calligraphy* made great strides, and *stone carving* was of such fine cut and excellent *medium* selection that inscribed *pillars* dating back to 105 B.C. are in excellent condition today. All of the arts of the period are characterized by clarity of perception, mastery of *composition,* and gracefulness of *expression.* The work of this period has rarely, if ever, been surpassed.

HANGING CREEPERS—In Chinese *painting,* a brush stroke technique employed to give the effect of bird tracks on a slope, pointing downhill. Used frequently to represent gnarled trees and the irregular faults of angular rocks in *landscape* work.

HAN LIN—In Chinese a*rt,* a *painting* of trees without leaves. Known to Western artists as *cold forest.*

HANSA YELLOW—In *painting,* a valued yellow *pigment* of the *lake* class, derived from a synthetic permanent *dye.* Various greens are made from a base of *hansa yellow,* all possessing unusually strong *hiding power* and general *stability.*

HARRISON RED—In *painting,* a fine *lake color* having strong tinting power, used successfully as a substitute for *vermilion;* possesses considerably more *stability* than the reds prepared with *alizarin* or *madder* (qq.v.). Though the origin of the term is obscure, it is believed by some that it is in honor of Birge Harrison, distinguished American artist.

HASHIRA—In Japanese *art, hashira,* a *pillar*; *hashirae,* a *painting.* Thus, a pillar painting or a narrow, painted *panel* to hang on a pillar. Generally applied to a long, narrow form of Japanese *print,* approximately 28 inches in height by 5 inches in width.

HEAVY MAGNESIA—A white powder of varying weight, used in the making of *paints* and *varnishes, cements* and other adhesives, fine *lacquers,* and *artifical stone, brick,* and *plaster tiles*; employed also as a substitute for *platinum.* Chemically it is magnesium oxide, MgO.

HEBREW GRANITE—In *sculpture,* a variety of *graphic granite* in which the *quartz* crystals imbedded in the body of the stone are in such form as to suggest characters of the Hebrew alphabet.

HEIEN—In Japanese *art,* a term indicating *level distance,* shown in *paintings* of mountains supported by clouds, lakes, mists, etc., to lend depth. In this technique, colors are characterized by both clarity and obscurity, while figures are invariably indistinct. Chinese counterpart is *level distance* (q.v.).

HEI-TIKI—In *Maori carving* (q.v.) the *symbolic* pendants on the neck cords of *totemic* figures. Exquisitely *carved* (usually of *greenstone*) these pieces are treasured as heirlooms.

HELIOTROPE—In *painting,* a pale *purple* or *mauve* color; also, any *pigment* or *dye* imparting such a color.

HEMP—A tough *fiber* derived from the tall-growing annual plant CANNABIS SATIVA, originating in Asia but now cultivated in many parts of the world, esp. tropical. Used in the making of ropes, coarse *fabrics, rug*-lining, etc. In China, used for making a variety of *paper* employed as a *ground* in *painting* and *calligraphy.* See *chih.*

HEMPSEED OIL—In *painting,* one of the materials found to be effective as a *drying oil* (q.v.).

HÊNG FU—In Chinese *art,* a *scroll painting* (see *chüan*

chou) so designed and executed that it is hung horizontally. Different techniques are required in the arrangement and size of the *chou* and *chou shou* (qq.v.) in mounting the picture. Compare with *kua fu.*

HERACLES—Same as the Latin *Hercules,* leading pioneer hero of the Greeks, son of *Zeus;* by sheer physical strength overcame many natural and human obstacles during his spectacular career, and eventually was received into Olympus as a demigod. He is usually *represented* in the *arts* wearing a lionskin and armed with a bow and club. His exploits were treated extensively by 6th and 5th century B.C. *vase* painters of Greece, and he appeared in *architectural* sculpture at Delphi (*Athenian Treasury*), Olympia (*Temple of Zeus*), and Athens, (*Temple of Hephaestus*), as well as in many famous *metopes.*

HERMA—In Greek *sculpture,* esp. common in ancient Athens, a type of monument or *statue* consisting of a head fully sculptured *in the round,* but supported on a quadrangular pillar which, though not representing the lower part of the body, corresponded roughly thereto in mass. Known also as *herm* and *hermes,* the term derives from the fact that the head of such *statuary* was most frequently that of *Hermes.*

HERMES—The Latin *Mercury,* Greek god of fertility and commerce, and messenger of the gods. Frequently *represented* as a handsome youth with winged *helmet* and sandals, carrying a herald's staff. On Greek funerary *vases* he was often pictured escorting the souls of the dead to Hades.

HEROIC—In *sculpture,* a term used to describe a *statue* that is larger than life size (whether man or animal) but not reaching *colossal* proportions. The average *heroic statue* represents a human figure at between six and seven feet in height.

HEXAMINE—A white crystalline substance used as a hardening agent in the type of *resins* employed as *surface films* over *paintings* and *statuary.*

HIDING POWER—In *painting,* the power of a *pigment, paint,* painting material, etc., to obscure the surface to which it is applied. The extent of *opacity* found in a paint or pigment. *Body-colors* are frequently employed for their *hiding power,* i.e., their ability to conceal the texture of the *ground.*

HIERACOSPHINX—In Egyptian *archaeology* and *sculpture,* a variety of *sphinx* having the head of a hawk, as distinguished from the human-headed *androsphinx* and the goat-headed *criosphinx.*

HIGH—In *painting,* a term used by artists to describe the greatest possible degree of *gloss* or *luster* obtainable. See *gloss.*

HIGH DISTANCE—In Chinese *painting,* the term applied to a view from the foot of mountains looking up to the peaks, the aspect being abrupt. *Colors* are clear and bright, and figures are clear and visible from afar. In the proper execution of this technique, height and distance must be combined or the height will lose its effect. The inclusion of waterfalls helps to furnish the *illusion* of height. Compare with *deep distance* and *level distance* (qq.v.).

HIGH KEY—A term in *painting;* see *key.*

HIGHLIGHT—In an *oil painting,* (1) the one point posessing the most *intense* light; (2) the small portion of the *light* surface which receives the rays of the source of light at right angles and which, when wet, *glitters.* This can be observed in the vicinity of a street light on a rainy night.

HIGH RELIEF—A mode of *sculpturing* in which the figures and other raised portions stand out boldly and strongly from the background. Known also as *alto-relievo* (q.v.). See also *bas-relief.*

HIGH RENAISSANCE—See *Renaissance.*

HIGH WARP—A *painting* so arranged that its *warp* is in a vertical position when it is *framed* and hung.

HITSUI—In Japanese *painting,* a term generally meaning *brush stroke.*

HOGBACK—In Chinese *painting,* a brush stroke technique giving the effect of large axe splits, or the cleavage caused by striking the back of an axe with a hammer, into wood. This style differs from *axe cuts* (q.v.) in that the strokes are longer and fewer, and the ridges are left white instead of being outlined. Used in representing large, ragged-edge rocks.

HOHENSTAUFEN ART—Paralleling the reign of the German HOHENSTAUFEN DYNASTY (1138-1254), this period was one of tremendous tension and antagonism in the *arts.* In *architecture,* the disputes centered about the central *dome* idea, with some designers seeking exact periphery encircling the dome, and others favoring the Greek cross plan and the anti-*Gothic* handling of *vault* pressure, i.e., removal of the pressure-resisting supports from within. In *sculpture,* though all gave importance to the human figure, one group stressed the metaphysical aspect while another took the *natural,* human view of life in *stone.* Opposing trends extended also to *painting,* some *artists* showing life in spiritual *emotion* and *ecstasy* of soul, others insisting upon strict, severe, formal representation as in life, and still others favoring a lavish, richly embellished style of *fantasy.* The *Hohenstaufen arts* are considered by many to be the *proto-Renaissance,* or predecessor influences of the *Renaissance.*

HOLLOWING—In *sculpture,* the technique of creating gently-sloping depressions in the surface of a large work, at carefully chosen points; intended to enhance the light and shadow effects and make greatest possible use of natural *chiaroscuro,* keeping the *statue* in the original color of the *stone, granite, marble,* etc., used. The practice originated with Rodin (1840-1917), who frowned on 'painted shadows.' See also *bossing.*

HOLLOW RELIEF—In *sculpture,* not a true *relief,* since it has no background, but it may be used as the *mold* for true relief. Creates the impression of roundness by *optical illusion,* because its sculptural forms are not *convex* or plastic, but *concave* or hollow. As the light touches an inverted relief, light and shade are reversed. When highlighted from above, shadows form on the upper parts of the relief, and light appears below; this is in contrast to a projected relief, which would be lighted on top and shaded below. It is rarely encountered today, the only modern example existing on the walls of the British and French buildings of Rockefeller Center, New York. The Greeks and Romans used it on *gems* for *seal*ing rings; the Babylonians carved it into *stone* cylinders which were rolled over *clay* and left a plastic imprint. It is now used mainly in *negative carving* (q.v.) for *bas-relief,* and in modern *abstract* relief sculpture; also in sculptural *cut glass.*

HONEY—Used in mixture with a *painting pigment,* producing a *tempera* which will give a true *matte* (q.v.) finish. See *tempera.*

HONZON—In Japanese *art* and religion, the principal *sculptured image* in a Buddhist *temple.*

HOO BIRD—Japanese name for the Chinese *fêng-huang,* or bird of good omen. Used in *painting* and fine *sensu* work, in which it appears as a long-tailed pheasant-like bird. Known commonly as the *phoenix,* and technically as the *ocellated argus.* See *phoenix.*

HOOKER'S GREEN—A valued *pigment* on the artist's *palette,* made by mixing *phthalocyanine* in green with *cadmium* orange. Although completely permanent and *stable,* it possesses the same *shade* and *transparency* as the green *fugitive* color which employs *gamboge* in the mixture. In the early 20th century, prior to the discovery of phthalocyanine, it was mixed with *Prussian blue* and *cadmium,* producing a highly *unstable* pigment. Named for the artist who first introduced it in *painting.*

HOPEWELL CULTURE—An aboriginal American *culture* centering in southern Ohio but widespread in the eastern United States. Its name derives from the owner of a site near Chillicothe, Ohio, where remains of it were first discovered and where some of its finest products were found, including *temple* and domicile *foundations,* stone pipes, *mica* and *copper* ornaments, intricately woven *textiles,* necklaces, and ornaments of fresh-water *pearls.* Also found were *carvings* of bird, animals, and human figures, depicted naturalistically and with great vitality on *stone.* See *Adena Culture.*

HOPI KACHINAS—In Hopi Indian *art,* a famous series of more than 200 carved *figurines* or dolls, used in various *ceremonies.* After the representation of the particular god or other figure is created in *wood,* the doll is *painted* in bright colors and ornamented with hawk feathers. The word *kachina* is used by the Hopis in three different meanings: (1) any divine or supernatural being; (2) a masked dancer impersonating a spirit; (3) the small carved effigies representing both of the others. After being put to their use in various rituals, the dolls are given to the children as toys, and as visual aids in teaching them the important deities and ceremonies.

HORSE TOOTH—In Chinese *painting,* a brush stroke technique intended to give the effect suggested by the name. Stiff, hard strokes are applied with the point of the brush; used for the representation of upright angular rocks and vertical jointing. Known natively as *ma ya ts'un.*

HOSO—In Japanese *art,* a *print* about six by twelve inches in size, hung vertically only.

HOT COLORS—A popular term applied to all *colors* exhibiting the *tones* of fire, the sun, the glow of embers, and the like. The group includes all hues of red and those approaching red, e.g., yellow, and even yellow-green. These colors are associated with heat, and the fact that they produce a sensation of warmth can be demonstrated by the use of a sensitive thermometer.

HSIANG—In Chinese *painting,* any individual *portrait,* as distinguished from *ch'uan shên jên wu,* referring to portraiture broadly, as a subject.

HSIEH I—In Chinese *art,* the term applied to any free *sketch* or *painting* characterized by spontaneous expression, as distinguished from *kung pi,* which displays meticulous attention to detail and strict adherence to forms and standards.

HSING LÊ T'U—In Chinese *painting,* a life *portrait* as distinguished from *chui ying* (q.v.), especially one in which there is a generous amount of setting or background. Many pictures showing the emperors of the great CH'ING DYNASTY in the palace gardens and pavilions are in this class.

HSI PI—In Chinese *art,* a small *pi* (q.v.), used as an *ornamental jade* girdle pendant.

HSIUNG HUANG—In Chinese *painting,* a bright *yellow* color known also as *Princeton yellow,* prepared from *realgar* (q.v.) in the manner of *shih ch'ing.* Stones that are originally red and shaped like a cockscomb are believed by Oriental artists to yield the best *pigment.* The color is *stable* and has many uses; however, if used in any combination with *gold,* a blackening reaction occurs. See *shih ch'ing.*

HSÜAN CHIH—In Chinese *art,* a fine white *paper* made of *bamboo,* esp. suitable for *painting* and *calligraphy.* Of double thickness, it is generally un-*sized,* though the *ink* is more difficult to control without the sizing. See *chih.*

HUA—In Chinese *art,* the general term for a *picture* of any kind; also, the verb 'to paint.' See *t'u.*

HUA CH'I—In Chinese *art* and *ceramics,* any *painting* or *pottery* upon which *lacquer* has been used as the *medium.*

HUA CH'ING—In Chinese *painting,* a blue *pigment* resembling *indigo,* known also as *flower blue.* Often used as an undercoat, or applied to the back of a painting to soften the texture and prevent it from cracking when rolled up. See *t'ou ch'ing.*

HUA CHÜAN—*Picture silk;* silk especially adapted by the Chinese to *painting,* as ready-*sized* silk. Formerly, artists undertook the laborious process of sizing, but this *ground* now comes prepared, all of it being accomplished in Soochow. Not synonymous with *chüan,* which refers generally to all varieties of silk used in painting. See also *hung pien* and *tz'ü ch'ing.*

HUA HUI—Flowers and plants; in Chinese *art* schools, one of the stipulated subjects required of students prior to advancement.

HUE—The *color* of a visual *stimulus,* determined by its *wavelength.* The general term distinguishing one color from another. Simply, *hue* is color. The primary *hues* are *red, blue,* and *yellow,* which, when taken together with *orange, green,* and *violet,* make up the chief colors of the *spectrum.* Between these are the *intermediates,* which take on the characteristics of the adjoining *hues*. The word is defined by some authorities (e.g., Munsell) as the identity of a color in terms of its being simply a variety of red, green, or other identifiable colors. See *color vision* and *Munsell System.*

HUNGARY BLUE–A term in *painting;* see *cobalt blue.*

HUNG PIEN–In Chinese *painting,* a variety of ready-*sized silk* used as a *ground,* distinguished from *hua chüan* (q.v.) by its *red* stripes (in the *selvage*) and its barely perceptible *yellow* cast.

HYDROFLUORIC ACID–A corrosive liquid compound which readily attacks silica, used widely for *etching* on *glass.*

HYDRO-PLASTIC–The term applied to any number of *plastic* materials prepared in paste form; will harden permanently upon exposure to air, the hardening time varying according to the thickness of application. Used widely as a *modeling* material, for *relief* decoration, and for the *inlaying* of *carvings* on works of art. Prepared in a range of colors.

HYDROSTONE–In *sculpture,* one of the hardest and strongest *casting plasters* known; used with remarkable success in the making of *molds* for *carved* objects. Chemically it is a *gypsum* plaster, *hydrostone* being a trade name.

I

ICE SNOW PAPER—A *ground* in Chinese *calligraphy* and *painting*. See *ping hsüeh.*

ICHI-MAI—A single-sheet Japanese *woodblock print* in *black* and *white.*

ICON—The *representation* of some sacred personage, as Christ, or an angel or saint, in *paint, enamel, fresco,* or other material, the object being revered as sacred because of the holy resemblance it bears. Many religious disputes throughout the centuries were centered about the *icon* and its purpose, giving rise to *iconoclasm* (rejection of the use of *images* in religion) and the *iconophiles* (friends of images). Some of the greatest works of *art* in all of art's history have been accomplished as *icons.*

ICONOGRAPHY—The *art* of representation by *pictures* or *images*; the study or description of *portraiture* or representation. The identification of religious characters, incidents, and *symbols* in the arts. See *icon.*

ICONOSTASIS—In 14th century Russian *art,* an '*icon*-screen' separating the church from the *sanctuary.* Such *altarpieces* consisting of a single row of *paintings* had been used in earlier centuries, but the structure of the *iconostasis* now became a tall, wide screen with as many as five registers of painting, completely shutting off the *altar.* In the central row, or *tschin,* was the *Deesis* (Christ flanked by the Madonna and John the Baptist); on either side of the Deesis were *panels* representing Saints Peter, Paul, Michael and Gabriel. The upper rows were given over to various feasts and holy figures. See *polyptych.*

IDIOM—An exceedingly broad, general term of vague and undefined meaning, usually indicative of a wide classification, pecularity of *character,* distinctiveness of *style,* or period of creation, as an *expresssion* in any of the *arts;* e.g., the *idiom* of 18th century *hymns* was the pleasing *melody,* in contrast to the *idiom* of the older *psalms,* characterized by strength and dignity. The *idiom* of *rococo* was the almost uncontrolled *ornamentation;* that of *classic architecture,* the formal lines; that of *pre-Raphaelite painting,* the emphasis on *naturalism,* etc.

IDOLINO—A famous *bronze statute* in Florence *representing* a graceful, standing youth. Though its creator is unknown, it has many of the characteristics of Polyclitus' *sculpture,* particularly the wavy *pattern* of the hair and the serene pose of the body and facial expression.

IGNEOUS ROCK—In *sculpture* and *architecture,* one of the three great classifications of *stone* (q.v.), this group including *granite,* feldspar, and others formed by solidification of molten masses from within the earth.

IKEBANA—Japanese term generally applied to the *art* of flower arrangement. Describes models for *still-life paintings* as well as *vase*-contained flowers for ordinary *decorative* use.

ILLUMINATE—In *art,* to *decorate* pages, letters, *manuscripts,* etc., with *gold* or *color;* finest examples are found in *illuminated manuscripts* and *Evangeliars* (qq.v.).

ILLUMINATED MANUSCRIPT—A book, usually of the *Middle Ages,* in which the text is written by hand and *illustrated* with *drawings* or small *paintings.* An extensively practiced *art* at the time, it declined after the growth of *easel* painting in the *Renaissance.* An excellent specimen is one of the first collections of AESOP'S FABLES now in the New York Public Library. See *illumination.*

ILLUMINATION—In *painting,* the *technique* of creating small, well-executed *pictures* as accompaniment to texts, Especially popular in the *Middle Ages,* when some of the finest *miniatures* were thus made. See *illuminated manuscript* and *Evangeliars.* The embellishments, chiefly in *red, blue* and *gold,* were often added to the initial letters and borders of the *manuscripts* and printed books of early times, with independently designed *miniatures* illustrating the subject matter of the text.

ILLUSIONISM—The effort in *painting* or *sculpture* to create as nearly as possible an *illusion* of visual reality; the painting or *modeling* of *substitute objects,* i.e., objects so like their prototypes as to serve as substitutes for them. Proper *illusionism* can be executed with careful attention devoted to *perspective, foreshortening, chiaroscuro, representional line drawing,* and microscopic detail, all of which combine to create the desired effect. *Naturalism* and *impressionism* (qq.v.) are forms of *illusionism.*

ILLUSTRATE—In *art,* to *ornament* or explain by means of *pictures, drawings, illuminations, photographs,* etc., esp. as a part of printed text, as in a book; any such individual item is an *illustration.*

ILLUSTRATED MANUSCRIPT—An early form of *book art,* emphasized during the *Carolingian* epoch; great *artistic* effort and talent were devoted to the *decorating* and *illustrating* of hand-written *Evangeliars* (q.v.) and other religious volumes. See *Ada Group.*

ILLUSTRATION BOARD—In *drawing,* a variety of *ground* produced in a great number of qualities, *textures* and thicknesses. Used for *pen* work, *wash drawings, airbrush, crayon, water-colors,* and *tempera.* Generally made up of a high grade *paper* mounted on heavy cardboard, with the back counter-mounted to prevent curling or warping.

IMAGE—(1) A *representation* or similitude of any person or thing, made of a material substance, e.g., an *image* wrought of *wood, stone, metal, wax, canvas, paper,* etc. (2) An *idol;* the representation of any person or thing that is an object of worship; see *icon.* (3) An idea; a re-*creation,* through a *medium,* of anything coming to the mind; a conception; a *picture* drawn by *fancy.* (4) Any likeness of an object produced by reflection or *refraction,* whether enlarged or diminished, erect or inverted, virtual or real, as in *photography.*

IMITATION VERMILION—A *painting pigment* of brilliant, *vermilion*-like red, properly known as *victoria red* (q.v.).

IMITATIVE ARTS—Term applied to those *fine arts* devoted principally to representation or re-creation of figures or objects already in existence, subject only to the accuracy and interpretation of the *artist.* Most frequently considered the *imitative arts* are *sculpture* and *painting.* See *work of art.*

IMPASTO—In *painting,* the *technique* of laying *colors* on thickly, usually with the aid of a knife. The heavy application causes the *paint* to stand out in *relief.* Known commonly as *palette knife work.* Also, the term used to describe the mixture of *pigment* and *medium* (*oil* or *turpentine* or both) with which a *picture* is painted.

IMPRESSIONISM—In *art,* a variety of *naturalism* (q.v.) which depicts objectively the world of ephemeral appearance; it differs from *illusionism* in that it gives no heed to details, although it is generally considered a form of *illusionism* (q.v.). Developed in the latter 19th century, it deals with a type of *painting* with informal subject matter and the effects of *light* as they impress the *artist.* It is a method of expressing *luminosity* with *juxtaposed* touches of pure *color;* the effort to present a general impression of an incident, view, or object, rather than to record it in detail or to depict what the eye sees at a glance. See *synthetism.*

IMPRIMATURA—In *painting,* a type of *glaze* applied as a toner to the *canvas* or other *ground* that is to receive the projected work; an *underpainting,* intended to relieve the monotony of a white or gray background behind light or *transparent* colors. Any one of a number of *varnish* or *resin* substances may be used, in the color best suited to the colors intended for the final painting. See *pentimenti.*

IN—In Oriental *art,* a Japanese *seal* in *relief* or *intaglio,* accompanying the *colophon* or signature of the artist at a corner of the *painting.* Similar to the Chinese *yin chang* (q.v.).

INAURATE—In the *arts* generally, a term applied to any surface or object having a golden *luster.*

INCISED RELIEF—Not a true *relief* (q.v.), since it consists only of a frontal plane without background. It is made up of incised outlines and rounded-out forms cut into a flat surface in *intaglio* fashion. The impression of depth and roundness is created by *light* and *shade* on the forms, through overlapping and *foreshortening* (q.v.).

INCRUSTATION—(1) A technique of ornamentation that consists of applying or *inlay*ing one (usually a finer) material upon another, as colored *mosaics,* marbles, *lacquers* or *enamels* upon *wood, stone* or *metal.* (2) The materials so applied.

INDIA INK—A black *ink* which is treated by the addition of suspended carbon, rendering it indelible to erasure and moisture. Used widely in informal *drawing.* Also known as *Chinese ink* and *mo* (qq.v.), it is used chiefly in drawings to be *photographed* for *engravings;* made by adding *size* or *glue* to *lamp-black.*

INDIAN LAKE—A *natural* organic *red dye*-stuff more properly known as *lac* (q.v.). It is in little demand as a modern *lake color,* chiefly because of its lack of *brilliance* and *stability;* it was replaced on the artist's *palette* by the safer *alizarins* and *madders.* It is an old *pigment,* and many 13th century *manuscripts* attest to its early use. Originally made from the insect COCCUS IACCA.

INDIAN PURPLE—In *painting,* a semi- transparent *pigment* made by mixing *madder* with *ultramarine blue.* Its hue is easily duplicated directly on the *palette* of the artist, although this process will generally result in a pigment of low *brilliance* and *stability.* Experiments with *Antwerp blue* and *carmine*-tinted *vermilion* have increased brilliance, but reduced still further the stability. Despite modern techniques, *purple* in all of its shades is still the most *fugitive* of all colors.

INDIAN RED—In *painting,* one of the *iron pigments* in the *red* iron oxide class. It differs from other varieties of red earth in *purple tinge.* Synonyms include *colcothar* and *caput mortuum* (and *rouge,* used as a *jewelry*-polishing material).

INDIAN YELLOW—An artist's *pigment,* always rather rare, and now practically out of use. First prepared in Bengal, it was a dried extract from the urine of cows that were fed on mango leaves. The *color* is a deep, *translucent yellow-orange,* it is fairly *stable* (even on long exposure to *light*), and is slightly soluble in water. A synthetic subtitute is now sold under the same name, and compares favorably with the *natural* variety. Known also as *piuri, purree, giallo indiano,* and *Indischgelb.*

INDIA PAPER—A thin, strong variety of *paper,* a thousand sheets of which measure less than one inch in thickness; made by a secret process involving *linen* rags treated and blended with a superior grade of *flax, hemp,* and other materials. It has a soft, silky *texture,* and takes *ink* well. When originally made in China and Japan, it had a creamy, off-white color, and was used chiefly for the taking of *prints* from fine *engravings.* Numerous imitations, many of excellent quality, are available.

INDIGO—A deep *blue dye,* valued for its consistently rich *color.* Formerly extracted from various plants of the genus INDIGO FERA, but now made on a large scale artificially, in comparable quality. The oldest of all blue colors, it was widely used as a *fabric* dye. Unlike most organic colors used as a painter's *pigment,* this was not precipitated on a base, but was ground to a fine dye powder, and thus mixed well with different *mediums.* It is more satisfactory in water than in *oil,* and is moderately *stable* when well bound and covered with *varnish* or other *surface film* (q.v.); also known as *intense blue* and *indico.*

INDISCHGELB—In *painting,* a deep, translucent, orange-yellow *pigment* of moderate *stability,* commonly known as *Indian yellow* (q.v.).

INK—A deeply colored liquid of varied composition, practically unlimited as to *color* range. Oriental *art,* for many years, centered about *ink drawings.* The common variety of *black* and *blue*-black *inks* owe their color to organic iron compounds. Applied by *pen*point in varying thickness, and by thin *brush.* The chemical mixture itself has no color, but turns black when exposed to the air.

IN KEEPING—In *painting,* a term used by some *artists* when referring to the proper prominence or subserviency of *tone* and *color* in every part of a picture.

INK SPLASH—A Japanese *ink-painting* technique of the 13th century, characterized by remarkable simplicity and effect. With a few strokes of the *brush* (so few that they can be quickly counted) an excellent *landscape* is depicted.

INKSTONE—A very fine-*grained* whet-*stone* used by Japanese *ink* makers. The stick or cake of mixed carbon and *glue* is rubbed into water on the *inkstone* or *suzuri* (q.v.), creating the *medium* common to the writer and *painter.* Compare with the *grinding slab* and *muller* (qq.v.) of the *Renaissance* painter. See also *sumi.*

INSECT WAX—A pale yellow *wax* in flat cake form, soluble in naphtha and benzene, used as a protective *surface film* on *paintings* and *statuary,* as a *leather* finisher, and as a substitute for *beeswax* in all of its uses in the *arts. Insect wax* is a misnomer, since it is obtained from a species of the botanical RHUS by boiling the fruit in water. Known also as *vegetable wax, Japan wax,* and *sumac wax.* Not synonymous with *Chinese insect wax* (q.v.).

INSTABILITY—In *oil painting* and *water-color,* a term applied to any *color, pigment, surface film,* etc. that is not permanent, e.g., will fade, blister, cloud, etc., upon exposure to light, heat, moisture, or other elements. Opposite of *stability* (q.v.); see also *stable.*

INTAGLIO—Depth *carving,* incised, as distinguished from carving in *relief.* Any *decoration, design* or *figure* cut or sunk below the surface of the object. In *engraving,* any *paint*-manufacturing process in which the *color* or *ink* is applied to the final product from parts of the *plate* sunk into the surface. The word also applies to any print or engraved object so produced. *Intaglio* was used extensively by the Egyptians, and made its reappearance in the 20th century. It is now used largely in the *decoration* of *architectural* surfaces which do not allow projections. See *aquatint.*

INTAGLIO CRAYON AQUATINT—A variation of the *aquatint* process. The *plate* is cleaned, and a porous aquatint *ground* is laid on it, after which a *drawing* is made on it with a cheap *paraffin* or *wax crayon.* Where the ax protects the plate from the *biting* of the *acid bath,* it will leave a *white,* crayon-textured line on the plate. Usually, only the pure whites are drawn before the plate is immersed in the bath for a short bite. Each subsequent drawing and biting produces a darker line. This method is often used by itself to produce an interesting, coarse, white, crayon-textured *print;* at other times it is used in combination with *soft ground etching, pen process,* and other *intaglio* process.

INTENSE—In *painting,* the description applied to any piece of work in which the *colors* are strong, *vivid,* and full. See *intensity of color;* see also *highlight.*

INTENSE BLUE—In *painting,* the name given to a deep blue *pigment* made by a technique involving the refining of *indigo.*

INTENSITY OF COLOR—The strength of an *artist's color* in comparison with *gray;* often expressed as more or *less brilliant,* rich, etc. See *intense.*

INTERMEDIATE HUES—Those *colors* between the six essential *hues* of the *spectrum,* which partake of *blended* combinations of the adjacent colors. See *hue.*

IN THE ROUND—A term in *sculpture.* See *round.*

IONIC FRIEZE—In *classical architecture,* the middle member of the *entablature,* over the *epistyle* or *architrave.* In the *Ionic order,* a plain *band* with a crowning *molding* or *decorated* with a continuous *band* of figures, or *ornamented* in *relief.*

IRIS GREEN—A rare *pigment* with fine *green color,* classed among *painting* materials now obsolete. It was used extensively in *illustrated manuscripts* during the 14th and 15th centuries. An organic *dye*stuff made from the juice of the iris flower, the best *hue* was obtained by mixing it with alum.

IRON BRUSH—A Chinese *art* known also as *seal cutting.* So called because the *stylus* or scalpel was the tool of artistic application. The *carvings,* a form a *calligraphy,* were exquisitely executed on iron, *jade, stone, wood,* and other materials.

IRON PIGMENTS—A range of *colors* created by oxidation of iron in nature. Best known are the earth *reds* and *yel-*

lows, and *green earth* (q.v.). The red iron oxides found as natural deposits include *Indian red, light red, Tuscan red, Venetian red, English red,* and others of lesser importance and use. Among the most popular mixing and *glazing iron pigments,* are *umber* and *sienna* (q.v.). See also *burnt sienna* and *mars pigments.*

IRON WIRE—In Chinese *painting,* the term applied to a brush stroke technique in which stiff, straight strokes of unvarying thickness are applied, suggesting vertical jointing. This method is frequently employed in conjunction with the *horse tooth* (q.v.) technique, first mastered by the *artist* Ku K'ai-chih in the 5th century.

ISHZURI—The *technique* of securing an impression by taking a *rubbing from* a *stone.* The term is also used to describe any *print* seemingly made by that process. See *rubbing.*

ISOCEPHALY—A style of composition in the *visual arts* in which the subject persons are so arranged that they are of the same height; a manner of *representation* pertaining mainly to the *classical* period of Greek art. The principle by which *natural* proportion is distorted so as to bring all the objects in a composition to an equal height for purposes of *design.*

ISOMERIC COLORS—Those *colors* which appear to be identical, but which actually contain different chemical or physical properties, the atomic structures possessing different arrangements.

ISOMETRIC DRAWING—A type of *drawing* taking as its points of departure three axes known as the isometric axes; the dimensions of the object to be drawn are marked off on these axes, and through the points marked off, lines are drawn parallel to the isometric axes. It is to be noted that angles in *isometric drawings* do not show their true size, and therefore cannot be measured in degrees; circles appear as ellipses, preventing true readings. See *cabinet drawing* and *oblique drawings.*

ISOMETRIC PROJECTION—A geometrical *drawing* showing an object in three dimensions. The plan is set up with lines at an equal angle to the horizontal, and verticals are projected from it to scale. This method gives the object a more realistic appearance than *axonometric projection,* but all diagonals and curves are distorted.

ISTRIAN MARBLE—In *sculpture,* a fine variety of large-grained *marble* quarried on the Dalmatian Islands. It is buff-colored, and is held in high esteem by sculptors throughout the world for its excellence in *statuary* work. Used also in *architecture,* it was employed almost exclusively in the building of the city of Venice.

ITALIAN BLUE—In *painting,* a *lake color* of beautiful *hue,* introduced into the *fine arts* in the early 20th century. It approaches the prized color of *cerulean blue,* but is lacking in *stability* and should be avoided where any degree of permanency is required. Known also as *Venetian blue* and *turquoise blue.*

ITALIANIZERS—A group of Flemish *artists* of the 16th and 17th centuries who sojourned to Italy and imitated the *Italian style* (q.v.). This influence created a fusion of the two schools. Those of the group who worked in Rome called themselves *Romanists.* See *Flemish style.*

ITALIAN OCHRE—In *painting,* a variety of deep, rich, golden *ochre* having a translucent quality, used as a *pigment* since ancient times. It is *stable* and possesses a strong degree of *hiding* power, featuring the chemical and physical properties of the other ochres; is suited to practically all techniques.

ITALIAN PINK—One of the several *lakes* of *yellow* or *greenish hue,* used in *water-color* work. It is made by precipitating vegetable juices on a *white* earth product, such as *alumina* or *chalk.* It is highly *fugitive* in nature, and will generally produce *unstable* colors in mixture, as in *green lake* (q.v.).

ITALIAN STYLE—A style of *art,* essentially different from the *Flemish* in that the emphasis was on the plastic effect of *form* and *color,* while Flemish art strove for literal *representation* according to strict *realism.* See also *Italianizers.*

I TUNG PI HUA—In Chinese *art,* large movable *murals* often executed on a fabric *ground,* folded when not in used. Usually hung on temple walls during certain *ceremonies.* Technically, the name should be *i tung pi tzu,* since the painting is not applied directly to the wall, but executed elsewhere. See *pi tzu, pi hua,* and *chêng.*

IVORY—Widely used as a material for *carving* and as a support for *paintings,* it has been a material familiar to *artists* from ancient times. Strictly, the word is limited to the tusk of an elephant, although those of the walrus, hippopotamus and other animals (some even from prehistoric remains) have been used. Unlike bone, it can be worked as soon as it is cut, since it is a solid tooth formed of phosphates lying in layers deposited by the growth process. The enormous *chryselephantine* cult *statue* of *Athena* was made largely of *ivory.* See *Pangani.*

IVORY BLACK—A *pigment* prized in *drawing* and *painting,* essentially a *black* carbon. Supposedly made by charring *ivory* in a sealed vessel, many authorities are of the opinion that the substance charred is actually animal bone, as used in the making of *bone black* (q.v.). Also known as *ivory drop black, nero d'avoiro, noir d'ivorie, negro de marfil,* and *Elfenbeinschwarz.*

J

JACK OF DIAMONDS—A Russian *art* group formed by the followers of Cézanne four years after his death. At this time (1910), when the *artists* of Paris came under the influence of *primitive* and *exotic* arts, certain Russian artists went back to their own past for new sources of *inspiration.* Related to the *fauves* and *expressionists* (qq.v.), they were interested in *forms* and *colors* that did not imitate nature. Among the best was Marc Chagall, whose *motifs* from Jewish folklore created a fantastic dream world of lyric beauty in which *cubist* elements were mated successfully with primitive color and expressionist mood.

JADE—A mineral ranging in *color* from *white* to *black,* though most often recognized in an emerald *green hue,* used extensively in Oriental *art,* especially *carving.* It is a hard and exceedingly tough substance of varying composition; some of the finer varieties of *serpentine* (q.v.) are often mistaken for *jade.*

JADE TABLET PAPER—In Chinese *art,* a variety of coarse *paper,* un-*sized,* used as a *ground* in *painting* and *calligraphy.* See *yü pan hsüan.*

JAN—In Chinese *art,* to *dye;* to apply a *tincture* or *tint* of *ink* or *color.* It is one of the steps in creating *paintings* of mountains, distinguished by the necessity that individual *brush* strokes must not appear. *Jan* is usually a verb, with the name of the color or *pigment* as the object; sometimes used in a verbal compound.

JANUS—In Roman *art* and mythology, the god of the doorway, shown in *painting* and *sculpture* as a two-faced human, the faces behind each other on one head. Thus, his famous *bronze temple* in the Roman Forum faces both east and west; the temple was open in time of war, and closed in time of peace.

JAPANESE PRINTS – Names, *techniques, mediums, grounds,* implements, etc., include:

beni
benie
beni-zurie
chuban
dai-bon
diptych
hashira
hoso
ichi-mae
kakemono
keyblock
kira
koban
lacquer print
nima tsuzuki
nishiki
oban
pentatych
surimono
tan
tane
triptych
wood-block
wood-block print
yoko

Each of the terms is described in its appropriate alphabetical location.

JAPANESE VELLUM–A costly variety of Japanese hand-beaten *paper,* made from the inner bark of the mulberry tree.

JAPAN LAC VARNISH–One of the *balsam* group, it flows from incisions in the trunk of the RHUS VERNIX, becomes black on exposure to air, and dissolves in very little *oil* when purified. Mixed with coloring matter, it constitutes the world-famous *varnish* of Japanese *art* work.

JAPAN WAX–A pale yellow *wax* in flat cake form, soluble in benzene and naphtha, used in the making of protective *surface films,* in *leather* finishing, and as a substitute for *beeswax* (q.v.). Obtained from a species of RHUS when the fruit is boiled in water; known also as *Japan tallow, sumac wax, insect wax,* and *vegetable wax.*

JAPONISM–The term used by French writers of the late 19th century to cover the entire complex of interest in the *art* of Japan. The term today is limited to the influence of Japanese art (especially that of the Japanese *color print*) upon the *graphic arts, painting, crafts,* and *interior archi-*

tecture of Europe and America during the late 19th and early 20th century.

JASPURE—In *sculpture,* a name applied to any *marble* that is veined or colored, naturally or artificially, in resemblance of *jasper.*

JAUNE BRILLIANT—In *painting,* a yellow *pigment* approaching *Naples yellow* in color, produced by an admixture of *white lead, vermilion,* and *cadmium yellow.* The presence of the white lead renders it *opaque,* and imparts a good degree of *hiding power;* however, it is generally considered unsafe because of poor *stability* and the resulting discoloration.

JAUNE INDIAN—In *painting,* a fine yellow *pigment* having a *cobalt* base. Although possessing a high degree of *stability,* it tends to assume a brownish hue when mixed with certain *lakes,* e.g., *indigo, cochineal,* etc. It is chemically similar to *cobalt yellow,* and is known also as *Kobaltgelb;* the quality of its transparency is such that it is best used as a *water-color.*

JÊN WU—In Chinese *painting,* the term applied to all pictorial representations of men and objects, including all branches of portraiture and figure painting together with the man-made or natural environment of man. *Jên wu* is one of the major classes of subject matter, embracing all rustic and domestic scenes and objects.

JET—(1) Name applied to any variety of *marble* that is full black, without veins, blotches or clouds. (2) A type of dense black lignite that takes an unusually high polish, sometimese used in *jewelry.* (3) Black *tourmaline* (q.v.), known also as *jetstone.*

JEWEL POINT—In *etching,* an incising tool with a *diamond* or *ruby* point; used with extraordinary freedom in the making of *drypoints.*

JIKU—The *ornamental* knob at each end of the cylindrical stick upon which Japanese *paintings* are mounted and rolled.

JU CHIN—In Chinese *painting,* 'milk gold' made by rubbing *gold leaf* with the fingers under water until a creamy 'mud' is formed. The leaf must be rubbed in circular motion, always in the same direction, and in taking up the gold the *brush* must follow the direction of the rubbing. This brush technique is required even when using commercially prepared *ju chin* if a smooth and *lustrous* effect is to be obtained. Used for outlining rocks in *ch'ing lü* landscapes, and to give a bright highlight in birds and flowers; used also in the garments of portraiture and in Buddhistic painting. Its popularity in China is increasing, due in part to Japanese influence.

JUDAS HAIR—The term popularly applied to fiery red hair; derives from the fact that in *paintings* of the *Middle Ages,* Judas Iscariot is invariably represented with bright red hair and beard.

JUGENDSTIL—In Germany, the name applied to the *art nouveau* movement, popular from 1890 to 1905, and affecting all of the *visual arts.* See *art nouveau.*

JUXTAPOSITION—In *painting,* the position of *colors,* usually close together or side by side, so placed that each will enhance the other. See *simultaneous contrast* and *successive contrast.*

K

KABE—A Japanese *mural* or *wall-painting.*

KACHO—A composite Japanese *painting,* always containing a rock, a tree, a flower, and a bird.

KAILĀSANĀTHA—The vast *sculptural* edifice in India, commonly known as *stūpikā* (q.v.).

KAKEMONO—A Japanese *painting* or example of *calligraphy* mounted with *brocade* margins incorporating a cylindrical rod at the bottom, on which the painting, etc., can be rolled up when not in use, and a small, pierced stick at the top, by means of which the *picture* can be hung on a wall.

KAKEMONOE—A long, vertical Japanese *wood-block print,* about 10 by 28 inches; also, any horizontal *print* of unusual size.

KALI—Mythological Hindu goddess, often *represented* in the *arts,* esp. *sculpture,* as a woman with four hands. One hand *symbolizes* nature's creative powers; another, the cosmic preservative functions; the third is an *emblem* of the purifying forces of dissolution, and the fourth is outstretched in a gesture of blessing salvation. Through these means she supposedly calls all of creation back to her soul. Also called *Kali Divine.*

KAMAKURA-BORI—Japanese carved *wood,* thickly *lacquered* in *red* or *black;* named for the city of *Kamakura,* where this lacquer style was particularly favored.

KAMI—In Japanese *art,* the term applied to any type of *paper* used for *prints, painting, calligraphy,* or other artistic purpose. Chinese equivalent, *chih* (q.v.).

KANE STONE—In *sculpture,* a variety of fine-grained *limestone* having a buff color, responsive to high polish, and easy *carving*. Somewhat on the soft side, it is best used for indoor work. The term developed through usage from *Caen stone, a*fter the locality in France where it occurs. See *limestone.*

KANGA SCHOOL—A Japanese style of *painting* which was created solely for the purpose of imitating that of the Chinese. Known also as *Kano School.*

KAN PI—In Chinese *art,* a technique of *painting* popularly termed *dry brush,* used by Ni Tsan and others. The *ink* is used sparingly with little moisture in the *brush.* In furthering this process, Chinese art students are taught to be *hsi mo ju chin* (economical of ink as if it were gold).

KANSHITSU—In Japanese *art,* a *technique* whereby cloth is saturated with *lacquer* and *modeled* over *armatures* to produce *sculptural* forms. In vogue in China and Japan in the 8th and 9th centuries. Also known as *dried lacquer work* and, in ancient times, *soku.*

KAOLIN—Decomposed *granite* rock, ingredient of all *porcelain* deriving its name from the Chinese mountain KAO-LING, now a great *pottery* center. First made in 206 B.C., this porcelain is of dazzling whiteness, so hard that steel will not scratch it, impermeable to liquids, and unaffected by acids. Also known as *china clay.* See *argilla.*

KARASHISHI—The popular Chinese lion *motif* in Japanese *art.*

KATA-KIRIBORI—In Japanese *art,* incised chiseling in which the *carved* lines imitate *brush* strokes.

KAURI GUM—In the *arts,* a hard, *lustrous* transparent *resin* obtained from the *kauri pine,* prized for its qualities as a *surface film* over *paintings* and *sculpture.* It is dissolved in *linseed oil* and diluted with *turpentine,* forming an excellent *varnish* which, when carefully applied and slowly dried, is remarkably hard and durable, taking a high polish.

KENCHI—In Oriental *ivory-carving,* an instrument in the nature of a pair of pliers with one of the handle extremities considerably shorter than the other. It is used to cut flat sheets of ivory into small sections or strips.

KERMES—A famous red *dye* of the ancient Egyptians, derived from the dried body of the insects COCCUS ILICIS which lived on the leaves of the *kermes* oak. Not fully permanent, it was replaced in medieval times by *cochineal* (q.v.) from India and later by the *lac lakes* from Mexico. Some experts believe that the word is the ancestor of the term *crimson,* tracing it through Arabic, Latin and English. The color was not *brilliant,* and left a *matte* finish, even on the *leather* the Egyptians dyed with it. Known also as *grain lake,* it is not listed by artists' colormen today. Sometimes referred to as *Venetian scarlet.*

KEY—In *painting,* the terminology applied to the *color value,* the *key* color being the *dominant* one. Dull or dark values create a *low key;* light or bright values a *high key.*

KEY-BLOCK—A *wood-block* (q.v.) on which only *contour* lines are cut. When applied to a *print,* this block outlines all *color* areas with a *black* line. Known also as *dai-bon.*

KEY PLATE—In *etching,* the *blue* or *black plate* used in multiple-plate *color aquatint* work. This plate carries most of the outlines and is used to *offset* onto the other plates.

KIESELGUHR—A fine variety of *clay* used in both *ceramics* and *painting;* commonly known as *tonerde* (q.v.).

KINDLING STYLE—In Chinese *painting,* a brush stroke technique creating lines having the effect of brushwood or faggots. A stiff, large-pointed brush is used in *side brush technique* (q.v.), rendering the lines coarse and rigid. Considered a strongly *impressionistic* style.

KINGLY POSE—In *art,* a formal pose often seen in the *painting* and *sculpture* of India. The right foot is raised to seat level, and the right arm rests on the raised knee.

KING'S BLUE—A term in *painting;* see *smalt.*

KING'S YELLOW—One of the oldest *pigments* known in the history of *painting,* used widely in *ancient* and *medieval* art. Identified on many *illuminated manuscripts* of the *Middle Ages* and the *Renaissance,* it is closely related to the *orange*-colored *realgar* (q.v.) Known also as *Chinese yellow* and *orpiment* (qq.v.).

KINJI—A Japanese *lacquer* technique in which the *colors* are applied directly to a plain *ground* of *gold.*

KIRA—A variety of Japanese *wood-block print,* unusual in that the background is invariably sprinkled with powdered *mica,* giving it the same effect obtained by the use of *flitters.*

KIRIKANE—In Japanese *art,* (1) a *painting* technique whereby *gold foil* is cut into hairline strips and applied to the painting; intended to *represent* the thin *patterns* of *fabrics;* (2) a *lacquer* process in which foil of gold or *silver* is cut into small rectangular pieces and applied to lacquer to make an all-over pattern.

KIYOSE-HO—In *sculpture,* a technique originating in Japan. The *statue* is formed from several sections (usually *carved wood*) and then joined, instead of carving in from a single piece.

KOBALTGELB—In *painting,* a pure yellow *pigment* commonly known as *Jaune Indian* (q.v.).

KOBAN—A vertical variety of *wood-block print,* somewhat smaller than a *chūban* (q.v.).

K'O FÊN—In Chinese *painting,* a product of white lime made through an Oriental technique of burning seashells. Considerably better than *ch'ien fên* (white lead), particularly with respect to *stability;* however, it is more difficult and expensive to obtain.

KOKA-RYOKUGO—A *lacquer* technique local to Japan. The object is first coated with alternating layers of *red* and *green* lacquer, and then *carved* deeply, bringing out crimson flowers among green leaves.

KONDO—Any work of *art* (esp. *sculpture* or *metalwork*) having a *gilt-bronze* finish.

KOPOL—A series of *synthetic resins* containing a wide variety of *copal* ingredients. Used in the making of *varnishes, enamels* and *paints,* it is chemically an esterified copal with modified alkyds, *kopol* being a trade name.

KORAI—In Greek *sculpture,* figures of girls or young women. Youths represented in *statuary* are known as *kouroi.*

KOU CHIN—In Chinese *painting,* to outline an object in *gold;* the technique of outlining in gold. Used chiefly in *landscapes* and bird work, and to some extent in the representation of the folds of garments in portraiture.

KOUKLIA—Site of the temple of *Aphrodite,* goddess of love, excavated in late 1950. Among the treasures unearthed were many pieces of ancient Greek *sculpture,* remains of *architectural* members, and what is perhaps the finest specimen of Greek *painting* in full color, all dating from the 6th century B.C. A particularly valuable find was the curved wing of a marble *sphinx,* painted in brilliant blue, red and green, rivaling the best works of the period. The discoveries are considered proof of the extended existence of the City of Aphrodite into and after the *Bronze Age.*

KOUROI—In Greek *sculpture,* figures of young men. Representations of girls and young women are known as *korai.* See *Argive School.*

KREMNITZ WHITE—A variety of pure *white lead* made by adding carbon dioxide to *litharge* and lead acetate, forming tablets of the resulting substance; used in fine *painting.*

KUA FU—In Chinese *art,* a variety of *scroll painting* (q.v.) so designed and executed that it can be hung vertically; popularly referred to as *li chou.* Compare with *hêng fu.*

K'UAN—In Chinese *painting,* the signature or *colophon.* It may also bear the name of the person for whom the picture was made, the place and date of painting, and the artist's name. A poem or essay is not properly a part of the *k'uan,* even when written with it. In Oriental art the *k'uan* is actually considered part of the painting, and not merely a means of identification. Consequently, great care is exerted in executing it artistically. See also *fang* and *yin chang.*

KUANG CHIAO—In Chinese *painting,* a famous *glue* used as a *surface film.* Almost odorless and colorless, it possesses remarkable *stability.* See also *o chiao.*

KUAN P'AI—In Chinese *painting,* the term applied during the late CH'ING DYNASTY to a style characterized by strict and unwavering observance of rules and customs without regard to individuality or invention. Properly known as *yüan t'i* (q.v.).

KU CHOU—In Chinese *art,* literally 'lonely scroll' referring to a *painting* that is hung singly, as distinguished from those displayed in groups, as *p'ing chang* (q.v.).

KUNG PI—In Chinese *painting,* the term applied to any

work displaying great attention to detail; care and precision with respect to form and standards, as distinguished from *hsieh i* which is a free sketch in spontaneous expression. See *ch'ing lü.*

KWAIGETSUDO—A large and unusually rare variety of Japanese *ukiyoye,* 17th century print. Emphasizing everyday scenes, these prints gained more popularity than did the religious and official *motifs* prevailing in art at the time. An extensive exhibit of *ukiyoye* and *kwaigetsudo* at the New York Metropolitan Museum of Art in 1949-1950 drew wide attention. See *ukiyoye.*

L

LAC—A *natural* organic *red dye*stuff also known as *lac lake* and *Indian lake.* Native to India and the Far East, it is similar to the *seed lac* or *shellac* derived from the same larvae. It is similar, also, in *color* and composition, to the *carmine lakes* made from *cochineal* (q.v.), although *lac* is duller in *tone* and somewhat more *stable.* It appears to have been used more extensively in the East than in Europe, but became moderately familiar to Western *artists* during the *Middle Ages.* See also *kermes.*

LACCA GERANIO—A term in *painting;* see *geranium lake.*

LACCA SCARLATTA—In *painting,* a fine *pigment* of deep rich *scarlet*-red, extracted from the dried dead wingless female *cochineal* insect; it lacks only in *stability* (q.v.). The *fugitive* nature of the pigment induced its imitation through the medium of *alizarin madder* which not only reproduced the fine *hue,* but imparted the needed *permanence.* Its transparency renders its esp. valuable in *water-color* work. Known popularly as *scarlet lake* and *purple lake* (qq.v.).

LAC LAKE—A *natural* organic *red dye*stuff better known as *lac* (q.v.).

LACQUER PRINT—The informal term applied to a *broadsheet,* actually classified as a *print,* but painted in certain parts to give the effect of a *lacquer medium.*

LACQUERWARE—A *technique,* peculiar to the Orient, whereby the sap of a poisonous tree is used as a *painting medium* in the *fine arts.* In the *crafts* it is used over a *wooden* base, producing a permanent surface of great beauty, with all the aspects of the painter's art.

LAKE COLORS— *Paint colors* made from a *dye* in combination with a *mordant.* Usually, a dye is used in coloring tissue, *fiber,* etc., the "lakes" being the only paint colors so used. The word may have come from *lac,* a natural *red* dye. *Lake colors* are completely soluble as *pigments* when combined with the solution of a *metal* to form a precipitate with body, grain, and some amount of hiding power. Generally *transparent,* they are slow in drying, and make good *glazing pigment* when the metal solution (as *alumina*) is added. *Lake colors* include, among others, *crimson, green, red, purple,* and *yellow.* See *paint* and *pigment.*

LA LIBRE ESTHETIQUE—An *art* group in Belgium associated with the popular *art nouveau* movement between 1890 and 1905. Previously, the movement had as its supporting "school" in that country the group known as *Les XXs.* See *art nouveau.*

LAMP-BLACK—Finest-*textured* of all the carbon *blacks,* it was known in *ancient* times and has been in continuous use since. It was formerly the most important black *pigment* used in the manufacture of printing *inks,* now largely surpassed by *gas black.* Made from the condensed smoke of *oil,* tar and *resin* burning with an insufficient supply of air. The soot thus formed is allowed to settle in large chambers and is collected from time to time. Still used extensively as an important ingredient in the making of *carbon paper;* known also as *Chinese ink* and *vegetable black.*

LANDSCAPE—In *art,* a *picture* representing the scene of a section of country as far as the eye can reach, or a particular extent of land and the objects it contains, or the various aspects of its scenery; also, such pictures collectively, as distiguished from *marine pictures* (*seascapes*), or *portraits,* or those wherein figures are prominent.

LANDSCAPE MARBLE—In *sculpture,* a variety of *limestone* showing veins, blotches, etc., suggesting woodlands or open country when polished. Caused by the infiltrations of iron oxide, these markings are particularly representative of the name when seen in cross-section or along certain planes. Known also as *forest marble* (q.v.).

LANGUEDOC MARBLE—In *sculpture,* a brilliant red or

scarlet *marble* blotched sporadically with white; occurs in the French Pyrenees, chiefly at Montagne Noire.

LAO HUNG—In Chinese *painting,* a *pepper red* pigment used chiefly for outlining tree leaves, and representing full maple leaves. It is prepared by mixing *yin chu* with *che shih* (qq.v.).

LAO LÜ—In Chinese *paintings,* an excellent *green* pigment belonging to the *ts'ao lü* (q.v.) class. Known in the West as *old green.*

LAPIDARY—In *sculpture,* anything inscribed upon *stone;* of or pertaining to inscriptions on stone; monumental, as *lapidary lettering.* Also, any *style* in *literature* found to be appropriate for monumental or other inscriptions.

LAPIS LAZULI—A somewhat rare mineral of beautiful *blue color,* considered one of the accepted *semi-precious stones* of *jewelry.* It serves as a material for *carving,* and also as the source from which genuine or true *ultramarine blue,* the painter's *pigment,* is derived. This pigment comes directly from pulverized *lapis lazuli* and is made even more *intense* in color by a process which separates out the more highly colored particles from those which are colorless or have a contrasting color. Chemically, *lapis lazuli* is a sodium aluminium *silicate* containing sulphur. Often referred to as *azure.* See *ultramarine blue* and *French ultramarine blue.*

LAPIS LAZULI BLUE—In *painting,* the famous blue *pigment* popularly known as *ultramarine* (q.v.).

LAQUE ÉCARLATE—In *painting,* a fine *pigment* of deep, rich *scarlet* red obtained from the dried dead wingless female *cochineal* insect, lacking only in *stability.* The color was later imitated in *hue* by use of *alizarin madder,* which also imparted the needed *permanence.* Its transparency renders it esp. valuable in *water-color* work. Known popularly as *scarlet lake* and *purple lake* (qq.v.).

LAQUE GÉRANIUM—A term in *painting;* see *geranium lake.*

LARDSTONE—A variety of soft stone found in the Orient, used in Chinese *carvings.* Known also as *agalmatolite* (q.v.).

LATE PALEOLITHIC—Last of the three significant *archaeological periods,* making up the *Paleolithic,* or *Stone Age,* featured by the first appearance of *homo sapiens* in Europe (Cro-magnon man), and the great development of cave painting in southwestern Europe; characterized also by a marked advance in the *arts,* and crafts. Bodies were often buried with ornaments, and the first *stone, ivory,* and bone *statuettes* of nude women appeared. The *figurines* and cave paintings probably indicate advanced religious or magical beliefs or pursuits, although precise information is thus far lacking. See also *Early-* and *Middle Paleolithic.*

LATE RENAISSANCE—See *Renaissance.*

LAVENDER—One of the many shades of *purple* (q.v.).

LAY FIGURE—A mechanical figure so jointed that it can be given a pose resembling a human figure; often used as an *artist's model,* sometimes as a *support* for drapery. Though like a *manikin* (q.v.), the term usually applies to more realistic devices in which the joints and mechanism are concealed. It does not appear to have been in wide use prior to the 19th century. The *lay figure* permits the *painter* or *sculptor* to work without the presence of a living model. Finer varieties are jointed even to the finger knuckles, and may be arranged into any human position.

LEAD POINT—A *drawing* instrument developed from the ancient *stylus,* functioning in the same manner as the *silver point* (q.v.).

LEAD SILICATE—A crystalline white powder, insoluble in practically all solvents, used (1) in *ceramics* as an ingredient of *enamels* and *glazes;* (2) in the making of fine *glass;* (3) in *paints* and *varnishes* as a white *pigment.* It is obtained by a reaction between lead acetate and sodium silicate, $PbSiO_3$.

LEAF—In *metalwork* and *gilding,* an extremely thin sheet or plate of metal, as *gold.*

LEDGER BOND—In *drawing,* a fine variety of heavy white *paper* used extensively as a *ground* for *ink* and *wash drawings.* Best varieties are fully *opaque.*

LEDGER PAPER—A *drawing* and *water-color* ground better known as *ledger bond* (q.v.).

LEF—A Russian *art* group formed primarily from the *Cubist-Futurists,* 1923-1929, declaring that art was destined to create "new material values." When Vladimir Mayakovski, its leader, abandoned it, the group disbanded. Name derives from the Russian LEVY FRONT ISKUSSTVA, Left Front of Art.

LEIOCOM—A substance having unusually strong adhesive qualities, derived from *starch.* Used extensively in *collage,* it is employed also as a *sizing* for *paper,* for various purposes in *bookbinding,* and as a substitute for *tragacanth* and *arabic gum.*

LEITHNER'S BLUE—A term in *painting;* see *cobalt blue.*

LEMNIAN ATHENA—In *sculpture,* a famous *statue* of *Athena* by Phidias having, in addition to its artistic mastery, the unusual feature of *representing* Athena in a gentle, graceful pose, as distinguished from almost all other portrayals, showing her as a warrior. See *Athena.*

LEMNIAN REDDLE—In *painting,* a fine *ocher* of deep red color found in mixture with various earth substances. Used as a *pigment.*

LEMON YELLOW—Better known as *barium yellow* (q.v.), it has a slight *greenish tinge* and is rather pale. It is fairly *stable,* being little affected by light, but is decomposed at high temperatures. See also *strontium yellow,* and *yellow pigments.*

LEPANTO MARBLE—In *sculpture,* the trade name given to a variety of gray *marble* enlivened by pink and white *fossils;* found chiefly in the Plattsburg area of New York.

LESBIAN LEAF—An ancient Greek *pattern* used in *architecture* and *sculpture,* frequently in *moldings* and *cornices.* It is a highly *decorative* design consisting of a series of heart-shaped leaves with a deeply marked midrib. Known also as *Lesbian wave, water leaf,* and *cyma Lesbian.*

LES XXs—An *art* group in Belgium, associated with the popular *art nouveau* movement from 1890 to 1905, affecting all of the *visual arts.* See *art nouveau.*

LEVEL DISTANCE—In Chinese *painting,* the term applied to a view in which one important mountain in the foreground is supported by the peaks of distant mountains behind, with the latter blending together almost to the point of vanishing in mists. The *illusion* is enhanced by the inclusion of clouds, bodies of water, mists, etc., without which the view would be confined. In this technique, the effect is or should be one of serenity; colors partake of both clarity and obscurity and figures are blended and indistinct. Compare with *deep distance* and *high distance.* Japanese equivalent is *heien.*

LI CHOU—In Chinese *art,* the popular name for *scroll paintings* of the vertical-hanging variety, properly termed *kua fu.*

LIEN CHÜAN—In Chinese *painting,* a metallic cloth, usually *silk,* used widely in the T'ANG DYNASTY. The preparation process consisted of placing the silk on a smooth stone and beating it with a *silver-* or *gold*-covered battering device until all the spaces between the threads were filled, and the surface was one of continuous metal.

LIGHT MAGNESIA—A white powder of varying weight, used in the making of *paints* and *varnishes,* cements and other adhesives, fine *lacquers,* and artificial *stone, brick* and *plaster tiles;* employed also as a substitute for *platinum.* Chemically it is magnesium oxide, MgO.

LIGHT RED—In *painting,* one of the *pigments* occurring in nature as a *red* iron oxide, belonging to the class of *iron pigments* (q.v.).

LIGNITE WAX—A variety of *wax* derived from lignite coal, occurring in dark brown color when crude, but invariably *bleached* white for use in the *arts.* Employed in the making of artists' *paints,* adhesives, *leather* finishes, and various waterproofing materials.

LIME—Made by burning *limestone, marble* or *chalk,* this is known in the *arts* as the principal ingredient of *plaster* and an important factor in *fresco painting.* Combined with suitable amounts of water and sand or other granular material, it forms the traditional *lime plaster. Pigments* mixed with water and applied to its surface are held in place by changes in crystalline *character.* Used also in the making of *architectural mortar.* See *marble dust* and *oyster white.*

LIME BLUE—A *painting pigment* of fine sky-blue color,

but lacking in *hiding power* and *stability;* commonly known as *mountain* blue (q.v.).

LIME PLASTER—In *art* and *architecture,* the proper term for the substance commonly known as *plaster* (q.v.). See also *lime.*

LIMESTONE—A coarse, granular, crystaline variety of *stone,* used from time immemorial as a *medium* in *sculpture* and *carving;* it is the basic material of many fine *marbles;* although the latter are generally harder, and more difficult to incise. It occurs in numerous colors, the whitish type being the purest and most desirable for *statuary* work. The fine-grained *limestone* of buff color, when possessing even *texture,* is also an excellent stone for use in sculpture.

LIMN—In *painting* and *drawing,* (1) to add *illuminations* to *manuscripts* (obs.); (2) to draw or paint; portray; illustrate; delineate; (3) to paint, using *water-colors. Limner*: an illuminator of books or *parchments;* a *portrait* painter.

LINEAR—In *art,* having to do with line, *contour,* and form, as distinguished from the *painterly* (q.v.) which stresses *color, tone, shade* and *shadow;* the term describing the act of *drawing,* rather than coloring. See *linear perspective* as contrasted with *aerial perspective.*

LINEAR PERSPECTIVE—The term applied to the effects of distance upon the appearance of size and form; e.g., in a typical view down a railroad track, the rails and telegraph wires appear to converge to a vanishing point on the horizon, while the successive poles seem to become progressively smaller and closer together as they recede in the distance. Such apparent reduction in the intervening spaces because they are seen from an acute angle is known as *foreshortening.* Compare with *aerial perspective* (q.v.). This *illusion* is used by *artists* to obtain the effect of depth. See *illusionism.*

LINE DOUBLING—In Chinese *painting,* a brush stroke technique creating lines having the effect of double thickness. The first is drawn lightly with thin *ink* and then retraced with heavier ink to intensify certain places and add depth and roundness. Both lines remain, side by side or partially overlapping. Not to be confused with the practice of obliterating the under line with the second line, as done in *yung hsiu* (q.v.) .

LINE DRAWING—A *drawing* in which the lines are solid rather than shaded; may be made with *pen, crayon* or *brush,* and is used in *printing* as copy for *line etchings.*

LINE ENGRAVING—An *intaglio* process older than *etching,* having been used by 15th century armorers and *jewelers.* The metal is cut away with a *burin,* instead of using the *biting* (q.v.) technique, and instead of using a metal point to raise a *burr* as in a *drypoint* (q.v.) . It is easier to make a straight line with the engraving tool than a curved one, but although the lines have a clear, regular perfection, the process gives the *engraving* a stiff, angular effect. Sometimes the *print* is made by using dots of varying size and depth instead of using lines; this is called *stipple engraving.* Included in this general classification are *copper* and steel engravings made by direct incision of the *graver* or drypoint, *wood* engravings, and zinc *etchings* made from *pen drawings.*

LINE ETCHING—An *intaglio* process devised in the 16th century as a short cut to *engraving.* The *design* is carried by deep indentations instead of by raised parts, as in *relief* printing. A *copper plate* is heated, and the *ground* (usually *wax asphaltum)* is applied. The ground must be acid resistant. The drawing is then made with a pointed *stylus* which breaks through the ground to the copper, exposing it at those points. In the *acid bath* which follows, the copper is etched by the acid only in those places where it was laid bare by the stylus. This is known as *biting.* The three acids most often used for biting are nitric, Dutch *mordant,* and iron chloride. Certain areas are exposed to the acid longer, to make the line deeper or blacker, while others are subjected to a *stopping out* after a short bite. The entire plate is covered with *ink,* which is wiped off the surface, leaving ink in the lines only. It is then ready for transference to the etching paper. See *intaglio* and *aquatint.*

LINER—In *painting,* a type of *brush* having a thick grouping of camel hair gradually tapering from the ferrule to a very fine point; used principally for the creating of fine-line contours, although often used successfully as a *scroller*.

LING MAO—Literally 'feathers and fur,' the class of Chinese *painting* devoted to birds and animals. This is one of the four major categories of subject matter in Chinese art; excludes horses and cattle which come within the broad *jên wu* group.

LING TZŪ—In Chinese *painting*, a fine *silk* made up of unusually thin threads in varying weave, used chiefly for the mountings of pictures. It occurs as a *damask* and as a *gauze*, as well as in conventional silk form. See also *tz'ŭ ch'ing* and *hu chüan*.

LINING—In *art restoration*, the *technique* of backing a painter's old and weakened *canvas* with a new, strong one. The process is commonly known as *relining* (q.v.).

LINOLEUM BLOCK—A *picture* or *design* cut into *linoleum* with a sharp tool in the same manner as in the *medium* of the *wood-block*. This technique has grown in popularity in recent years, and the *engravings* thus produced are used for poster and other flat-color *printing*.

LINOXYN—Though rarely used in the technology of the *arts*, this term is common in general *paint* technology, referring to the fully dried and hardened *film* of *linseed oil* (q.v.).

LIN PEN—In Chinese *art*, a copy of a *painting* made with the the original before the artist as a *model*. Some interesting aspects of the art of copying are found in *ying hsiang* (q.v.).

LINSEED OIL—Although many *drying* and *hardening oils* have been used as *painting* media, *linseed oil* is employed most widely. It is extracted from the seed of the *flax* plant, and the better grade for *artists' paint* comes from cold pressing. Un-*bleached*, it has a bright golden-*yellow color*. It has been supposed that the finest quality comes from India, and is known as *Calcutta oil*. Its history in the past of the painting *art* is indefinite; known as early as the 8th century, but had its greatest use beginning at some time in the early 15th century. See *binder*.

LITHARGE—A form of *lead monoxide*, combined with various *colors* and used as a *painting medium*. Frequently called *massicot,* although the latter is a clear *yellow,* while *litharge* tends toward *orange* in its truest state. Also used as a *glaze* in *ceramics,* and as a base material in the making of camera *lenses* and *flint glass.* See *antimony pigments* and *mitsudaso.*

LITHOGRAPHIC STONE—A variety of fine-grained *limestone* which responds well to *carving* and *etching.* In wide use when *lithography* employed stone for the basic pattern.

LITHOGRAPHY—A *technique* of graphic reproduction developed at the close of the 18th century based upon a chemical combination of *ink* and *oil,* Modern *lithography* employs metal *plates,* as contrasted with the original block of *stone, wood,* or other crude material. The *design* to be printed is drawn on a metal *ground* with an ink especially prepared for clinging and drying on such a surface. The surface is then exposed to a weak *acid bath,* hardening the ink and slightly *etching* and lowering the unprotected parts. Printing ink is then rolled over the *face,* repelled by the blank parts but adhering to lines of the design, and the *lithograph* plate is ready to make an impression on paper.

LITHOL RED—A deep bluish-red *dye*stuff, first prepared synthetically at the end of the 19th century. Non-*bleeding* and highly *stable,* it is one of the most important and extensively used substances in the making of fine *lake colors.* Known also as *lithol toner.*

LITHOPHONE—A *white pigment* having little use in the *fine arts,* though common in commercial *paints.* It is comparatively recent in origin, first produced in England in 1874. It is used chiefly as an *extender,* by mixture with other pigments of more *intense color.* Also spelled *lithopone,* it is occasionally found in poster colors and other items of *commercial art.* Its lack of favor may be due to its tendency to darken under strong light and re-brighten in darkness, a defect which has since been corrected by elimination of metallic impurities; however, the confidence of the artist has not been restored. Known also as *silver white* and *Orr's white.*

LIU YEH MIAO—In Chinese *painting,* a brush stroke technique known to Western artists as *willow line,* starting narrow, widening, and then tapering to a fine point, somewhat resembling the willow leaf. The term is also applied to a series of such modulations in a single line. Despite the delicacy of the thin ends, the stroke is a strong one, executed with firm pressure of the *brush;* there is no *tien* or dotting. This technique was used extensively by WU TAO-TZU in his famous paintings of KUAN YIN. Compare with *bamboo line* (q.v.).

LIZARD STONE—In *sculpture,* a variety of *serpentine* named for Lizard Point, Cornwall, England, where it is found.

LOAM BEATER—In *casting,* a ramming device used in the forming of a *mold* made of *loam.*

LOCAL COLOR—In *painting,* (1) the *hue* or combination of hues special to any represented object or part thereof; (2) a general system of *light* and *shadow* upon which the *model*ing and *tint*ing of details is extecuted; (3) *chiaroscuro* (q.v.); (4) distinct characteristics, peculiarities, or individuality in a painting, as applied to the *artist,* his *technique,* or to the *picture* itself.

LONDON WHITE—A series of *pigments* having wide use in the *arts* as fine coloring matter; the various pigments within the group differ from each other principally in the quantity of lead oxide they contain.

LONELY SCROLL—In Chinese *art,* the popular term referring to a *painting* that is hung and displayed singly, as distinguished from those exhibited in groups, as *p'ing chang* (q.v.).

LOST WAX PROCESS—A technique of *bronze-casting* whereby the shell or form of the *statue* or other object is duplicated in *wax* which is then melted off and replaced by the molten metal. Better known as *cire perdue* (q.v.).

LOTUS THRONE—A *pedestal* designed with *lotus* petals surrounding a lotus pod *motif* on which, in *painting* and *sculpture,* the Buddha is usually seated.

LOUVAIN SCHOOL—A *painting* school of 15th century

Flemish artists at Louvain. It was here that Dierick Bouts developed his famous style of *landscape* which influenced all of Europe for centuries thereafter.

LOW COLOR—In *painting,* a term descriptive of any *color* possessing little *chromatic intensity.* This is not necessarily a defect in the *work of art,* since many subjects and *techniques* are *best* rendered when *brilliance* is contrasted with *low color.*

LOW KEY—A term in *painting;* see *key.*

LOW RELIEF—*Sculpture* in which the raised portions stand out but little from the background; a mode of sculpturing with the figures almost flat. Same as *bas-relief* (q.v.).

LUCIDOL—A *bleaching* agent for artists' *oils* and *waxes;* it is an odorless white solid, crystalline in structure, slightly soluble in *alcohol* and insoluble in water. It is obtained as a product of the reaction between benzoyl chloride and barium peroxide.

LUCULLITE—In *sculpture,* a fine variety of *marble* colored dense black by carbon; occurs only in Egypt.

LUMACHELLE—In *sculpture,* a shell variety of dark brown *marble,* having brilliant fire or *chatoyant* reflection from within; known also as *fire marble.*

LUMINOSITY—In *painting,* a term referring generally to the quality of *brightness* in *colors.* The word is frequently found in *art criticism.*

LUN K'UO—In Chinese *painting,* the arrangement of the peaks in a mountain range in such manner that the finished picture appears to resemble a stack of barrel hoops or wheel rims. In this unusual style, the peaks are all of the rounded, or *dome*-top variety.

LUSTER—In *painting,* the name given to a certain variety of *enamel* or *varnish* (and by extension to any *surface film*) added to *porcelain* for the purpose of enhancing its *gloss.*

LUTE—In the *arts* generally, any *plastic* substance, e.g., *gum, resin,* etc., used for adhesive purposes or for sealing. Applies particularly to *surface films* (q.v.).

LUTSCHISM—Native Russian name for the revised theory of *Impressionism* known as *Rayonism,* dealing with *paint-*

ing showing dispersion and interpenetration of light rays emanating from objects. *Abstract* in style, it was founded in 1911 by Michael Larinov and his wife, both of whom remained its only adherents. However, it had a stimulating effect on *theatre* decoration.

LYNCURIUM—A stone used for *intaglio* work. While it is believed to be *hyacinth* (q.v.), it is not identified with certainty. In 77 A.D. the word was used by Pliny in describing *amber*.

M

MADDER—One of the *lake* or *dye pigments;* it was as well known as any of the *red* coloring materials used by painters since *classical* times. It is believed to be the *rubia* mentioned by Pliny, and specimens of it have been found on *paintings* of Egyptian and Greco-Roman times. It is a *natural* dye extracted from the root of the RUBIA TINCTORIUM. Synthetic *dyes* such as *alizarin* have totally displaced it. See *alizarin.*

MADDER BROWN—A term in *painting;* see *garance brun rouge.*

MADDER PLANT—See *alizarin.*

MADONNA—A *picture, statue,* or other *image* or representation of the mother of Christ, generally with the Child in her arms. The term is occasionally used in devotions to her.

MADREPERLA LUSTER—The term applied to any surface having a *luster* or reflection resembling that of *mother-of-pearl.* See *luster.*

MADREPORE MARBLE—In *sculpture* and *architecture,* a *fossil*-bearing variety of *limestone* of the Devonian Age, occurring in numerous colors; it is receptive to *carving* and a high polish. Name derives from *madrepore,* the branched, perforated type of coral, one of the most characaeristic forms of fossil extant.

MAGATAMA—In Japenese *art,* a *carved* bead or pendant in the shape of a comma. Its significance is lost in *antiquity.*

MAGENTA—A deep, *brilliant red*dish *purple* color; also the name applied to a particular synthetic *aniline,* used as a *dye.* It was first prepared in the mid-19th century, and although it is a *fugitive* material, it is still used as a *water-color.* Also known as *aniline red* and *fuchsin.*

MAGILP—Same as *megilp* (q.v.).

MAGNESITE—A *natural* substance occurring in colors ranging from white to brown, having a dull, vitreous *luster.* A magnesium carbonate ($MgCO_3$), it is used in the making of *ceramics,* as an ingredient in *paints* and *varnishes,* in the manufacture of *celluloid,* and artificial *stone, brick* and *plaster tiles;* employed also as a *textile* finishing agent.

MAHLSTICK—A rod held in the *palette* hand for the *painter* and used as a rest for his painting hand, especially in the execution of fine, detailed work. Evidence of its use goes back to the 16th century. It is of light-weight *wood,* usually with a soft, *leather*-covered ball at one end. The ball is made to rest against the painting, if necessary, or against a part of the *easel.* Commercially-made *mahlsticks* are of hard-wood or *bamboo,* jointed to give a total length of four feet; literally, *paint-stick.* Known in France as *appuiemain;* occasionally spelled *maulstick.* Many modern varieties of *mahlstick* are made of *aluminum* or other light-weight metal ,and are available in separable-section form or in collapsible telescopic form, for portability. Sometimes referred to as *rest-stick.*

MAKIMONO—A Japanese rolled horizontal *scroll,* usually containing text alone, as distinguished from the *e-makimono* (q.v.) which is *illustrated.*

MALACHITE—A basic *idiochromatic* variety of *copper* associated with the *blue* known as *azurite* (q.v.) *Green* in *hue,* it has often been referred to as *mountain green.* The mineral is prepared as a *pigment* by selection, grinding (see *grinding slab*), and sieving. Formerly much used in Europe through the *Middle Ages* and the *Renaissance,* it is now no longer prepared by the *artists'* colormen. It still appears in the Far East with azurite as a pigment, and has evidently been on the *palette* of artists of that region since the *Han dynasty* (206 B.C.-220 A.D.). Known also as *green mineral. .See shih-lu.*

MANAIA—In *sculpture,* a squat human figure; originally, the basic and recurrent *motif* in *Maori carving* (q.v.).

MANAKIN—See *manikin.*

MANDALA—In Arabic *art,* a *temple painting* showing a portion or all of a *pantheon* (q.v.), with mystic *symbols* often *geometrically* arranged. Known also as *mandara.*

MANDARA—In the *art of old* Arabia, *same as mandala* (q.v.).

MANDORLA—A soft light emanating from a figure in sacred *art,* differing from the *aureole* in that the shape of the mist is oval, while the aureole follows the precise lines of the body it surrounds. Used extensively in medieval art, through rarely to be found thereafter.

MANGANESE PIGMENTS—*Blue* and *violet* colors derived from manganese metal. The violet appeared first (1890) and is a synthetic pigment, quite *stable* to light and heat. Although its hue is not high in *brilliance,* it is nevertheless a strong, *opaque,* dense color of god permanence. The blue, still more recent in origin (1935), is *inert* and unaffected by heat or strong acid or alkalis; light *greenish* in effect, it is weak in tinting strength but has high *luminosity* and is especially useful in *seascape* and sky work. The violets are particularly varied, some of the *shades* including *mineral-, permanent-,* and *Nuernberger violet.*

MANIKIN—An adjustable *model* made to imitate the human figure, used chiefly in the *representation* of *costume* and drapery, and ranging in height from 12 inches to life size. Known as early as the 16th century, it probably existed in *artists' studios* at an earlier date. Compare with *lay figure* (q.v.). See also *ecorché.*

MANNERISM—The *late Renaissance,* embracing the period 1530 to 1600; see *Renaissnace.*

MANNERISM—In *painting,* the term applied by some critics to any distinctive or peculiar method or technique that has been carried to excess; the inartistic extension of *manner.*

MAN OF SORROW—In religious *sculpture,* the name given the famous late-*medieval* devotional *image representing* Christ upright, suffering from the wounds inflicted. Frequently exhibited during the *Passion,* occasionally showing the actual injuries, thereby inviting the compassion of the beholder.

MAO LIN—In Chinese *art,* the term applied to any *painting* of a forest showing heavy, thick foliage on the trees, as distinguished from the *han lin* which represents leafless trees. Known to Western artists as *flourishing forest.*

MAORI CARVING—A local *art* style distinctive from and far surpassing that of other south sea island groups. Discovering the fine-*grained medium* of *totara wood* and the sharp-cutting *nephrite greenstone,* the *Maoris* turned to the wood *craving* to preserve their art *forms.* Their work was exquisitely detailed and strongly *symbolic,* with frequent *representations* of things in nature which, to them, had meaning in life and death, e.g., the lizard, which symbolizes death in most aboriginal *cultures.* Huge *panels* are characterized by intricate circular carving; *totemic* figures exhibit extensive detail, and *tradition* is pursued through the ages. Eyes in the figures are made of *paua* shells, and the pendants on neck cords (known as *hei-tiki*) are treasured heirlooms of greenstone. See *manaia, tohunga, Salish art,* and *marakihau.*

MARAKIHAU—The widely-used sea monster *motif* in *Maori carving* (q.v.).

MARBLE—The most extensively used *medium* of the *sculptor,* far exceeding all other varieties of stone combined; used widely in decorative *architecture* as well. It is more durable than *limestone* and other forms of *sedimentary* rock, and softer (and consequently easier to *carve*) than *igneous* rock. Its use in *statuary* work was started by the Romans, and grew more and more popular through the centuries. Of metaphoric origin, marble is related geologically to limestone, although differing structurally. Many dozens of fine types of *marble* are used in *sculpture,* each variety possessing a different name (as *Carrara, forest, scagliola, graphic,* etc.) in accordance with its markings, the locale of its occurrance, its color, or other identifying feature. Generally, *marbles* are responsive to *carving,* take a high polish, do not *fracture* under the sculptor's tools, and have ageless durability.

MARBLE DUST—Finely-powdered *marble,* mixed with *lime*

to obtain the *plaster* used by some artists as a *ground* for *fresco* (q.v.) painting. Popularly known as *whiting* (q.v.).

MARBLE POLISHER—In *sculpture,* a linen cushion with which the final rubbing of *marble* is accomplished; it is generally charged with *emery* dust. The term is sometimes applied to the block of *sandstone* used for rubbing the marble in the preliminary polishing; also, any machine, wheel, or other device employed for such purpose.

MARINE PAINTING—In *art,* any painting on *canvas, porcelain,* etc., having as its principal subject an expanse of water and/or a marine object or objects. Frequently referred to as a *seascape,* esp. in *oil painting* and *water-color.*

MARLY HORSES—In *sculpture,* a name given to any *statue* (generally executed in *stone* or *bronze*) depicting two or more horses in a rearing position. The term derives from the specific name of such a group sculptured by Coustou, situated in Paris at the entrance to the Champs Élysées.

MARMOLITE—In *sculpture,* a scaly, foliated variety of *serpentine* (q.v.), pale green in color.

MAROON—A *shade* of deep *red* having unusually little *luminosity;* generally, any deep red *color* modified by addition of a *tinge* of blue. Also, a coal-tar *dyestuff* obtained in the manufacture of *magenta* (q.v.).

MARS—*Ares,* god of war; *represented* in many fine works of *sculpture.* See *Ares.*

MARS PIGMENTS—A range of *colors* from *yellow* to *violet* through *orange* and *red,* made artificially; generally similar to the *earth* yellows and reds, though somewhat *brighter* in in color and finer in *grain* than the *natural* products. Sometimes considered members of the *iron pigment* family, they are made on a base of iron oxide.

MARTIN—In *sculpture,* a stone-faced, perforated plate or runner, used for grinding and polishing stone and *marble.*

MARUYAMA SCHOOL—A Japanese school of *painting* depicting subjects of nature in the strictest form of *realism.* See *Shijo School.*

MASSGEFÜHL—A *sculpture* movement of the early 20th century originating in Germany. It marked a strong and sudden change from what was believed to be the outworn *realism* and over-sentimental *romanticism* of the late 19th century, and sought a new, simple, essentially decorative *naturalism*. It combined technical ability of a high level with expression of power, often to the point of brutality. Pursued extensively in *modeling, casting,* and *carving* as well. The most striking examples of sculpture emerging from the *Massgefühl* (figuratively, the feeling of the *statue* for its surroundings) school are found in a series of German national monuments.

MASSICOT—In *painting,* a lead monoxide having a clear *yellow color.* It is made by the gentle roasting of *white lead* at 300 degrees centigrade. *Litharge* is another name given it , although that is often used to designate a *pigment* more *orange* in *hue. Massicot* was used extensively by painters during the *Middle Ages* and the *Renaissance,* and it was known from predynastic times in Egypt. See *antimony pigments* and *litharge.* Also, *Naples yellow.*

MASS TONE—A term in *painting;* see *top tone.*

MASTERPIECE—In the *arts,* especially *painting* and *sculpture,* a term now used to indicate a certain high level of excellence. The word in earlier times was reserved for the one finest item in a given group. The term suggests relative *values,* sometimes with limited comparisons, and is employed chiefly to record widely accepted *judgments* over a period of time. Under the pressure of exacting standards of modern art study, the word appears to be losing some of its former glamour. Careless application has also contributed to its loss of stature. See *chef-d'ouvre.*

MASTIC—The most commonly-used *varnish*-making *resin.* Prepared from pure resin by solution with *turpentine* and addition of a *drying* oil or other plasticizer. See *resin, varnish, balsam.* Resin is also an adhesive used in repairing sheet materials, as *glass,* rubber *tile,* etc. Used widely as the substance into which the *tesserae* are set, in the making of *mosaics;* also as a protective addition in the *restoration* of *oil paintings.*

MATERIALISM—In *art,* the *representation* of that which is taken exclusively from nature, as it is perceived by the senses. The only focal point in this purusuit is material nature, which has as its essential characteristic the *accidental,* i.e., *color,* shape, etc., and to be successful, it must eliminate all human *values* and *artifacts.* Approaching nearest to the *materialistic* program were the 19th century *artists* devoted to *naturalism* and *impressionism* (qq.v.).

MATTE—The term describing any object of *art* having such *texture* that it gives off no shiny reflections, e.g., un*glazed pottery.* Characteristic of any paint *medium,* esp. *tempera,* which leaves a dull finish. Compare with *luster* (q.v.).

MAULSTICK—In *painting,* the *leather*-tipped rod (usually *bamboo*) upon which the *artist* rests his working hand in the execution of fine detail work; approx. four feet in length. Known also as *mahlstick* (q.v.), *appuie-main,* and *rest-stick.*

MAURESQUE—The *painting* and *sculpture* style of the Arabic and Moorish peoples, often incorrectly referred to as *arabesque.* See *arabesque* and *grottesque.*

MAYAN BLUE—A fine blue *pigment* used widely in *Maya art,* esp. in the execution of *murals,* and *wall paintings.* Microscopic examinations by various museums show the presence of iron and copper, and it has been established definitely as inorganic. Practically every ancient Mayan site has produced paintings or *ceramics* possessing this lost pigment.

MA YA TS'UN—In Chinese *painting,* a brush stroke technique in which stiff, hard strokes are applied with the point of the *brush, giving the effect of a horse's teeth* (see *horse tooth*). Used chiefly for rock representation in *landscape* work.

MEASURED PAINTING—In Chinese *art,* a *style* popular in the 10th century A.D. The painters pursuing it, including Kuo Chung Hsi, the outstanding *artist* of his time, used only *architectural* wholes or parts as their *themes,* sometimes with surrounding *landscape* in the background. Examples extant are carefully preserved in *museums* and in *private collections.*

MEDIA PAPER—A variety of *coated paper* used as a *ground*

for three-dimensional effects in *pencil, crayon, charcoal,* and *pastel* work.

MEDIUM—Specifically, the *vehicle* or material added to *pigment* to give it fluency or brushability. It may be *linseed oil,* water, *wax, oil,* egg, etc. Generally, it is any method, agency, or material through which an *artist* sets forth his ideas, thoughts or feelings. May appear in the form of *metal, wood,* words, musical *tones, stone, colors, enamel, dance* movements, etc. Pl. *media* is grammatically correct, but *mediums* appears to be Anglicized. See *ground.*

MEDIUM VALUE—In *painting,* an in-between *value* of a *color,* being neither *intense* nor unduly pale. Also known as *middle value.*

MEGILP—Name of a 19th century mixture of *mastic resin* and *linseed oil* which was added to commercially prepared oil *paints* during the *painting* process. With the change in painting *styles* and methods, it has been largely abandoned, although some artists persist in its use for its *siccative* qualities. Also spelled *magilp.*

MEI—In Chinese *art,* the *plum, symbol* of longevity; corresponding Japanese term is *ume.*

MELAMINE RESIN— A series of *synthetic resins* characterized by high heat resistance, speed of conversion, and remarkable *stability* to color. Used in the making of *enamels, ceramics,* and *laminated plastics;* successful also as a substitute for *linseed oil* in *paint* and *linoleum.*

MELDRUM SCHOOL—The term refers to a group of Australian *painters* who follow the *art* and teaching of Duncan Max Meldrum (20th cent.). Meldrum, in stating what he believes to be the true principles of *painting,* contends that painting "is a pure science, the science of optical analysis," and he maintains that the *artist* has the task of translating optical impressions in terms of his *medium,* and in the precise scientific order in which these impressions come to the eye; *tone* being first, proportion second, and *color* third. Meldrum exerted considerable influence, finding both accord and objections throughout the art world.

MELPOMENE—In Greek *mythology,* one of the nine famous

daughters of Zeus and Mnemosyne. She was the *Muse* of tragedy, song, and harmony, and was frequently represented in the *arts* with a sword, a tragic *mask,* and a garland of vine leaves as her *attributes.* See *Muse.*

MEMENTO MORI—Any skull-shaped ornament or *amulet,* often exquisitely carved and sometimes *gem*-studded, carried or worn by some persons as a reminder of the inevitabiliy of death.

MEMORY COLOR—Inexact perception of the *color* of an object because of a former experience, usually a recent one. See *after-image.*

MEMORY PICTURE—In *art,* a *representation* of the most characteristic features and aspects of *forms;* found principally in *primitive* and early art. See *fractional concept.*

MENISCUS—The curved top-surface of a liquid in a vessel, important to *artists* in representing correct picturization in applicable *still-life* work. All liquids which wet the surfaces of their containers, e.g., water, have a depressed *meniscus* (*concave*) ; other liquids, non-wetting, e.g., mercury, have a raised (*convex*) *meniscus.*

MESOPOTAMIAN ART—A convenient general name embracing the kindred *arts* of ancient *Chaldea, Babylonia* and *Assyria*—though these arts were not definitely limited to Mesopotamia proper. They constitute together one of the chief diversions of art development, and exerted an important influence upon Greek art, and hence upon suceeding arts for all time. See *Chaldean Art, Babylonian Art* and *Assyrian Art.*

METAL—One of many elementary substances, used widely in the *arts,* possessing in a substantial degree the *qualities* and properties of hardness, *opacity,* fusibility, *malleability, ductility,* conductivity, etc., as *gold, platinum, silver, copper,* etc. Distinct from non-*metals,* those elements whose oxides will unite with water to form bases. The term includes *alloys,* such as *brass, bronze,* etc. See *metalwork* and *metallography.*

METALWORK—One of the *arts,* embracing such diverse creative *artists* as *sculptors, silver*smiths, *gold*smiths, *pewter*-makers, and all other *metallographers.* Though general in scope, the term does not include *etchers* and *engravers* who create *metal* art works not complete in themselves, but serving as the foundations for reproduction. The function of the *metal-worker* is to create a finished object of art, by forming, treating, decorating, and for all purposes rendering complete a work of art, using one or more metals as the *medium.*

METAMORPHIC ROCK—In *sculpture* and *architecture,* one of the three great classifications of *stone* (q.v.), including of any of those in the *igneous* (q.v.) and all other classes that have been changed in character by movement of the earth's crust or by chemical action; e.g., *marble,* which is a *metamorphic* condition of sedimentary *limestone* and *chalk.*

METHOCEL—A non-toxic white powder, soluble in water, clear and viscous. Used in adhesives, as a *size* for *paper,* and in the making of some *paints;* employed also as a *gum* in *textile printing* and in the manufacture of *pencils* and *crayons* as a *binder* for the *pigments.* Chemically it is methyl cellulose, *methocel* being a trade name.

METOPE—The *panel* between *triglyphs* in a *Doric frieze,* popular during the 5th century B.C., usually *decorated* with *sculptured* figures, but sometimes with a *rosette* or *shield,* or left blank. The blending of the *metope* decoration with the rest of the building presented the greatest problems of the *art.* On the *Parthenon,* the figures of the *metopes* assumed a rich variety of geometric *patterns,* with drapery skillfully used to bind them into a unified whole. As a rule ,the background was *blue,* with the details of the figures in *red* and *gold,* causing them to stand out in apparently *high relief.* The most popular subjects were *Heracles* and *Theseus,* the battles of gods against giants, Greeks against *Amazons,* etc. After the 5th century B.C., no *metope sculpture* of importance was created.

METZ SCHOOL—An *art* group of the *Carolingian* period (9th to 10th centuries) specializing in the making of *Evangeliars* (q.v.)

MEXICAN ONYX—In *architecture,* a calcitic stone resembling *marble,* occurring chiefly in Tecali, Mexico; used extensively for interior ornamentation, occasionally for *sculpture.* See *onyx marble.*

MEZZOTINT—An *intaglio engraving* process similar to the making of *drypoint,* except that that procedure is reversed. A *burr* is raised over the surface of the entire *plate,* and this roughening process is so laborious that few *artists* have had the courage to carry it through. It is accomplished by use of a tool known as a *rocker* which cuts *ridges* in many directions, until the surface of the *copper* is cut all over into a minutely-dotted surface which holds the *ink* as does the burr of the drypoint. *Mezzotints* are outstanding for their richness of *blacks.* The process is one that will reward the artist who has the will to do the work and explore the subtle range of *tones.* See *aquatint mezzotint.*

MICA—A group of mineral silicates, the powder of which is used in the making of *paints, wallpaper, tiles,* and *textile printing* substances; employed also as a substitute for *aluminium* powder. In its natural state, it appears in crystalline layers that peel readily, used as such in stove doors, goggles, gas masks, etc. It is believed that the *lapis specularis* mentioned in literature as the *window* material of the Romans was made up of thin sheets of *mica.* See *muscovite.*

MIDDLE AGES—The period in European history between *classical antiquity* and the Italian *Renaissance,* extending from the late 5th century to about 1350; occasionally limited to the latter portion fo this period alone, e.g., after 1100; sometimes extended to 1450 or 1500. Adj. *medieval.*

MIDDLE VALUE—See *medium value.*

MILK GOLD—In Chinese *painting,* a creamy gold 'mud' used for outlining rocks in *ch'ing lü* landscapes and to give a bright highlight in bird and flower work; used also for garments in portraiture and in Buddhistic painting. Known natively as *ju chin,* it is made by rubbing *gold leaf* with the fingers in a circular motion under water. In taking up the gold, the *brush* must follow the same motion in order to insure a smooth and *lustrous* effect.

MILKWEED—Many important uses have been uncovered for this apparently insignificant plant. Its floss is warmer than *wool,* though six times lighter in weight; its seed oil is semi-drying, rendering it valuable in the making of *paints* and finishes; used also in *paper* making, *rayon* and *textile* prcoesses, wallboards, and *plastics.*

MILORI BLUE—In *painting,* one of the many names by which the famous *Prussian blue* (q.v.) is known.

MINERAL BLUE—In *painting,* the name given to *azurite* when it is reduced to an impalpable powder for use as a *pigment.*

MINERAL GRAY—In *painting,* a gray *pigment* of fine drying power, translucent and *stable,* but possessing little tinting strength. It is in small demand, since the average artist can mix it on his *palette* by using *lamp black, zincweiss,* and *ultramarine* in combination. The finer product is obtained from *lapis lazuli.* A substance known as *gangue (vein-stone)* is often offered as *mineral gray,* but is not a successful substitute.

MINERAL GREEN—In *painting,* a bright bluish-green *pigment* commonly known as *emerald green* (q.v.).

MINERAL LAKE—In *painting,* a variety of tin-chromate glass used as a pink *pigment.*

MINERAL VIOLET—In *painting,* one of the fine *manganese pigments* (q.v.).

MINERAL WHITE—In *painting,* same as *permanent white;* a fine grade of *gypsum* ground to a powder and used as a *pigment.*

MINIATURE—A small, highly-detailed *painting* or *drawing.* This *art* found great popularity during the *Middle Ages,* possibly through the need for *miniatures* in the making of *illuminated manuscripts* (.v.) The term may have its origin in the fact that the artists executing these works used *minimum,* or *red lead,* the use of the word subsequently growing to embrace any small *portrait* or picture on *vellum* or *ivory.*

MINIUM—A bright scarlet *color* made by heating *litharge* for long periods at high temperatures. It has good hiding power, and a smooth *texture* in *oil.* It has been used generally in European and Asiatic *paintings* since *ancient* times, and the word was often applied to *cinnabar* (q.v.).

MIRASOL RESIN—A variety of *synthetic resin* used as a *drying oil, surface film* or coating over *painting* and *statuary,* and in the making of *paints, textile* finishes, and *printing inks.* Chemically it is a *resin* of the alkyd class, *mirasol* being a trade name.

MIR ISKUSSTVA—A Russian *art* movement growing out of the *Blue Rose* (q.v.) following the 1905 revolution; known in the West as *World of Art. Painting* was restored to a stylized form in decorative *linear*ism, spreading its influence to *settings* in the Russian *theatre* and *ballet.* It was also a protest against the *Wanderers* (q.v.), seeking true pursuit of 'art for art's sake,' which was the slogan. This new decorative art was quickly taken up in the *graphic arts,* book *illustration* and *mural* painting, as well as in the theatre.

MIRROR—In *painting,* a term used by artists to describe a finish that a somewhat *glossy* and lustrous, although not approaching the reflecting power of the *high* and *enamel* finish.

MISCHIO MARBLE—In *sculpture,* a fine variety of violet-red *breccia marble* found in Serravezza, Italy; known also as *African breccia* or *breche Africaine.*

MISERABLISM—Word *coined* by an *art* critic of Paris in 1950, alluding to the *paintings* by artists who are 'obsessed by their own firsthand experience in misery.' In fierce morbidity, the works represent humans in the throes of despair; thin, sorrowful and apparently helpless in the grasp of circumstances, often emmeshed in a *geometric* net. The pathos of the 'school' is best illustrated by Bernard Buffet's SELF-PORTRAIT and Louis Smith's WOMAN IN YELLOW. Admirers claim it to be the first truly new *style* in years.

MITIS GREEN—In *painting,* a bright bluish-green *pigment* commonly known as *emerald green* (q.v.).

MITSUDA—The term describing certain *ancient* Buddhist *paintings* which were long thought to be a lost *technique* of *oil painting.* The process is now believed to have been fine *lacquer* work. Finest examples are on the doors of the *Tamamushi shrine* in Horyuji, near Nara. As *mitsudaso,* the term applies to a painting *medium* in the nature of *litharge,* sometimes difficult to distinguish from true lacquer work.

MITSUDASO—See *mitsuda.*

MIXTEC—A linguistic group inhabiting northern Oaxaca and southern Puebla, Mexico. They were the authors of an important religious *art* which seems, from its *relics,* to have flourished during the 11th century, and it supplanted previous independent religious arts of Middle America. Later aspects of this *culture* are referred to as Mixteca-Puebla, since the area appears to have been its center of origin and it was participated in by both the Aztecan Nahaus and the Mixtec-speaking peoples.

MIZU—In Japanese *art,* a *water-color painting.*

MO—In Chinese *art,* a fine variety of *ink* made by mixing carbon with *glue;* usually in form of a cake or stick, some finely decorated. It is made ready for use by rubbing in water on a *palette* of stone or other suitable material. It is an extraordinarily versatile *pigment,* attested by the rich black of *calligraphy* and the varied *tones* of *landscapes* in *monochrome.* Known also as *Chinese ink* and *India ink,* the latter deriving from the fact of its having been produced in India by European and Asiatic traders.

MODEL—Anything in particular shape, size, construction, *quality,* etc., intended for purposes of imitation; a form in miniature, *natural* size or *enlargement* to be remade in similar proportion; any plan or *pattern;* a copy in imitation of something already existing, as a *model* of the White House. Also, any person posing for a *painter, sculptor,* etc., known generally as *artist's model.*

MODELING BOARD—An essential item of equipment in *ceramics* and *sculpture;* used for the working of *clay* into desired shapes. Usually owned in sets of three, each of a different size, but all being square or almost square, made of hard wood, and highly *varnished.* Frequently furnished with short legs or cleats, elevating it from the table or other surface upon which it is placed.

MODELING CLAY—In *sculpture,* a fine *plastic clay,* especially prepared for *artists* in modeling by kneading it in glycerin or similar substance.

MODEL LIGHT—In *ceramics,* a variety of *clay* possessing the unusual feature of self-hardening; will dry and harden practically to the *texture* and durability of fired *pottery,* with *casting* or *baking* unnecassary. Care must be taken to keep the unfinished model covered with a damp cloth, to preserve its pasticity until ready for drying. Used successfully in *sculpture* as well, the substance is its own dehydrating and setting agent, *model light* being a trade name.

MODERNIST—In the *arts,* (1) one whose general treatment or interpretation of a subject departs radically from accepted method; (2) one who upholds the value of new *techniques* and teachings as opposed to the *classical;* (3) an advocate of new trends, thoughts and methods in a given field, e.g., *music, literature, painting,* etc.

MOIST CLAY—In *sculpture,* a variety of modeling *clay* that is both popular and inexpensive. Light gray in color, it dries to gray-white. It possesses a fine uniformity of *texture,* offering ease of manipulation, and responds well to all sculptors' tools; can be *cast* with *plaster* or *gelatin* when dried to a leather-like hardness.

MOKUGA—Literally, "*wood* picture"; a Japanese *picture* in *marquetry* or wood *inlay.*

MOLD—Any *form,* usually of *stone* or *metal,* the inner surface of which has been previously *carved* or laid out in *design* or *pattern.* It is lined or filled with any substance having hardening qualities, and upon solidifying, the substance is removed and is found to bear the imprint of the *mold's* design. The process in its entirety is known as *casting,* and the material most commonly used is *gypsum,* better known as *plaster of Paris* (qq.v.). Its origin lost in *antiquity,* the *mold* was used in the famous *cire perdue* (q.v.) or *lost wax process.*

IOLD BURLAP—In *sculpture,* the *fabric* used for the reinforcing of plaster *casts* or *molds.* The loose, stringy weave f ordinary burlap is well adapted for this purpose.

LD FACING—A fine powder or wash applied to the face a *mold* to insure a smooth, clean *casting.*

MOLD SEPARATOR—In *sculpture,* any one of a number of chemical preparations applied as a thin coat over the *carved* object before it is set into the moist *plaster.* After hardening, the *mold* or *cast* is easily separated from the *model.* Care must be exercised in keeping the coat as thin as possible; a thick application will dull the clean edges of the reproduction. See also *shim brass.*

MONASTRAL BLUE—In *painting,* a fine organic blue *pigment* made available to artists in 1938. Fairly *stable* and permanently *fast* to light, it approaches the perfect pure blue because of its ability to absorb within itself its yellow and red constituents, reflecting only blue and blue-green. It has twice the strength of *Prussian blue,* and about thirty times that of *ultramarine.* Chemically it is PHTHALOGYANINE ($C_{32}H_{16}N_8Cu$), *monastral* blue being a trade name.

MONOCHROME—Any work of *art* that has been treated with *color,* but with one color only. Although the object itself is generally referred to as *monochromatic,* the *technique* is usually described as *monochrome painting, monocrome porcelain work,* etc.

MONOLITH—In *archeology, architecture* and *sculpture,* an upright monument, *column* or *statue* of great proportions, made of a single *stone;* e.g., the Egyptian *obelisk.* Usually commemorative, it may be in any form.

MONOTYPE—A *print technique* usually classified among the *graphic arts.* The picture is *painted* in full *color* on a non-absorbent surface, as a sheet of *glass* or metal, with any sufficiently slow-drying *paint.* It is then transferred to *paper* by direct contact with it, using a *rubbing* pressure on the back of the paper with any smooth, hard, rounded implement. Various effects may be produced by manipulating the paint prior to the making of the impression. To make additional copies of the same subject, the *plate* must be repainted; thus, the variations in color and *design* cause each print to be a unique *proof* rather than an exact replica. See *rubbing.*

MONTAGE—Generally, the *art* or *technique* of combining in one composition a number of pictorial elements acquired from several sources, with the result that the individual parts are distinct, and still blend into one overall *picture* through super-imposition and arrangement. From the French, *mounting; putting together.* When *montage* is made up of purely *photographic* elements, the resulting combination is known as *photomontage,* and the artist, *photomonteur.* See *collage.*

MONTAN WAX—A variety of *wax* derived from lignite coal, dark *brown* when crude, but invariably *bleached* to a *white* state, *amorphous,* for use in the *arts.* It is employed in the making of *paints,* adhesives, *leather* finishes, and waterproofiing materials; used also as a substitute for *carnauba wax* and *beeswax* (qq.v.). In turn, *synprowax* and *candelilla* are effective as substitutes for *montan wax.*

MONTHIER BLUE—In *painting,* the name given to a special kind of *Prussian blue* (q.v.) in the making of which ammonia is used.

MOORISH ART—The *art* (chiefly *decorative*) of the Mohammedan people of northern Africa both at home and in Spain during their occupation of that country. It is a branch of the *Saracenic* art, and bears a close general resemblance to Arabic art (as seen in old Syria, and esp. in Egypt), but it is generally inferior in dignity, refinement, and variety. Like other Saracenic art, it is nearly devoid of the representation of animal or vegetable life, and is esp. rich in purely conventional or geometrical patterns, such as interlacings, produced in stamped and colored *plaster,* in *glazed* and *painted tiles,* in *carving,* etc. *Alhambraic* art is a late development of the *Moorish.*

MORDANT—In *etching,* a term applied to the acid employed in the *biting* (q.v.) operation. See *aqua fortis.*

MORDANT—In *painting* (esp. *gilding*), a *technique* involving the use of an adhesive *film* which remains *tacky* long enough to allow metal leaf applied over it to become firmly attached. It is contrasted with *water gilding* which is used for large flat areas on the *panals* of *altarpieces.* Distinguished also from the *shell gold process* by which powdered *gold* is mixed with a *medium* and applied to a work of *art* in the form of a thin *paint.*

MOTTLED—In the *arts* generally, the appearance of having

been spotted conspicuously, esp. with varying *colors;* any effect on *wood, marble, metal,* etc., seemingly maculated or stained; any irregularity of *texture, color* or *design* in continuous *pattern* throughout an entire surface, as in the effect created by *mottled glaze.*

MOULAGE—The *technique* of making a *mold,* generally in *plaster of Paris;* also, the plastic substance itself. Used successfully in making *masks* of living person, and death masks.

MOUNTAIN BLUE—In *painting,* a *pigment* of beautiful sky-colored blue. Although prized for its *hue,* it has been found deficient in *hiding power,* and while relatively *stable* it is nevertheless sensitive to extreme changes of light, moisture, and heat. These defects result in its being used chiefly in *fresco* work, into the *plaster* of which it has good 'bite.' Known also as *lime blue* and *neuwied blue.*

MOUNTAIN GREEN—A *pigment* famous through the centuries, closely associated with *azurite;* properly known as *malachite* (q.v.).

MOUNTAIN-WATER PAINTING—In Chinese *art,* the general term embracing all *landscape paintings.*

MPONGWE—Name of an African group famous for its artistry in the *carving* of human figures, esp. in wood. The tribe was probably the most advanced in all of Africa, exhibiting great merit in the construction of *musical instruments* in addition to its recognized craftmanship in *sculpture.*

MU—In Chinese *art,* to copy, but only by the methods of *tracing* or transfer; general term embracing all techniques of copying is *mu fang.* See *fên lin.*

MU FANG—In Chinese painting, an exact copy; the term *mu* (q.v.) indicates a copy either by *tracing,* or transfer, and by no other technique. *Mu fang,* however, when found in a *colophon,* means that a faithful representation has been made, regardless of method.

MULLER—A rounded *stone,* flat at the bottom, moved over a *grinding slab* (q.v.) by hand to grind *pigments* which were placed on the slab in a paste mixture with *oil* or water. The *muller* was usually of the same material as the slab, *porphyry* (q.v.) having been the *traditional* preference since *ancient* Egypt. The discovery of the *color mill* led to the abandonment of the hand grinding process. See *slice.*

MULTIPLE GRAVER—In *engraving,* a pointed, chisel-like tool with a split tip, giving two or more scratching points, enabling its user to cut parallel lines at one stroke. Particularly useful in drawing *graph* forms. See *graver.*

MUMMY—In *painting,* a brown *color* prepared from the *asphaltum* taken from Egyptian *mummies,* and used as an *oil* color by *artist.* Resembling asphaltum generally, it possessed the added feature of being less liable to crack, and it was believed for many years that the finest colors were produced from the ingredients taken from Egyptian mummies.

MUMMY PIGMENT—The dull *brown* coloring material taken from the bones and bodily remains of Egyptian *mummies* in which *bitumen* or *asphaltum* (qq.v.) had been used in the embalming process. Employed chiefly as an *oil paint* in the 17th to 19th centuries.

MUNSELL SYSTEM—A procedure for identifying *colors* by reference to standard *tints* and shades of various *hues,* thus objectifying color nomenclature. The *Munsell photometer* is an instrument for testing *pigments, paper,* and other materials that reflect light rather than produce it. See *Ostwald System.*

MURAL—A *decoration* on a *wall* and, by extension of its meaning, on a *ceiling,* by use of *fresco, oil,* or *encaustic techniques.* The term excludes from consideration other forms of interior surface decoration such as *relief sculpture, mosaics, marble encrustations,* and *paneling.* Generally, a *mural* is subordinate to the *architectural* surfaces it embellishes, although some examples, e.g., Michelangelo's painted *architecture* and *sculpturesque* figures on the Sistine ceiling, and Coreggio's paintings at Parma, have far surpassed in *art* recognition the structures to which they were originally affixed as mere incidentals.

MUSE—In Greek *mythology,* any one of the nine goddesses, all daughters of Zeus and Mnemosyne (Memory). They were originally goddesses of memory, after their mother, but each was later identified with a particular *art* or science as the inspirer thereof. The term has general use in referring to the spirit which presides over all artistic and scientific endeavors. Loosely, the 'genius,' spirit or *inspiration* which dominates the poet, dancer, composer, etc., in creative moments. First venerated on Mount Olympus, their activities centered on Mount Helicon. The *paintings* of Herculaneum depicted the *Muses* with their individual *attributes.* The nine were *Calliope* (epic poetry); *Clio* (history); *Euterpe* (lyric poetry); *Thalia* (pastoral comedy); *Urania* (astronomy); *Erato* (erotic poetry); *Polyhymnia* (chant and hymn); *Melpomene* (tragedy); *Terpsichore* (dance). The word *museum* is literally the home or seat of the *Muses,* and the first building so named was erected by Ptolemy at Alexandria, about 300 B.C.

MUSEUM—Establishment for the preservation, study, and exhibition of *artifacts* and *natural* objects. For educational purposes, *museums* make use of reproductions and other *representative* devices, *restorations,* rearrangements, charts, *photographs,* and lectures, along with the display of the objects themselves. The objects are assembled in collections classified by various categories, and are acquired by purchase, gift and bequest, as well as through exploration and excavation. Literally, *museum* means the home or seat of the *Muses,* nine famous daughters of Zeus and Mnemosyne.

MU TAN HUNG—In Chinese *painting,* a pink-colored *pigment* prepared from *yen chih* (q.v.) especially for the painting of peonies; known also as *peony red.*

MUZHIK—The Russian peasant, famous subject of many masterpieces in *painting* and *culpture;* generally represented as a strong, intelligent, loyal man of the soil, invariably bearded. Russian painters specializing in this *theme* include Ilya Repin, Vassili Perov, and Spiro Rossolimo. Sometimes appears as *mujik* or *moujik.*

N

NAGASAKI SCHOOL—A Japanese school of *painting,* named after the city of its origin; emphasis was placed on the imitation of Chinese painting *styles,* materials, and subjects.

NANGA SCHOOL—In Japanese *art,* a style of *painting* depicting *genre* subjects in a manner of Chinese *idealism.* See *Shijo School.*

NAPHTHA—A diluent for *oil* as a *painting medium,* second only to *turpentine* (q.v.). Active on fluid oils, and on *wax* as a solvent, it has little effect upon the *resins* with the exception of *dammar.* It has been known since *ancient* times, although its *value* to the *arts* was not explored until the 19th century, when it became popular in painting.

NAPLES YELLOW—Now rare as a painter's *pigment,* this lead antimoniate was used during the *Middle Ages* and the *Renaissance.* As a *glaze* for *ceramics* it has been familiar to potters since Babylonian and Assyrian times. It is *yellow* to *orange* in *color,* and is made synthetically from the salts of lead and antimony. See *massicot, antimony pigments,* and *yellow pigments.*

NARODNIKI—A Russian *art* movement of the early to mid-19th century, characterized by realistic *painting* strongly tinged with academic romanticism. The school was led by Alexander Ivanov, one of the most talented of Russian artists, an early disciple of *realism.* Creative works of the movement showed an acute observation of nature marked by deep sincerity; many notable BIBLICAL sketches emerged. Nicholas Kramskoy, one of Ivanov's students, broke away in 1872 to form the *Wanderers* (q.v.).

NATIVE PARAFFIN—See *ozokerite.*

NATURAL—In *painting* and *water-color,* the name given to the *color* most closely resembling the skin color of the Caucasian race in temperate zones; formerly known as *carnation* (q.v.). See also *flesh color* and *tan.*

NATURALISM—The doctrine in *art* proposing that nature should be represented objectively, without interpretation, aberration, or editorializing; that any *representation* of the *natural* must appear in such manner that the influence of man is not an obvious feature. Compare with *impressionism* and *illusionism* (qq.v.).

NAVJE—In Russian *mythology,* heaven. Frequently represented in *painting* as a colorful country scene with festive throngs dancing. See also *peklo.*

NAZARENES—A movement of German *painters* in 1809 who sought to establish or renew *art* on the basis of Christian ideals and principles; all were Roman Catholics, holding that art is not essentially a purely creative quality, but should serve the expression of religious ideas. Of brief popularity, the 'school' included Overbeck, Pforr, Philipp Veit, Karl Begas, and Julius Schnorr.

NEEDLE—In *etching,* the name applied to any fine-pointed instrument used in the *drypoint* technique on copper plates.

NEGATIVE CARVING—A *technique* in low and very low *relief* used since the Babylonian era. It is simple reversed *carving* in which the form is cut into a surface instead of projecting upward from a surface, and may be used as a *hollow relief* (q.v.) or as the *mold* for a *bas relief.* Especially suitable for smaller *designs,* it has been used successfully in the creation of *plaques, coins,* and *medals,* and in the carving of *sculptural* designs into *ceramic* molds. The process allows the *sculptor* the quick preparation of *sketches* of large reliefs, for the study of scale, composition, and light and shade. See *hollow relief.*

NEGRO AZULADO—A fine black *painting pigment* made on a carbon base, permanent in its pure state, and blue-black (its name) with a gray *tint* when in admixture with any good white pigment. It is produced by the dry or destructive distillation of vine twigs, grape husks, and even the yeast of spent wine (the carbon exists in the 'tartar'). Although somewhat low in *opacity* and *hiding power,* it *possesses* an usually high degree of *stability,* and is suited to practically all techniques. Known also as *nero bleustro.*

NEGRO DE MARFIL—In *drawing* and *painting,* a fine black *pigment* made by charring chips of *ivory;* commonly known as *ivory black* (q.v.).

NEGRO DE NUESO—In *painting,* a *pigment* of warm brown color, made by the calcining of *ivory* and bone chips. It is not particularly *stable,* and will fade on exposure to light; hence, it is not recommended where permanency is required. However, it gains enormously in admixture with *ivory black* and *burnt umber* (qq.v.), acquiring a high degree of stability that is completely reliable in all painting techniques.

NEN LÜ—In Chinese *painting,* a fine *green* pigment in the *ts'ao lü* class, known in the West as *fresh green.* The color approximates that of *celadon.*

NEO-CLASSIC—A term in *art* and *architecture* applied to the period centering about the turn of the 19th century, representing a reaction to the luxury and elegance of *Louis XV.* There was a suave refining of lines and contrasts, the growth of dignity and simplicity, the stressing of horizontal lines, and a general sincerity in the re-creation of *classic* forms in subdued fashion. In *painting,* subjects went back to heroic events and *mythological* characters of antiquity, along with romantic and academic *representations.* Since little *ancient* painting was known, the *neo-classic* painters imitated antique *sculpture.* In architecture, modified forms of Roman *temples,* bath, *basilicas* and other public structures were adapted to all modern buildings, including schools, churches, banks, *museums,* legislative halls, and dwellings. Any work failing to recapture the classic spirit is *pseudo-classic.* Originated in Germany as *Neuklassik,* and appears to have been induced by the discovery of Pompeian art in the 18th century.

NEO-IMPRESSIONISM—A *painting* style of the 1880's, incorporating the *paint*-applying *technique* and rainbow *brilliance* of the *colors* of *impressionism,* but stressing *design* and personal *emotion* rather than impressionist objectivity, and emphasizing the use of *line, form* and color as a psychological science. It is essentially a variety of *post-impressionism* (q.v.).

NEO-PLASTICISM—A Dutch *geometric-abstract* movement in *sculpture, painting,* interior *decoration* and poster *design,* founded in 1920 by Piet Mondrain as a phase of *de Stijl* (q.v.).

NEO-ROMANTICISM—The movement of the 1890's which developed into *expressionism.* Irrational in its orientation, it contained two opposing forms: (1) *estheticism,* aristocratic aloofness, decadence, and escapism; (2) the worship of strength, heroism, blood, soil, and race. Both, however, emphasized *imagination, color,* the dream, and the music of words. Originated in Germany as *Neuromantik.*

NEO-TRADITIONALISM—An *art* movement developed by Gauguin in the late 1880's, better known as *synthetism* (q.v.).

NEPHRITE—In *carving,* an unusually hard variety of *greenstone* found in some of the South Pacific islands. Used extensively in *Maori carving* (q.v.) with *totara wood* as the principal *medium. Nephrite* was the material used in the making of practically all the cutting tools employed by the *Maoris.*

NERO-ANTICO—In *sculpture,* (1) specifically, a highly polished block of fine black *marble* found among the fragments of certain ancient Roman ruins; never *carved,* although apparently intended therefor; (2) generally, any variety of black marble found at the ruins of Cape Taenarus, Greece, and used today in sculpture.

NERO BLEUSTRO—A term in *painting;* see *negro azulado.*

NERO D'AVOIRO—In *painting* and *drawing,* a fine black *pigment* made by charring chips of *ivory.* Commonly known as *ivory black* (q.v.).

NEST SAUCERS—In *painting,* a series of small scoop-shaped trays with flat bottoms, used for the mixing and blending of *colors;* name derives from the fact that they stack neatly into each other perpendicularly when not in use. A more practical device employed for the same purpose is the *well slab* (q.v.).

NEUTRAL COLOR—(1) A term denoting any *color,* the *hue* of which is broken because it absorbs the reflected colors of the objects surrounding it. Compare with *positive color.* (2) Any color which will not clash with a mixture of *black* and *white;* any hue sympathetic to *gray.*

NEUTRALIZING HARMONY— In *painting,* the addition of *gray* to two or more *colors,* creating a certain subtle harmony which causes the original colors to recede in prominence; produced by an admixture of *complementary colors.*

NEUWIED BLUE—A *painting pigment* of fine *sky-blue* color, commonly known as *mountain blue* (q.v.).

NIGGLING—In *art,* a term describing minute and exceedingly careful workmanship, especially on unimportant detail.

NIGHT BLUE—In *painting,* the name popularly applied to any *blue* that is completely devoid of *violet,* and retains a true blue color in artificial light. Compare with *parma blue.*

NIGHT PIECE—In *painting,* the term commonly applied to any *picture* representing a scene at night.

NIHIL ALBUM—A term in *painting;* see *zinc oxide.*

NIMAI TSUZUKI—In Japanese *art,* same as *diptych* (q.v.).

NIMBUS—A circular *halo,* or soft, misted light emanating from and surrounding the head of a sacred figure, indicating divine *attribute.* Not synonymous with the *aureole,* which surrounds the entire figure, nor the *mandorla,* which effuses from the entire figure in pure oval shape. Used widely in *medieval art,* though rarely to be found thereafter. Occasionally square in shape.

NIPOCER—A tan-colored synthetic *wax* used chiefly as a *surface film* or coating on *paintings* and *statuary;* blends readily with *Japan wax, paraffin, beeswax* and *carnauba,* creating emulsions that are remarkably *stable* to light, heat and air. It is made in chemical combination of a number of freely available raw materials, *nipocer* being a trade name.

NISE—In Japanese *art,* the general term applied to any type of *portrait painting.*

NISHIKI—In *weaving,* a variety of rich *brocade* made in Japan; also, a *color print.* Hence, any 'brocaded' or colorful *picture.*

NOBLE SERPENTINE—In *sculpture,* a variety of rich, dark-green *marble* of the *serpentine* (q.v.) family. Considered one of the rare minerals, it is sufficiently hard to take a high polish; it is *translucent* and often contains imbedded *garnets* which form red spots and add to the surface beauty. Known also as *precious serpentine.*

NOIR BELGE—In *sculpture,* the finest black *marble* known, occurring in Belgium and known also as *Black Belgian;* prized for its compactness, hardness, and the fact that it is responsive to a high polish. It is dense black without veins or other discoloration. Its one drawback is in its inherent tendency to *fracture* in *conchoidal* lines under the chisel; great care must be exercised in this regard, and the marble is not recommended for beginners.

NOIR DE VIGNE—A fine black *pigment* having a carbon base, produced by the dry or destructive distillation of vine twigs, grape husks, and even the yeast of spent wine (the carbon exists in the 'tartar'). A pure gray *tint* with a bluish *tinge* is obtained when it is mixed with any good white pigment. Although somewhat low in *opacity* and *hiding power,* it possesses an unusually high degree of *stability,* and is suited to practically all techniques. Known also as *noire bleuâtre.*

NOIR D'IVORIE—In *painting* and *drawing,* a fine black *pigment* made by charring chips of *ivory;* commonly known as *ivory black* (q.v.).

NOIRE BLEUÂTRE—See *noir de vigne.*

NON-CREEP—Any one of a number of liquids produced in a variety of *colors,* a few drops of which are added to a substantial quantity of *Chinese ink, water-color,* etc., to make it adhere evenly to any *waxed* or *glazed* surface; used also in *retouch varnishes.* Gives complete and *opaque* coverage over all types of *grounds* if properly prepared.

NON-DRYING OIL—See *plasticizer.*

NON-OBJECTIVE PAINTING—First used in Russia by Alexander Rodchenko, and developed in 1913 by Kasimir Malevich who was the first to concentrate on entirely *abstract, non-objective paintings.* The *artists* partaking of this movement used their *line, color* and *medium* not to portray any event, historical scene, *still life, portrait,* etc., but to create freely, following their intuition without the introduction of *light* and *shadow, perpective, texture,* psychological features, or resemblance. The movement, still strong in 1950, found many American abstract artists turning to *Non-Objectivity.* The Russians frequently termed the school *Suprematism* (q.v.).

NORDIC STYLE—The term used to describe the *art* of Teutonic, Celtic, Anglo-Saxon and other northern barbaric peoples of the *Middle Ages,* characterized in style by a dynamic, linear *Expressionism* often suggesting a chained or suppressed energy. In subject matter it exhibited a preference for animal *motives.* It contrasts stylistically with Latin *Illusionism* (q.v.) and with *Byzantine* symmetrical *design,* proportion, restraint and *balance.* In Nazi Germany the term *Nordic* was misused in art to describe 19th century international *Naturalism* and *Popular Romanticism* (qq.v.) which the Nazis erroneously considered the native racial style of their local ancestors.

NORMAL BUTYRIC—A colorless liquid used as an ingredient in the making of clear *lacquers* and *surface films;* possesses a high degree of *stability.*

NOTAN—In Japanese *art,* the general term applied to *light* and *shade* as affecting *paintings.*

NOTE—In *painting,* an *artist's* rough *sketch,* especially of a detail.

NUERNBERGER VIOLET—In *painting,* one of the fine *manganese pigments* (q.v.).

NUMIDIAN MARBLE—In *sculpture,* a general name given to a wide variety of celebrated *marbles* of cream, yellow, red and pink colors, found chiefly in northern Africa. Most experts believe the name to be incorrect, since the true source of the stone is not the province of Numidia, but rather Mauritania. The quarries were first worked by the ancient Romans.

NUNOME—In *painting, ceramics,* etc., any pattern made up of small nodules simulating the *texture* of regular *weaving* or of a woven surface.

NUREMBERG SCHOOL—A private *art* academy founded by Joachim Nutzel in 1662 in order that the youth, especially underprivileged children, might learn the art of *drawing* and establish Nuremberg as a future *culture* center. Many *painters* of international reputation joined the faculty. It became a public institution later in the century, dedicated to the purposes of its origin, and has gained world-wide fame through its motives and accomplishments.

NYMPHS—In Greek *mythology* and in world-wide *painting* and *sculpture,* the lithe, graceful female sprites who are sportive and gay, usually friendly, but occasionally destructive. They reside in various natural objects, as springs, lakes, trees, mountains, etc., and possess certain divine gifts such as prophecy; they are long-lived, though not inmortal.

O

OBAN—In Japanese *art,* a rather larger *print,* approximating 15 inches by 10 inches in size.

OBLIQUE DRAWING—A *drawing* executed on three axes: similar to an *isometric drawing* except that one axis is drawn horizontally, one vertically, and one at an angle. Measurements are laid out along these axes representing the length, breadth and thickness of the object. See *isometric drawing* except that one axis is drawn horizontally, one vertically, and one at an angle. Measurements are laid out along these axes representing the length, breadth and thickness of the object. See *isometric drawing* and *cabinet drawing.*

OBVERSE—(1) The front, or main face of any two-sided object of *art;* the side bearing the principal *design* or *motif.* (2) Any object whose top is narrower than its base; e.g., an uppointed leaf represented in *painting, sculpture,* etc.

OCCULT LINES—In *drawing,* a term applied to the lines that are used in the original construction of the project, but do not appear in the finished work.

O CHIAO—In Chinese *painting,* a famous *glue* made by boiling donkey skins, used as a *surface film.* Other fine glues of ancient and modern China include *tung-o hsien* (or *tunga*), *kuangtung,* and *kuang chiao*; the last is almost odorless and colorless, and possesses remarkable *stability.*

OCHRE—A *painting* term embracing a wide range of *colors,* all of them natural *earth hues,* called *red-ochre, yellow-ochre, brown-ochre,* etc. All are *clay* mixtures, owing their color to iron oxide. As a *painter's pigment, ochre* has been known since prehistoric times. Also spelled *ocher,* it is a pulverulent iron oxide of impure state. Brown and yellow *ochres* consist of limonite (or geothite) in combination with red *ochre* of *hematite.* The term is applied generally to any natural earth mixture used as a pigment.

ODIN—Norse god to whom the warriors appeal for help, occasionally receiving human sacrifices. Under Christian influence he is also honored as the creator and director of the world, a sky-god, and an all-father god; his omens are carried by wolves and ravens. In his numerous representations in the *arts* (esp. *painting* and *sculpture*) he is generally shown riding a gray horse, wearing a long cloak, and carrying a spear. Also *Odhin.*

ODYSSEUS—Leading Greek hero of the Trojan War (Latin *Ulysses*), famous for his wit, wisdom and endurance as told in Homer's ODYSSEY. His exploits were often pictured in Greek *vase paintings,* as well as in post-*classical sculpture.*

OFFICIAL SCHOOL—In Chinese *painting,* the term applied during the late CH'ING DYNASTY to a style of representation characterized by impeccable observance of forms, rules and customs, completely devoid of individuality or invention. Properly known as *yüan t'i* (q.v.).

OIL—See *oils.*

OIL COLOR—Any *pigment* that has been ground in *linseed oil* or *poppy oil,* the latter producing the finer artist's colors. The term is popularly interchanged with *tube color* (q.v.).

OILING OUT—In *painting,* the technique of rubbing a thin coating of *drying oil* over the parts of the picture intended to be retouched. The slight *film* left behind takes a fresh *pigment* more readily than a perfectly dry surface would.

OIL OF ANTS—In the making of artist's *lacquers, resins, varnishes,* and *surface films,* a colorless liquid which has a tendency to become faintly *amber* upon exposure to light and air. The pale *hue* is often desired as a softening device over an *oil painting.*

OIL PAINTING—(1) The *art* of *painting* with *pigments* mixed with a *drying oil* (as *linseed oil, poppy-seed oil,* etc.) Oleoresinous *varnishes* to protect painted surfaces had been used prior to the 15th century, at which time the invention of a dry, colorless, and sufficiently liquid vehicle (as one of the above *oils*) came about, attributed to the noted Flemish painter Van Eyck. (2) Any picture painted in *oil-colors;* any painting executed with a *pigment* made by grinding a coloring substance in oil; in medieval times, by the *muller* and *grinding slab* (qq.v.), and later by the *color mill. Oil paintings* are most commonly rendered on *canvas* which has been stretched on a frame and covered with a *size* containing *white lead.*

OILS—The general term embracing all vegetable *oils* used chiefly as *surface films* and *painting mediums,* especially the *linseed, poppy-seed* and *walnut oils,* capable of drying or forming a firm and hardened *film* on exposure to air. Known from the early 15th century, there is extensive evidence pointing to their use prior to that time in European painting. The Far East never showed active interest in *oils,* although rare examples, e.g., the *representations* on the doors of the *Tamamushi Shrine* at Nara, Japan, indicate that *drying oils* were known to the Orient. Care must be exercised in the use of *oils;* too little renders the paint brittle, and too much may bring about early yellowing. See *drying oils.*

OIL VARNISH—In *painting* and *sculpture,* a coating or *surface film* that contains *resin* and *drying* oil as the basic *film*-forming ingredients, and is converted (after application) to a solid protective shell or film. See *resin.*

OITICICA OIL—A substance having extensive use as a *drying oil* (q.v.) in *paints,* and as a substitute for *tung oil* in all of its uses in the *arts.* Occurs in three forms: (1) a white or cream-colored semi-liquid crude oil; (2) an *amber*-colored viscous fluid; (3) a clear light oil mixed with mineral spirits.

OLD GOLD—In Chinese *painting,* a fine *gray-green* pigment known natively as *ts'ang lü,* used most frequently in representing tree leaves at the time of the first frost, mountain slopes in early autumn, and roads and paths. Prepared by mixing *ts'ao lü* with *chê shih* (qq.v.).

OLD GREEN—In Chinese *painting,* a prized *green* pigment known natively as *lao lü,* prepared from *ts'ao lü* (q.v.).

OLD MASTERS—In *painting,* popular term applied to the great *artists,* esp. of Italy and the Low Countries, who executed their works between the 15th and 16th centuries; also the paintings themselves.

OLEIC ACID—Colorless crystals, soluble in ether and benzene but insoluble in alcohol, used in *painting* as a *siccative* and in *textile* processing as a water-proofing agent.

OLEORESIN—The term applied in the *fine arts* to a natural *balsam* or soft semi-liquid which exudes from coniferous trees; employed as an ingredient in *surface films* and in *painting media.* The best known are *Venice turpentine, Strasbourg turpentine, Canada balsam,* and *Copaiba balsam,* and all are likely to form dark, brittle *film* on long standing. The term is also applied to various combinations of *oil* and *resin.*

OLIVE GREEN—In *painting,* a color made by mixtures of several other colors, varying in *shade* according to the type and proportion of the ingredients employed. The *hue* is basically a deep green with a brownish or yellowish *tinge.* If a *lake color* is desired, a mixture of transparent browns and blues is used; where *opacity* is required, a *chrome* or *cadmium* yellow in combination with *indigo, Prussian blue* or *ultramarine* will yield an *olive green* of good color and body.

OLIVE PIT TECHNIQUE—In Chinese *painting,* a brush stroke technique creating lines having the appearance of strung-out olive pits in a series; actually, it is a series of connected *tien* (q.v.), fine at the ends and thick at the centers, though not as pointed as *liu yeh miao* (q.v.). A large, stiff-pointed *brush* is used with a zizag motion, with the brush brought up promptly at the end of each stroke.

OLMEC—A term originally applied to peoples inhabiting southeastern Vera Cruz, and at one time, central Mexico. No *arts or crafts* have as yet been surely identified as their work, but the term has been tentatively applied to highly stylized *sculptures* of men and tiger gods found in southern and central Mexico.

OLTREMARE—In *painting,* the famous blue *pigment* popularly known as *ultramarine* (q.v.).

ONE-POINT DRAWING—A *drawing* in which the object presented is viewed in such manner that one face is parallel to the front plane. In this style of *perspective,* the horizontal lines of the front plane remain parallel, but the lines of all planes perpendicular to it meet at one point. Known also as *parallel perpective drawing.*

ONYCHITE—In *sculpture,* a variety of *alabaster* or calcite (*stalagmite*) with yellow and brown veins. Used by the ancients for the *carving* of *vases* and *statuettes.*

ONYX MARBLE—In *sculpture* and *architecture,* a type of calcite somewhat resembling true *onyx* in appearance, used for *carving* and as an ornamental stone. It is usually found in *stalactite* and *stalagmite* formations, its chief source at the present time. It is a material of great beauty, and was used by the ancients for making small *vases* for containing precious liquids; it was the alabastrite of the Romans, and is sometimes referred to as *Oriental alabaster.* The lost ancient quarries were rediscovered in Egypt in 1850, and furnished a quantity of *onyx marble* since. A similar stone, known as *Mexican onyx* or *Tecalli marble,* was discovered in Mexico in the late 19th century, and supplies of it have been sent to the U. S. and elsewhere.

OPACITY—The state or quality of being *opaque;* neither *transparent* nor *translucent;* of such material, *color, texture* or finish that light, in any form, cannot penetrate. *Wood* and *metal* normally possesses *opacity; glass* normally does not. In *painting,* the term is applied to any *pigment* or other *medium* possessing a high degree of *hiding power* (q.v.), i.e., the power to conceal the *ground* or undercoating.

OPAQUE—Of such nature that wave motions (usually *light*) cannot pass through. Any substance not *transparent* or *translucent.* Also, a variety of *water-color.* See *gouache* and *opacity.*

OPAQUE WHITE—A white *drawing* fluid possessing a remarkable degree of *hiding power* and *stability,* used chiefly in corrective work. It will completely cover *Chinese* or *India ink,* restoring the white *ground* for further *paint* or *ink* work. Will adhere well to any type of surface.

OPHITE—In *sculpture,* a variety of *marble* to which a green color has been imparted by the presence of *serpentine.* As *ophicalcite,* the term has reference to a crystalline form of *limestone* that has been spotted by serpentine. The word *ophiolite* is employed by some authorities in describing the entire classification of all serpentines.

OPPOSITION—A term in *dance* applied to the means by which the body is rendered more plastic by contrast of its members arranged in *asymmetrical* balance; e.g., the left arm and leg do not move together, but rather the left arm and the right leg. This *opposition* is also the basis for the *natural,* unconscious human walk which effects a mechanical *balance* of weight whereby the body manages to remain in equilibrium despite shifts of its center of gravity. From this essential principle, opposition further consciously enhances and emphasizes the normal elegance of the body. In *sculpture* of the *baroque,* the Italian term *Contrapposto* expresses the same idea in static version.

ORANGE—A bright *color* placing itself between *yellow* and *red* in the *spectrum;* any of the numerous *hues* made up in varying mixtures of red and yellow. The color of the fruit bearing the name.

ORANT—(1) In ancient *art,* a female figure in an attitude of prayer; a female adorant. Such *figures* are commonly distinguished or indicated by the raising of the hand and arm or forearm, with the palm outward, as well as by the smaller size of the *orants* when divinities are represented in the same scene. (2) In early Christian art, a female figure standing with arms outspread or slightly raised in prayer, *symbolizing* the church as engaged in adoration or intercession. Such figures are frequently found as *paintings* in the *catacombs,* and some have been regarded as *representations* of the Virgin Mary.

ORGANIC COLORS—A broad term embracing all *pigments* deriving from animal and vegetable dyestuff.

ORIENTAL ALABASTER—A term in *sculpture;* see *onyx marble.*

ORMOLU—(1) An imitation *gold,* made of *zinc* and *copper* in *alloy.* Scaly in appearance, it was used widely in France in the 18th and early 19th centuries as a decorative accessory to *furniture* and as a *gilding* agent. Also known as *mosaic gold,* it is now employed in the making of *costume jewelry,* chandeliers, and other ornamental objects. (2) *Gold leaf* that has been ground for use as a *pigment* for *bronzes, brasses,* and other materials amenable to gilding.

ORPHEUS—The greatest of Greek musicians, founder of the ORPHIC MYSTERIES which promised worshippers a blessed immortality; famous also for his tragic attempt to bring his wife *Eurydice* back from Hades. In *ancient art* he was frequently *represented* on *vase-paintings;* in *music* there is the excellent ORPHEUS IN HADES; among the post-*classical sculptors* who used him as a subject were Rodin, Crawford, Gregory, Stewart, and Carl Milles.

ORPHISM—A French school of *painting* in the early 20th century, known later as *simultaneism.* It taught a lyrical *color* expression that extended into *cubism* (q.v.), producing a *prismatic* effect by separate coloring of the innumerable *geometric* planes in enormous pictures. Known also as the *Synchromist School,* it was essentially an *abstract* style founded in Paris by Apollinaire (1912) who called it "An art of pure musical lyricism of color."

ORPIMENT—Known also as *king's yellow,* a painters' *pigment* widely used in *ancient* and *medieval* times, identified on many *illuminated manuscripts* of the *Middle Ages* and *Renaissance.* It is closely related to the *orange*-colored *realgar* (q.v.), and is a *natural,* crystalline, *yellow* sulphide of arsenic, occurring as a deposit in Macedonia, Asia Minor, Hungary, and in various points of Central Asia. Sometimes referred to as *Chinese yellow;* see also *shih huang.*

ORTHOGRAPIC PROJECTION—In *drawing,* the technique of projecting accurate outlines of views of an object and properly arranging them. This method may best be explained through a process of *tracing* views of an object on the sides of a transparent box, and then manipulating the sides of the box (and consequently the traced views) in a mechanical fashion, simulating the theory controlling the location and arrangement of the views necessary to present a picture of the object.

OSIRIS—In the religion of *ancient* Egypt, the god of the underworld and judge of the dead. The husband of *Isis,* he was the enemy of his brother *Set* (q.v.), the god of evil. *Osiris* is the father of every king of Egypt, and is pictured in the *arts* (esp. *painting*) seated on a throne with a *scepter* and scourge in his hand. In *sculpture,* he is usually represented as a *mummy* wearing the plume-flanked *crown* of Upper Egypt.

OSTWALD SYSTEM—A *color*-identifying process whereby all *stimuli of color vision* (q.v.) are arranged and described in terms of *hue,* full color, *white* content, and *black* content. The system is aided by a device consisting of a color-solid formed by two squatty cones joined at their bases, upon which 24 selected 'foundation' hues are arranged at the equator, with *gradations* extending to black at the lower apex and white at the upper. See also *Munsell System.*

OTSU SCHOOL—Name applied to a Japanese group fostering a crude style of *painting;* was one of the steps in the creation of the *Ukiyoye School* (q.v.).

OTTONIAN ART—A period in German *art* reaching roughly from 919 to 1024 while the German Saxon kings reigned. Starting in late *Carolingian* style, the transition to true German came under Henry II. In *architecture,* the best examples of the period are the *cathedrals* of Mainz, Worms, Essen, and Augsburg. In *painting,* the style was one of dynamic and dramatic *expression* and considerable time and effort went into the making of some excellent *Evangeliars* (q.v.) under the supervision of the Archbishop of Trier. *Sculpture* was concerned especially with *reliefs* made of *metal, ivory, stone* and *wood,* many showing late Carolingian characteristics. One of the most famous treasures of the *Middle Ages* is the *Ottonian* crown of the German emperors, re-made by Konrad II in 1025.

OUTLINE VIGNETTE—A term in *etching;* see *half-tone, vignette.*

OUTREMER—In *painting,* the famous blue *pigment* popularly known as *ultramarine* (q.v.).

OXFORD OCHER—In *painting,* a variety of native *ocher* found near Oxford, England. It is the purest and best type of *yellow ocher* known. Sometimes referred to as *stone ocher.*

OXGALL—A fine yellowish powder added in minute quantity to any coloring matter having unusually thin consistency (e.g., *inks,* certain *paints,* etc.). Gives the liquid a clinging quality which permits it to spread and adhere to the *ground* without bubbling or running.

OYSTER WHITE—In *painting,* the shell of any mollusk ground to fine powder, mixed with *lime* to create a type of *plaster* used as the undersurface for *fresco* (q.v.) work. It is believed that the Orientals burned the shells (under control) prior to pulverizing them.

OZOKERITE—A natural, *wax*-like substance, yellow-brown to green or black in color, possessing a greasy 'feel' in its pure, *translucent* state; used as a *surface film* or coating over *paintings* and *statuary,* and as a successful substitute for *beeswax* and *carnauba* (qq.v.) in all their uses in the *arts.* Known also as *native paraffan.*

P

PAGODA STONE—A variety of Chinese *limestone* which, when cut sectionally, shows certain natural figures fancifully likened to *pagodas;* these markings are due to the *fossil* content.

PAGODITE—A variety of soft stone (pinite or *agalmatolite)* out of which the Chinese *carve* figures of *pagodas,* idols, etc. Not synonymous with (or even resembling) *pagoda stone.*

PAINT—Usually a *liquid,* containing a *pigment* (any colored material) in a state of suspension. After application to a surface, evaporation and hardening take place, the pigment remaining as a skin. Ingredients of *paint* in addition to the pigment are usually *linseed oil,* a thinner such as *turpentine* or other volatile liquid, and a *drier* (see *siccative)* to accelerate the hardening of the linseed oil and pigment. The linseed oil operates as a *binder.* The term may be defined simply as a mixture of pigment with vehicle, intended to be spread in thin coats for decoration, protection, or both.

PAINT CONFIGURATION—In *painting,* a term having reference to the high and low, or *plastic* aspects of the surface; see *impasto* and *pastose.*

PAINTED GLASS—A variety of ornamental *glass* painted in vitrifiable *pigments* or *enamels;* often used colloquially to include colored or *stained glass,* and compositions of such glass. Many authorities consider *painted glass* a more important formative principle of *Gothic architecture* than the *pointed arch,* as e.g., J. Fergusson in his HISTORY OF ARCHITECTURE, I, 526. See *glass-painting.*

PAINTED PANEL—See *panel.*

PAINTER—An *artist;* one employing *paint* as the *medium* in *decorative* or *creative* work, whether professional or *amateur.*

PAINTERLY—A theory in *art* emphasizing the rendition of masses and their relation to light, appearing as *color, tone, shade* or *shadow,* as distinguished from the *linear,* which stresses the expression of *forms* or ideas by lines, with the main accent on the *contour.* It is termed *painterly* because it indicates more the painter's handling of color or *brush* than the *linear,* which refers to the act of *drawing,* and not coloring.

PAINTER'S ETCHING—Term applied to an *etching* which in first conception, composition, delineation, and mechanical execution is entirely the work of one *artist,* as distinguished from an etching executed by one artist after a design or picture by another.

PAINTER STAINER—In *heraldry,* the name given the *artist* who restricts his work to the *painting* of *coats-of-arms* (q.v.). Does not appear to have existed outside of England.

PAINTING—The *art* of laying *colors* or *paints* on *canvas, panels* or other *supports,* forming figures, objects and scenes intended to be *represented* to the eye; the art of forming a colored likeness upon a flat surface. Also, the *picture* itself; any likeness or resemblance in color. The three basic materials required are, a colored powder, a liquid adhesive, and a support; the accessories usually include *brush, pen, palette knife, model, varnish, stretcher* and *frame.* Charles Marriot defines *painting* as "primarily the characteristic use of materials. The representation of nature and direct action of design are both incidental to that." This appears to support the doctrine "an artist cannot exceed his materials." The most popular method of *painting* at the present time is in *oil,* first made practicable in the 15th century and quickly adopted in Italy and north Europe. Next in popularity is the *water-color* (at least until recently), and it appears that *tempera* may be replacing it. See *oils* and *oil painting.*

PAINTING—In the making of *stained glass* (q.v.), the process following directly upon that of *waxing-up* (q.v.). Using a *pigment* of one *color,* consisting of powdered *glass* melted and mixed with copper and iron oxide, desired detail and shading are applied to the stained glass.

PAINT MILL—A term applied by artists to any device, manual or mechanical, with which mineral substances are ground into *pigment.*

PAINT-OUT—In *painting,* a sample dab of *color,* applied to a part of the *palette* or other convenient surface, to test the mixture prior to its use on the painting itself.

PAINT PROCESS—See *silk screen stencil.*

PAINT SCREEN PROCESS—See *silk screen stencil.*

PAI WÊN—In Chinese *art,* an *intaglio seal* or *yin chang* so arranged with respect to color that the raised characters imprint white against a background of red. Known also as *yang wên.* The *vermilion pigment* used for this purpose is known as *yin sê.*

PALAPORE—A *painted* or *printed* wall-hanging or bed cover, usually of *cotton* (q.v.). Reached high popularity in the 18th century. Inexpensive East Indian prints are used in large quantities throughout the world today. Named for *Palanpur,* India.

PALETTE—Figuratively, the system of *color* employed by a *painter* in a given work, or in his usual style of coloring. Literally, any surface on which *paint* is mixed in actual *painting* processes. The typical *palette* is a thin piece of hardwood, with a *handle* or *thumb-hole* providing easy grip. The paint, ordinarily in an *oil medium,* is disposed in small lumps around the edge, and mixtures are made toward the center. Modern *palettes* are made also of steel, aluminum, *plastics,* and other substances. See *disposable palette.*

PALETTE KNIFE—According to modern usage in *painting,* a spatula with a thin, rounded, flexible blade, used for mixing the paste-like *oil paint* and placing it on the *palette.* The *palette knife* of the *Renaissance,* frequently *represented* in paintings of that period, was usually of heavy blade and pointed. It was probably not designed specifically for the purpose to which it is now put. Many of today's *palette knives* are somewhat trowel-shaped.

PALETTE KNIFE WORK—In *painting,* the popular term applied to the technique of laying thick, lumpy colors on the *canvas;* properly known as *impasto* (q.v.).

PALLADIUM—Any *statue* or other *image* of the goddess *Pallas* (q.v.); in *art* and *legend,* any such *xoanon* image. On the preservation of such an image, according to the legend, depended the safety of Troy.

PALLAS—In Greek *mythology,* the goddess of wisdom and war, identified fully as *Pallas Athene.* Known to the Romans as *Minerva,* she was also the goddess of the liberal *arts.* She was represented in *painting* and *sculpture* with a serious, majestic countenance, armed with helmet, shield and spear, and wearing long, full drapery. See *palladium.*

PANEL—In *painting,* the term applied to an early variety of *support,* usually of *wood.* The great bulk of European *easel* painting from early Christian times until the mid-17th century was executed on such supports. Large *panels* were made of many pieces of wood joined together with *dowels* and frequently with *cross battens* for added strength. The kinds of wood varied regionally, *oak* and *pine* being common in the north, and *poplar, lime, willow* and *nutwood* in Italy.

PANGANI—One of the finest varieties of *ivory* known, used chiefly for *carving.* It has unusually fine grain, is hard and heavy, responds well to polishing, and does not *fracture* under the carver's tools. Known also as *green ivory,* it comes from the region of Pangani on the east coast of Africa.

PANNETIERS GREEN—In *paintings,* one of the finest and most brilliant greens on the artist's *palette;* now commonly known as *Guignet green* (q.v.).

PANTOGRAPH—In *drawing,* an instrument operated by a system of levers, used for the mechanical copying, *tracing* or cutting of a *design* or drawing, usually with a change of scale. It generally consists of four rods or arms held together by adjustable pins. Two points of this frame move in unison if a third point is held stationary, and when one of the two points is moved over the *pattern,* a *pen, pencil* or cutting tool at the other point will reproduce the *illustration.*

PAPER—A substance made from *wood,* rags, or other fibrous matter, usually prepared in the form of sheets for receiving *drawing, writing, printing, etc.* As a *support* for *paintings, prints* and *drawings,* it is found in the earliest recorded history of *art* in the Far East. The Chinese were manufacturing *paper* in the 2nd century A.D., and the *technique* was well established in Europe in the 12th century, resulting in the displacement of *parchment.* Oriental *paper* seems to have been made directly from plant *fiber,* while in Europe it was made from the fibers of *cotton* and *linen* rags; both varieties were made by hand. Machine-made *pulp paper* appeared at the end of the 18th century, displacing the *rag product* for less important work. It is weaker and more apt to discolor than that made from rags, but it varies in strength and stability according to the method of manufacture.

PAPYRUS—The forerunner of *paper.* It was an ancient writing material developed in Egypt and made largely in the Nile delta, from at least the time of the Old Kingdom. It was formed directly from the reed CYPERUS PAPYRUS of Linnaeus. Strips of the cut *reed* were placed across each other at right angles, soaked, pounded flat, and dried in the sun. By the 10th century A.D. paper had replaced it completely. See *tchama, rotulus,* and *biblion.*

PARALLEL PERSPECTIVE—A term in *drawing;* see *one-point drawing.*

PARDO VANDYCK—In *painting,* the rich brown *pigment* commonly known as *Van Dyke brown* (q.v.).

PARIAN MARBLE—The finest *marble* known to the Greeks for *sculpture,* used as the *medium* for their best *statues.* Quarried on the island of Paros, it has coarse crystals which absorb and reflect the light, giving a remarkably lively, *luminous* glow to the surface. Consequently, it is unexcelled for the *representation* of vitality and sensuous charm.

PARIAN PORCELAIN—A fine, natural variety of very

hard *porcelain,* used more in *sculpture* than in *ceramics,* principally for the *carving* of *statuettes* and *bas-reliefs;* so-called because of its resemblance to the famous *Parian* marble.

PARIS BLUE—The first *blue pigment* to be made synthetically on a large scale, betetr known as *Prussian blue* (q.v.). See also *cobalt blue.*

PARIS GREEN—In *painting,* a bright bluish-green *pigment* commonly known as *emerald green* (q.v.).

PARIS WHITE—A natural substance occurring as a white, *amorphous* powder, having extensive use in *painting, gilding and ceramics.* Better known as *whiting* (q.v.).

PARMA BLUE—In *painting,* a fine *blue pigment* characterized by a decided *violet* tone whih keeps it from the *night blue* (q.v.) classification.

PARMAZO MARBLE—In *sculpture,* a variety of white *marble* traversed by a coarse network or veining of dark lines. Occurs chiefly in northern Italy.

PARQUETAGE DE CHAMP—A *technique* employed in the *restoration* of *panel paintings* whereby thin stationary strips were placed edgewise on the back of the *panel,* with the narrow edge affixed to the panel with *glue.* This method prevented the characteristic buckling that occurred when a solid new backing was applied, and it appears to be replacing the *cradling* (q.v.) technique.

PARSUNA—In Russian *oil painting,* the general term applied to all 17th century *portraits,* usually representing highly-placed persons.

PARTHENON—A magnificent Greek structure used as a *temple,* dedicated to *Athena,* whose *ivory and gold chryselephantine,* forty feet high, occupied the center of the *cella.* The tremendous cult *statue* (as well as the *frieze*) was executed by Phidias. Part of the frieze, known as the *Elgin Marbles,* has been in the British Museum since 1816. The *Parthenon* was begun in 447 B.C. and completed in 438 B.C.; located on the *acropolis* at Athens.

PASITELEAN SCHOOL—An important school of ancient Greek *sculpture,* founded by Pasiteles in Rome toward the close of the republic, and continuing to flourish under the early empire. The school was *archaistic,* seeking inspiration in the works of the powerful Hellenic artists who preceded the bloom of *art* in the 5th century; but with its studied archaism in proportions, attitudes and types, it combined careful work from the living *model.* Surviving works of the followers of Pasiteles exhibit genuine merit and charm, and rise above the feeble imitations of the later Hellenistic sculptors. An excellent specimen is the *statue* ORESTE AND ELECTRA, now in the Museo Nazionale, Naples.

PASTE BLUE—In *painting,* the term applied to *Prussian blue* when it is in a thick or pasty state, requiring the addition of a thinner to render it brushable.

PASTEL—In *painting,* (1) any of the pale *hues,* as light *pink, blue, yellow,* etc.; (2) a type of painting made with *crayon* pigment in combination with *resin* or *gum. Pastel colors* are made up of finely-ground pigments having a small quantity of binding medium to hold the particles together. They allow soft effects, retain their freshness, and permit the artist to continue his work in various colors without waiting for any to dry. However, they cannot be mixed on a *palette,* and are blended on the painting itself. This requires a far larger assortment of *tints* and *shades* than *oil* paints or other color *mediums.* It is a permanent form of painting.

PASTEL PAPER—A variety of *paper,* either rough or velvety in finish, used as a *ground* for *pastel* painting. Heavy weight and possessing 'depth,' it has high rag content and is generally *deckle*-edged.

PASTOSE—In *painting,* the technique of applying the colors in thick layers; also, any painting featuring such work. Some artists apply their colors *pastosely.* Loosely synonymous with *impasto* (.v.).

PATENT YELLOW—In *painting,* a popular clear, golden *yellow color,* used as a *pigment;* known also as *cassel yellow.*

PATINA—A green encrustation formed on the surface of old *bronze* by oxidation, often deemed ornamental; any surface calcification indicating substantial age.

PATRON—One who supports and/or encourages a person or a work; one who finds favor with a *style, artist,* or *art* project, as a *patron* of *modern art,* etc.

PAVONAZZA—In *sculpture,* a type of *limestone* possessing various shades of green, blue or gray, alternating with bands of white; so called because of its resemblance to the plumage of the peacock. Formerly much used in southern Italy. Known also as *pavonazetta marble* and *Phrygian marble.*

PAYNE's GRAY—A famous *pigment* on the artist's *palette,* in particular demand by *water-colorists.* Made by proper mixing of *ivory black* (q.v.) with several *ultramarines.* When carefully combined, the result is a thoroughly *stable* and permanent *gray* pigment. Known also as *gris de payne* and *grigio di payne.*

PAYSAGE—In *painting,* any *landscape* picture.

PEACH BLACK—In *painting,* a variety of *lamp black* that is unusually *stable* and reliable in all techniques; may be used safely in mixture with other good *pigments.*

PEDESTAL—The *base* for a *column, statue,* etc. Usually circular, square, or rectangular; rarely polygonal.

PEKING BLUE—In Chinese *painting,* a famous deep *blue* mineral *pigment* obtained from the bottom layer of the *azurite* stone when it is rubbed down in water. Frequently used on the back of *silk* paintings to intensify the *brilliance* of the surface tone, it is also used in fine outline and filling-in work in connection with leaves and foliage. Known natively at *t'ou ch'ing;* see *shih ch'ing.*

PEKLO—In Russian *mythology,* hell. Frequently represented in *painting* as a dark, misty cavern inhabited by *legendary* monsters, with the condemned humans cowering in corners and crevices. See also *navje.*

PELOPONNESIAN SCHOOL—In Greek *art,* one of the chief schools of classic *sculpture,* differing from others in its notably robust quality, and its less minute elaboration of detail. Phidias, whose chief teacher was Ageladas the Dorian, united the excellence of both features. A famous product of the school is the *statue* THE NIKE OF PAEONIUS, dedicated at Olympia by the Messenians in commemoration of the Spartan defeat at Sphacteria, 425 B.C. See *Athena* and *Parthenon.*

PEN—The implement used traditionally for *writing* and *drawing,* originating in Europe as a split or pointed quill, as the draftsman or writer desired. The *reed pen* was probably used from earlier times, made from the tubular stock of fine, hollow *bamboo* or coarse grass, cut in much the same manner as the quill. Although *metal pens* have been known since *ancient* times, machine manufacture during the 19th century displaced the older varieties completely.

PENCIL—A *writing* and *drawing* device of wide use in the *arts,* usually in the form of a thin, round strip of black 'lead' or colored *chalk* or *crayon* enclosed in a cylindrical or hexagonal case of wood, pointed at one end and either flat or having an eraser at the other. Loosely, any writing instrument not employing *ink.* Of all misnomers extant, that of 'lead pencil' is probably the greatest, since there is no *lead* in *pencils.*

PENCIL—In *painting,* (1) a *brush* of hair or bristles used in the laying-on of *colors;* (2) the manner or skill of an *artist;* his own artistic *style.* In the sense of brush (1), it is invariably small and fine, made of the hair of the camel, badger, or squirrel, or the down of the swan, ferruled in a quill. Larker varieties come into the conventional *brush* class.

PEN PROCESS—An *intaglio aquatint* process lost since Gainsborough, but rediscovered by modern artists in search of new, unique media. The finished *proof* is similar to a *pen* or *brush drawing.* An *ink* with high sugar content is applied with *pen* or *brush* to the *copper plate, and* a *ground* is rolled on the plate over the ink drawing. A cold water bath dissolves the ink, leaving the copper bare wherever ink had originally been placed. If *biting* were now permitted, *crevé* would result. To overcome this, a new *aquatint* ground is placed over the entire plate, and the pen or brush lines, lower than the rest of the new ground, now make it a perfectly *etched* plate. The *pen process* is quick, certain, and comparatively easy. It is capable of almost as many variations and nuances as brush and pen, with the added charm of a *print.* See *aquatint.*

PENTALYN—A variety of *resin* characterized by unusual hardness and *stability* to heat. Since it produces rapid drying without the aid of *tung oil,* it is used in the preparation of hard-surfaced, fast-drying *varnishes.* Chemically it is pentaery-thritylabietate resin, *pentalyn* being a trade name.

PENTAPTYCH—In *art,* a term often used in reference to a series of five *prints* which have been composed as a related group.

PENTELIC MARBLE—In *sculpture,* one of the most famous and highly prized of all ancient *marbles* used in *statuary* work. The quarries were opened in the 6th century B.C. at Mount Pentellicus (Pentelicon), near Athens; in early use it was also employed widely in *architecture.* Most of the buildings of ancient Athens were made of *Pentelic marble.* It is valued chiefly for its unusual durability, its structure of small crystals, and its high sparkle. The rusty gold tints of the *Parthenon* are the result of oxidation of the iron content in the *Pentelic marble* of which it is made. The heads of certain statues are found to have been made separately, of *Parian marble* (q.v.).

PENTIMENTI—The term applied to the *paint* ridges existing under the finished surface of an *oil painting.* These marks usually indicate earlier states of the *picture,* prior to repair or *restoration.* In many instances, however, the phenomenon occurs because the colors become *transparent* through the years, revealing the original *imprimature* or *underpainting* (qq.v.).

PEONY RED—In Chiese *art,* a pink-colored *pigment* prepared especially for the *painting* of peonies. Known natively as *mu tan hung,* it is a product of *yen chih* (q.v.)

PEPERINO—A variety of volcanic rock used widely in Italian *sculpture* and *masonry* before the era of *marble.* It is formed by the natural cementing together of volcanic sand, cinders, scoriae, etc. Known also as *albani stone.*

PEPPER DOTS—In Chinese *painting,* a variety of *brush* stroke technique in the *tien* (q.v.) class, giving the effect of tiny dots or black pepper. Used chiefly in the representation of *cedar* leaves.

PEPPER RED—In Chinese painting, a red pigment used extensively in outlining tree leaves. Known natively as *lao hung,* it is made by mixing *yin chu* with *chê shih* (qq.v.).

PEREDVIZHNIKI—A group of Russian *painters* of the school of *realism* in the latter half of the 19th century. They transferred their exhibitions from town to town, hence the name, a derivative of the verb *peredvigatj,* to move from place to place. The leader of the group appears to have been Ivan Kramskoi. Although all were defenders of ideological realism, they were divided into two general classes: those preferring subjects in the life of the peasants and lower classes of the population, and those chiefly interested in the lives of the merchants and office workers in the towns. In addition, the *landscape* painters were made up of two groups: those who painted the countryside exclusively, and those who preferred *seascapes.* The serious *art* of the *Peredvizhniki* gradually degenerated toward the end of the 19th century, its *esthetic* essence collapsed, and its society ceased to be the center of artistic life. One of the numerous groups intended to replace it was *Mir Iskusstva* (q.v.), or *World of Art.*

PEREVAL—A 20th century Russian *art* group organized by A. K. Voronski as a nucleus in "preserving the artistic heritage." Disbanded in 1932 along with the abandonment of its periodical, KRASNAYA NOV'.

PERGAMENE ART—A *Renaissance* school of Greek *sculpture* which found its *inspiration* and its most frequent *theme* in the victories, important for civilization, won by King Attalus I of Pergamum in the last half of the 3rd century B.C. over the threatening advance of barbarism represented by Gallic invasions. The work of this school appears to be remarkably able, and considerably more modern in spirit than older Greek work; it possesses a force and originality raising it far above contemporaneous Hellenistic art. Prior to 1875 *Pergamene Art* was known only by a number of detached fragments from battle-pieces scattered throughout European *museums;* some of these have long figured in the list of the most notable ancient sculptures, e.g., THE DYING GAUL (The Gladiator) in the U. S. Capitol, and the ARRIA AND PAETUS in the Villa Ludovisi, at Rome. Knowledge of the school and its work was enlarged by subsequent discoveries. Probably the finest specimen now know is the famous Athene group from the great *frieze* of the *altar* at Pergamum, executed in *high relief,* unearthed after 1875 and now in the Berlin Museum.

PERILLA—A light yellow oil, soluble in alcohol and ether, used as a substitute for *linseed oil* in the mixing of artists' *paints.*

PERITO—In the *art* of Mexico, a general term referring to a skilled craftsman in any of the arts, *fine* or *applied;* also, an art appraiser or *restorer.*

PERMALBA—In *painting,* a fine white *pigment* of great *opacity,* tinting strength, and *stability.* It is not acted upon by other mediums used in any painting technique, will not discolor with age, and has no tendency to crack or become horny or brittle. Used in *oil painting, tempera,* and *water-color* work.

PERMANENCE—In *oil painting,* the *quality* of changeless characteristics in the *pigments* employed. See *stable.*

PERMANENT VIOLET—In *painting,* one of the fine *manganese pigments* (q.v.).

PERMANENT WHITE—A fine white *pigment* used extensively in *paints,* and also in the making of *photographic* paper. It is a heavy white powder, soluble in water, requiring application of a *surface film* after completion of the *art* work. Chemically it is a precipitated barium sulphate; known also as *blanc fixe* and *terra ponderosa* to artists' colormen.

PERSIAN LAKES—In *painting,* a series of fine yellow *lake colors* used extensively by French and English artists of the 18th century. Fairly *stable,* they were obtained from the dried berries of the buckthorn or RHAMNUS shrub of Orient. Known also as *buckthorn lakes,* they are no longer listed by artists' colormen.

PERSIAN RED—In *painting,* a brilliant red *pigment* in the general hue of *vermilion.* Commonly known as *victoria red* (q.v.).

PERSPECTIVE—(1) Generally, the science of *optics.* (2) The *illusion* of three dimensions created on a flat surface. (3) The proportion of parts of a *picture* to each other, considered in relation to depth or distance; that which suggests the effects of angle and distance upon the appearance of objects, e.g., (a) *aerial perspective,* concerned with the effects of distance upon *color* and clarity; (b) *linear perspective,* pertaining to similar effects upon size form, and outline. See *illusionism, aerial perspective,* and *linear perspective.*

PERSPECTIVE DRAWING—A *drawing* which represents an object on a plane surface as it appears to the eye; affords a better pictorial effect than most other types of drawings. See *one-point drawing.*

PETIT GRANITE MARBLE—In *sculpture,* a bluish variety of *marble* studded with innumerable fine white dots or points formed by *fossil* content; occurs chiefly in Ecuasines, Belgium.

PETREX—A variety of *resin* obtained from petrex acid, used in the making of fine *lacquers, varnishes, aniline inks, shellacs,* and *surface films* for the coating of *paintings* and *statuary.* Chemically it is an alkyd resin derived from polybasic acid and terpenes, *petrex* being a trade name.

PETRIFIED CITY—Name applied to the city of Ishmonie in upper Egypt because of the vast number of *statues* there (men, women, children and animals are all represented). *Legend* has it that all were once alive, but were turned into stone by a divine miracle.

PETWORTH MARBLE—In *sculpture* and *architecture,* a variously colored type of *limestone* containing markings caused by the remains of certain fresh-water shells. Known also as *Sussex* marble, both names arise from the fact that it is quarried at Petworth in Sussex.

PEWTER—In *sculpture,* a type of polishing material made by calcining tin, used in bringing a high *gloss* to a finished work in *marble.*

PHANTOM SECTION—In *drawing,* a cross-*hatching* executed on an outside view to show interior construction; the use of an additional view or drawing may thus be eliminated on occasion. *Phantom sections* are also used to indicate adjacent parts.

PHARAOH'S CHAIRS—In Egyptian *archaeology,* the name applied by natives to the ruins of the *pedestals* supporting the twin 40-feet-high *statues* of Amenemhat III, greatest ruler of the XII DYNASTY (2212-2000 B.C.). Erected at the ruler's own direction, the statues were part of a large temple dedicated to *Sebek,* the crocodile-god. The reign of Amenemhat was also featured by the construction of the Hawarah *Pyramid* (to be his *tomb*), and numerous *sphinxes.* It is believed that the face of the famous sphinx at Gizah is in his image.

PHENOL RESINS—A group of unusually strong *film* materials, known chemically as the phenol-formaldehyde *resins,* and commercially as *bakelite.* Used industrially as surface coating; thus far little use has been found in the *arts* for them.

PHIGALIAN MARBLES—A series of 23 *sculptures* in *alto-relievo,* discovered in 1812 at Arcadia. They are part of the *Elgin Marbles,* now in the British Museum. These works show the combat of the *centaurs* and Lapithae, and that of the Greeks and the *Amazons.*

PHILOSOPHER'S WOOL—A term in *painting;* see *zinc oxide.*

PHLOGOPITE—A variety of *mica* (q.v.) used chiefly as a substitute for *aluminum* powder in the making of fine *paints.*

PHOENIX—The bird of good omen in Chinese *art* and *mythology;* known technically as the *ocellated argus,* and in China as the *fêng-huang.* Japanese version, including the same bird and meaning, is the *hoo bird.* It is used extensively in the *decoration* of Oriental *musical instruments, usually* surrounded by red flames executed in *lacquer,* symbolizing immortality.

PHOTO-AQUATINT—An *engraving* made by a photochemical process, the result being an *intaglio* copper *plate* from which impressions similar to *photogravures* may be made. Also, any *print* made by this technique.

PHOTOMACROGRAPH—A direct *enlargment* of a *painting* or other object; an enlargement of a thing visible to the naked eye as distinguished from a *photomicrograph,* which is the enlargement of an object invisible without magnification, *photographed* through a microscope. The *photomacrograph* is made with an ordinary *camera* and enlarging *lens,* without the grain usually found in projected enlargements.

PHRYGIAN MARBLE—In *sculpture,* the variety of colored *limestone* resembling the plumage of the peacock in its markings; properly known as *pavonazza* (q.v.).

PHTHALOCYANINE BLUE—A prize blue *pigment* favored by artists who do not fully trust the complex, synthetic *Prusian blue* (q.v.). Although the latter has been dropped from a considerable number of *palettes* in recent years, it can still be made in thoroughly reliable fashion. Nevertheless, *phthalocyanine blue,* equally desirable, appears to be replacing it. Valued esp. for its clear, semi-transparent, middle hue of blue. In the same class is *phthalocyanine green,* a deep, strong, very clear *blue-green,* unmatched by any other for mixtures from *yellow*-green through blue-green in *hues* of the highest *intensity* and *luminosity;* not only deeper, but seven times stronger than *viridian.* Both *phthalocyanines* appeared on the market in quantity in the 1930's. They are chemically inactive, inert to normal destructive agents, and proven *stable,* having much greater light resistance than *alizarin.* See *monastral blue.*

PHYLOMORPHIC—In *painting* and *sculpture,* the term applied to any detail or *design* resembling a leaf.

PI—In Chinese *art,* (1) the *brush* used in *calligraphy* and *painting.* The typical brush consists of a graded bunch of hair (goat and wolf being most popular) inserted into the end of a *bamboo* tube and held by an adhesive. A well-equipped artist usually has four or five different types, each being so constructed that it has a fine point; (2) any stylistic brush stroke characterizing an *artist,* locality, era, etc.; (3) a *jade* disc having a perforation in its center, used ritually as a *symbol* of heaven.

PIAO—In Chinese *art,* (1) narrow strips or labels (usually of *paper*) affixed to the outsides of *chüan chou* or *school paintings,* citing the dynasty, artist's name, and title of the *painting.* The notation is often found to have been made by famous persons at the request of the *artists,* usually to enhance the value of the work. For this reason it is not uncommon to find old *piao* transferred to the scroll in *restorations* and remountings; (2) the *technique of* mounting a picture by pasting it to a paper backing.

PIAO CHU—In Chinese *painting,* a fine *vermilion pigment* of mineral origin, deriving from *cinnabar* (q.v.). Known also as *Satsuma red,* it is used in portraiture *(jên wu)* as decorative addition to the garments of men. It is the first layer removed from the stone in emulsion (see *chu sha*), but is also available today in prepared form, requiring (like *chê shih*) only the addition of water.

PIAO PEI—In Chinese *painting,* the mount or *margin* of a *picture;* usually a *brocaded* area around the painting, evenly spaced, and applied in formal fashion. The ends of the rod of a *scroll painting* are considered essential parts of the mounting, and are frequently decorated with *ivory, jade,* horn, *porcelain* or *metal.* See *chou shou.*

PICTORIAL REPRESENTATION—Generally, the *art* of rendering the shape, *design,* and *character* of objects through the *medium* of a *graphic art.*

PICTORIAL VIEW—In *drawing,* the representation of an object as seen by the observer; seldom used by itself, but usually as an *illustration* where details of *orthographic projection* (q.v.) are not readily understood. Has the advantage of requiring less training of the *imagination* to visualize a complicated object, and in some instances, requires less time for the actual drawing.

PICTURE—A *painting* or *drawing,* the scene or subject of which bears resemblance to somebody or something; any *portrait* or drawing; a likeness, executed with or without *color.*

PICTURE SILK—In Chinese *painting,* a variety of ready-*sized silk* used as a *ground.* See *hua chüan.*

PIETÀ—A devotional *image* used extensively in the *arts,* representing St. Mary mourning over the body of Christ in her lap. This *motive* was first introduced into art in Germany shortly before 1300, and spread quickly to other parts of Europe. Many excellent portrayals of this scene are found in *painting, sculpture* and *architecture.*

PIGMENT—Although generally given over to any type of *color*ing matter, the term is applied in the *arts* to a powder that is ground into a *medium* to form *paint.* Extant since *ancient* times, the number of such coloring materials is large, with hundreds listed by *artists'* suppliers. A *pigment* is applied to a surface, leaving its color affixed. There must be a *pigment* in every *paint,* usually in combination with a *thinner* (as *turpentine*) to insure brushability, and a *binder* (as *linseed oil*) to give cohesion to the whole. A *drier* or *siccative* is often added. *Pigments* may be of mineral, vegetal, or animal origin. See *painting.*

PI HUA—In Chinese *art,* a *mural* or *wall painting* applied directly to the wall surface as a *ground,* as distinguished from the *pi tzu* which is executed elsewhere and later affixed to a wall. As a rule the *pi hua* resembles *fresco;* the term is also applied to a certain *brush*-stroke technique emphasizing *gradation* in straight lines.

PINAX—A *tablet* hung over cases of books in the Alexandrian Library, serving as a catalog. That of Callimachus added biography, list of works, etc., thus forming the first attempt at a history of Greek *literature.* Also, a *painting* on a tablet of wood.

PIN CHU—In Chinese *painting,* literally 'guest and host'; the principle of balancing large mountains by the inclusion of smaller ones; an important flower by lesser ones or by a butterfly, etc.

PINE-LEAF DOTS—In Chinese *painting,* a type of *brush* stroke technique used in the representation of *pine* leaves. Consists of fine strokes, sharply pointed, either curved or straight, usually arranged in groups of seven in a semicircle; the strokes have a notable stiffness, due to the strong necessity of keeping them from overlapping, or even touching. Compare with *water-grass dots* (q.v.).

PINE SOOT—A variety of *ink* used in Chinese *painting,* properly known as *sung yen mo* (q.v.).

P'ING CHANG—In Chinese *art,* sets of four, six, eight or twelve narrow vertical *scroll paintings* designed to be hung together; the flowers of the four seasons are typical subjects. Each individual member is so narrow that it is pleasing only when displayed in combination with the others. See also *kua fu.*

PING HSÜEH—In Chinese *art* literally *ice snow paper;* used as a *ground* in *painting,* it is creamy white and *sized,* with a soft *texture* and barely perceptible *mold* marks. See *chih.*

PINK—A light-*red* color. Also, any one of the many varieties of *lakes* of *yellow* or *green*ish *color,* made by precipitating vegetable juices on a *white* earth product, such as *alumina* or *chalk;* e.g., *Dutch pink, brown pink, rose pink* and *Italian pink.* These *hues* are valuable as *water-colors* only. Most *pinks* are high in *brilliance* and low in *saturation.*

PINXIT—The word added to the name or initials of an *artist* on a *painting.* Often used on a copy, to indicate that the artist whose name precedes *pinxit* painted the copy only. Frequently reduced to *pinx.*

PISCIFORM—In the *visual arts,* the general term applied to any object or *design* in the shape of a fish.

PISTACHIO—In Chinese *painting,* a famous pale *green pigment* derived from a mixture of the *blue* of *hua ch'ing* and the *rattan yellow* of *t'êng huang* (qq.v.). Often referred to as *vegetation green,* it belongs to the great green class known natively as *ts'ao lü* (q.v.). The *color* itself, high in *brilliance* and low in *saturation,* is in wide use throughout the world.

PITCHING CHISEL—In *sculpture,* a chisel-like tool made of steel, the cutting face of which is rectangular in outline.

PI TZU—In Chinese *art,* a *mural* or *wall painting* not applied to the wall directly as in the case of *pi hua,* but executed at a *studio* and later mounted on a wall.

PIURI—In *painting,* a deep, translucent, orange-yellow *pig-*

ment of moderate *stability,* commonly known as *Indian yellow* (q.v.).

PLANIGRAPH—In *drawing,* an instrument similar in principle to the *pantograph* (q.v.), used for the reduction or enlargement of any *illustration.*

PLASTER—The name carried by a great variety of materials, used in *architecture* for surfacing the *walls* of buildings. In the *arts,* it is used chiefly for *model*ing and as a *casting* substance, and for such purposes *gypsum* or *plaster of Paris* (qq.v.) is most common, since it has the advantage of setting or recrystallizing by the addition of water and of losing none of its volume in the process. Its tendency to harden rapidly can be modified by the addition of other materials. *Plaster* used on walls, usually with a *lime* base, serves as a *ground* for *painting,* the best known *technique* being that of true *fresco* (qv.).

PLASTER OF PARIS—Known also as *gypsum* (q.v.), it is the most common of all *molding* and *casting* materials, serving also as the inert substance used in *grounds.* First burned, it sets rapidly into a firm *plaster* when again combined with water. It is generally *stable,* slightly soluble in water, and fairly soluble in diluted hydrochloric acid. The name derives from the fact that it was first found in large quantities in the quarries of Montmartre, in Paris.

PLASTER TOOL—In *sculpture,* any one of a number of instruments used in the cutting, shaping, smoothing, grooving, etc., of *gypsum* or *plaster.* Usually all metal, the central handle extends both ways ending in square, angular, pointed, saw-toothed, etc., working edges, usually incorporating two different edges in one tool. See also *double end tool.*

PLASTIC—Generally having such consistency as to be workable; capable of being shaped or modeled; pertaining to or characteristic of forming or *molding;* e.g., *clay, plaster,* etc. Such substances possess *plasticity;* see also *plastics.*

PLASTIC ARTS—The general term embracing *sculpture* and all of its subordinate and related *arts* by which objects are represented *in the round* or in *relief* (qq.v.).

PLASTICIZER—A substance added to a *paint* or *varnish,* intended to reduce the tendency to dry too rapidly and become brittle and *friable. Binding mediums,* with a slow-drying *plasticizer* added, will create *film* surfaces of non-brittle *texture.* For the *resin* class, *drying oils* (q.v.) and a few *semi-drying* or *non-drying oils* have served this purpose. More recently, synthetic *plasticizers,* e.g., tricresol phosphate and dibutyl phthalate, have been used successfully with the *artificial resins.* See also *abalyn* and *surface film.*

PLASTICUM—In *sculpture,* a fine variety of modeling *clay* invariably prepared in some shade of green. Produced in brick form, it will not harden or crack, and has a smooth *texture* and consistency that will not vary. Responds well to all sculptors' tools.

PLATE—In *etching,* a piece of *copper, zinc,* or other appropriate metal constituting the *die* or form from which *prints* are made. It is covered with a *ground* (*wax asphaltum*) which is cut by a *graver* or *stylus,* and when the desired *pattern* or *design* is carved, the *plate* is immersed in an acid bath where the *biting* process allows for etching on the exposed parts of the *plate;* the ground, being acid-resistant, is not affected. Some lines are given longer acid treatment for heavier, darker lines; others are given a *stopping out,* to prevent overbiting. See *drypoint, line etching, aquatint,* and *biting.*

PLATE OIL—In *etching,* a light, medium or heavy *varnish,* made of burnt *linseed oil,* used with dry *pigments* in the making of etching *ink.*

PLUMBIC OCHER—Same as *massicot* (q.v.).

PLUMBO-PLUMBIC—A bright *scarlet* color made by heating *litharge* for long periods at high temperatures. It is *stable,* has good *hiding power,* and a smooth *texture* in *oil paints.* Used as a painting *pigment* since ancient times, the term was often confused with *cinnabar* (q.v.), esp. by Pliny. Used also as a base material in the making of *flint glass* and camera *lenses.*

PLYWOOD—Laminated boards with a heavy core and one or two faces of very thin *wood* attached by means of an adhesive. It has become popular in building, and some types of *plywood* have been taken up by *painters* for use as *panel* supports. When well-made, *plywood* is stronger, and warps less, than solid wood.

PNEUMATIC PEN—In *drawing,* a pneumatic instrument, now obsolete, formerly used for producing a copying *pencil.* It *traced* the lines to be reproduced by means of numerous minute perforations through the paper. *Ink* or *color* was then spread over the surface and filled the perforations, and the pattern thus created was filled out in detail for reproduction on numerous other surfaces.

POINTILLISM—A technique in *oil painting* in which the *color* is applied to the *canvas* or other *support* by tapping with a stiff *brush* rather than by the *traditional* stroking with the brush. It grew in popularity during the 20th century, leading to development of the bristle brush which had to be produced in quantity because of the fast distortion brought to it in the tapping process.

POINTING—In *sculpture,* the technique by which a *stone* or *clay* reproduction of a *plaster* model is made. Holes are drilled to the proper depth in a stone block, at points corresponding to points indicated on the *model* by the *sculptor.* See *taille directe.*

PO KU—In Chinese *painting,* curios or *antiques* as subject matter, coming within the broad *jên wu* classification; the painting of pictures of old bronzes (see *sacrificial bronze*), *porcelains,* and similar objects. This is regarded as a low class of *art* because the pictures are easily executed, they admit of no *creative* originality, and even when painstakingly accurate they are of interest chiefly as records or for minor decoration.

POLISH—(1) To render smooth and *glossy,* as a surface of *marble, wood,* etc., whether by rubbing or by coating with *varnish* or other surface application, or by both. *Polishing* is frequently undertaken with the object of bringing out the color, grain, markings, etc., of the material as of colored marble, *agate, jasper,* etc., and richly veined wood.

POLYCHROMY—Decoration or execution in many *colors;* specifically, the practice of coloring *statuary* and *architectural* work more or less completely. The technique dates from remote *antiquity,* and reached its greatest artistic perfection in Greece, where it was consistently applied to all *sculpture* and architecture. In *archaic* (q.v.) examples the coloring was complete and strong, and in the case of sculpture was to a great extent conventional, with men's flesh colored deep-*brown* and women's *white* or *yellow*ish. While architectural surfaces were still brilliantly colored, as in *red* or *blue,* the chief part of many features (as of *columns*) was left in the natural color of the *marble,* or perhaps merely *tinted,* and discreetly set off with *meanders* or other ornaments in *gilding* or strong color. During the 12th and 13th centuries architectural *polychromy* was employed with admirable effect throughout Europe.

POLYCHTAN—A term in *sculpture* pertaining to the school of *art* inspired by the great Greek sculptor Polyclitus (or Polycletus) of Argos and Sycyon, the contemporary and emulator of Phidias. The word is also applied to the sculptural canon of perfect human proportions which he established. See *Doryphoros* and *Argive School.*

POLYMERIZED OIL—A comparatively modern term in *oil painting,* although this substance, in one form or another, was used from early times as a painting *medium.* Distinguished from the common *drying oils* (q.v.) by molecular arrangement, resulting in greater viscosity and a more *stable* paint.

POLYMNITE—In *sculpture,* a variety of stone veined with black streaks and dendrites, having a fancied resemblance to rivers, marshes and ponds. See *forest marble, landscape marble, river marble, fortification marble.*

POLYPTYCH—A variety of *altarpiece* consisting of a group of five hinged *panels,* so arranged that the outer sections or wings would fold over and conceal the inner sections. The panels were pictorially treated, enriched with *paintings* or *sculpture* in *relief;* also known as *retable. See triptych* and *iconostasis.*

POLYVINYL RESIN—A synthetic material used in recent years as a *surface film* and *varnish* for *pictures,* and taken up sparingly as a *medium* in *oil painting.* It is insoluble in water (although otherwise affected by moisture), fairly flexible, and *stable* to light. However, it is easily permeable and is readily dissolved by most organic solvents. Its future in oil painting is speculative.

POMEGRANATE—In *painting,* a variety of *purple* color consisting of 50% red, 40% black, and 10% blue.

P'O MO— In Chinese *painting,* (1) literally 'broken ink'; having an outline and general configuration of rocks, shaded or modeled by means of wrinkles or *ts'un* (q.v.) which gradually build up depth for *perspective.* Found in the works of WANG MÊNG and other artists of the northern *Sung Period.* (2) A variety of *ink* painting known popularly as *spilled ink;* painting with broad full strokes and no defined outline.

POMPADOUR RED—A light crimson or rose-pink *color,* popular in *painting* and *water-color* work.

POMPEIAN BLUE—A synthetic *blue pigment* resembling *Egyptian blue* (q.v.), made by heating a mixture of silica, *copper,* and calcium carbonate. The result is a *bright,* yet pale blue *color.*

POONA—In *painting,* a large stub-nosed *brush* of bristle or badger, used chiefly for dabbing. Now obsolete, it was replaced by the *dabber* which is employed almost exclusively in smudge and *stencil* work.

POPPY-SEED OIL—One of the better *drying oils* (q.v.), long in use as a *painting medium,* though lighter in *color* and slower in drying than *linseed oil.* Known in *classical* times, it achieved its greatest popularity in 17th century Italy. Extracted from the seeds of the opium poppy, grown largely in India, Russia, France, and Asia Minor. See also *walnut oil* and *binder.*

POPULAR ROMANTICISM—A term used in *painting* and *sculpture* criticism to describe that type of *romanticism* (q.v.) concerned with the appeal of popular subject matter, rather than with the invention of new *visual* or formal *values.* Typically, the *Popular Romanticist* is a formal naturalist (see *Naturalism*) who chooses subjects of romantic appeal, e.g., subjects from the *Middle Ages* or the Near East, from Goethe, Shakespeare and other poets, literary illustration in general, and subjects of sentimental interest stressing the home, family, adventure, courage, motherhood, nationalism, hero workship, and the like.

PORCELAIN BLUE SILK—A good grade of *silk,* dyed a deep *blue,* used as a *ground* in Chinese *painting.* See *tz'ŭ ch'ing.*

PORCELAIN COLOR—In *painting,* the general term applied to any *pigment* in the nature of those used for the decorating of *porcelain;* also, any pigment actually used in the coloring of porcelain. Such pigments are colored *glasses* reduced to fine powder which, when *fired* or subjected to the action of heat, fuse upon the surface of the *biscuit.*

PORPHYRY—In *sculpture,* a type of very hard rock quarried first in *ancient* Egypt; has a dark *purplish-red* ground and takes a fine *polish.* Although used traditionally through the centuries to make the important *muller* and *grinding slab* (qq.v.) for *painters,* it is prized for its strength and durability in *statuary* work. See also *verd antique* and *slice.*

PORPORINO—In the *art* of the *Middle Ages,* a type of *glaze* used for protection and ornamentation, made of mercury, tin and sulphur, and resembling *gold.* Used chiefly by Italian artists of the era.

PORT-CRAYON—A holder for *chalk, charcoal, crayon,* or the like, used in *drawing.* It is usually a kind of metal tube, split at one or both ends, and tending to spring open, but held fast by rings which slide upon it, so that the drawing material is gripped and held firmly. Also spelled *porte-crayon.*

PORTFOLIO—Any container for loose sheets of *paper. Artists* generally use the type made with heavy boards hinged at one side, provided with strings or tape for securing the other three sides.

PORTO MARBLE—In *sculpture,* a kind of dense black *limestone* traversed by *gold*-colored veins; occurs chiefly at Porto Venere and the Isle of Palmeria, in the Gulf of Spezia, Known also as *black and gold marble.*

PORTRAIT—In *painting,* a likeness of a person, especially of the face, usually made from life; a painted *picture* or *representation* of a person. The term is also used generally to denote the same type of subject in *engraving, drawing,* and *photography* of this character. In some *art* circles, the term is extended in meaning to include *portraits* accomplished in *sculpture.*

PORTRAITURE—In *painting,* (1) *portraits* (q.v.) collectively; (2) the *art* of making portraits; (3) any pictorial *representation* emphasizing the likeness of a face.

POST-IMPRESSIONISM—A term used to describe French *painting* following *impressionism,* from about 1885 to 1905, in which a *subjective art* of self-expression succeeded objective *naturalism* and impressionism. *Post-impressionists* were thus *expressionists* rather than impressionists. The *post-impressionists,* who included Cézanne, van Gogh, Gauguin, Seurat, Signac, late Renoir and late Degas, were followed by the *Fauves,* who were more radical in departing from objective naturalism in order to express their personal *emotions.* See *absolute art;* also, *synthetism.*

POTASSIUM FERRICYANIDE—A poisonous chemical appearing as *lustrous* red crystals, soluble in water, used in the making of *pigments, paper,* and blue-print paper, and in numerous *textile* processes including *calico printing* and *wool dyeing.* Also employed in *electroplating.* Chemically, $K_4Fe\ (CN)_6$.

POTSTONE—In Chinese *carving,* a coarse or impure variety of *soapstone* (q.v.) so called because of the ease with which it is cut into *pots* and other hollow vessels owing to its unusual softness.

POTTERY WHEEL METHOD—One of the three *techniques* employed in the *sculpture* which uses the *medium* of *terra cotta* (q.v.).

POUR MOLD—In *ceramics* and *sculpture,* any one of a number of forms commercially available for the addition of *plaster* or *clay* in the making of various objects of art. Relieving the sculptor of the *carving* work normally required in the making of an original for the *casting,* the *pour mold* may be purchased in the shape of any animal, flower, bowl, vessel, etc., ready for the *moist clay* or other *plastic* substance.

POZZOLANA—A volcanic *clay* or *cement* found at Pozzuoli near Naples, and along the Rhine; was probably used in the *ancient* figure *models* and *reliefs* classified as *stucco.* It is made up of easily decomposable silicates formed by the action of volcanic fires, and when mixed with *lime* (q.v.) it provides a cement that is moderately strong and slow to harden.

POZZUOLI—In *painting,* a fine red *pigment* of volcanic origin, found in the general area of *Pozzuoli,* near Naples.

PRAXITELES CURVE—In *sculpture,* the term describing the sensuous representation of human bodies in repose. PRAXITELES (370-330 B.C.), famous Athenian *sculptor,* secured this effect by placing the *figure* in a relaxed upright position with the weight on the forward right foot, the left foot swung lightly back, the left arm extended to the side (often resting on a tree or *ornamental vase*), the right hip curved out, and the head turned to the right. The entire body assumed the position of an inverted s-curve, or *Praxiteles curve.* See *contrapposto.*

PRECIOUS SERPENTINE—A material in *sculpture* better known as *noble serpentine* (q.v.).

PREDELLA—In *painting,* the lower section of an *iconostasis* (q.v.); the series of small *panels* below the center panels of an *altarpiece.*

PRE-RAPHAELITISM—A movement in late 19th century English *art* and *literature,* referring especially to *painting.* Its adherents considered art before Raphael more sincere and genuine, less artificial and formalized than it was thereafter. *Forms* stressed *naturalism* with almost *photographic* vision. From the point of view of content, the *Pre-Raphaelites* were sentimentalists and *Popular Romanticists* who preferred to depict moral, religious, historical, or *anecdotal* subjects. Their aims: to express genuine ideas; to study nature with a view toward gaining experience for such *expression;* to sympathize with what is direct and sincere and heartfelt in art, to the exclusion of what is conventional, self-parading, and acquired by rote; and to produce fine *works of art,* as those of the earlier Italian artists. The average age of the founding group was twenty years.

PREUSSISCHBLAU—Original native name for the famous

Prussian blue (q.v.), first fine blue *pigment* to be made synthetically on a large scale.

PRIMARY COLORS—In a strict sense, there are three *primary colors* only, *red, green,* and *violet* (or *blue*); in *pigmentation* they are red, blue and *yellow*. Loosely, *indigo* and *orange* may be included, all possessed of a vast number of *gradations* and *shades*. The *primary colors,* by common definition, are those into which *white* light is broken by passing through a *prism*. White and *black* are not considered colors, white reflecting and black absorbing all the rays of light without separating them. Two *primary colors* in combination create a *secondary color*; two secondary colors in combination create a *tertiary color*.

PRIMER—The first coat of *paint* applied to a *ground;* the paint or analogous substance applied to the surface of the material to be painted. Not synonymous with *size* (q.v.).

PRIMITIVE—In *painting,* the term applied to an *artist* active in a rudimentary period in the development of a *style* or movement, particularly a period prior to the *Renaissance*. Also, a *provincial* or naive painter, or one of his works.

PRIMITIVE COLORS—In *painting,* the colors *red, yellow* and *blue,* so called because it was erroneously believed at one time that from mixtures of these all other colors could be obtained. With respect to mixtures of *pigments,* this very rudely approximates the truth; in regard to true mixtures of *colors,* it is strikingly false.

PRINCETON YELLOW—In Chinese *painting,* a bright yellow color of mineral origin prepared from *realgar* in the manner of *shih ch'ing* (q.v.). Stones that are *red* in the natural state, and shaped like a cockscomb, are believed by Oriental artists to yield the best color. Known natively as *hsiung huang,* it is comparatively *stable* and has many uses; however, if mixed with *gold,* a blackening reaction occurs.

PROFILE—The forwardmost edge of the human face as seen from a side. Also, a vertical section *drawing* through an object. Loosely, any outline.

PROGNATHOUS—In *portraiture,* characterized by a relatively projecting jaw and sloping face, i.e., by a facial *profile* angle of less than 80 degrees. See also *facial angle* and *facial asymmetry.*

PROLETCULT—A Russian group founded in 1917 to work out the questions of proletarian culture on the basis of 'collective cooperation' so as to give the laboring class a wholesome education which would 'direct its will and trend of thought.' In 1920 a group known as *Kuznitsa* broke away and into the field of writing. Name is abbreviation of PROLETARSKIE KULTURNO-PROSVETITELSKIE ORGANIZATSII. Its periodicals were THE FORGE, THE FUTURE, and THE WHISTLES.

PROMACHOS—In Greek *mythology* and *archaeology,* a deity who fights before some person, army or state, as a protector or guardian; said esp. of *Athena* and *Apollo.* In *art* (esp. *sculpture*) the type is distinguished by a definite attitude of combat, often with upraised shield and the spear or other offensive weapon extended threateningly, as in the famous example ATHENE THE DEFENDER, a *statue* executed in *marble* (*Herculaneum*) now in the Museo Nazionale, Naples.

PROOF BEFORE LETTER—In *engraving* and *etching,* a *proof* impression taken before the title or inscription is *engraved.*

PROPAGANDA ART—Ideological *art,* executed primarily to persuade the spectator to favor in a literary idea, philosophical opinion, religious conviction, political, social or economic doctrine, or any other course of thought or action. The term is not applied unless the *esthetic* merit of the work was, in the mind of the *artist,* clearly a secondary consideration as contrasted with the *propaganda* value.

PROPORTION—A term in *criticism* used in a sense similar to that of *balance* (q.v.), although restricted in application to the artist's treatment of his subject-matter. An *artist* (and hence, his work) is said to exhibit *proportion* when he respects and adheres to the true worth and significance of the different elements of his subject, placing appropriate emphasis upon each aspect thereof. The accordant interrelationship of all parts of a work so that each receives due measure of stress, space, attention, etc., while contributing to the *harmony* and balance of the whole.

PROTEAN STONE—In *architecture* (and sometimes in *sculpture*), an *alabaster*-like artificial stone of strength and beauty, made from a *gypsum* base.

PROTO-RENAISSANCE—In *art,* any period or movement which exerted influence on the *Renaissance* era, as *Hohenstaufen Art* (q.v.).

PRUSSIAN BLUE—The first *blue pigment* made synthetically on a large scale (early 18th century). Chemically it is complex, but it can be described as a ferric ferrocyanide, usually made by a precipitation process. Because the approximate date of its entry into the *arts* is known, analytical identification of *Prussian blue* is often the means of placing a limiting date upon a *picture* in which it has been used. Known also as *Berlin blue* (situs of its origin), *Paris blue, Antwerp blue,* and *Chinese blue.* It appears to be disappearing from a number of *palettes* in recent years, with *phthalocyanine blue* (q.v.) replacing it as a less speculative pigment.

PRUSSIAN BROWN—In *painting,* a fine brown *pigment* used by artists, prepared by calcining an aluminous *Prussian blue* (q.v.), forming a compound of sequioxide of iron and *alumina.* It is *orange-brown* and resembles *burnt sienna,* but is not so rich in tone.

PULLING PLIERS—An instrument used by *painters* to pull the *canvas* tightly around the under-frame; better known as *canvas pliers* (q.v.).

PURE COLOR—(1) Any *color* produced by homogeneous light. (2) Any very *brilliant* or decided color. (3) In *painting,* a general color *pattern* in which each *hue* is lighted or *shaded* only with a modification of itself (see *confluent colors),* and not with a totally different hue. Thus, a *red* in *pure color* will be red in both sunlight and shadow, as distinguished from an impure red which will be true in sunlight, but *purple, blue,* or *gray* in the shade.

PURE DRAWING—In *art,* the essence of *drawing* with emphasis on the *abstract character* rather than the pictorial or *natural.*

PURE SCARLET—In *water-color* work, a *pigment* of *fugitive* character commonly known as *royal scarlet* (q.v.).

PURISM—An *art* movement in revolt against *cubism* (q.v.), flourishing in France from 1916 to 1925. It emphasized semi-*abstrac*t painting in which precision, clarity, elegance of line and form, and an impersonal, mechanical cleanliness prevailed. It differs from cubist *paintings* in that objects are clearly recognizable. It is two-dimensional, frankly *decorative,* and constructed on the basis of an elaborate, systematic *color* theory. *Architecture* followed painting, using the 'machine age' *motif.*

PURPLE—Any *color,* such as *violet, mauve, lavender, orchid, magenta,* etc., having as essentials the components of both *red* and *blue.* This was the color of the dress worn through the centuries by persons high in ecclesiastical rank and by royalty. It is one of the most highly *fugitive* colors known.

PURPLE LAKE—In *painting,* a fine *pigment* of deep, rich *carmine* red, obtained from the dried dead wingless female cochineal insect COCCUS CACTI; *prepared* in either powder or compressed block form for subsequent grinding. Though prized for its color, it is generally considered unsafe where permanency is required because of its *fugitive* quality in light. In addition, the presence of any metallic pigment in the mixture will bring on fading, usually into brown. Known also as *scarlet lake,* it was later imitated in *hue* by *alizarin madder,* which also imparted a greater degree of *stability.*

PURREE—In *painting,* a deep, translucent, orange-yellow *pigment* of moderate *stability,* commonly known as *Indian yellow* (q.v.).

PUTTI—In European *art,* esp. *sculpture,* figures of nude Cupid-like children usually embellishing a larger work; a favorite subject in Italian *Renaissance, putti* were also frequent in *painting* and *architecture* of the period. (Sing. *putto*).

PYSANKY—The Ukrainian *tradition* and *art* of *painting*

eggs, and the eggs themselves. The practice dates back to pagan times when the egg, like newborn life, *symbolized* the sun god who gave life to all; after Christ's death the egg became a symbol of eternal life to Slavonic peoples. Designs such as the *swastika,* triangle, and *rosette* were used as expressions of success, health, and happiness. Some *pysanky* have been so expertly executed that they are now *museum* pieces.

Q

QUADRA—In classical *sculpture* and *architecture,* (1) a square frame or border enclosing a *bas-relief;* (2) the *plinth* of a *podium;* (3) any small *molding* of plain or square section, as one of the *fillets* above and below the *scotia* of the *Ionic base;* (4) generally, any outline, border or framework. An excellent specimen is the *quadra* ANNUNCIATION by Luca della Robbia, in the Borgo San Jacopo, Florence, showing a double frame surrounding religious figures *carved* in *relief.*

QUATTROCENTO—A term applied to the *style* of *art* flourishing in Europe (esp. Italy) during most of the 15th century. It was featured by rigid formality of line and strong positiveness of *color,* both tempered with rich warmth and sentiment. Though the word means 'four hundred,' it actually refers to 'fourteen hundred,' the century of its popularity.

QUERCITRON LAKE—In *painting* and *watercolor* work, a series of yellow *lake colors* deriving from the inner bark of the botanical QUERCUS TINCTORIA. Never popular with *artists* because of their tendency to fade in sunlight; however they are fairly *stable* in artificial light. Known also as *yellow lake* and *flavine lake.*

QUETZALCOATL—In *Aztec art* and religion, the god of the atmospheric elements and the creator of men; often represented in *painting* as a feathered snake.

QUIVERING BRUSH—In Chinese *painting,* a fine brush stroke technique intended to give the effect of water waves. A *vertical brush* style is used, and in proper execution the line appears nervous and oscillating.

R

RABOT—In *sculpture,* a hardwood block used in the polishing of *marble.*

RACK—In *painting,* a 19th century device consisting of a stone or wood tablet having a number of grooves running length-wise, in which *brushes* were placed. Used chiefly by *water-color* and *miniature* specialists, it kept the wet brush tips from each other and from rolling.

RAG-WIPED PRINT—See *wiping.*

RAHJ AL GHAT—See *realgar.*

RAINDROP STROKE—In Chinese *painting,* the technique of shading *developed* during the T'ANG DYNASTY. It consists of exquisite, detailed shading accomplished by using small, pointed, oval strokes.

RAKKAN—In Japanese *art,* the signature on a *painting* or *drawing*; may appear as the artist's *seal* rather than name.

RANCE—In *sculpture* and *architecture,* a dull red *marble* with blue and white streaks and veins, occurring in Belgium and brought to other countries as *Belgian marble,* the name by which it is best known.

RANCHITO GROUP—In *archaeology,* name given to the series of mounds located on the east promontory at the site of the *Tres Zapotes* excavations. Principal among the discoveries were *burial* chambers, *sculptured* works, *figurines,* pieces of ornamental *ceramic* ware, and numerous *sherds* of various materials. One *tomb* contained a series of telescoped sections of clay tubing, supposedly for the escape of the soul. See also *mastaba* and *Zapotec.*

RANDA—In Oriental *ivory-carving,* an instrument having any number of points at the working end, used chiefly for final ornamentation of the object, esp. at the base. The multipointed extremity allows for the incising of more than one line, ridge, etc., in one operation.

RAT-FOOT DOTS—In Chinese *painting,* a technique of *brush* stroke by which leaves are executed in the shape of the print of a rat's foot. Groups of four or five slightly curved strokes are arranged fanwise, with a white center indicating the open top of the downward-pointed leaf. Appears to be limited to representation of *pines* in autumn and winter, or for distant pines in all seasons.

RATTAN YELLOW—In Chinese *painting,* a bright *yellow* vegetable *pigment* approaching goldenrod, known natively as *t'êng huang.* The plant sap is allowed to solidify in a mixture with glue, forming slender sticks for the artist's use. It is somewhat poisonous and irritating, and the charged *brush* must not be 'tipped' on the tongue or lips. Used extensively in bird, flower and *landscape* work.

RAW SIENNA—An *earth color* similar to the *ochres,* but somewhat finer in grain and more *translucent.* In color it is comparable to *yellow* ochre; *burnt sienna* (q.v.) becomes a warm, *red*dish-*brown.* Both belong to the group known as the *iron pigments,* and both are used as a *glaze* (q.v.) to *tone* or soften the color effect of *paintings.* At certain angles it appears to have a strong *green-gray* depth amid the brown. Classified also in the large *yellow pigment* (q.v.) group, it works well in both *oil* and *watercolor,* as well as in other techniques. The rich, transparent yellow color for which this pigment has been prized on the *palette* since ancient times is due to the large percentage of iron hydroxides present. It has the *stability* and absolute *permanency* of all other pigments related to the ochres. Known also as *rohe sienna* and *terre de sienne.*

RAW UMBER—In *painting,* a variety of *ochre* deriving its deep *brown* color from the presence of various oxides. When the native earth is properly washed, finely ground and dried, it produces one of the most *stable* and durable *pigments* known to artists, and it is adaptable safely to all techniques. Identified by its piercing, disagreeable odor.

RAYONISM—In *art,* a style of *abstract painting* founded by

Michael Larinov in Russia in 1911, characterized by radiating lines of light. Known locally as *Lutschism,* the theory dealt with dispersion and interpenetration of rays emanating from objects. This revised *Impressionism* had no real adherents, although it had a stimulating effect on *theatre* decoration.

REALGAR—A *painters' pigment* closely resembling the pigment *orpiment* (q.v.), both being sulphides of arsenic. *Realgar,* however, is *orange-red,* and derives its name from the Arabic *Rahj al ghar.* It appears to have been used largely in the Far East, and has been identified on *wall paintings* in Central Asia; frequently mentioned in *ancient* and *medieval* treatises. See *hsiung huang.*

REALISM—In *art* and *literature,* the treatment of subjects as they actually are, rather than as the *artist* or writer believes, in his imagination, they should or might be; the *representation* of things actual and real, with strict fidelity to nature and to real life, as distinguished from the *abstract,* speculative, etc., aspects of *idealism* (q.v.).

REALISTIC PAINTERS—An informal term applied to those painters in history and *legend* whose representations deceived spectators into believing they were observing the actual objects represented; e.g., Matsys, the Dutch artist, painted a bee so realistically that Mandyn, a fellow artist, attempted to sweep it from the *canvas* with a brush; Parrhasios painted a huge drape in such manner that Zeuxis strode up to it and tried to draw the folds to one side; Zeuxis himself painted a bunch of grapes at which birds pecked; Apelles (334 B.C.) painted a horse so like the real animal that mares approached the canvas and neighed. See also *trompe-l'oeil.*

REBENSCHWARZ—In *painting,* a fine *pigment* made on a carbon base, permanent black in its pure state, and blue-black with a gray *tint* when in admixture with any good white pigment. It is produced by the dry or destructive distillation of grape husks, vine twigs, and even the yeast of spent wine (the carbon exists in the 'tartar'). Although somewhat low in *opacity* and *hiding power,* it possesses an unusually high degree of *stability,* and is suited to practically all techniques.

RECEDING COLORS—In *painting* and *watercolor* work, those *hues* so *blended* or applied as to give an *illusion* of distance; excellent *technique* when executed in works showing the spatial aspects of *perspective* (q.v.).

RED—The *color* seen at the end of the *spectrum,* farthest from violet; the color of fresh human blood; the response to *light-waves* which are 670 to 760 *millimicrons* in length. One of the most popular colors on the artist's *palette, red* embraces approximately eighty different *shades,* each bearing its own descriptive name.

RED LEAD—A bright *scarlet* powder made and used as a *pigment* since *ancient* times. Pliny and other writers seem to confuse it with other bright *orange-red* pigments such as *cinnabar* (q.v.) but analysis has discovered it on objects whose origins have been lost in *antiquity.* The widespread use of artificial *vermilion* in the late *Middle Ages* caused a decline in the use of *red lead* by *artists,* although it is widely used industrially as an undercoat for dark *colors* in *architectural* painting. Its color is moderately *stable,* but has been found to darken and turn *brownish* with long exposure, particularly in light and in high moisture. Used also as a base material in the making of *flint glass* and *camera lenses.*

RED OCHER—In *painting,* a name common to a wide variety of *pigments,* rather than designating an individual *color.* The term comprehends *Indian red, light red, Venetian red, scarlet* ocher, Indian ocher, *reddle, bole,* and other oxides of iron. As a mineral, *red ocher* has reference to a soft, earthy variety of *hematite.*

RED OIL—A substance in the form of colorless crystals, insoluble in alcohol, used in *painting* as a *siccative.*

REGISTER—In *etching* and *printing,* (1) small dents appearing in multi-color *aquatint* plates, used as guides to insure that the various color impressions will match each other in the final *proof.* Known also as *register marks;* (2) any color reproduction is said to be *in register* when the color or type plates print exactly where intended.

REGISTER MARKS—A term in *etching;* see *register.*

REIMS SCHOOL—An *art* group of the 9th and 10th century *Carolingian* period, stressing the *decorations* and *illustrations* in the famous *Evangeliars* (q.v.).

RELIEF—In *painting, drawing, etc.,* (1) the effect of solidity, depth, or detachment given to a design on a plane or curved depth, or detachment given to a *design* on a plane or curved surface by the *lines, shading,* or *colors* of which the *pattern* is composed; (2) in a figurative sense, the vividness and sharpness of outline obtained by contrast or technical rendering, such as a figure in bold relief against the sky.

RELIEF—A *technique* in *sculpture* in which *designs,* figures, *patterns,* etc., are raised above the flat background in varying degrees of prominence. In *bas-relief (low relief, basso-relievo)* the figures are almost flat; in *alto-relievo (high relief)* the raised portions project boldly and strongly from the background; in *demi-relief (half relief)* they are given a medium prominence. From French *relever,* to lift up.

RELIEF CARVING KNIFE—A knife featured by long handle and short, chisel-like blade, either straight or diagonal at the cutting edge. Used widely for *relief* carving into *plywood,* where it is intended that the upper or *veneer* ply be incised without disturbing the lower plies. Used also in *chip carving.*

RELINING—In *restoration* work, the technique of backing a painter's old and weakened *canvas* with a strong, fresh one; sometimes termed lining. In this treatment the original canvas is not removed from the structure, but is merely given further support by the new one attached. Until the late 19th century a mixture of *glue* or paste and glue was the common adhesive, but since that time there has been a growing tendency to affix the new canvas with a *wax* or a combination of wax and *resin.*

REMARQUE—In *etching,* a *sketch* originally made by the *artist* on the *margin* of his *plate* to test his tools. In the 19th century such sketches came to be valued as part of the finished *print,* but they are no longer made on the margins, and consequently no longer appear as part of the prints.

RENAISSANCE—The term generally applied to the re-awakening of the *arts,* of learning, and of living in the in the spirit of the *classical* past of Greece and Rome; the revival of *artistic* activity in Europe during the 14th, 15th and 16th centuries, establishing the transition from the *medieval* to the modern world. The term is also applied to the various forms, *techniques* and treatments characteristic of the period, which is further classified into *early Renaissance* (1378-1500), *high Renaissance* (1500-1530), and *late Renaissance* or *Mannerism* (1530-1600), all three of which are identified by their efforts to rationalize and systematize the steadily increasing amount of empirically-gained observations and to apply them in the *fine arts.* (French *renaitre,* to be born again.)

REPAINTED WRECK—The popular term applied by art dealers to an old *picture* in a state of dilapidation which has, by cleverly forged *restoration,* been reborn. In many cases the extent of the original *paint* is less than 10%, and this rather large class of forgeries is worthless, except for study purposes. Since the *fluorescence* (q.v.) test cannot be used, because the forger's *varnish* prevents detection, x-ray and *infra-red* ray *photographs* are employed, and they quickly reveal the fraud.

REPOUSSAGE—A *technique* in *etching.* When a *plate* is repaired, scraped and rubbed, a hollow is left which would print a *gray* smudge. To prevent this, the plate is laid on a flat steel surface and the hollow is eliminated by tapping gently upon the plate with the ball of the *repoussage* hammer. This process is known as *repoussage.*

RESIN—Ingredient of most *varnishes* used for *surface coatings* on *works* of *art.* The *resin* is dissolved in a suitable solvent rendering the coating fluid brushable. It is not a new practice; Egyptians of the 19th dynasty were familiar with it, and the Incas of South America used it in their embalming processes. The general term is applied to any of a large number of hardened secretions or excretions of plants, most of those taken (by tapping) being known as *balsam.* *Resins* are classified into the *oil-varnish* group and the *spirit-varnish* group, the latter including the famed *dammar, mastic,* and *sandarac* varnishes, dissolved in an appropriate solvent; the former is made by fusing the *resin* with an *oil.* See *balsam* and *oleo-resin.* See also *resin, synthetic.*

RESINOUS—One of the classifications of luster (q.v.). Also, resembling, pertaining to, possessing, or having the appearance or consistency of *resin* (q.v.).

RESIN, SYNTHETIC—Scarcely established in the *fine arts,* artificial *resins* are complex, *amorphous* solids or semisolids made by chemical processes from a variety of raw materials. Resembling *natural* resins, they are less brittle, somewhat less colored, and more *stable..* Dissolved, they are useful as *surface films,* and in the solid form serve as *carving* and *molding* materials. See *amyl acetate.*

RESTORATION—In the *arts,* especially *painting,* the aim by reputable dealers and *artists* to preserve *works of art* by detecting and correcting their causes of deterioration, and returning them as nearly as possible to their original state. See *cradle, relining,* and *repainted wreck.*

REST-STICK—In *painting,* the *leather*-tipped rod (usually *bamboo*) upon which the artist relaxes his working hand in the execution of fine detail work; approx. four feet long, it is known also as *mahlstick* (q.v.), *maulstick,* and *appuie-main.*

RETHI—In Oriental *ivory-carving,* the general name applied to any instrument serving the function of a file. The usual type has a thick wooden handle to which a long, thin, rasped extension of *metal* is ferruled. The pointed extremity allows for boring as well as filing.

RETOUCH COLORS—In *painting,* a series of finely-ground colors having complete covering quality, used for *bringing up* the dull or dried-in colors previously applied. If properly made they should affix themselves without creeping, cracking or chipping, and should be *spectrophotometer*-tested in advance by the manufacturer. Used with *brush* or *airbrush,* they will dry to a *matte* surface, with no *gloss* apparent. Used chiefly by photo retouchers, *engravers, painters, illustrators* and *letterers.*

RETOUCH VARNISH—A variety of transparent, colorless *varnish* intended to bring life and color to dull spots in *oil paintings.* Also available at art supply sources are a number of *retouch colors* used for the brightening of *paintings, photographs, negatives, illustrations,* etc.; may be used with *brush* or *spray. Retouch varnish* often has a *dammar* base, and may be used at any stage in painting. In addition to bringing out dried-in colors, it establishes better cohesion between *paint* layers, prevents stringiness and trickling, and temporarily protects a superficially dry painting. Since it does not seal off the paint from the air, the paint will continue to dry, but is protected from dust until ready for the heavy protective coat of *surface film.*

RETROUSSAGE—In *etching,* a technique of raising the *ink* from the deep grooves of an *intaglio plate* in order to widen lines and render certain parts darker and richer. This is accomplished by drawing a soft cloth across the ink-filled incisions prior to *printing.*

REUBENS MADDER—In *painting,* a fine *lake color* of orange-brown *hue,* made from the *madder* root. After the 1st quarter of the 20th century, it was replaced on the palette by a *coal-tar alizarin* product possessing a higher degree of *stability.*

RHENISH SCHOOL—The term describing *works of art,* primarily *reliefs* (q.v.), of the 12th and early 13th centuries in the Cologne area. This style presents an interesting combination of French *Gothic,* German *Romanesque,* and *Carolingian Renaissance.* The figures of prophets and apostles are not treated with the *archaic,* cube-like simplicity of the German Romanesque, but are clearly and plastically developed. The softly flowing folds of their robes show strong individual expression which is carried over into the attitudes of the bodies.

RHODIAN SCHOOL—An important school of Hellenistic *sculpture,* of which the famous group known as the LAOCOÖN (three men being crushed by a giant serpent), now in the Vatican, is the outstanding work. The *artists* of this school sought their *inspiration* in the works of Lysippus. The intensity of *expression* attained in the LAOCOÖN has never been surpassed, and its many exaggerations are more than redeemed by its genuine power. The group, however, falls far short of the supreme excellence attributed to it by Pliny and by the art *amateurs* of the late 18th century.

RIDGE—In *etching,* the *burr* or torn edge left by the cutting action of the *stylus* or *graver* in cutting through the *ground* to the *plate,* preparatory to the *biting* process. See *burr* and *drypoint.*

RIGGER—In *painting,* a type of *brush* having the sable emerge from the thin end of a conical ferrule, broaden toward the center, and end in one of the finest points found in any brush. Used chiefly for extremely fine line work and in *relief* painting. So called because of its frequent use by *seascape* artists in executing the fine lines of ship riggings.

RILIEVO SCHIACCIATO—In *sculpture,* literally 'crushed relief'; unusually flat *relief* having only faintly discernible projection, the *figures* appearing to blend down to the background.

RIVER MARBLE—In *sculpture,* a variety of *limestone* which, when highly polished or cut along certain planes, exhibits veins and blotches so distributed throughout as to suggest flowing rivers. The markings are caused by infiltration of iron oxide.

ROCKER—In *etching,* an instrument used in roughening a *plate* to the extent that its entire surface is one extended *burr.* This is necessary in creating a *mezzotint,* in which an intense, uniform, velvety *black* is required. The *rocker* itself is a steel chisel having a curved edge, serrated with very fine teeth, the handle springing from the center of the curve. See *mezzotint.*

ROCK SOAP—An important ingredient in *crayons,* known also as *mountain soap.* It is a pitch-black or bluish-black variety of aluminum silicate, greasy to the touch, which crumbles in water. Functions as a filler.

ROCOCO—A florid style of *decoration* and *architecture* which came into prominence in the late *Renaissance,* about 1720. The term, however (Fr., *rocaille,* rockwork or shellwork), was first used between 1830 and 1840. It is generally a meaningless mass of extravagant forms *embellishing* or concealing structural lines, featuring a profusion of wheels, *scrolls,* shells, etc. Distinguished from the *Baroque* by its 'wedding cake' elegance, use of many materials (*wood, stucco, tapestries, mirrors, metal,* etc.), and by its delicate foliage and definite femininity as contrasted with the heavy and the pompous. It was often without *expression* and individuality, and many of the wrought forms were totally indescribable. *Rococo* reflected the growing sophistication of the French court under *Louis XV* and the increasing influence of woman's taste in its circle. The term is sometimes applied in contempt to anything bad or tasteless in decorative *art,* or an object or style overelaborated or exaggerated.

RODENT TAIL—In Chinese *painting,* a variety of brush stroke technique creating lines like rat tails, long and tapering, with beginnings like nail heads. The *brush* is applied with firmness to produce a strong dot, and is then trailed off in a tapering line to a fine point.

ROHE SIENNA—In *painting,* a famous *earth* color prized on the *palette* since ancient times, commonly known as *raw sienna* (q.v.).

ROJO VÁGETAL—The red *dye* of the ancient Egyptians originally extracted from botanical sources, later produced as a *pigment* on a base of *coal-tar;* commonly known as *safflower* (q.v.).

ROMAN CANVAS—A *ground* used by artists for *oil painting;* consists of thick *linen* sheeting previously coated with *paint* on one side. See *canvas.*

ROMAN GREEN—In *painting,* a fine yellowish-green *color* of low *brilliance* and high *saturation,* a trifle higher in saturation than *olive green* (q.v.).

ROMANISTS—A group of Flemish *painters* who worked in Rome under the influence of Raphael and Michelangelo. They were part of the group who sojourned to Italy and imitated the *Italian style,* thereby fusing it with the *Flemish style* (q.v.). See *Italianizers.*

ROMAN NOSE—A human nose-shape somewhat aquiline in

outline, popular in representation by *painters* and *sculptors* through the centuries.

ROMAN OCHER—In *painting,* a fine *pigment* of rich, deep, and powerful *orange-yellow* color. It is used, both raw and burnt, in *oils* and in *water-color* painting, and is transparent and *stable.*

ROMAN PURPLE—In *painting,* a prized *color* of bluish-red *hue,* somewhat brighter than *royal* (q.v.). It is generally of low *brilliance* and high *saturation.*

ROMAN SCHOOL—The term applied to the style of *painting* popular in 16th century Rome, esp. to that of Giulio Romano.

ROMAN SEPIA—A *painting pigment* of warm sepia *hue,* obtained by mixing *sepia* and *burnt sienna* in careful proportion; the resulting product possesses the durability and *stability* common to both ingredients. The *color* is the same as that of *Vandyke brown.*

ROMANTICISM—The term applied in any period to a *style* or movement in which the *emotional* and imaginative qualities in *art* are stressed. In this general sense, one hears of *romantic* trends in Venetian *painting,* German *art,* etc. It thus becomes the *expression* of a basic attitude opposed to the *classical* with its historical emphasis on the rational, the definite, and the harmonious. See *popular romanticism.*

RONDEL—In *sculpture,* a steel instrument about 8½ inches in length, somewhat thicker than the ordinary pencil, used in the cutting of *stone;* characterized by a somewhat rounded head, often incised to various depths.

RONDELLE—Any one of the colored *glass* discs used in the making of *stained glass* (q.v.) windows.

ROODSTONE—(Rare) In religious *art,* any *cross* or *crucifix* made of *stone.*

ROSE—A name given to any of the *colors* of the many varieties of the *rose,* generally *red* in a vast range of *hues,* having a medium degree of *brilliance* and *saturation.* The broad scale of *rose* colors extends from light *yellowish*-red to deep *bluish*-red, varying from low to high in brilliance. The common interpretation of the word has reference to a dusty *pink* shade, characteristic of the petal color of the common *rose* of rather light hue.

ROSEAKER—In *painting,* ancient name for *realgar* (q.v.).

ROSEBUD—In *painting,* a prized *color* on the artist's *palette,* deep bluish-red in *hue,* high in both *brilliance* and *saturation.*

ROSE CARTHAME—In *painting,* a transparent, brilliant-red *lake color* produced upon a basic ingredient of *coal-tar.* It is a 20th century *pigment* having good *stability* to light, and possesses the physical and chemical properties common to the lake pigments generally.

ROSE D'ALTHAEA—In *painting,* a fine red *color* on the artist's *palette,* high in *brilliance* and medium in *saturation*

ROSE DE NYMPHE—In *painting,* the *color* popularly identified as ivory, eggshell or off-white, often tinged with yellow.

ROSE DORÉE—In *painting,* a *color,* red in *hue,* popular on the artist's *palette.* It is medium in *brillance* and high in *saturation.*

ROSE GRAY—In *painting,* a neutral color of slightly red-yellow *hue,* possessing medium *brilliance.* It occurs most frequently as a *neutral* gray.

ROSE HERMOSA—In *painting,* a prized *color* of yellowish-red *hue,* high in *brilliance* and medium to high in *saturation.* Found on the *palette* of the modern artist.

ROSE HORTENSIA—In *painting,* a *color* of reddish red-yellow in *hue,* high in *brilliance* and low in *saturation.*

ROSE LAKE—In *painting,* a prized *pigment* of red-yellow *hue,* low in *brilliance* and high in *saturation.* Primarily red, it is a prized *color* on the artist's *palette.*

ROSE MADDER—In *painting,* a *color* of fine red hue, medium to high in *saturation.* Also, an alumina *lake ofalizarin* or *madder,* pale *rose* in color.

ROSE NEYRON—In *painting,* a valued *pigment* of fine red hue, medium in *brilliance* and extremely high in *saturation.*

ROSE PINK—One of the several *lakes* of *yellow* or *greenish* *hue,* used in *water-color* work. It is made by precipitating vegetable juices on a *white earth* product, such as *alumina* or *chalk*. Made also from *Brazilwood,* all varieties are somewhat *fugitive* and not recommended where *permanency* is desired.

ROSE PURPLE—In *painting,* a prized *pigment* of blue-red *color,* medium in *brilliance* and medium to high in *saturation.*

ROSET—Obsolote term for a red *pigment* of deep *hue* used on the artist's *palette.*

ROSE TAUPE—An artist's *color* of yellowish-red *hue,* low in *brilliance* and unusually low in *saturation.*

ROSIN—In *oil* products, a term often confused with *resin* (q.v.). It is used as a substitute for *colophony* (q.v.), being the hard residue left after *turpentine* has been distilled away from the pine *balsam.* In a strictly technical sense the word is a variant of resin, deriving from similar sources and possessing similar qualities and *texture.* Used widely on the bows of *violins* and similar instruments, for better grip or 'bite' on the *strings.*

ROSSO ANTICO—In *sculpture,* a fine red *marble* having white markings and thin black veins, used by the Etruscans and ancient Romans. Said to have been obtained from Cynopolis and Damariscita. Known also as *rouge antique.*

ROSSO VEGETALE—A term in *painting;* see *safflower.*

ROUCOU—In French *painting,* a pale pink *color* similar to that of *salmon.*

ROUGE—In *painting,* one of the *iron pigments* (q.v.) identified by its *tinge* of *purple;* commonly known as *Indian red* (q.v.).

ROUGE ANTIQUE—See *rosso antico.*

ROUGE VÉGÉTAL—In *painting,* a *pigment* of good permanency and *stability,* derived from *coal-tar;* earlier varieties going back to the ancient Egyptians were used as *dyes* only, extracted from the botanical CARTHAMUS TINCTORIUS. Commonly known as safflower (q.v.).

ROUGHHEW—In *sculpture* and *carving,* to shape or hew in coarse fashion, as to *roughhew* marble or timber in the first stages of preparation.

ROUGHING STONE—In *litography,* a stone with an intentionally roughened surface upon which *prints* are impressed to impart to them the appearance of *water-colors* or *oil paintings.*

ROUGHSETTER—A *sculptor* or *mason* who constructs raw-quarried stones into rough or semi-rough slabs or sections. *Roughsetting* is the first process undertaken in rendering quarried *stone* into shape usable for *architecture* or *sculpture.*

ROULETTE—In *etching,* a small wheel running in a socket attached to a handle, which leaves the indentations of its teeth upon the *metal* as it is rolled across the *plate.* It is used to correct *mezzotint* plates, as well as to make *designs* which take on a special character because of the tool used. A *roulette*-made *print* is distinguished by the *pattern* of small tooth marks on the plate. Difficult to handle, it is not often used. See *roulette intaglio.*

ROULETTE INTAGLIO—An *etching* process practically identical to the *drypoint* technique, the only difference being that a small wheel, rather than a point, is used to create the *burr* (q.v.); employed by *mezzotinters* to add darks in spots scraped too light. Also used on *aquatint* and drypoint for corrections and additions. Though difficult to handle, it yields remarkably fine work in the hands of an expert. The wheel is known as a *roulette* (q.v.).

ROUND—In *sculpture,* a figure done completely, front, back and sides, as distinguished from *relief* work, showing front and partial sides only. Also known as work in *the round.* See *bust.*

ROYAL—A variety of *purple color* made by a mixture of 55% *red,* 33% *black,* and 12% *blue.*

ROYAL BLUE—A term in *painting;* see *smalt.*

ROYAL SCARLET—In *painting,* a *pigment* of fine *scarlet-vermilion* hue, formerly popular in *water-color* work. However, it rapidly fell into disfavor in the early 20th century because of its lack of even reasonable *permanency.* Its lack of *stability* was surprising, in view of its high degree of *opacity.* Known also as *pure scarlet.*

RUBBER CEMENT—A colorless, *transparent* adhesive

usually made of fine crepe *rubber;* produced in liquid form under a wide range of trade names, it is used in mounting work, in the affixing of mats, and in other *art* work requiring extreme thinness and complete absence of wrinkling.

RUBBING—The *technique* of making an impression on thin, tough *paper* by moistening it and patting it into the interstices or lines of the *relief* upon which it is placed, or into the incised parts of a *carved* or *modeled* surface. The paper, still on the *designed* object, is then tapped with an inked pad, producing an actual-size *image* in *ink* on the paper. See *ishizuri.*

RUBBING BLOCK—In *sculpture,* a smoothing or *polishing* block used in the early stages of the refinement of *marble;* consists of a heavy, coarse-grained stone, usually artificial. Known also as *rubbing brick.*

RUBENS SCHOOL—A school of *art* originating in the *studio* of Peter Paul Rubens at Antwerp in the early 17th century. Here Rubens' *baroque* style influenced such *artists* as Van Dyck, Seghers, Snyders, and others, producing a fusion of the Italian and *Flemish* styles which proved a strong guide in the later course of *painting..* See *Romanists, Flemish style,* and *Italianizers.*

RUBIA—A rare *red pigment* mentioned by Pliny and believed to have been in use as long as any known *color* employed in *painting.* Derives from the botanical RUBIA TINCTORIUM (q.v.). See also *madder.*

RUBIA TINCTORIUM—The root source of *rubia,* the famous *red color* used by painters since ancient times. Mentioned by Pliny, and found on many *paintings* of the Egyptian and Greco-Roman periods, it has since been completely replaced by synthetic *dyes.* See *madder* and *alizarin.*

RUBIC—In *painting,* to redden, to *color* with *red.*

RUBY—A *color* of rich, deep *carmine red,* as that of the *true,* or *Oriental ruby;* the *hue* of *ruby glass.* Generally, the quality of being red; redness; any object *ruby*-like in color.

RUSSIAN SCULPTURE—A *cosmopolitan* type of *sculpture* growing out of the fact that practically all Russian *sculp-*

tors studied abroad. Among the most representative were Lanceray, who specialized in *bronzes* of spirited action in meticulous detail; Lieberich, who limited his fine talents to animal work; and most eminent in all of Russia, if not in all the world, was Marc Antokolski (1843-1902), who resided permanently in Paris. His portrait *statues* are prized *museum* pieces, and his IVAN THE TERRIBLE was purchased by Emperor Alexander II who had it cast in *bronze* as everlasting tribute to its creator. His representation of TURGENEV is considered one of the greatest pieces of sculpture since the *Renaissance.* In *Russian sculpture* generally, outside influence in apparent, esp. in the numerous national monuments found throughout the country.

RUSTIC WARE—In *sculpture,* a *glazed* variety of *terra cotta* in brown, buff or tan, sometimes with green *mottling.* Used chiefly for ornamental work in *architecture.*

RYŪ—In the *painting* and *carving* of Japan, the *representation* of a *dragon* (q.v.).

S

SABLE—General name for a type of small animal, having become a synonym for a painter's *brush.* This, the finest of all brushes, is made from the hair of the *kolinsky,* one of several species of Asiatic minks.

SACCHAROIDAL MARBLE—Any variety of *marble* having a granular crystalline structure; highly esteemed by *sculptors* for *statuary* work, esp. the type known as *statuary marble* (q.v.).

SAFFLOWER—A red *dye* extracted from the dried petals of the botanical CARTHAMUS TINCTORIUS, put to many uses by the ancient Egyptians. Commonly known as *carthame* (q.v.), it is expensive and *fugitive* as a *dye,* but is *permanent* and *stable* as a *pigment,* esp. in a *lake color* made upon a *coal-tar base.* Known also as *rouge végétal, rosso vegetale,* and *rojo vágetal,* even in English-speaking countries.

SAFLOWER OIL— An *oil* prized as a *siccative* in artists' *paints* and *varnishes.* Unlike *tung oil,* it is soluble in *turpentine* and other thinners, and its rapid-drying qualities are superior to those of *soy bean oil.* Obtained from the seeds of the CARTHAMUS TINCTORIUS, native to India, but now cultured in the U. S. The same plant produces the red dye *safflower* or *cathame,* used in the making of *pigments.* See *carthame.*

SAFFRON—An unusual *color*ing material, more a *dye* than a *pigment.* Producing a pale *yellow* golden color, it is extracted from the dried stigma of the crocus flower, and seems to have been a favorite among the *painters* of the *Middle Ages.* It was probably used more for *illumination* (q.v.) than for larger works.

SAFTGRUEN—In *water-color* work, a coloring agent of dark yellow-green *hue* extracted from the unripe berries of the buckthorn, or RHAMNUS. It is not very *stable,* and is really imitated by the more permanent *lakes* produced on a base of *coal-tar;* however, its transparency gives it value as a *glazing* color. Commonly known as *sap green* (q.v.).

SAINT ANNE MARBLE—In *sculpture,* a deep blue-black variety of *marble* having white veins; occurs chiefly in Biesme, Belgium (but is not the well-known *Belgian marble*).

SAINT BAUME MARBLE—In *sculpture,* a hard yellow stone (not strictly a *marble*) with veinings of brown or red, quarried in the province of Var, France.

SAINT-BEAT—In *sculpture,* a fine-grained variety of *marble* quarried in France, prized for its compact structure and pure white color. Employed widely in *heroic* and *colossal* statuary work, to which it is adapted because it occurs in large blocks.

SAKU—In Japanese *painting,* the word placed in the corner of the finished work beside the artist's signature, meaning 'made by.'

SAKURA—In Japanese *art,* the cherry blossom, *symbolizing* the soul of Japan and the transient aspects of human life.

SALIAN ART—The period paralleling the epoch of the German emperors of the Salian Frankish House, 1024-1137. *Painting* and *sculpture* favored the static, *linear,* and symmetrical elements of style, inclined toward a one-sided metaphysical and ascetic expression, deriving strong influence from the *Byzantine* (q.v.).

SALISH ART—A mature *art culture,* expressed particularly in wood *sculpture,* originating with the old *Salish* Indian tribes of northwest U.S. Though not as elaborate as the west coast art which emerged from it, the rigid stylization and utter simplicity of this sculpture echoes recent trends in truly *modern art.* The better pieces compare favorable with the now well-known creation of the Pacific islands (see *Maori carving*) and the west portions of Africa.

SALMON—A comparatively old *color* on the artist's *palette,* being the color of the flesh of the fish. The *hue* varies among different manufacturers, ranging from pale off-white tints to deep pink.

SAMOTHRACE—Aegean island upon which the famous VICTORY *statue* was found in 1863. A product of the 2nd century B.C., VICTORY is one of the finest examples of the *sculpture* of the period, and is now in the Louvre, Paris. Another *marble* statue, said to equal its predecessor in beauty and craftsmanship, was discovered on *Samothrace* late in 1949.

SAN CH'ING—In Chinese *painting,* the pale *blue* mineral *pigment* obtained from the first layer of the *azurite* stone when it is rubbed down in water. Known also as *beryl blue,* it is used chiefly for the painting of garments in *figure* studies. See *shih ch'ing.*

SANDARAC—A *resinous* substance now little used as a *varnish* material because it produces a brittle *surface film* with a tendency toward *crazing.* It was highly regarded in *ancient* times, and according to some authorities, was supposed to have given rise to the name *varnish* through corruptions of the names of various South American locations of its production. See *resin.*

SANDERS BLUE—In *painting,* a corrupt name for the French CENDRES BLEUES *(ash ultramarine).* Sometimes termed (also improperly) *saunders blue.*

SAND PAINTING—An *art* expression of unknown origin, practiced by many tribes of American Indians, especially the Navaho. The *paintings* vary from three to twenty feet in diameter, always executed on the floor. Sand is spread to a depth of one-third of an inch and smoothed with a batten. The *pigments* consist of five *colors* of finely-ground sand: *white, red, yellow, black,* and a *gray-blue,* each used *symbolically.* The *artist* takes a pinch of the colored sand between his fingers and allows it to trickle to the *ground*-base of neutral sand, working from the center outward, developing the *design* according to *traditional* rules of exactitude. From one to a dozen artists work on a picture simultaneously, depending upon its size, and the finished *representation* (usually gods, the rainbow, lightning, mountains, etc.) must be started at dawn and finished before nightfall. After certain *ceremonies,* the sand is taken up and thrown away. Reproductions are made from memory by white men permitted to witness the rite. See Hasteen Klah, NAVAJO CREATION MYTH (1942); Reichard & Newcomb, SHOOTING CHANT; SAND-PAINTING OF THE NAVAHO (1937); Laura Armer, SAND PAINTING OF THE NAVAJO INDIANS (1931).

SANDPAPER PAINTING—A *technique* of *painting* or *drawing* on sandpaper for reproduction. A waxed *crayon* is used to build up an impression on the sandpaper which is then *inked* and *printed.*

SAND THREADS—In Chinese *painting,* a technique giving the effect of shallow water dotted with grass; usually accomplished by a combination of horizontal strokes and *pien* (q.v.). For deeper water, the *dotting* is eliminated, and slightly wavy, approximately parallel horizontal strokes are used, with an occasional S curve of flowing line.

SANSUI—In Japanese *art,* a type of *landscape painting* emphasizing mountains and water. Chinese equivalent is *shan shui* (q.v.).

SAP GREEN—In *painting,* a substance made from the berries of the botanical RHAMNUS since medieval days. While it is one of the most *fugitive* of all colors, it is still popular among *water-color* artists and will be fairly *stable* under proper conditions, esp. constancy of light and temperature. Proof of its permanency is found in the *illuminated manuscripts* which still exhibit strong *sap green* color after hundreds of years. It is available today, although the modern variety generally contains an added *coal-tar* ingredient. Known also as *vert de vessie, verde vejiga,* and *saftgruen,* even in English-speaking countries.

SAPONIN—In the *restoration* of *paintings,* an *amorphous* powder which forms a soap-like foam when mixed with water, used for the general cleaning of oil paintings. Less harmful than common soap, it will effectively remove accumulated smoke, dust and grease. However, excess rubbing may penetrate the *canvas* and result in irreparable damage.

SARCOPHAGUS—A stone coffin, grave, or chest-like *tomb,* usually *sculptured* and inscribed in a manner relating to its occupant. A great number of Egyptian *sarcophagi* are extant in excellent preservation. Perhaps the most beautiful is the famous *sarcophagus of Alexander* (q.v.). In most cases it was the final, or outer coffin containing an *inner coffin* or a *cartonnage case* which, in turn, contained the *mummy.* The oldest examples were made in IV DYNASTY Egypt, of *granite.* The term is loosely applied to all coffins, of all materials.

SARCOPHAGUS OF ALEXANDER – A *sarcophagus* found at Sidon, and now at Constantinople. It is undoubtedly the most beautiful of all *classical* sarcophagi, as well as an outstanding work of 4th century B.C. *relief sculpture.* Its top is in the form of a *temple* roof, and the reliefs on the sides are framed by exquisitely carved *moldings.* The sculpture, embellished with delicate *red, blue* and *yellow,* represents dramatic battle and hunting scenes, with ALEXANDER THE GREAT playing a prominent role. See *sarcophagus.*

SARDINE OIL—A pale yellowish liquid derived from sardines by a boiling and pressing technique. Soluble in alcohol, ether, and other fluids, it is used extensively as an ingredient in *surface films* or coatings applied to *paintings* and *statuary.* Employed also in the making of *asbestos* cements, *printing inks,* and waterproofing substances.

SARRANCOLIN MARBLE—In *sculpture,* one of the most beautiful of all *marbles.* The prevailing colors are red, white, brown, green and orange, with variegated streaks, blotches and veins of contrasting color. Chief source is the valley of Aure in the French Pyrenees.

SATSUMA RED—In Chinese *painting,* a *vermilion* pigment used in the coloring of garments in portraiture (*jên wu*). It derives from *cinnabar,* and is the first layer skimmed from the stone in emulsion. Available today in prepared form, requiring (like *chê shih*) only the addition of water.

SATURATION—In *painting,* the extent of *chroma* or purity; the degree of freedom from relation to *white;* the *attribute* of chroma at a maximum. In general terms, the *intensity* or purity of a *color.* See *chroma.*

SAUNDERS BLUE–See *sanders blue.*

SAUROKTONOS– (Greek, *lizard slayer*) In *sculpture,* the name given to a famous *statue* executed by *Praxiteles.* The *bronze* original was made about 325 B.C., and is listed among the works described in Pliny's NATURAL HISTORY XXXIV, 70. There are Roman copies in *marble* in the Vatican and the Louvre, and a small bronze replica in the Villa Albani in Rome. All *represent* the young *Apollo* as he watches a lizard climbing a tree. He holds an arrow, evidently awaiting the moment for the kill. Illustrated in SCULPTURE AND SCULPTORS OF THE GREEKS, Gisela M. A. Richter, New Haven, 1929, Figs. 674-5.

SCAGLIOLA–In *sculpture* and *architecture,* a material composed of *cement,* isinglass and coloring matter, generally used to imitate *marble.* Receptive to high *polishing* and unusually durable, it is valuable for use in simulating *granite* as well. Colored by the addition of tinted *glue* while in the soft state.

SCALE DRAWING–A copy of a *drawing* so made that all distances are in the same ratio with the corresponding distances in the original; a copy with all distances multiplied by a constant factor, usually a fraction. The technique is of strong importance in *cartography.*

SCALE PATTERN–In the *art* of ancient Mesopotamia and Greece, an *ornamental pattern* in which rows of pointed or round-tipped scales overlap; arranged so that the tips of one row come over the joints of the lower row.

SCALE STONE–In *sculpture,* one of a pair of blocks upon which the *model* and the block stone are placed. Known also as *scale stone stool.*

SCARLET–A bright red *color* inclining toward *orange.* Most *vivid* of all the *reds,* it was originally obtained from the *cochineal* (q.v.) insect exclusively, and treated with *zinc* and tartar. Now produced successfully from *coal-tar.* The *hue* bears a strong similarity to that of *carmine;* see also *royal scarlet.*

SCARLET LAKE–A term in *painting* referring to a coloring agent formerly prepared from *cochineal,* lacking *stability* in its *fugitive* character. It was subsequently imitated in *hue* by the permanent *alizarin madder* toned with a permanent yellow to produce a true *scarlet* color; as such, it is a dependable, transparent *lake color* having considerable durability and stability, esp. in *water-color* work. Known also as *purple lake* (q.v.), *laque écarlate, lacca scarlatta,* and *scharlachrot.*

SCAUPER—In *engraving,* a tool used for clearing out open spaces between lines. Known also as *scorper.*

SCHARLACHROT—In *painting,* a fine *pigment* of deep rich *scarlet*-red, extracted from the dried dead wingless female *cochineal* insect; it lacks only in *stability.* The *fugitive* character of the pigment induced its imitation through the medium of *alizarin madder* which not only reproduced the fine *hue,* but imparted the needed *permanence.* Its transparency renders it esp. valuable in *water-color* work. Known popularly as *scarlet lake* and *purple lake* (qq.v.).

SCHEELE GREEN—A *painter's pigment* discovered in 1778, named for the Swedish chemist who first prepared it. It is similar to *emerald green* (q.v.), being a compound of copper and arsenic. It is easily discolored in sulphur-bearing air, and has been largely abandoned. Its highly poisonous nature was another reason for its loss of favor after strong popularity during the 18th and 19th centuries. Severe illness came to artists who pointed or 'tipped' the *brush* with the tongue or lips.

SCHIZZO—In Italian *art,* any *sketch,* whether preliminary to a *painting,* or the final work itself.

SCHOOL OF BOLOGNA—A famous school of *painting* founded in Bologna by Lodovico, Agostino, and Anniable Carracci in 1589, in which they stressed the style of Raphael and Correggio rather than that of the then popular 'Caravaggismo' favored by Michelangelo. The most famous of the Carraccis' works is the painting (1600) of the *gallery* of Cardinal Farnese's *palace* in Rome, executed by Anniable and Agostino.

SCHWEINFURT GREEN—A bright bluish-green *pigment* commonly known as *emerald green* (q.v.).

SCIPIOS—Term in *sculpture* applied to the famous *tomb,* located on the Appian Way in Rome, which once enclosed the *sarcophagus* of Scipio Barbatus (consul 298 B.C.). It was discovered in 1780 when it was rifled and defaced.

SCORPER—Same as *scauper* (q.v.).

SCOTCH STONE—A term in *sculpture;* see *ayr stone.*

SCRAPER—In *etching,* a sharp, three-cornered tool used in scraping a *lithographic plate* to correct errors. When the *stylus* or *graver* leaves an upraised *burr* or ridge on the *ground,* the *scraper* levels it down, although in the *drypoint* process, the raised edge is allowed to remain, since it enhances the quality of the *print,* giving it the appearance of a *drawing.* See *drypoint* and *burr.*

SCRATCHBOARD—A type of *chalk*-covered cardboard covered cardboard upon which *drawings* are made with *pen* and *ink, crayon,* etc. It has a smooth surface with line or *stipple tint,* and the desired lighting is achieved by scratching out parts of the surface with a steel tool.

SCRATCH KNIFE—In *painting,* etc., a tool having a triangular blade with a sharp, pointed tip, used for removing unwanted or damaged spots from a painting or *drawing;* employed where the use of an eraser or solvent is inexpedient. Some artists prefer a razor blade.

SCRIMSHAW—The *art* of decorating *ivory,* shells, and the like by incising or *engraving* scenes and patterns, sometimes adding coloring matter as a final ornamental feature.

SCROLLER—In *painting,* a type of *brush* having a very gradual thinning to a point, used in the creating of *scroll* designs; the camel-hair brushing end is ferruled to the handle. Available in a wide range of sizes, some varieties of *scroller* taper out from a thin ferrule to a broad, rounded tip, depending upon the thickness of the lines to be drawn or painted.

SCROLL PAINTING—In Chinese *art,* the most common form of *painting,* rolled up when not on view. Developed because of the need for portability in the event of moving, war, fire, etc., after loss of many fine *murals* through these events. The finished picture is mounted, and a rod *(chou)* with ornamented ends (*chou shou*) is affixed to the bottom edge. See *chüan chou.*

SCUDDING CLOUD—In Chinese *painting,* a technique of executing wavy lines giving the effect of fast-moving clouds or running water; a *vertical brush* is used, and complete figures are often made with a single line. Although the appearance is one of freedom, the *brush* is carefully controlled and brought up at the end of each stroke.

SCULPSTONE—In *sculpture* and *carving,* an unusual *medium* possessing sufficient softness to be cut with a knife, yet hard enough to last through the centuries. Used sporadically since ancient times, a mid-20th century revival has produced numerous *art* works of high merit. Available at art supply sources, *sculpstone* may be had in simulation of *marble, granite, alabaster, basalt,* and other conventional materials of the sculptor, in a wide range of colors. Many varieties exhibit the properties of diorite and obsidian; it is mined in practically all parts of the world. A display of *sculpstone* creations in New York late in 1950 drew wide interest.

SCULPTOR—One who pursues the *art* of *sculpture* as a profession, inclination or hobby; an *artist* who practices *sculpture* (q.v.).

SCULPTURE—(1) The *art* of *carving, cutting* or hewing *stone, wood,* or any other hard material into figures; also, the *modeling* of figures in *wax, clay,* or other soft substances to be cast afterward in *bronze* or other *metal.* The term has been extended to include the designing and executing of medals, *medallions,* and *bas reliefs,* and to the carving or *engraving* of *gems.* (2) A work that has been *sculptured;* carved work; a figure cut or carved in wood, stone or metal, *representing* some real or imaginary object or person; a *statue;* an *icon, image,* or other figure in *round* or in *relief.* (3) An engraved *illustration* (obs.). Generally, *sculpture* is three-dimensional art creation, as distinguished from such two-dimensional works as *paintings* and other flat-surface creations. The origin of *sculpture* is lost in antiquity, and numerous *primitive* examples of the art are extant.

SCULPTURE IN WAX—See *wax sculpture.*

SCULPTURE PAINTING—See *bas-relief.*

SCUMBLE—In *painting,* a light, semi-transparent color that is applied over a darker *underpainting* or *imprimatura* (qq.v.). In the technique of *scumbling,* the artist may apply a thin film of *opaque* color in an almost dry state over other color, intending to alter it, but not to cover it completely.

SEAL—In Oriental *art,* an impression made with a stamp, generally accompanying the signature on East Asiatic *paintings;* usually applied with *vermilion pigment.* See *yin chang* and *in.*

SEAL CUTTING—The Chinese *art* of *calligraphic carving,* more commonly known as *iron brush* (q.v.).

SEALER—In *painting,* a liquid coating composition, usually *transparent* (such as *varnish*), that also contains *pigment* for sealing porous surfaces, esp. *plaster,* preparatory to application of the finish coating of *colors.* In a strict sense it is a *size* (q.v.).

SEALING-WAX—A *medium* used for receiving and retaining the impression of *seals,* usually consisting of a mixture of *shellac, rosin* and *turpentine,* colored with *vermilion* or other *pigment.* In its earliest form it was *beeswax* mixed with one of the *earth colors* (q.v.); the modern variety, known also as *Indian sealing-wax,* originated in Venice.

SEASCAPE—In *art,* the common term for *marine painting,* in which water and/or marine objects are emphasized.

SECANT—A *pattern* frequently found in modern *design* and *painting,* consisting of a straight line cutting a circle at two points.

SECCO—A variety of large *painting,* frequently of *mural* proportions, executed on dry *plaster.* The technique produces a dull, *matte* finish, as contrasted with *fresco* (q.v.). See also *fresco secco.*

SECESSIONISTS—See *Sezessionists.*

SECONDARY COLOR—A combination of two *primary*

colors in equal proportion. See *primary colors;* see also *tertiary colors.*

SECTION—In *drawing,* a view obtained by imagining the object cut away, as if by sawing. The path of the saw is considered the cutting plane; i.e., the plane upon which the cut is made. If one portion is then removed and a drawing made of the remaining portion, the lines formerly invisible are exposed to view. Known also as *sectional view.*

SECTION LINES—In *drawing,* lines used to indicate material in a *section* (q.v.) or view 'through a part.' Known also as *cross-hatch lines.*

SEDIMENTARY STONE—In *sculpture* and *architecture,* one of the three great classifications of *stone* (q.v.), this category including *gypsum, limestone,* slate, shale, and *sandstone.*

SEMI-ABSTRACTION—In *painting,* the name applied, under Picasso's leadership, to *abstraction* (q.v.).

SEMI-DRYING OIL—See *plasticizer.*

SEMIK—In Russia, the traditional *day of the dead,* observed once a year in memory of all of the deceased of the nation since the earliest days of the country's existence; particularly strong during the *druzhina period.* Frequently represented in 11th and 12th cent. *painting,* showing the grief of the throngs alleviated by antics of professional buffoons retained for that purpose.

SENEGAL GUM—A *white* or *yellow* powder derived from numerous varieties of ACACIA; used in *inks,* adhesives, *textile printing,* and in the making of *surface films* for *paintings* and *statuary.* Known also as *Arabic gum.*

SENOFO—An African tribe famed for its artistry in wood sculpture, esp. in the representation of human *figures.* While not on a par with the exquisite *Maori carvings* (q.v.), *Senofo* pieces are nevertheless prized collectors' items today.

SENSU—A type of folding *fan* of Japan, representing the highest point in the application of fine *painting* to this type of device. The greatest artists of Japan exerted their efforts in the painting of paper fans. See *fan* and *uchiwa.*

SEPIA—A term familiar in the *fine arts* as both a specific coloring material and as the name of a *color* (neutral *brown*). The coloring material provided an *ink* that was known in *classical* times, but apparently little used in Europe until the late 18th century. It was then taken up for ink *drawings* and *water-color* painting. The source is a secretion from the ink sac of the common cuttlefish or squid, and from related species. Superior to all other water-colors with respect to evenness of spread when applied with a *brush.*

SEPIA UMBER—A special *hue* of *burnt umber* and *ivory black;* appears to be as deep, *stable, effective,* and valuable as the prized original *umber.*

SERIGRAPHY—Name applied to the *silk screen* process as a reproduction printing *medium* in the *fine arts.* The screen is prepared in the customary manner (see *silk screen*) and a lithographic *tusche* is painted on the *silk* where the flat *color* is to be printed. When the tusche is dry, a watery *glue* is applied, filling in the mesh spaces without adhering to the tusche. The latter is removed by *turpentine*-soaked cloths, leaving the *design* capable of clear *printing.*

SERPENTINE—In *sculpture,* a variety of *marble* having a basically *green color,* sometimes *tinged* with *red* or *brownish-yellow.* It has a smooth, often greasy 'feel' and is responsive to high polishing and sharp cutting. The name derives from the irregular, winding veins streaked throughout. Numerous varieties of *serpentine* abound, ranging from rare mineral to plain rock. See *noble serpentine, verd antique, common serpentine* and *marmolite.*

SEZESSIONISTS—An *art* group in Vienna associated with the *art nouveau* movement, popular between 1890 and 1905. See *art nouveau.*

SFUMATO—In *painting,* a hazy atmospheric form or outline created by meticulous attention to fine shading and color blending. The blurred and misty effect is frequently found in *marine* and *landscape* work. From Italian, 'smoked.'

SHADE—(1) The term applied to any *color* which lies below mid-*gray* in *brilliance*. Also, a trace or light *value* of a color. (2) A degree of any color darker than normal, as when *black* is added; when the color is rendered lighter by the addition of *white,* it is a *tint.*

SHADE—In *art,* the darkness of certain areas on objects caused by those parts being faced away from the source of direct *light.* Distinguished from *shadow* in that the latter's darkness is due to the fact that the light has been cut off by some intercepting material. See *chiaroscuro.*

SHADER—In *painting,* a type of *brush* having a square finish at the bristle ends; used in smudge and shadow work, it cannot be employed in fine line and contour work. Available in a variety of thicknesses, ranging from 7/16" to 1-11/16"; curiously absent from the working equipment of the Chinese painter.

SHADING—In *art,* especially *painting,* the gradual passing in color from one *tint* or *shade* to another. Known also as *gradation.*

SHAN MIEN—In Chinese *art,* the face of a *fan;* the *paper* or *silk* portion bearing the *painting,* as distinguished from the frame and ribs.

SHAN SHUI—In Chinese *painting,* the two classes of pictures embracing (a) pure *landscape,* and (b) water and mountains together. This group constitutes one of the four major categories of subject matter in the painting art of China, where supremacy in landscape work is considered the ultimate in painting mastery. Japanese equivalent is *sansui* (q.v.).

SHAPING METHOD—In *ceramics,* the simplest technique by which objects may be formed. A ball of tightly-wedged *clay* is manipulated by action of the hands and fingers alone, so handled as to create the desired shape. Compare with *coil method* and *slab system* (qq.v.).

SHARP DOT TECHNIQUE—In Chinese *painting,* a style of *brush* stroke consisting of short, upright, pointed movements, creating the effect of tacks sticking point upward; made only with the tip of the brush. This is the most common form of *tien* (q.v.), and may represent distant trees, grass on low levels or gentle slopes, etc. Chief use, however, as with all landscape *dotting,* is to add variety to a scene and to emphasize planes and *contours.*

SHELL MARBLE—A highly ornamental variety of architectural *marble* containing *fossil* shells.

SHÊNG—In Chinese *painting,* a term applied to any type of *silk* that is un-*sized* and used as a *ground,* as contrasted with *shu,* or sized silk. See *hua chüan* and *su ling.*

SHIH CH'ING—In Chinese *painting,* a famous *blue pigment* of mineral origin. *Azurite* stone is rubbed down in water, taking off the *color.* The upper stratum of the emulsion yields a light blue (*san ch'ing*), the middle layer a medium blue (*êr-ch'ing*), and the heavy bottom layer a rich dark blue (*t'ou ch'ing*). After securing the color, of which only one day's supply is taken at a time, the artist mixes it in a heated state. Now available by purchase, there are blues, *greens, yellows* and *reds* in stick form which are rubbed in water on a *grinding slab* (q.v.) or stone *palette,* as is *Chinese ink.*

SHIH HUANG—In Chinese *painting,* a fine *yellow pigment* of mineral origin. The source is believed to be *orpiment* (q.v.) stone which is baked until *friable* and then ground to powder and mixed with *glue.* The color resembles, and is also known as, *sunflower yellow;* used extensively in portraiture (*jên wu*) and in butterfly painting.

SHIH K'O—A term in Chinese *sculpture* applied to any type of *carving* executed in *stone* or *marble.*

SHIH LÜ—In Chinese *painting,* a fine *green* mineral *pigment* prepared from *malachite* in the same manner in which the famous *shih ch'ing* mineral *blues* are derived from *azurite;* obtained similarly in three degrees of intensity. Oriental artists state that malachite stones shaped "like prawns' tails" yield the finest colors. See *shih ch'ing.*

SHIH NÜ JÊN WU—In Chinese *painting,* portraits of women—usually women of remarkable beauty—presented with the primary purpose of displaying their beautiful features; categorized in the *jên wu* class.

SHIJO SCHOOL—A Japanese school of *painting,* combining the *naturalism* and *realism* of the *Maruyama School* and the *idealism* of the *Nanga School.*

SHIM BRASS—In *sculpture,* thin sheets of *brass* employed for the purpose of separating the carved *model* from the *cast* or *mold* without damage to either. Prepared in rolls, *shim brass* is found to be as effective as the chemical *mold separators* in dividing the *plaster* and *carved* object.

SHIN-EN—In Japanese *art, a* term meaning 'deep distance' in a *painting;* mountains are painted as though seen through a break in a range of hills.

SHIVER—In *masonry* and *sculpture,* a flake, chip or splinter, as from a *stone,* usually worked off in dressing or chiseling. Known also as *spall.*

SHO-CHIKU-BAI—In Japanese *art,* the trio of pine, *bamboo,* and plum, *symbolic* of longevity, happiness, and good fortune. Frequently found in *painting* and *sculpture.*

SHOHEI-GA—In Oriental *art,* the general term applied to all *paintings* on Japanese *screens, partitions,* and sliding doors.

SHOU CHÜAN—In Chinese *art,* a *scroll painting* that is never seen in its entirety. Its *theme* unfolds as part is displayed between the end rods or *chou* (q.v.). This *technique* of exhibition is based on the belief that pictorial art should unfold or reveal itself as though it were a *poem* or *musical score.* The problem of *composition,* therefore, is an exacting one.

SHOZO—In Japanese *painting,* a general term applied to any *portrait.*

SHU—In Chinese *painting,* any variety of *sized silk* used as a *ground,* as distinguished from *shêng,* which is un-sized. See *hua chüan* and *su ling.*

SHUANG K'UAN—In Chinese *art,* a signature or *colophon* on a *painting* which contains the name of the person for whom the picture was painted or to whom it was dedicated, along with the artist's name. See *k'uan* and *tan k'uan.*

SICCATIVE—In *oil painting,* a chemical substance added to paints by the *artist* in order to promote more rapid drying. *Siccatives* in popular favor are *litharge,* manganese, and *cobalt* oxide. They are not *drying oils* but are added after the drying oil has been blended with the *pigment.* Their use, esp. in excessive amounts, is believed to be detrimental to the life of the *paint,* and consequently, to the painting. See *dryer.*

SIDE BRUSH TECHNIQUE—In Chinese *painting,* a technique in which the *brush* is held and used in an oblique position with respect to the *ground,* as in writing. Known natively as *ts'ê pi,* it is used chiefly in *wash drawings* and certain types of *dotting* (see *tien*) and shading.

SIENA SCHOOL—The final artistic *expression* of the twilight of the *Middle Ages* in 14th and 15th century Siena, city of *pageants* and mystics, and the last stronghold of *medievalism* in Italy. The artistic *tradition* was essentially untouched by the progress of the neighboring school of Florence, and rigorous prohibitions discouraged the work of foreign *artists* who might have introduced the innovations of the onsweeping *Renaissance.* Francesco di Giorgio broke loose from tradition and succeeded in rivalling Botticeli in his mastery of poignant line and the *luminous* quality of his style (1439-1502). Compare with *Tenebrists* (q.v.).

SIENNA PIGMENT—*Earth colors,* similar to the *ochres,* but more *translucent* and finer in grain. *Raw sienna* is comparable to *yellow* ochre; when *burnt,* it becomes a warm, brown-*red.* Both are used as a *glaze* (q.v.) to tone down the effect of colors previously applied to *paintings.*

SIGNBOARDS—Generally, *art* work of a commercial nature in large size for outdoor display. *Signboards* were known to both the Greeks and Romans, and there are numerous references to them in *classic* writings. Excellent specimens have been found at Herculaneum and Pompeii, sometimes *painted,* more often *carved.* Among the great *artists* who have painted *signboards* are Correggio, Holbein, Hogarth, Millais, and others; numerous of their works in this category are extant.

SIGNWRITER'S BLACK—A variety of deep black, waterproof *lettering* ink used extensively in *commercial art, photography, mechanical* drawing, etc. It is free-flowing for *brush, spray* or *pen,* covers the *ground* in solid *opaque* in one stroke, and dries with a rich, velvety *luster.*

SILENE—In *painting,* a fine white *pigment.* Chemically it is a variety of calcium silicate, *silene* being a trade name.

SILENUS—Companion of *Bacchus* (q.v.), and the most famous of the *Satyrs.* Archaic *sileni* were *represented* as half animal, half human. Later they tended more toward human beings, retaining only long ears and tail, in which form they appear frequently in Greek *vase painting* and *sculpture.* A famous example is SATYR by *Praxiteles,* a lost work known only through *literature.* Many other replicas are extant, all showing Satyrs pouring wine.

SILHOUETTE—A dark *image,* usually *black,* standing out in contrast to its lighter background; an outline *drawing,* uniformly filled with solid black. A representation in *black* of the outlines of an object; a *profile portrait,* appearing as a shadow cast by candlelight. The name derives from Étienne de Silhouette, French minister of finance, whose rigid economy in 1759 caused his name to be applied to anything incomplete; hence, to this type of likeness, then popular in Paris.

SILICA—A substance well known in the *arts* for its importance in *glass* making, *glazing,* and *enamel-firing;* also provides filler or extender in the manufacture of *artists' paints.* A *natural* product, it is mixed with *pigments* of high *tint*ing strength or intense *color* to increase the bulk and reduce the cost.

SILK SCREEN PRINT—A *technique* of *printing* a flat color *design* through a piece of silk, known as *Swiss bolting cloth,* which has been tightly stretched over a wooden frame firmly fastened to a table by means of hinges with removable pins. All parts of the design not to be printed are *stopped out* by a resistance *medium,* and the balance is transferred to the *silk. Silk screen printing* can be applied to many surfaces, such as *glass, plastics, wood, metal, leather, paper* and *cloth.* The printing medium, e.g., *lacquer, water-color,* or *oil* base, is slowly pushed through the open meshes of the exposed silk by means of a long wooden handled squeegee edged with hard rubber; only one *color* can be printed at a time. The same silk and frame can be cleaned and used repeatedly for different designs.

SILK SCREEN STENCIL—A recent development in *silk screen painting.* A light-hardened photographic *emulsion* is applied to the screen at the non-printing parts, permitting the *paint* to go through the screen when the excess emulsion is washed out to open up the printing areas. Fine line-cuts and even *half-tones* are reproduced by this technique, along with reproduction of *type.* In hand work, a filler is painted on the screen's non-printing areas to stop the *ink* or paint from going through. Known also as *paint process* and *paint screen process.*

SILVER POINT—A *drawing* instrument developed from the ancient *stylus,* along with points of *copper, lead,* and *gold.* It can be used only on prepared *paper, coated* with a fine abrasive which will take off and hold small *grains* of the *metal.* The line of the *silver point* corrodes to a dark dull, warm *tone.*

SILVERSMITH—One pursuing the *art* of forming *silver* objects as a profession or hobby. His occupation may embrace any or all of the various techniques of shaping, incising, hammering, soldering, *chasing,* etc.

SILVER WHITE—In *commercial art,* a fine white *pigment* commonly known as *lithophone* (q.v.).

SIMULTANEISM—A 20th century French school of *art* flourishing at its height just prior to the outbreak of World War I. Originally a form of *cubism* and *futurism* (qq.v.), it was soon rejected by the cubists in favor of *synthetic cubism,* but became an important principle of futurism since it contributed to the *expression* of dynamic movement. Known also as *orphism.* (q.v.).

SIMULTANEISM—In *painting,* the simultaneous presentation of different views of an object in the same *picture,* more or less superimposed upon each other.

SIMULTANEOUS CONTRAST—In *painting,* an optical effect acquired when one *color* is influenced in *hue* by an adjacent color, and vica versa. The spatial *juxtaposition* of opposed sensory impressions (usually *primary colors*) whereby the *value* of each is enhanced by the other.

SI-MURGH—In the *art* of old Persia, a fabulous monster made up of the parts of numerous animals, actual and legendary. This composite creature, known also as *senmurv,* was frequently represented in *paintings, rugs, tapestries* and *ceramics.*

SINOPSIS—In *painting,* one of the many names given to the famous *pigment* known popularly as *vermilion* (q.v.).

SINUATE—A general term in the *arts* applied to any technique by which serpentine or wavy lines are *carved, engraved, inlaid,* etc., into the *ground* by the artist. Any object so decorated is said to be *sinuated.*

SIVA—One of the supreme deities of Hinduism, frequently re-created in the *arts,* esp. *sculpture,* as a many-armed human figure. *Siva* represents both the principle of destruction and the power of reproduction or restoration. Often spelled (and always pronounced) *Shiva;* see also *Vishnu.*

SIZE—In *painting,* a *glue* used as a binding agent, and sometimes applied under *paint* or *distemper* to eliminate absorption. There has been a tendency to use this term in referring to the type of animal glue derived from skins and bones, which would render it synonymous with *gelatin.* The word *glue* would be then applied specifically to the adhesive material obtained from cartilage and sinew. *Size,* however, is somewhat different since it contains *chondrin.* Many varieties of *paper* used in Chinese *calligraphy* and *painting* are *sized* (see *ping hsüeh* and *fan hsüan*), as are numerous types of *silk* used as *grounds* in the same *arts* (see *hua chüan* and *shu*).

SIZING—In *woodworking* and *painting,* (1) any working material prepared to the proper dimensions is said to have *sizing;* (2) any coating of *glue,* shellac, or other substance applied to a surface to prepare it for *painting* or other method of finish.

SKETCH—In *painting, drawing,* etc., the first outline or general embodiment of an artist's idea on *paper,* in *clay,* etc., from which to work out subsequent plans or the final creation itself; a rough or incomplete draft of any *design* or project. Also, a transcript of any figure or object in *chalk* or *pencil,* with simple *shades* only, or a coarse draft of the same in *colors.* The term is sometimes extended to apply to a short and simple musical, literary, or dramatic composition.

SKETCH BOOK—Popular term applied to a fine grade of white *drawing* paper usually produced in pad form; suitable for *crayon, pencil, ink,* and *water-color* work.

SKETCHING EASEL—A type of *easel* which folds compactly, designed for portable use by the *landscape* artist. See *easel.*

SKETCHING UMBRELLA—A device used by the *landscape* painter to enable him to pursue his work in inclement weather. It consists of a small canopy on a collapsible frame of steel ribs, fitted with one principal spike that is pressed into the ground for support. When opened it has an average diameter of four feet. A set-screw allows for placement of the 'umbrella' at any desired angle.

SKEW CHISEL—An instrument used for the *carving* of *wood-blocks* and *linoleum blocks.* Extending from a wooden handle by a ferrule, the blade has angular lengthwise construction, the cutting edge appearing as a *V*-shaped affair having two arms, one thick and blunt, the other thin and sharp.

SKY BLUE—In *painting,* a mixed *pigment* containing *zinc oxide* and *ultramarine blue* as its principal ingredients, producing a warm, light blue color. It possesses a high degree of *stability* and *hiding power,* rendering it suitable to all techniques.

SLAB—The smooth surface on which early *painters* ground their *colors* with the aid of a *muller,* both items traditionally made of *porphyry* (q.v.) See *grinding slab.*

SLAB SYSTEM—One of the three techniques employed in the *sculpture* which uses the *medium* of *terra cotta* (q.v.). When used for the making of *plaques, tiles,* and other substantially flat objects, the process consists simply of pressing *clay* with a rolling pin or similar instrument until the desired thickness is obtained; the finishing work is accomplished with cutting or abrasive tools. In making animal or flower figures, thin wires or pipe cleaners may be used as inner foundations to support the clay. Compare with *coil method* and *shaping method.*

SLANT—In *water-color* work, a metal or *porcelain* tablet in which three or six wedge-shaped wells or depressions are fashioned to a depth of a quarter inch at one end, elevating gradually to the surface level of the tablet. Each such depression is for a color. Other varities have circular scoops, some with a *thinner* well opposite each cut-out See *well slab.*

SLANT LINER—In *painting,* a type of *brush* broadening widely from a narow ferrule to a thick painting end, finished with a diagonal edge. Used in creating slanting lines, and lines intended to have varying thickness; usually made of camel hair, it is available in a wide range of sizes. Compare with *liner* (q.v.).

SLICE—A scraper, apparently used in early times to pick up *paint* from the *grinding slab.* It was made of *metal* or *wood* and resembled a putty knife, though the scraping edge was often at an irregular angle and the blade was broader. See *grinding slab, muller,* and *slab.*

SMALL AXE STROKE—In Chinese *painting,* the technique of *shading* developed by the Northern School of the T'ANG DYNASTY; i.e., shading by small strokes resembling axe splits.

SMALT—Although literally one of the *cobalt pigments,* this dates from a much earlier time, with some evidence that it may have been known to the *ancient* Egyptians. However, as a dark *blue color* on the *artist's palette* it has not been identified on European pictures earlier than the 15th century. Like the other cobalts it is *permanent,* but unlike them, it has a weak *tinting* strength and poor *hiding power.* It will not keep its color with extremely fine grinding, and its weakness probably led to its displacement by the much stronger *Prussian blue* in the 18th century (see *cobalt pigments* and *azure*). Known also as *zaffre, royal blue, dumont blue* and *king's blue.*

SMOCK—The customary outer garment worn in the *studio* by the followers of most of the *arts,* consisting of a loose fitting wrap-around, usually made of *cotton,* belted, buttoned, or put on over the head in the manner of a *poncho.* The term appears to derive from one or more Icelandic words: SMOKER OR SMOG, a loose garment; SMJUGAN, to creep into or through; SMOKKA, to don part of a garment, as a sleeve, loop, etc. Also known (esp. in England) as *smock-frock.*

SMOKING—In *etching,* the technique of employing a specially-constructed taper to impart a smoked appearance to the hard *ground* employed in *line etching* (q.v.). The melted ground combines with the *lamp-black* from the taper to form a *black* surface upon which the *drawing* is easily seen.

SOAPSTONE—A type of rock, green to bluish-gray in color, sufficiently soft to be *carved* with a knife. Its qualities of smoothness and heat resistance render it valuable in the making of *statuary* and other items of decorative art. Known also as *talc rock* and *steatite,* it is readily identified by its greasy or soapy feel. Used chiefly by the Chinese and Japanese.

SOCLE—In *sculpture* and *architecture,* a low foundation or *pedestal* supporting a large *vase* or other ornament, as distinguished from a *base* or *plinth.* Found frequently as the step at the foot of a *column* or *statue.*

SOFT GROUND—In *etching,* same as ground (q.v.) except that about 50% of tallow is added, rendering it usable for the making of *soft ground etchings* or *acquaints.*

SOFT GROUND ETCHING—A type of *etching* having a soft, broken line resembling a *pencil* or *crayon line.* It does not have the decisive *quality* or control that characterizes *line etching,* but has a pleasing line well suited for masses, *textures,* and use in conjunction with *aquatint.* Also known as *vernis mou,* an important feature is the tallow-softened *ground.* Its popularity has long been waning, chiefly because the same effects can be obtained by *lithography.*

SOFT GROUND OFFSET—In *etching,* a method of transferring a *chalk drawing* to a copper *plate* for *intaglio printing.* The *proof* resembles *crayon lithography* to a greater extent than does the regular *soft ground etching* (q.v.), which tends to resemble a *pencil drawing.* The masses of dark area are richer and easier to handle.

SOHAN—In Oriental *ivory-carving,* an instrument resembling the ordinary file, used for applying the first rough finish to large pieces; made in varying degrees of rasp or roughness.

SOKU—The ancient Japanese *technique* of covering *armatures* with *lacquer*-saturated cloth, producing *sculptural* forms. Now known as *kanshitsu* (q.v.).

SOLENHOFEN STONE—A prized variety of *limestone,* particularly valuable in *lithography* (where the stone block method is still employed). Found as an UPPER JURASSIC deposit at Solenhofen (vicinity of Pappenheim), Bavaria.

SOLFERINO—A variety of *purple* color produced by a mixture of 83% red and 17% blue.

SOOT BROWN—In *water-color painting,* a deep brown *pigment* occurring as the tarry soot of *resinous beech* or *pine,* ground from its lumpy consistency to a fine powder. Although substantially *stable,* it is rendered somewhat *fugitive* by the tarry matter present, and changes to a *cooler,* paler hue in time.

SOYA BEAN OIL—A natural, pale yellow oil obtained by pressing out the bean; has a wide variety of uses in the *arts:* (1) as a *drying oil* in artists' *paints,* instead of *linseed oil* or *tung oil* (qq.v.); (2) in the making of *glycerin, enamels, varnishes,* and *printing inks;* (3) as a *sizing* for coated paper; (4) as an ingredient in various *fibers* and *plastics.* Known also as *bean oil, soy oil, soja-bean oil,* and *Chinese bean oil.*

SPACE ARTS—A term applied to those *arts* having to do with such elements as *color,* light, space; e.g., *architecture, sculpture, painting,* etc., as distinguished from non-space-occupying arts such as *literature* and *music.* See *visual arts.*

SPALL—In *sculpture,* a chip, splinter or flake, as from a *stone,* usually worked off in dressing or chiseling. Known also as *shiver.*

SPANISH BROWN—In early *painting,* a brown *pigment* of inferior quality, consisting of a highly adulterated dark oxide of iron. Now completely abandoned by *artists,* it is used chiefly by masons for the coloring of *mortar.*

SPANISH RED—A *color* prized by the artist for its unusual lasting quality; a deep *shade* of *red,* it is commonly known as *Venetian red* (q.v.).

SPANISH WHITE—A substance used in *gilding,* and as an adulterant in the making of *lake colors;* commonly known as *whiting* (q.v.).

SPECULUM METAL—In metal *sculpture,* a bronze-like *alloy* consisting of *copper* (67%) and tin (33%). See *bronze.*

SPHINX—In Egyptian *archaeology* and *sculpture,* any one of the figures usually executed in great size, having a human or animal head and generally an animal's body. Three principal classes are (1) *androsphinx,* having a human head; (2) *criosphinx,* having a goat's head; (3) *hieracosphinx,* the hawk-headed variety. The Greek *sphinx* deriving from *mythology* was a woman monster shown in *art* as a winged lion with female head and breasts; said to have propounded a riddle and to have killed all who could not solve it. This colossal recumbent stone figure, near the *pyramids* of Gizeh, is the most famous example extant.

SPIDER WEB TECHNIQUE—In Chinese *painting,* a method of executing lines resembling the long, waving, loose strands of a spider's web, used extensively in former epochs for Buddhistic figures, flowing robes, and garment representation generally. The finest *brush* is used, pointed and *vertical.* Care is emphasized in showing the similarity of the lines to the strands of silk emitted by the silkworm.

SPILLED INK—In Chinese *art,* a *painting* technique employing broad full strokes, with the result that the objects in the picture have no defined outline. See *p'o mo.*

SPINACH GREEN—A very dark *green color* used on the *palette.* The term was most often used in the Orient to describe a certain *hue* of *jade* as *spinach-green* jade.

SPOSALIZIO—Sobriquet for Raphael's famous *painting* in the Brera Museum, Milan, relating the story of the wedding of Mary and Joseph. It was painted in 1504 for the

Church of St. Francis at Citta di Castello, where it remained until brought to Milan in 1798. The picture is signed "Raphael Urbinas MDIIII" and was painted shortly after Raphael had left his teacher, Perugino. The term derives from the Italian, "marriage."

SPRAY GUN—A device having many uses in the *arts,* the simplest variety of which resembles generally the construction of the ordinary insecticide gun. Used in solid-color *painting,* spraying mists of water on unfinished *models* of *clay* in *sculpture* and *ceramics,* spraying *engobes* and *glazes,* etc. Often referred to as *airbrush,* many elaborate, effective, powered types are available. See *airbrush.*

SPRUCE OCHER—In *paintings,* a popular name given to brown or yellow *ocher* (q.v.).

SSŪ HSIANG—In Chinese *art,* the quadruple margin of border around a *painting,* immediately surrounding the *ink* or *paint.* The upper margin is always wider than the lower. See *yang chü.*

STABILITY—In *painting,* the quality of permanence, steadfastness or constancy in any *color, pigment, surface film,* etc. See *stable.*

STABILIZER—The ingredient in artists' *pigments* rendering them brushable, keeping the oil from separating, preventing running and stringiness, and contributing to the durability of the colors. Aluminum stearate is used successfully as a *stabilizer.*

STABLE—In *painting,* the term describing an artists' *pigment* that is not readily *bleached,* clouded, softened, decomposed, or otherwise altered from original *color* or *texture* upon exposure to air, light, heat, and other elements; firm; steadfast; constant. Compare with *fugitive colors* (q.v.).

STAINED GLASS—A pictorial or *decorative* composition made by uniting various sizes and shapes of *colored, translucent glass* together with strips of lead. Detail and shading are painted in afterward. Except for a wider range of colors and *textures* now available, in addition to certain minor technical developments, the *art* of *stained glass* making is essentially the same today as it was in the 12th century. The color may be produced by (1) metallic oxides in the melting pot; (2) coating the surface with a film of colored glass (thus making *flashed glass*) which is *etched* away where the color is not wanted; (3) applying a silver solution under fire, which turns clear glass yellow (the etched portions of the flashed glass will become green); (4) covering the surface with colored *enamels* and fusing them into the glass. The cathedral of Chartres has 146 important *stained glass* windows embracing 1,350 pictures containing more than 5,000 human figures. Modern attempts to equal the beauty of this work have been unsuccessful, even though the processes are known. See *gather.*

STAND OIL–An *oil* (used by *painters*) thickened by exposing it to the sun in a shallow vessel; appears to have been used widely in 15th to 18th century European *oil painting.* Also made by heating raw *linseed oil* for long periods at a high temperature; in either case, it is thickened by heat alone. It tends to yellow slightly less than raw linseed oil, produces a more impervious surface with *glossy* finish, increases the fluidity and transparency of the paint, and prevents absorption into the *ground* or underpainting. Popular again, it is readily available at art supply sources. See *sun thickening.*

STATUARY–In *sculpture,* (1) statues considered collectively; a group of statues; (2) the *art of carving* statues or *images;* (3) (rare) one who pursues the art of making or carving statues or images.

STATUARY MARBLE–In *sculpture,* a pure white variety of *saccharoidal marble,* highly prized for all the qualities lending themselves to that *art.* The finest varieties are brought from the Apuan Alps. It responds excellently to cutting, takes a high finish, and is of unusual strength and durability.

STATUE–A product of the *art* of *sculpture;* any lifelike representation of a human figure or animal in a solid substance, as *marble, wood, iron, bronze,* etc., or in an apparently solid substance. Also, any sculptured, *cast* or *molded* figure of appreciable size, executed in the *round,* as a *statue* of *Hercules,* etc.

STATUETTE—A small *statue,* usually of perfect proportion in reduction.

STAYBELITE—A clear, pale yellow solid substance of *resinous* texture derived from the southern *pine,* used in the making of *plasticizers,* in the *sizing* of *paper,* in *ceramic printing,* and as a *surface film* or coating for *paintings* and *statuary.* Chemically it is a hydrogenated rosin, *staybelite* being a trade name.

STEADY—In *sculpture,* a support used for blocking up a piece of stone or *marble* that is to be worked.

STEATITE—A variety of soft, smooth rock used in *carving,* commonly known as *soapstone* (q.v.).

STECCA—In *painting,* a blade of wood or animal horn kept on the *palette* of the medieval artist to spread the *gesso* on the wooden *panel* or *support.* Another variety, having a metal edge, was used for smoothing, scraping, or removing paint during the actual painting process. Not synonymous with *palette knite* (q.v.).

STEEL BLUE—In *oil painting,* one of the many names by which the famous *Prussian blue* (q.v.) is known.

STEEL FACING—In *etching,* an electroplated chromium-steel *plate* used to prevent the *intaglio* metal *design* from wearing out in the *printing* of a large *edition.* Delicate plates, especially *drypoints,* are likewise protected in this fashion.

STELE—A stone *pillar* used as a gravestone or to mark a site. The oldest known *stele* decorated with *sculpture* is Sumerian (Mesopotamian), dating from 2,550 B.C., representing the king leading his army. Another pictures King Urnammu pouring a libation to a god. Buddhist and Mayan *stelai* have been found, decorated with religious scenes. The most beautiful are those made in Athens in the 5th and 4th centuries B.C. to serve as *tombstones.* The earliest were high and narrow, with a single figure, but by the middle of the 5th century the slab was made wider, allowing for more elaborate *relief.* The scene pictured was usually a characteristic episode from the life of the deceased, as a knight dealing the death blow to a foe, a boy with a pet animal, a woman holding her jewels, or the final farewell in the home. After the decree of Demetrios of Phaleron against the display of wealth, the market for this sculpture in Athens disappeared, but similar grave reliefs continued popular elsewhere. Today the term refers generally to any memorial slab or tablet of stone. See *Aristion.*

STEREOCHROMY—Known also as *water-glass painting,* a *technique* characterized largely by the *medium* employed. Waterglass, a thick, syrupy, clear liquid, is an aqueous solution of potassium or sodium silicate. Into this substance, *pigments* are ground; or, a thinner water-glass is used as a *fixative* with pigments that have been applied with water alone. This process has been widely advocated for *mural* painting.

STIACCIATO—In *carving,* a general term applied to any object or technique containing or embodying *low relief.*

STIL DE GRAIN—A term in *painting;* see *brown-pink.*

STILE LIBERTY—In Italy, the name applied to the *art nouveau* movement, popular from 1890 to 1905, and affecting all of the *visual arts.* See *art nouveau.*

STILL LIFE—In *art,* a *picture* of inanimate objects. Frequently, flowers or fruit in a *vase* or bowl.

STIPPLE—In *painting,* the effect obtained by using small touches or dots of *color* instead of strokes and lines. By employing this technique in proper fashion, the artist will obtain evenness of surface, *gradation* of *shade,* or *intensity of shadow.* It was used extensively by English *water-colorists* of the 19th century. See also *stipple engraving.*

STIPPLE ENGRAVING—In various *etching* processes, the *technique* of piercing the *varnish ground* with a multitude of small dots, and adding further dots or flecks on the plate with a *stipple engraver;* generally, the use of dots instead of lines in the making of a *line engraving* (q.v.).

STOMP—A *pencil*-like device usually made of strips of rolled paper having a blunt end and no coloring matter; used for spreading and shading *pastel* and *charcoal* effects by smear technique after dipping. Known also as *tortillon* and *stump*.

STONE—Highly honored as an *architectural* material from *ancient* times, *stone* early became the substance of *sculptured designs* and, to a slight extent, a *support* for *painting*. Broadly, the kinds of *stone* in use in the *arts* can be placed in three general categories: (1) *sedimentary* (e.g., *sandstone*, slate, *limestone*, shale and *gypsum*) ; (2) *igneous* or primary rocks, formed by solidification of molten masses from within the earth, including *granite*, feldspar, *quartz*, diorite and *basalt;* (3) *metamorphic rocks*, which are either sedimentary or igneous in origin, but have been changed in character by movement of the earth's crust or by chemical action; e.g., *marble* (q.v.) is the metamorphic combination of sedimentary limestone and *chalk*.

STONE NOSE—In Chinese *landscape paintings* showing mountains, the first straight rock or peak; the nearest peak, from which the others arise, or from behind which additional peaks appear in the background.

STONE OCHER—A term in *painting;* see *Oxford ocher*.

STONE YELLOW—In *painting*, same as yellow *ocher*.

STOP-OFF—In metal *casting*, to fill part of the *mold* with sand or earth, to prevent access of the molten metal to that part.

STOPPING OUT—In *etching*, the act of stopping certain sections of a *plate* from further *biting* (q.v.) while exposed to the *acid bath;* this process also keeps the unwaxed or ungrounded back of the plate from being etched. Quick-drying *varnishes* are successful in *stopping out*. See *line etching* and *crayon aquatint*.

STRASBOURG TURPENTINE—One of the *balsams* used directly in the *arts*, as an ingredient in *painters' varnishes*. It is the exudate from coniferous trees, and the volatile oil is derived by distillation, with a crude *resin* remaining as residue. See *oleoresin* and *balsam*.

STRETCHER—An accessory to the canvas *support* of a painted *picture*. It is a *frame* of four or more pieces over which the *canvas* is fixed, usually by tacks. As a rule, *stretchers* are provided with keys or small wedges for slight enlargement to take up the slack from the canvas.

STRETCHING—A *technique* employed in the drying of *intaglio prints;* see *flattening.*

STRETCHING PINCERS—A device used by painters to pull the *canvas* tightly around the under-frame; better known as *canvas pliers* (q.v.).

STROBA WAX—A light-colored hard *wax,* compatible with most waxes and *resins,* used in the making of *paints* and *varnishes, surface films* for *paintings* and *sculpture,* and as a successful substitute for *carnauba wax.* This trade product is also employed in the manufacture of insulating and recording waxes.

STROGANOV SCHOOL—A Russian school of *art* named in honor of its patrons, the Stroganovs, an influential and wealthy family of merchants, who were *connoisseurs* of the arts of the East, of Persian *miniatures,* and Indian textiles and *jewelry,* as well as of the *icon,* outstanding for its rich Oriental display of colors and ornamentation. The school itself furnished detailed study of these arts, along with creative teachings intended to surpass then in artistic merit. The school dropped to its decadence with the fall of the Stroganovs in the early 17th century.

STROKE—In *sculpture,* to give a finely *fluted* surface (esp. at the edges) to a piece of stone or *marble.*

STRONG—In oil *painting,* the adjective describing full, *intense colors.* The term is frequently employed in *criticism* which may refer to such work as *strong art.*

STRONTIUM YELLOW—In *painting,* a color strongly related to *barium yellow* (q.v.), being a strontium chromate instead of a barium chromate. Like its barium counterpart, this *pigment* has a *lemon hue,* but is slightly deeper in *tint* and has greater *hiding power.* Prized on the *palette* because it will produce the brightest known *greens* in mixture.

STUDIO—Generally, the *atelier* or workroom of an *artist;* the place or room in which some form of creative *art,* e.g., *painting, sculpture,* is pursued.

STUDIO EASEL—An improved but complex variety of

easel having screw adjustments for both height and the angle of the *painting*. See *easel*.

STUDY—In *oil painting,* any reproduced *picture* utilized by students as a practice *model*.

STUMP—A small instrument, consisting of rolled up *chamois* skin or *paper,* used for smoothing out the *tones* of *crayon* or *charcoal drawings*. A smaller tool of the same type, pointed at one end only, is called a *tortillon* (q.v.).

STUN—A white or discolored spot or area in *marble,* caused by a blow from a blunt-edged or blunt-pointed hammer. See also *terrace*.

STUPIKĀ—In the *archaeology* of India, a vast *sculptural* decoration hewn directly from a great quarry of rock. Carved under the CALUKYA DYNASTY (650-750 A.D.), the *shrine* is in the shape of a *terraced pyramid,* dominated by the huge, *bulbous* shape which is repeated in smaller scale on the *tiers* of this enormous *stupa*. One of the greatest monuments in Indian art, it is known in religion as the *Kailāsanātha,* and is located at Ellura.

STYLE—A broad term, deriving from the Greek *stylos* and Latin *stilus* (see *stylus*) now all-inclusive and transferred to the entire field of the *arts*. Generally, those characteristics of *form* or *technique* which are peculiar to a certain work or group of works, or to an artist, school or movement, period, or locality. Many theories concerning *style* are extant: Gottfried Semper, in DER STIL, argues that *style* in art is identified only by the materials used, as *clay, wood, metal, silk,* etc., because each demands different treatment. His followers are numerous, even today. Aloys Riegl opposes this in his SPAETROEMISCHE KUNST-INDUSTRIE, taking the position that *style* originates in a subjective will-to-art lying in the artist himself, and that the spiritual structure of the artist seeks *expression* in accordance with the individual peculiarities of his own will. A compromise theory had been found by the Chinese in 350 B.C. through Dsuang Dsi's parable THE CARVER OF THE STAND FOR CHIMES, in which he stated that the natures of the material and of the man must be united before a real work of art can be created.

STYLOTINT—A *technique* in *etching,* not fully explored. It is an *intaglio* process, capable of great freedom, variation, and a wide range of curious *textures,* and when combined with *aquatint tones,* it can produce results resembling the Japanese *monochrome water-color.* The coating on the *plate* is soft, and easily displaced with a stick, stiff *brush,* piece of cloth, or steel point. If the *stylus* is in chisel form, a line of variable thickness will result. This is the type of line most resembling the Japanese brushline. The beauty of this process lies in the quality of the lines and textures, the ease with which large areas of black are produced, and in the smooth, easy resistance of the drawing tool on the surface of the *copper. Stylotint* belongs to the family which includes *pen process* and *offset soft ground* (qq.v.), but its control in *stopping out* is far greater.

STYLUS—In the history of *art,* a metal point used for markings, having wide and varied use since metals were discovered. It was a common writing instrument in *ancient* times, preceding the quill. It marked preparatory lines on *pottery* and on walls where *paintings* were to be executed; in some cases it indicated the lines for writing in *manuscripts.* It is used widely today in *etching* the *grounds* of *plates,* preparing them for the *biting* process of the *acid bath.* From this core, the broad term *style* was born. See *drypoint* and *line etching.*

SUBSTITUTE OBJECTS—In *painting* and *sculpture, models* so closely resembling their prototypes as to serve as substitutes for them in *illusionism* (q.v.).

SUIBOKU—In Japanese *art,* any *painting* or *drawing* executed in black and white only. The sole medium employed is *sumi* (q.v.) or *ink.*

SUISAIGA—In Japanese *art,* the general term applied to any *water-color painting.*

SU LING—In Chinese *painting,* a plain variety of thin *silk* (see *ling tzu*) ordinarily used for mountings, although preferred in this sense as an actual *ground* for painting. Un-*sized,* it is very white and has a compact cloth weave. See also *hua chüan* and *tz'u ch'ing.*

SUMAC WAX—A pale yellow *wax* in flat cake form, soluble in naphtha and benzene, used as a protective *surface film* for *paintings* and *statuary,* and as a *leather* finisher. Employed also as a substitute for *beeswax* (q.v.) in all of its uses in the *arts.* It is obtained from a species of RHUS by boiling the fruit in water. Known also as *Japan wax, insect wax,* and *vegetable wax.*

SUMI—Japanese *ink* or blacking, composed of a mixture of carbon and *glue molded* into sticks or cakes. When rubbed into water on an *inkstone,* it becomes the common medium of the *painter* and writer. See *suiboku* and *suzuri.*

SUNFLOWER OIL—In *painting,* one of the materials found to be effective as a *drying oil* (q.v.).

SUNFLOWER YELLOW—In Chinese *painting,* a brilliant *yellow pigment* of mineral origin, made by baking *orpiment* (q.v.) until *friable,* grinding it into powder, and then mixing it with *glue.* Used widely in portraiture (*jên wu*) and in butterfly painting; known natively as *shih huang.*

SUNG YEN MO—In Chinese *art,* a variety of *ink* also known as *pine soot;* found excellent in *painting,* it is rarely used in *calligraphy.*

SUN THICKENING—A technique in the making of artists' *pigments,* used for many centuries. The colors are exposed to the sun in shallow pans, and this treatment eliminates the need for added *siccatives, oils, resins* and *waxes.* Among the benefits claimed for this process are: (1) the oils acquire an inherent drying power, faster in actual operation than found in the use of *linseed oil;* (2) all of the colors on the *palette* will be of the same consistency and ready for use at the same time; (3) the oils dry hard, forming a more durable *film;* (4) the oils are more *brilliant,* and stronger in color, since the action of the sun *polymerizes* the oil. This provides them with greater affinity for the pigment particles and better 'wetting' power; (5) the oils require less thinning agent for fluid *painting* and *glazing;* (6) the oils still retain the valuable *plasticity* normally given by linseed oil; (7) there is less 'soaking-in' and the paint dries to an even *luster* without 'shiners' or flat spots. *Sun thickening,* however, is not suited to certain grinding colors.

SUOVETAURILIA—A scene appearing widely in early *art,* representing a boar, a ram, and a bull together. (q.v.).

SUPERREALISM—Original name of the radical *art* revolt (super-*realism*), subsequently corrupted to *surrealism* (q.v.).

SUPPORT—In *painting,* the structure or material which holds the *pigment.* The chief support of the *Middle Ages* was the *wooden panel,* replaced with the modern *canvas.* The *support* is covered with the *ground* (q.v.) for evenness, and is then ready to receive the actual painting.

SUPREMATISM – An *abstract* movement in *painting* founded in Moscow in 1913 by Kasimir Malevich. Flourishing during World War I and through the ensuing years, it was more commonly termed *Non-Objective Painting* (q.v.) and disregarded reality completely. Outstanding examples of works created in the movement are Malevich's WHITE ON WHITE (1919) and Rodchenko's BLACK ON BLACK (1919).

SURFACE BOARD—In *drawing,* a variety of *stippled ground,* used also for *cartoon* and *crayon* work, and *watercolor* painting. Interesting effects result when a lithographic pencil is used.

SURFACE COLORS—In the *arts* generally, the term referring to the outermost *color* or colors of *works of art;* e.g., the color of the *glaze* or *pottery,* as distinct from that of the *underglaze* or of the *ware* beneath; the color of the finish, or outer sheet in *veneer* work, as distinct from the non-surface sections.

SURFACED PAPER—A variety of *paper* having an added film of *whiting.* This extra layer fills minute pits and adapts the surface for the *printing* of *woodcuts.*

SURFACE FILM—In the *arts* generally, any *coating* material which may be used on *paintings, sculpture,* or other *works of art.* Includes *varnishes, oils, waxes,* and all other substances capable of forming a thin, *transparent* surface of reasonable *stability.*

SURIMONO—A Japanese *wood-block print* used as a greeting card.

SURINAM SNAKEWOOD—In *woodworking,* a straight-*grained* timber of French Guiana, used in fine *carving;* properly known as *zebrawood* (q.v.).

SURREALISM—A 20th century movement in *art* and *litera-*which claims to find a 'super reality' in the objects of subconscious mental reality. It is sharply opposed to both *naturalism* and to purely *abstract painting. Surrealism* is influenced by psychoanalysis, and is based on the expression of imagination completely uncontrolled by reason. Spreading to many parts of the world, it has expanded from *painting* and *poetry* to *drama, photography, stagesettings, motion pictures, commercial art,* and *architecture.* Much *surrealism* has found expression in *collage* (q.v.). See *automatism* and *art d'avant-garde.*

SUSSEX MARBLE—See *Petworth marble.*

SUZURI—A very fine-grained whet-stone slab on which *sumi* (q.v.) is rubbed with water; an *inkstone.*

SUZURI-BAKU—The supply cabinet or box of the Japanese *painter,* containing *ink-stone* (q.v.), writing *brushes,* and a small water pot; a writing box.

SWASTIKA—In *ancient* Mesopotamian and Greek *art,* an *ornament* composed of an equal-armed cross, with the ends of the arms bent at right angles, all four in the same direction. The *swastika* was first found to have been used in *primitive,* tribal inscriptions. See *filling motifs, fret,* and *meander motif.* Japanese equivalent, *manji* (q.v.), symbol of the sun; in India and China it is the *symbol* of good luck, as it was in Germany, under the Nazis.

SWISS BOLTING CLOTH—A variety of *silk* found to be exceptionally well adapted to the making of *silk screen prints* (q.v.).

SWIVEL KNIFE—A device consisting of a handle at one end of which a socket holds a sharp, chisel-like blade at an angle; the blade swings, allowing for good cutting in curves and circles. Used in *silk screen work,* cutting *stencils,* etc.

SYMBOLISM—An *art* movement developed by Gauguin in the late 1880's, better known as *synthetism* (q.v.).

SYMMETRY—In the *arts* generally, *harmony* within the work, of part to part, and of parts to the whole. Its use in a too-regular form destroys its quality, as in many machine-made objects. Even races have been marked by *symmetrophobia* (Egyptian temples: Japanese art). Some artists prize a ruggedness or roughness above a smooth and rounded *symmetry*. The term may be defined technically as the precise correspondence of an even number of parts of a figure with reference to a common line or point. A circle is *symmetrical* with reference to any true diameter. See *asymmetry*.

SYNCHROMIST SCHOOL—A French school of *painting* in the early 20th century, more commonly known as *orphism* (q.v.). Its doctrine favored *abstract* color designs as the proper aim of *painting*. *Synchromism* usually displayed its purposes in pictures of huge size, the *colors* forming *prismatic patterns*. The founders (1913) were MacDonald-Wright and Morgan Russell.

SYNTHENOL—A variety of rapid-drying, non-yellowing oil, used as a substitute for *tung oil* in the *arts*. It is dehydrated castor oil, *synthenol* being a trade name.

SYNTHETISM—In *painting*, a variety of *post-impressionism* developed by Gauguin in the late 1880's, challenging the analytic procedure of *impressionism;* supported synthetic painting in broad, simple, flat *tones* or *color*, often with definite edges, distorted in form and color for the sake of *decoration* and heightened *expressive* power, and influenced by Japanese *prints*, medieval *stained glass* and *enamels*, Italian *primitives*, and Egyptian painting. Known also as *symbolism* and *neo-traditionalism*.

T

TABLATURE—In *sculpture* and *carving,* any *surface* (usually *stone*) sufficiently smooth and hard for the receiving of lettering; a *plaque* before application of the inscription; any surface suitable for permanent marking, as a tombstone, historical marker, etc. Loosely, any *painting,* on a *table, wall,* or *ceiling.*

TABLE EASEL—Any one of the numerous varieties of small *easel,* designed for use on a table or other flat surface; does not stand on the floor. See *easel.*

TABLETS OF MOSES—In *sculpture,* a variety of *granite* occurring chiefly in Scotland; so called because when polished, esp. in cross section, it resembles the appearance of Hebrew characters on a white ground.

TABRÉEZ—In *sculpture,* a beautiful, transparent variety of *limestone,* composed of innumerable laminae, thin as paper, formed by deposition from a celebrated calcareous spring near Maragha, Iran.

TACK— Stickiness, as of a *painted, varnished,* oiled or *inked* surface that is partly dry; adhesiviness possessed by a *printing ink,* due to the addition of a stiff varnish. Any surface or object in such state is said to be *tacky.*

TAILLE DIRECT—In *sculpture,* the practice by the artist of cutting the stone of the final *statue* himself, instead of turning a *plaster model* of his work over to a stone-cutter for conversion into stone by *pointing* (q.v.). The latter practice was widely employed by 19th century *sculptors.*

TAMAMUSHI SHRINE—See *oils.*

TAN—A *color* like that imparted to Caucasian skin by the sun upon substantial exposure; a tawny, yellowish-brown or copper color; the color of tanned *leather; natural.*

TAN—In Japanese *wood-block printing,* a *color* derived from *red lead* (q.v.). The completed work, usually consisting of this one color only, is known as *tane* (q.v.).

TANAGRA FIGURINES—A famous serious of small figures or *figurines* made by the ancient Greeks for decorative purposes and as offerings to the gods. Though occasionally found in various locations throughout the areas of the old empire, the finest examples, as well as the first-discovered, came from Tanagra, for which they are named.

TANAGROA—One of the principal Polynesian gods, frequently represented in *primitive sculpture* and *carving.*

TAN CHÉ—In Chinese *painting,* pale *umber; ink* painting with only a *tincture* of color, the *pigment* made by mixing ink with *ché shih* (q.v.). The term is used as an adjective, describing a *landscape,* bird scene, etc., having faint color.

TANE—A *primitive,* Japanese *wood-block print* in which the only *color,* or the predominating one, was *tan* (q.v.), a *red* oxide of lead, somewhat *orange* in *tone.*

TAN HSÜAN—In Chinese *art,* a variety of un-*sized* paper used as a *ground* in *painting.* Of single thickness (compare with *hsuan chih*), it is frequently used in *calligraphy.*

TAN K'UAN—In Chinese *art,* the term applied to the signature or *colophon* on a *painting* which does not make reference to the name of the person (if any) for whom the picture was painted. See *k'uan.*

TANSAI—A Japanese *suiboku* (q.v.) or *black* and *white painting,* with the added feature of light-colored *tints.*

TAN T'AO HUNG—In Chinese *landscape painting,* a pale peach-red *pigment* approaching pink, used widely in flower and sunset work. Prepared by mixing *yen chih* (q.v.) with white.

TANZAKU—In Japan, small, decorative *paintings* applied to the margins or borders of sheets of *parchment* containing *poetry.* The reverse of the Chinese *t'i-shih* (q.v.) technique.

TAO SHIH JÉN WU—In Chinese *painting,* the term applied to *portrait* work representing Taoist or Buddhist figures; e.g., Buddhas, Lohans, Bodhisattvas, the Eight Immortals, and the like.

TAPPING—A dabbing *technique* in *painting;* see *pointillism.*

TA P'U PU—In Chinese *landscape painting,* a large waterfall having substantial height and width. Frequently used in the *high distance* (q.v.) technique as a *perspective* device.

TARNISH—To dull or discolor the *luster* of a metallic surface, usually by ordinary oxidation. Especially characteristic of highly-polished *silver* and allied metals. Also, the discoloration itself. See *luster.*

TATLINISM—An *art* movement founded in Russia in 1916 by Vladimir Tatlin who proclaimed the death of *easel painting* and the birth of a new art which found its *rhythm,* construction, and logic in the machine. As in *Dadaism* (q.v.), this group found no material unworthy of use in art, employing *glass,* nails, *wood,* and wire to create a new art language in terms of modern *technique.* Known later as *Constructivism.*

T-CHISEL—In *sculpture,* a boring tool having its cutting edge in the shape of the letter *T.*

TECALLI MARBLE—A term in *sculpture;* see *onyx marble.*

TECHNIQUE—An expert method of executing the technical details of an *art,* as distinguished from the pure *creativeness* and *inspiration* impelling it. *Technique* is the most teachable aspect of an art, having to do with the skills in the manipulation of a given art *medium,* leading to *virtuosity* (see *virtuoso*) when exhaustively studied and practiced. The development of *technique* in the arts is theoretically, but not practically separable from the development of *expression.* While facility in the use of a medium may be stressed in education and developed by practice, it can never be completely divorced from the character of an artistic statement. Thus, while virtuosity may be the theoretical aim of technical studies, good *technique* must be defined in practice as the ability to employ a medium and materials with sufficient skill to achieve a predetermined expressive effect.

TECOZAHUITL—Name given by the *Aztecs* to yellow *ocher* (q.v.).

TELEMON—A *carved* male figure used instead of a *column* to support an *entablature.* Also known as *atlante.*

TEMPERA—Any one of the several *paint mediums* which leave the surface of the picture in a state of *matte* (q.v.). The yolk of egg will accomplish this end, in mixture with the *pigment,* giving a pliable, firm, and completely permanent *film* with a minimum of *color* and *value* loss. Also used with success are *fig milk, honey,* and various *gums.* The most popular modern *tempera,* used to acquire a dull finish, is *glue* (q.v.), referred to by *artists* as *size* (q.v.). Ordinary skin glue is satisfactory, except for its tendency to swell when exposed to moisture or even humidity. *Casein* glue is a newer development commercially, although it, too, goes back to the *Middle Ages,* at least for its origin. Used as a paint medium, casein is firmer, but more difficult and hazardous to manage than skin glue. Until the end of the 15th century, *tempera* techniques were employed in the finest paintings; they gradually disappeared in the early 16th century when *oil painting* was generally adopted. It is interesting to note that every *tempera* painting of the *Renaissance* remains practically unchanged to the present time.

TENEBRISTS—The *painters* of darkness; an international group of painters of the early 17th century, inspired by the *art* of Michelangelo di Caravaggio (1565-1609). Their works are charecterized by the use of violent contrasts of *light* and *shade* reminiscent of, and often derived from, conditions in basements and other rooms having artificial light. Most *Tenebrists* preferred drastic, unidealized, and even vulgar treatment of subject matter, whether religious, *mythological,* or *genre,* and upon that point rose the opposition by the *idealizing* academic painters of Bologna. Compare with *Siena School.*

TENGAI—In Japanese *art,* esp. *painting* and *sculpture,* the canopy often shown above a deity represented therein. Frequently associated (incorrectly) with *nimbus.*

T'ÊNG HUANG—In Chinese *painting,* a bright *yellow* vegetable *pigment* approaching *goldenrod,* known also as *rattan yellow.* It is a natural plant sap, allowed to solidify with the addition of a small quantity of *glue;* believed by Oriental artists to be best when formed into sticks resembling thin brush handles. It is slightly poisonous and irritating, and the charged *brush* must not be 'tipped' on the tongue or lips. Used extensively in flower, bird and *landscape* work.

TÊNG LO TZŪ—In Chinese *painting,* a pale wisteria *purple* pigment used extensively in flower and sunset work; approaches *orchid* in *hue.* It is prepared by mixing *yang hung* with *hua ch'ing* (qq.v.).

TERRA BLUE—In *painting,* a rare variety of blue earth prized as a *pigment.* It is not classified as one of the *earth colors* (q.v.).

TERRACE—In *sculpture,* the term commonly applied to the type of flaw in *marble* that can be cored out and filled up; any defective or disfigured area in marble, sufficiently small to warrant corrective filling with a composition material. May consist of a *stun* (q.v.). Also spelled *terras.*

TERRA COTTA—A hard variety of high quality *earthenware,* usually un*glazed,* used extensively for *architectural* decorations, *vases, statuettes,* etc. *Brown*ish-*orange* in *color,* it is made from fine brick earth, *fired* in *molds,* and is often seen in blocks or figures as a *facing* material. Direct *terra cotta sculpture* can be made by three processes: (1) the *coil method,* used in small and medium *sculpture,* may be used successfully by students and *amateurs* unfamiliar with *ceramics,* because of its simplicity; (2) the *slab system* is preferable in larger works for quicker results, though *technique* is required, and such factors as weight, pull, and stress must be taken into account; (3) the *pottery wheel method,* suitable for *decorative* sculpture, is advisable only for *sculptors* familiar with the wheel, and for those having the services of an experienced *potter* in the *studio.* It was in an urn of *terra cotta* that the bones of St. Peter were reported found in 1950 in the *hypogeum* under the present St. Peter's *basilica;* the bones were in the color of old *ivory,* and the *urn* was in excellent physical condition.

TERRA PONDEROSA—A fine white *pigment* used extensively in *paints* and in the making of *photographic* paper. It is a heavy white powder, soluble in water, requiring application of a *surface film* after completion of the *art* work. Chemically, it is a precipitated barium sulphate; known also as *blanc fixe* and *permanent white* to *artist's* colormen.

TERRE-VERTE—The highly popular *green pigment* used green earth prized as a *pigment;* not considered an *earth color* (q.v.).

TERRE CASSEL—In *painting,* the rich brown *pigment* commonly known as *Van Dyke brown* (q.v.).

TERRE DE SIENNE—In *painting* and *water-color* work, the famous *earth color* prized on the *palette* since ancient times, popularly known as *raw sienna* (q.v.).

TERRA-VERTE—The highly popular *green pigment* used by *painters* of the *Middle Ages* and the *Renaissance,* commonly known as *earth green* (q.v.).

TERTIARY COLORS—Any *color,* as russet, citrine, olive, and the like, produced by a mixture of two *secondary colors.* The *tertiaries* are *grays,* being either *red*-gray, *blue*-gray, or *yellow*-gray when these *primary colors* are in excess; if the secondary colors are in excess, the *tertiaries* will be *violet*-gray, *orange*-gray, or *green*-gray. From Latin TERTIARIUS, third; of the third rank or order.

THINNER—A term applied to either a solvent or a diluent of a *painting medium.* It may also describe a mixture of both, and designates any fluid used to reduce a *surface film* material to a consistency suitable for application. See *film.*

THUMB-HOLE—The opening in an artist's *palette,* providing easy grip. See *handle.*

THUMBNAIL SKETCH—A miniature *drawing.*

TIEN—In Chinese *painting,* a technique by which small dots of *color* or *ink* are added to a *landscape* picture for the purpose of emphasis or better definition of planes or *contours.* On rocks, mountains, trees, etc., *tien* may be interpreted as moss, grass, etc. Often applied by means of the *side brush technique* (q.v.). See also *sharp dot technique.*

TIEN HUA—In Chinese *painting,* a fine *indigo blue* approaching glacier blue when used at full strength. This vegetable *pigment* is pressed from the plant, then boiled and mixed with lime and *glue.* Resembling the cake *water-color* pigments of the West, it requires only the addition of water when commercially obtained. Indigo is one of the most popular of all Oriental colors and is used widely in all classes of subjects. Compare with the manufacturing technique of the mineral pigment *shih ch'ing* (q.v.).

TILT BOARD—In *painting* and *drawing,* a type of informal *easel* consisting of a vertical working surface which can be tilted backward to approximately fifteen angles; supported by two horizontal, toothed braces, into the notches of which the tilting angles are adjusted. Numerous varieties and sizes are available, most of which are furnished with wells for *pencils, brushes,* etc., and a clamp for holding *paper, ledger bond,* or other *grounds.*

TINCTURE—In *painting* and *water-color,* a *tinge* of *color;* usually so faint that it is taken up by a stronger adjoining color.

TINT—(1) Any *color tone* which has either more or less *brilliance* than it would have in its *spectral hue;* also, any pale or light *value* of color. Not synonymous with *tinge* or *tincture.* (2) A degree of color lighter than normal, as when *white* is added; when the color is darkened by the addition of *black,* it is a *shade.*

TINT BLOCK—An *engraved, grained,* or flat *plate* or *electro* employed for the *printing* of a faint color only, either as a back-ground, or to fill *panels* or other parts of a *design.* See *ground block* and *tinge.*

T'I PA—In Chinese *art,* an annotation on a *painting* or its mounting; may be added by the artist himself or by another person. When the writing is in the form of a short *poem* (usually in praise of or inspired by the painting) it is known as *t'i shih.*

T'I SHIH—In Chinese *art,* a *poem inscribed* on a *painting;* a procedure directly opposite the Japanese *tanzaku* (q.v.) technique.

TITANIUM WHITE—A painters' *pigment* having many excellent qualities, made from the white dioxide of titanium metal. It is distinguished by its *hiding power,* in which capacity it is stronger than *white lead* and far stronger than the *white* in *zinc pigments* (q.v.). Although it can be used in its pure state, it usually contains an amount of other white, the most common being *barium* sulphate. *Titanium white* is a relatively modern pigment; although the ore was known since the late 18th century, production of the white was not undertaken until 1916.

T-MOTIF—In Oriental *art,* a *design* or *pattern* frequently found in *ceramics* and *symbolic paintings,* suggesting the capital letter *T.*

TOBA-YE—In Japanese *art,* a style of *caricature* in which prominent persons were drawn in the guise of animals. So-called after the Buddhist priest Kakuyo, better known by his ecclesiastic title TOBA SOJO (1053-1140).

TOHUNGA—Any Maori leader skilled in the *arts* or schooled in *traditional* lore. See *Maori carving.*

TONDO—Any *painting, fresco, relief,* etc., executed on a circular base or *ground.*

TONE—In *painting,* (1) an intermediate *hue* used to reduce, soften or subdue the *intensity* of a *color;* (2) the *technique* or method of so reducing, etc., a color; (3) the designation of any color considered with respect to its *attributes,* but indefinite as to the characterization of its attributes; (4) the prevailing effect of color, or the general effect produced by the management of light and *shade* in a picture, as silvery *tone,* light *tone,* dark *tone,* etc.

TONER—In *painting,* a term applied to any *lake color* or *dye* possessing a high degree of strength concentration; used to *tint* or *shade* the *pigments* to bring them up to the desired *intensity.* Often added to a painted or decorated surface to enhance the *color* work previously executed.

TONERDE—A fine variety of *clay* used in the *arts;* occurs as a fine white *amorphous* powder, varying in color according to metallic content. It approaches *kaolin* (q.v.) in quality, and is used in the making of *porcelain, pottery, china, tile,* etc. As a *pigment* in *painting,* it is unusually *stable,* and resists the action of light, heat and atmosphere for a considerable time; however, because of its transparency, it is best suited for admixture with *lake colors.* Known also as *Kieselguhr.*

TONIC—In *painting,* a term relating generally to *tone,* or to light and shade in any picture; of or pertaining to the effect of the picture's *color* on the receptor.

TONING DOWN—In *painting,* to soften the coloring so that a subdued harmony of *tint* may prevail, and undue glare be avoided; to impart a more reticent *tone.*

TOOTH— (1) —In *painting,* that quality of the *canvas* or other *ground* by which it 'grips' and holds the colors; rough surfaces usually possess the greatest *tooth.*

TOPIA—In *painting,* the general term in Roman antiquity applied to any *mural* or large *landscape* depicting diverse and fanciful scenes.

TOPIATION—The *art* or *technique* of clipping hedges, shrubs, etc., into forms representing animals, pieces of furniture, terraces, and the like. The finished product is known as *topiary work.*

TOP TONE—In *painting,* the utmost *color* and strength of a *pigment* as displayed when viewed by reflected light; known also as *mass tone.*

TORCHON BOARD—In *water-color drawing,* a pasteboard *support* made of *torchon paper* (q.v.) .

TORCHON PAPER—A variety of handmade *paper* characterized by an unusually coarse surface and extreme hardness, used esp. by *water-color* artists.

TOREUTICS—The *art* of *sculpturing* by *embossing, damascening, chasing,* etc., especially in *metal.*

TORSION—In *sculpture,* the term applied to deformity in a body caused by twisting.

TORSO—In *sculpture,* the name applied to the trunk of a *statue* or of a human body which is lacking the head, arms and legs.

TORTILLON—Actually, a small *stump* (q.v.) ; a spreading or smoothing tool used on *crayon* or *charcoal drawings.* It is made of *chamois* or soft *paper* rolled in such fashion as to give a conical point at the end. Used chiefly in the execution of delicate work.

TOSA SCHOOL—A Japanese school of *painting,* emphasizing historic episodes after the *Yamato* (q.v.) style. Reached its peak in the mid-15th century.

TOTEM—In *painting,* a reddish-yellow *color* of medium *brilliance* and high *saturation;* one of the *mars* (q.v.) colors.

TOTEM POLE—A pole or post *carved* and *painted* by the northwest American coast Indians to display the *heraldic* devices and social rank of the family, to illustrate a *legend,* or to honor the dead. It was set up in front of or against the house, or served as a support for the *beams.* Carved from *red cedar,* abundant and gigantic in the region, the poles vary in height from three to seventy feet. The carvings *represent* animal, bird, or *mythical* guardian spirits with which the family is identified and from which it draws *qualities* peculiar to the being. *Totemic* myths and *ceremonies* take their character from the poles, which are usually *symbolic* of important experience or events.

TOUCH—In *sculpture,* any stone of unusually durable character, suitable for fine monumental work and for the preserving of inscriptions.

T'OU CH'ING—A fine deep *blue* mineral *pigment* in Chinese *painting,* obtained from the bottom stratum in rubbing *azurite.* Known also as *Peking blue,* it is used for filling in certain outlined leaves and for painting on the back of *silk* to intensify the blue on the surface. Since stone colors must not be too thick (or they will crack when the painting is rolled) either back painting or an undercoat of *hua-ch'ing* (q.v.) for blue *tones,* or *ts'ao lü* for green, is used when a particularly *brilliant* effect is desired. See *shih ch'ing.*

TOU FANG—In Chinese *art,* a small *album painting* (q.v.) usually square.

TOURNAI SCHOOL—A popular school of *art* in 15th century Tournai, stressing conventionally religious *representations.* It influenced the schools of *Ghent, Haarlem,* and *Louvain* (qq.v.).

TOURS SCHOOL—A 9th century *art* group of the *Carol-igian* epoch, specializing in the *decorating and illustrating* of the famous *Evangeliars* (q.v.) of the period.

TOWED PAPER—In Chinese *art,* a long strip of fine, decorated *paper* running alongside the picture in a *scroll painting;* used for receiving annotations in connection with the painting.

TRACING—The technique of transferring a *design, picture* or *pattern* from one surface to another through direct copying, the original *model* remaining undisturbed throughout the process. Numerous methods and materials are employed; e.g., see *calking.*

TRACING BOX—A device consisting of a flat, oblong box having a slanted *glass* surface upon which the *design, picture,* etc., and the *tracing paper* are placed. The interior contains two or more fluorescent tubes running crosswise, adjustable to forward and backward positions to bring the light directly below the section being worked on. Clamps at all four sides of the glass top hold the *art* work in place.

TRACING PAPER—In *drawing,* a variety of *paper* rendered *transparent* for direct copying purposes. Made by soaking the paper in a solution of *Canada balsam, turpentine,* and a small quantity of vegetable oil and hanging it in the air until dry. It is generally heavy in weight, unglazed, and has a clear *texture.* Suitable for *pen* and *pencil* work, it can stand numerous erasures without marring. See *calking.*

TRANSPARENT GOLD OCHER—In *painting,* a variety of *ocher* tending toward *raw sienna* but considerably more *yellow* in *tone.*

TRANSVERBERATION—In *art,* a mystic experience of St. Theresa; often represented in *painting* and *sculpture,* showing her heart pierced by a flaming arrow shot by an angel. Seen most frequently in *Baroque* (q.v.) art, the most famous rendition in *oil* is that by L. Bernini, now in the church of St. Maria della Vittoria, Rome.

TRIADIC COLORS—The term applied to any three *colors* so arranged on the *ground* as to form an equilateral triangle; frequently seen in *geometric style* of *painting,* and of *ceramic* decoration.

TRIAL PROOF—In *etching,* an impression taken from a *plate* that has not been completed. Generally done to observe the progress of the work.

TRICKLING—In *painting,* a situation in which the paint gathers itself into bubbles, acquiring height (rather than 'spread') upon its application. This usually indicates that the *imprimatura* (q.v.) on the *canvas* is too oily or waxy, preventing the paint from spreading. The addition of a *retouch varnish,* or merely rubbing the surface with a wad of soft cotton, will correct the condition.

TRIPTYCH—An *altarpiece* consisting of a group of three hinged *panels,* so arranged that the two outer sections or wings can fold over and enclose completely the center panel. Each section is *enriched* with *paintings* or *sculpture* in *relief.* Found frequently in Japanese *wood-block prints.* Known also as *retable;* see *polyptych, volet,* and *iconostasis.*

TRIUMPHAL ARCH—In *sculpture* and *architecture,* a monumental *arch* in honor of an individual, or in commemoration of an event. Such structures were first erected under the Roman emperors, and were originally temporary affairs, festooned and otherwise decorated, standing at a city's entrance for the triumphal return of a general and his victorious army. At a later period the *triumphal arch* became a richly sculptured, massive, and permanent structure, having a central archway passing through it, and a lesser arch on either side. An excellent example is the Arch of Constantine, Rome.

TROMPE-L'OEIL—In the *visual arts* (esp. *painting),* an accuracy of reproduction so *photographic* and detailed as to give an *illusion* of reality; the term has been extended by usage to include descriptions in *literature* of like impression. (French, 'deceiving the eye'.) See also *realistic painters.*

TRUE BLUE—In *art* generally, the name applied to the prized *blue color* having the *hue* of the clear sky, or of *lapis lazuli* (q.v.).

TRUNCATE—In *sculpture* and *architecture,* the term describing a cone or *pyramid* whose ascending lines are cut off by a plane parallel to its base; a *stepped pyramid;* appearing as if cut off at the tip, or at any lower point, or at regular intervals.

TS'ANG LÜ—In Chinese *painting,* a *gray-green* pigment prepared by mixing *ta'ao lü* with *chü shih* (qq.v.), known to Western artists as *old gold.* It is used for representation of tree leaves in the first frost, mountain slopes in early autumn, and paths and roads.

TS'AO CH'UNG—In Chinese schools of *painting,* grasses and insects; students were required to paint or draw these subjects prior to advancement.

TS'AO LÜ—In Chinese *painting,* the name applied to any one of the numerous *greens* made by mixing the *blue* of *hu ch'ing* and the *yellow* of *t'êng huang.* One of the most characteristic products of this combination is the pale *pistachio green;* known also as *vegetation green.*

TSCHIN—In Russian *art,* the central row of the 14th century *iconostasis* of five registers, portraying the *Deesis* (Christ flanked by the Madonna and John the Baptist); the remaining *panels* were devoted to various saints, other holy figures, and feasts. See *iconostasis.*

TS'Ê PI—In Chinese *painting,* a technique in which the *brush* is held and used in an oblique position with respect to the *ground,* as in writing. Used chiefly in *wash drawings* and certain types of shading and *dotting,* or *tien.* Known to Western artists as *side brush technique.*

TS'Ê YEH—In China, an album containing *paintings* only. See *tou fang* and *album painting.*

T-SQUARE—In *drawing,* a blade with transparent *celluloid* edges, securely fastened at right angles to a head by means of screws. Used for drawing horizontal lines; also, as a guide for drawing lines with *triangles* (q.v.).

TSUIKOKU—The Japanese technique of *carving* black *lacquered* surfaces.

TSUISHU—Japanese *carved* red *lacquer,* the *color* imparted through the addition of *cinnabar* (q.v.). Often referred to as *cinnabar lacquer.*

TSUITATE—In Japanese *art,* a solid, single-*paneled screen* with two low transverse feet, on the large face of which the *artist* paints *pictures,* generally of *landscape* character.

TS'UN—An important element in the *brush* technique of Chinese *painting;* literally, to shade, shading, modeling, contour lines, wrinkles. After a form is outlined, *ts'un* is employed to add character, as in giving wrinkled lines to the bark of an old tree, texturing the surface of natural rock, etc., in realistic and distinctive style. See *p'o mo.*

T'U—A general term in Chinese *art* referring to any variety of *picture;* however, actual use appears to limit it to a chart, plan or map rather than anything pictorial. The word of widest application is *hua* (q.v.), embracing all pictures.

TUBE COLORS—Popular term applied to *oil colors* put up in collapsible tin tubes for the use of *artists.* Most pigments available at *art* supply sources today are so prepared.

TUDOR PERIOD—The period in *art* and *architecture* marking England's transition from the *Middle Ages* into the *Renaissance.* In art, Henry VII commissioned Holbein and others to do some of the *paintings* that are now world *masterpieces,* chiefly *portraiture.*

TUDOR ROSE—A conventionalized rose, with petals open, used as a form of *enrichment* in *Tudor sculpture, architecture,* and *woodworking.* It has four rows of alternate petals, the second seven, the third eight, and the last, four. Known also as *union rose,* possibly because it is used in the badge of England.

T'UNG CHING—In Chinese *painting,* a combined scene made up of numerous elements; also, a variety of *p'ing chang* (q.v.) whose paired parts combine to present one over-all picture, as a large *landscape* or complex picture of birds, flowers, trees, mountains and grass.

TUNG-O HSIEN—In Chinese *painting,* a variety of *glue* used as a *surface film.* See *o chiao.*

TUNG OIL—A *painting* material derived from the seeds of the botanical ALEURITES CORDATA of China and surrounding countries. Although little used by painter as a *medium,* it has extensive use as a *surface film* or *varnish,* and is enjoying increasing popularity as a *drying oil* (q.v.). Known also as *Chinese wood oil* and *China-wood oil.*

TUN HUANG—An ancient Chinese *temple* in which many excellently preserved *works of art* were discovered; among the more valuable items were the fine examples of *fabric paintings* known natively as *chêng* (q.v.).

TURKEY RED—An artists' *color* of *intense* scarlet *red,* obtained from the *madder* plant; known also as *Adrianople red.* See *alizarin.*

TURKEY UMBER—A variety of *umber* found on the island of Cyprus; considered by *artists* to be the finest in the world.

TURKISH-CRESCENT RED—In *painting,* a *color* of red reddish-yellow *hue,* low in *brilliance and* high in *saturation.*

TURNSOLE—A fine bluish-purple *dye* of medieval times, extracted from the seeds of the botanical CROZOPHORA TINCTORIA of south Europe. Popular among 14th century artists as a *pigment* base, it was often deepened into purple by chemical additions, and was used widely for *illuminated manuscripts.* Occasionally employed as a *toner* for *azurite.*

TURNTABLE—A term in *sculpture* and *metalwork,* sometimes in *ceramics;* see *gentleman.*

TURPENTINE—A *balsam* distillate, or crude *resin* exuding from coniferous trees such as *pine, larch,* and *fir.* Distilled *turpentine* is a volatile solvent for *oil* and most *varnishes.* Although its general history reaches into the *ancient* world, it may not have been used in the *art* of *painting* before the *Renaissance.* Leonardo da Vinci spoke of it, but did not specifically mention it as an oil solvent. See *oleoresin* and *tracing paper.*

TURQUOISE BLUE—In *painting,* a *lake color* of excellent blue *hue,* prized for its appearance but dangerous because it is *unstable.* Commonly known as *Italian blue.* (q.v.).

TURQUOISE GREEN—In the *arts* generally, the name given to a somewhat pale *color* intermediate between green and blue. It is high in *brilliance* and medium in *saturation.*

TUSCAN RED—In *painting,* a *color* of low *brilliance* and

high *saturation,* varying in range from red to reddish-yellow. Also, a red *pigment* of purplish *cast* made by admixture of an *alizarin lake* with ferric oxide; belongs to the *pigment* (q.v.) class.

TUSCANY SCHOOL—The style of *painting* prevailing in Tuscany during the period reaching from Giotto to Michelangelo. The era is subdivided into two general sections, the division being applicable to the pursuits rather than to chronology: (1) SIENESE SCHOOL, famous for the sentamentality and dignity of its work, led by Simone Martini and Duccio di Buoninsegna; (2) FLORENTINE SCHOOL, noted for *drawing,* composition, and literary and intellectual superiority, represented by Andrea del Sarto, Fra Bartolommeo, Botticelli, and the Lippis.

TUSCHE—In *serigraphy* (q.v.), an oily *ink* used in applying *color* to the *silk screen.* It is later covered with a watery *glue,* used to fill in the *silk* mesh. The *tusche* is removed by *turpentine,* leaving the color affixed to the screen for *printing.*

TWO-POINT DRAWING—One in which the object to be drawn is viewed from an angle, and in which the two sets of horizontal lines meet at respective points on the horizon. Known also as *angular perspective drawing.*

TYRIAN BLUE—In *painting,* a bluish *pigment* low in both *brilliance* and *saturation.*

TYRIAN PINK—In *painting,* a *color* of medium *brilliance* and very high *saturation,* red to bluish-red in *hue.*

TZ'Ū CH'ING—A *ground* used in Chinese *painting,* known also as *porcelain blue silk.* It is usually a good grade of silk dyed a deep *blue,* used for the painting of flowers and Buddhistic subjects, as well as for writing in *gold.* There is also a type of *paper* of the same *color,* used for *calligraphy,* known as *tz'ü ch'ing chih.* See *hua chüan.*

TZŪ FÊN—In Chinese *painting,* a purple-pink *pigment* used extensively in flower and sunset work, made by mixing *yen chih* (q.v.) with white.

U

UCHIWA—A Japanese folding *fan,* usually painted by an *artist.* The *uchiwa* and *sensu* represent some of the finest examples of fan *painting* in the world. See *fan.*

UKIYOYE—17th and 18th century technique of Japanese *print-making;* literally, 'pictures of the floating world.' Popular in the sense that these prints depicted scenes from everyday life, they were consequently opposed in theory and practice to the religious and imperial *art motifs* favored by the upper classes. Particularly rare is the *kwaigetsudo* type of *ukiyoye,* of large size, only 39 of which are known to exist in the world. An extensive *ukiyoye* exhibit at the Metropolitan Museum of Art, New York, in 1949-1950, drew great interest.

ULINKA—In Russian *painting,* a style in which the *artist* makes deliberate effort to create pale, colorless figures; found in much of the work of Nikolai Gogol (1809-1852). Literally (Russian), 'dead souls.'

ULTRAISM—In the *arts,* a general term applied to the basic attitude of many of the radical schools of the 20th century. It sees man in one flow with all things and bound by the same laws; it seeks the essence, the *universal,* rather than the individual. Embraces *expressionism, surrealism, abstract art,* etc. An outstanding *ultraist* creation is Brancusi's THE GOLDEN BIRD in *sculpture.* See *creacionismo.*

ULTRAMARINE—The natural *blue pigment* used by the *ancients,* as distinguished from the artificial *French ultramarine blue* (q.v.) discovered in 1814. Made of powdered *lapis lazuli* (q.v.), its age is not known. The chief source appears to be Afghanistan, and it occurs in 6th and 7th century *wall paintings* in cave *temples* of that region. It appeared subsequently in Europe, and was used extensively until replaced by *smalt* (qv.) and other artificial blues, more *intense* and considerably less expensive, usually made of sulphur, *rosin,* burnt *clay,* and other ingredients in mixture. Commonly referred to as *ultramarine blue;* known also as *outremer, lapis lazuli blue,* and *oltremare.*

UMBER—In *painting,* a *raw* and *burnt* brown *earth pigment.* It is dark in *color,* inclined toward a neutral *green*ish-*brown,* and when burnt it is *red*der and warmer in *hue.* One of the best varieties is known as *Turkey umber,* coming from the island of Cyprus. See *iron pigments* and *sepia umber.*

UME—In Japanese *art,* the plum, *symbol* of long life, found extensively in *painting, sculpture,* and *architecture.* Chinese equivalent is *mei* (q.v.).

UNDERPAINTING—In *painting,* any treatment given to the *canvas* prior to application of the paint itself. Since many final colors are (or become) *transparent,* it is important that the *underpainting* be of such nature that it will harmonize with the projected subject, and the artist must pre-plan for such contingencies. Any 'foundation' separating the canvas or the *size* from the paint colors is an *underpainting.* See *imprimatura.*

UNDERTONE—In *painting* and *water-color,* (1) any *color* upon which other colors are imposed, usually for blending on the *ground* rather than on the *palette;* (2) any faint *tinge* or *tincture* of color, being close in *graduation* to the adjoining color.

UNION ROSE—See *Tudor rose.*

UNIVERSALITY THEORY—The theory, of German origin, propounding that all of the *arts, painting* included, can be combined into one unified object, study, and purpose. Commonly referred to as *Universal Artwork.*

UNPRINTED—In *etching* and *engraving,* the term applied to any area of a *print* or *plate* intended to be left white.

UNSTABLE—In the *arts,* esp. *painting,* a term applied to any *pigment, resin, varnish, color, surface film,* etc., lacking in resistance to change upon exposure to air, light, moisture, heat, etc. See *stable.*

UPRIGHT BRUSH TECHNIQUE– In Chinese *painting,* a technique in which the *brush* is held and used in a vertical position with respect to the *ground,* in the manner of writing. Used principally in dot work (see *tien*) and for some forms of shading. Known natively as *chêng pi.*

URAERUS–In *ancient* Egyptian *art,* the serpent used as a *symbol* of royalty; the *representation* of the sacred asp on the headdress of rulers. In the *sculpture* of the period, the symbol frequently occurred on either side of a winged solar disc, emblematic of the supremacy of the sun, or of good over evil, or of *Horus* over *Set.*

ŪRNĀ–In Buddhist *sculpture* and *painting,* the tuft of hair growing between the eyebrows (a mark of the Buddha), usually represented as a sort of *jewel* on the forehead. In this *form* it is considered a third, or divine eye, indicating supernatural spiritual insight.

UROTROPIN–A white crystalline substance used as a hardening agent in the *resins* employed as *surface films* or coatings over *paintings* and *statuary.*

URUSHIE–In Japan, a *lacquer picture;* the technique of *painting,* which employs lacquer as the *sole medium.*

USHNISHA–A protuberance or topknot on the skull of the Buddhas, always shown in *painted* or *sculptured* figures. The *usnisa* is the gnosis or knowledge of truth said to be signified by this cranial extension.

V

VAN DYKE BROWN—In *painting,* a rich brown *pigment* said to have been named for the *artist* who used it widely. It is an organic material, coming from such substances as brown coal and lignite. It is partially soluble in *oil,* and makes a *transparent film.* Though it fades when exposed to strong light, it is more permanent in oil than in *watercolor.* A good imitation is made by mixing *lamp black* with *Indian red,* but although the color is faithfully reproduced, it has little *hiding power* and is a slow drier in oil. Many items marketed today as *Van Dyke brown* are actually dark brown iron exides or *ochres,* but as such they are desirable for their durability and *stability.* Known also as *terre cassel* and *pardo Vandyck.*

VAN DYKE UMBER—In *painting,* a well-washed permanent *hue* of *burnt umber,* the same in *color* as the popular, partially tarry *Van Dyke brown* (q.v.).

VARNISH—Any protective coating laid over a *paint* or *film* material, or a shell-like coating over *sculpture* and other objects. Generally, *varnishes* are *resin*ous films with more or less *oil* added for strength and plasticity. It was originally supposed that the word alluded to a *resin* dissolved in an oil or mixed with it. See *balsam* and *turpentine.*

VARNISH COLORS— A class of *colors* used in fine *glass-painting* (q.v.) Soft in original form, they solidify into an impermeable *glaze* when properly applied to the surface of the *glass.*

VEGETABLE BLACK—In *painting, drawing,* and *printing,* one of the finest black *pigments* known; recently replaced to a large extent by *gas black,* after continual use in the *arts* since ancient times. Commonly known as *lamp-black.*

VEGETABLE WAX–A pale yellow *wax* in flat cake form, soluble in naphta and benzene, used as a protective *surface film* for *paintings* and *statuary,* and as a *leather* finish. Employed also as a substitute for *beeswax* (q.v.), it is obtained from a species of RHUS by boiling the fruit in water. Known also as *sumac wax* and *Japan wax.*

VEGETATION GREEN–In Chinese *painting,* a famous pale *green pigment* obtained from a proper mixture of the *blue* of *hua ch'ing* and the *rattan yellow of t'êng huang* (qq.v.). Often referred to in the West as *pistachio,* it belongs to the great class of greens known natively as *ts'ao lü* (q.v.).

VEIN-STONE–A term in *painting;* see *mineral gray.*

VENETIAN BLUE– In *painting,* a fine *lake color* resembling *cerulean blue,* but possessing little *stability;* commonly known as *Italian blue* (q.v.).

VENETIAN RED–A deep *shade* of *red,* darker than brick red, being one of the red iron oxides. Although the term was originally applied to *natural* red *pigment* only, it now embraces all mixtures of copperas and *whiting.* Known also as *Prussian red, Spanish red,* and *English red,* it is highly prized in the *arts* for its unusual lasting quality.

VENETIAN SCHOOL–A school of *painting* that originated and declined in the 16th century; outstanding characteristics are its mastery of *color* and a consummate knowledge of *chiaroscuro* (q.v.), combined with spirit, grace, and a faithful adherence to nature. Among its masters were Titian, Veronese, Giorgione, Tintoretto, and other illustrious artists. In the magnificence of its use of *pigments* and in technical perfection it has rarely has been surpassed, and in many artistic qualities its leaders rank with the first painters of the world.

VENICE TURPENTINE–One of the few *balsams* used directly in the *arts;* an ingredient in painters' *varnishes.* It has been in use since the *Renaissance,* although known since the 8th century. Derived from the European *larch* tree, it is now collected chiefly in the Tyrol. See *oleoresin.*

VENUS ACCROUPIE–In *sculpture,* a popular form of representation of the famous goddess in which she is depicted as unclothed, and crouching close to the ground. This position afford excellent opportunity for the display of body knowledge in sculpture, especially proportion. The most admired example is now in the Museo Pio Clementino in the Vatican.

VERD ANTIQUE—In *sculpture,* (1) a variety of *porphyry* (q.v.), *green* in *color,* used in fine *marble* work; known also as *Oriental verd antique;* (2) *serpentine* white marble of greenish *tint,* nicely *mottled,* which responds excellently to polishing. Used for ornamental sculpturing.

VERDE CENIZA—In *painting,* a fine green *pigment* commonly known as *emerald green* (q.v.).

VERDE VEJIGA—In *water-color work,* a *green* coloring agent made from the unripe berries of the botanical RHAMNUS; *fugitive* in character, it is readily imitated in more *stable* form on a base of *coal-tar.* Commonly known as *sap green* (q.v.)

VERDIGRIS—An artificial *green* pigment, known in *ancient* times as *vert de Grece.* Methods of preparing it from metallic *copper* by exposure to grape skins in vinegar were described by Theophrastus and Pliny. It is an *unstable,* reactive *pigment,* and it has been replaced on the artist's *palette* by more permanent greens. Also known as *aerugo.*

VERMEIL—In *painting,* a term known also as *vermil,* applied to a certain color falling a *shade* lighter than *scarlet.* The word is also used to describe *gilding* that is executed in *silver,* as distinguished from the usual *gold.*

VERMILION—A bright orange-red *pigment* of antiquity, in both natural and artifical form. The *natural* variety, *cinnabar* (though often given that name in the artificial), was displaced to a great extent during the *Middle Ages.* An Arabian *alchemist* of the 8th century writes of a red pigment produced by the union of sulphur and mercury, and from that time on, recipes for such preparation are common in the *literature* of *painting* and craftsmanship. Sulphide of mercury is the base of both types of *vermilion.* There is little difference between the two, although the artificial seems to have a somewhat higher *intensity* of *color.* Known also as *sinopis;* see *chu sha.*

VERMILIONETTE—A substitute for the famed pigment *vermilion,* made by precipitating certain *dyes* on a base of orange lead.

VERNIS MARTIN—A fine variety of *varnish* made by the 18th century French Martin family, first used as a *surface film* for coaches and *sedan chairs.* Recognition of the remarkably *lustrous* and *stable* quality of their product resulted in the granting of a monopoly to the Martins by the government in 1730, and later *panel paintings* and *furniture* work by some of Europe's greatest artists were protected with this varnish. Literally, 'Martin varnish.'

VERNIS MOU—A soft type of *etching* resembling *pencil* or *crayon* work, used in conjunction with *aquatint.* See *soft ground etching.*

VERONA BROWN—In *painting,* an artists' *pigment* of reddish-brown tone, prized as an *oil color.* It is a calcined ferruginous earth.

VERONESE GREEN—In *painting,* a bright bluish-green *pigment* commonly known as *emerald green* (q.v.).

VERT CENDRE—In *painting,* a bright bluish-green *pigment* commonly known as *emerald green* (q.v.).

VERT DE VESSIE—In *water-color* work, an extract of unripe buckthorn berries possessing a dark yellow-green hue; not very *stable,* it is readily imitated by the more permanent *lakes* made on a base of coaltar. Its transparency, however, gives it value as a *glazing* color. Commonly known as *sap green* (q.v.).

VERTICAL BRUSH TECHNIQUE—In Chinese *painting,* same as *upright brush technique* (q.v.).

VERTICAL SNAKE—In *archaeology,* name given to the *ceramic* figures suggesting the name, discovered in the *Tres Zapotes* excavations at the *Ranchito Group* site. Excellent *sculptures* in stone showed the same serpent in upright position, but most representations were in yellow and dark brown *earthenware.* Though its *symbolism* is unknown, it occurred most frequently in the vicinity of *tombs* and other *burial* chambers, giving rise to the supposition that it possessed religious significance.

VICTORIA RED—A *painting pigment* of brilliant red color,

approaching *vermilion.* It is made on a base of *red lead* which renders it *opaque* and imparts a high degree of *hiding power.* While *stable* to light, it is sensitive to extreme changes in temperature. Known also as *Persian red, imitation vermilion,* and *derby red.*

VICTORY—In *sculpture,* the name of the famous *statue* discovered on *Samothrace* Island in 1863, now in the Louvre, Paris. It is one of the finest examples of 2nd century B.C. *sculpture* extant. A second *Victory,* said to equal the first in beauty and craftsmanship, was found on the same island late in 1949.

VIGNETTE—In *painting,* a type of *color* application in which there is no border, and the subject is shaded off the the edges gradually. Any painting, *sketch* or *drawing* in which the colors are applied bit by bit, with no sharply-defined termination at top, bottom, or sides.

VIGNETTE HALF-TONE—See *half-tone, vignette.*

VINE BLACK—A fine black *pigment* having a carbon base; made by dry or destructive distillation of vine twigs, grape husks, and even the yeast from spent wine. When mixed with any good white pigment, it produces a pure gray *tint* with a bluish *tinge.* It has little *opacity* or *hiding power.* but is highly *stable,* rendering it adaptable to practically all techniques.

VINYL RESIN—A *surface film* or coating for *works of art,* esp. *paintings* and pieces of *sculpture.* A synthetic material, it is a polymerized derivative of vinyl alcohol, highly popular. It forms clear, *transparent films* when combined with a mild organic solvent, is capable of being brushed or sprayed, and can be removed safely from most types of painting. Used also in *lacquers, varnishes, enamels,* and various cements and adhesives.

VIOLET CARMINE—In *painting,* a semi-transparent *pigment* of the *lake color* series, prepared from the root of the botanical ANCHUSA TINCTORIA, from *Brazilwood,* and from mixtures of *alizarin madder* and *cobalt* or any other *stable blue.* It is only in admixture with one of the cobalts that the resulting product will possess sufficient *permanence* to be of value on the artist's *palette.*

VIORD—In *oil painting,* a general over-all impression of *brightness* or *intensity.*

VIRGIN DROP BLACK—A black carbon *pigment* of good covering value, used extensively in *drawing* and *painting.* Prepared through a process of destructive distillation of animal bones in an iron retort.

VIRIDIAN—A relatively modern contribution to the *art* of *painting,* this *pigment* first appeared on the market in crude form in 1838. It is slightly *bluish-green,* useful in both *oil* and *water-color,* and *stable* under even extreme conditions of exposure to *light* and to chemical reagents. Often confused with *emerald green* (q.v.); known also as *Guignet's green.* See *phthalocyanine blue.*

VIRTUOSO—(1) a person who excels in the *technique* of an *art,* esp. a *musical instrumentalist.* (2) In the *graphic* and *plastic* arts, one whose technical facility or skill in the use of a *medium* exceeds his conceptual power or originality of *expression* to such a degree as (apparently) to become an end in itself. Many Hellenistic *sculptors,* and 17th and 18th century *baroque* and *rococo* painters, sculptors and *architects* are said to have possessed 'mere *virtuositiy.*' See *technique.*

VISHNU—In Hindu *mythology,* the god who is found in the *trimurti,* or trinity, with the two other great gods, Brahma and Siva. Known also as *The Preserver,* the supreme god of the Hindu *pantheon.* He is most frequently represented in the *arts* as riding astride Garuda, a half bird and half man, and holding in one of his four hands a lotus, in another a conch-shell, in the third a mace, and in the fourth a disc as the *emblem* of supreme power.

VISUAL ARTS—Generally, those *arts* which manifest themselves and their creators through the agency of sight, e.g., *painting, sculpture, architecture, ceramics,* etc., as distinguished from an art such as *music* which, though visual to the extent of the written *notation,* displays *expression* through *sound.* The *visual arts* are frequently referred to as *space arts* (q.v.).

VIVID—As applied to *colors* generally, bright; strong; exhibiting the aspects of freshness and life; *intense.* An *artist* using bright colors extensively is said to have a *vivid palette.*

VOLET—The term applied to either of the two flanking sections or wings of a *triptych* (q.v.) .

VORTICISM—A movement in the *arts* established in London, 1914, carrying the manifestos of the American poet and critic Ezra Pound and the French sculptor Gaudier-Brzeska. Although the principles of the movement are not clear, the group as a whole opposed *naturalism, impressionism,* and *futurism,* esp. the last. It aimed to arouse an intensive awareness of *form* in the arts: *color* and *line* in *painting,* and the arrangement of planes in *sculpture.* Generally considered an ultramodernistic movement. See also *ultraism.*

VYATKA TOYS—A group of Russian toys prized as *caricatures* in *sculpture,* having historic and artistic significance. Although somewhat clumsy in form and coarsely tinted, each toy invariably contains some aspect of precision exhibiting a high degree of craftsmanship. They are likened by *archaeologists* to the famous *clay* toys of the ancient Greeks (after which they may have been patterned). Known also as the *dimtov toys.*

W

WALLING WAX—In *etching,* a type of *wax* employed in the forming of a miniature *wall* or bank around the edge of a *plate* to hold the etching acid, etc.

WALL PAINTING—A *picture,* often assuming the proportions of a *mural* (q.v.), painted on a full *wall* in either *fresco, oil,* or *tempera.* See *pi hua.*

WALNUT OIL—In *painting,* a popular *drying oil* (q.v.) used as a *medium.* Much favored in the latter part of the *Renaissance* in Europe, it comes from walnuts which run up to 65 % oil. It is rather slower drying than *linseed oil,* but it less apt to discolor or crack on drying. See *poppy-seed oil.*

WANDERERS—A Russian *art* movement started in 1872 by Kramskoy, intended to enlighten all of the people through art, just as various radical parties sought to enlighten them politically. The school attached more value to moral and literary aspects than to *esthetics,* and for twenty years it dominated the scene, sending works to the greatest art centers of the world. Its doctrine was *realism* in *landscape,* pictorial, and *seascape* work, many of the subjects displaying opposition to the growing absolutism of the czar. The most gifted of the *Wanderers* appears to have been Ilya Repin. See *Narodniki.*

WANTAGE WHITE HORSE—A huge work of *sculpture* consisting of the figure of a horse, 370 feet in length, *carved* into a chalk cliff at Wantage, Wiltshire, England. Numerous *legends* surround its origin, although the most prominent theory explains that it was accomplished under the direction of Alfred the Great to commemorate his victory over the Danes in 871. It can be seen from a distance of more than 20 miles in clear weather.

WARM COLORS—In *art,* the term applied to certain *hues* of *red* and those approaching red, e.g., *orange, yellow,* and possibly yellow-*green;* any *color* in which red, orange or yellow predominates. These colors are associated in the mind with heat, sun and fire, and the fact that they produce a *sensation* of warmth can be demonstrated by the use of a sensitive thermometer. Compare with *cool colors* (q.v.). See also *advancing color.*

WASH—A thin mixture of *water-color* with water. See *water-color.*

WASH DRAWING—A *drawing* made with *water-color* or diluted *Indian ink,* either of which will produce various shades of *gray.* It is used as preliminary copy for *half-tone engravings.* Also, any drawing made with *sepia* or *transparent* colors that have been washed lightly over the surface as with a *brush.*

WASP LINE—In Chinese *painting,* a brush stroke technique creating lines generally resembling the outline of a wasp's body. The point of the *brush* is used in vertical style, with frequent variations of pressure producing a characteristic thick and thin line.

WATER-COLOR—The *art* of *painting* on *paper* with a *medium* whose solvent is water; a process of painting with *transparent* or semi-transparent *washes* which distinguishes the medium from other types of painting. The *colors* are usually mixed with a *gum* product which acts as a *binder.* Although this art has developed principally since the mid-19th century, it was used by the Egyptians on *papyrus* rolls. In the *medieval* period, *illuminated manuscripts* were painted with a *water-color* medium. The development, passing through the *wash drawing* stage during the *Renaissance,* was from *monochrome* to neutral *tints* to full color. It has become a separate and distinct art form employing various *drawing* mediums such as *pencil, charcoal, ink, crayon,* or *pastel,* and then gone over with washes ranging from transparent to *opaque.* The paintings made with opaque *water-color* are often referred to as *gouache* (q.v.) *drawings,* esp. when a pliable adhesive is added to the binder to give a soft sheen to the surface. The purest water available should be used with *water-colors,* since impure water often discolors the *ground* and spots it; may also injure the working qualities of the *paint* and even affect the colors.

WATER-COLOR PAPER—A *ground* for *water-color* painting, made from *linen* rags that are boiled, beaten and shredded to separate the individual *fibers.* The *pulp* is then run over a fine *wire screen* in a thin layer, dried, and pressed. No chemicals are employed other than a mild *bleaching* agent. The paper is heavy (light paper would cockle and wrinkle, and is less manipulative) and will stay wetter longer, preserving its shape. The *grain* or *texture* takes the *color* from the *brush* in high and low spots, creating depth of *tone* and the type of sparkle rendering water-color the interesting *medium* that it is. Coarse and rough grains appear to be the most popular.

WATER-GLASS PAINTING—See *stereochromy.*

WATER-GRASS DOTS—In Chinese *painting,* a type of *brush* stroke technique employed in the representation of seaweed leaves. Somewhat similar to the effect in the *pine-leaf dot* (q.v.) method, the chief differences are that the strokes for seaweed are more delicate, softer, slightly more curved, and that they meet at the bottom in a defininte overlapping.

WATER OF AYR—A term in *sculpture;* see *ayr stone.*

WATTEAU BLUE—In Chinese *painting,* a famous *blue* mineral *pigment* obtained from the second stratum of the *azurite* stone when it is rubbed down in water. Known natively as *êr ch'ing,* it is used chiefly in painting the hills and rocks of *ch'ing lü* (*landscapes*). See *shih ch'ing.*

WAX—Long known in the *arts,* the *waxes* are esters of monohydric alcohols, though sources and variations are many. *Paraffin* is derived from shale oil, lignite, and petroleum; *montan* from lignite and peat; other common varieties are *beeswax, Chinese insect wax, candelilla,* and *carnauba.* All differ in hardness, *plasticity,* and melting point. The earliest records of art mention *wax,* in some form, as a *coating* material. *Sculpture* and *modeling* in *wax* were common in the *Renaissance,* and *wax* was at various times taken up as a *painting medium,* as in the early Christian era in the *Fayum* district of Egypt where *mummy portraits* were made with *wax* as a vehicle for the *pigment.* See *wax sculpture, encaustic painting, cire perdue* and *waxwork.*

WAXING-UP– In the making of *stained glass* windows, a *technique* following the process of *cutting.* After the required pieces of colored *glass* are cut, they are arranged on a sheet of clear glass and joined by hot *wax* applied to the corners of each piece. When thus located, the glass is ready for the next step, that of *painting.* Using a *pigment* of one *color,* consisting of powdered glass melted and mixed with copper and iron oxide, desired detail and shading are applied to the stained glass. See *gather, glass-painting* and *stained glass.*

WAX SCULPTURE–Because of its pliancy and its readiness to assume varied shapes, *wax* is well suited to the *art* of *sculpture*: (1) creation of *images* serving transitory needs and which may or may not be destroyed after use, e.g., *effigies* used in image magic; (2) creation of credible counterfeits of reality with the intention of deceiving the spectator; e.g., *manikins;* Mme. Tussaud's *waxworks.* In order to render the *illusion* more complete, the effects are heightened by additional garments and human hair. Great *realism* is often obtained, as illustrated by Roman portraiture which arose from the imitation of durable materials in wax effigies used in family cults and in various funerary *ceremonies.* See *waxwork.*

WAXWORK–In *sculpture,* a technique famous since the time of the *ancient* Egyptians who made *wax* figures of their deities; wax dolls were common in ancient Greece. Pliny writes that Lysistratus (about 300 B.C.) made colored *portraits* in wax from plaster *molds,* while in Rome, families made wax *masks* of ancestors and living members, placing them in their vestibules. In *medieval* times, many ecclesiastical figures were fashioned from wax, with superb specimens coming from Spain. Wax portraits acquired great vogue in the 18th century, and *statuary* in wax reached high popularity in the form of representations as exhibited at Madame Tussaud's in London, and Eden Musée in New York. Wax is used as a *medium,* with or without added material, for the execution of *statues, busts, medallions,* etc., as well as for modeling many objects from which metal *castings* are later to be made. Wax is employed extensively by *sculptors* to embody an initial conception to be worked out in *clay, plaster,* or other material in final form. See *wax* and *cire perdue.*

WAY OF THE CROSS—In *painting,* any series of pictures (usually in a *church;* occasionally in a *museum*) representing Christ's progress to Calvary. Sometimes called *Stations of the Cross.*

WELL SLAB—In *painting,* a color-mixing tray consisting of a rectangular *ceramic* plate having a series of oblong cut-outs arranged lengthwise. Opposite each such compartment is a circular, scoop-like well of water, thinner, *siccative,* etc. This device is superior to the *nest saucers* (q.v.) in that all of the materials are in a single, over-all container; preferred also to the *divided slant* which holds either the mixing elements or the finished paints, but not both. See also *slant.*

WHEEL OF LIFE—In Tibetan *art,* the famous wheel often seen in *paintings,* setting forth the basic beliefs in reincarnation found in Lamaism. The endless circumference represents immortality; three prominences at the hub are *symbolic* of the three great vices—ignorance, lust and anger, submission to which will render the wrongdoer an insect or other low form of creature in his next life. The six spokes represent the six principal divisions of life and religion: the gods, demi-gods, hell, tortured souls, men, and animals. See also *nirvana.*

WHEEL OF PRAYER—In Tibet, a barrel-shaped device of small proportions, made of *metal* or *wood* (often *silver*), filled with written entreaties to Buddha in preparation for death. The inscriptions, on *paper* or *parchment,* are stuffed into the hollow. Larger varieties are used for community purposes. One large *wheel of prayer,* near

Nathu-la, is powdered by a waterfall, and is filled with religious *paintings, statuettes,* cloth, and paper covered with written prayers. With each turn of the barrel, all of the prayers within are believed to be repeated again and again to Buddha. See also *prayer flag.*

WHELK RED—See *Tyrian purple.*

WHIRLING TABLE—In *sculpture* and *ceramics,* the name often applied to the *potter's wheel,* sometimes to the *gentleman* (q.v.).

WHIRLPOOL—In Chinese *painting,* a *brush* stroke technique intended to give the effect of a whirlpool, or of the marks of pellets dropped into soft mud; the strokes are circular. Employed also to represent the honeycombing under an overhanging cliff.

WHITE—The *color* of snow; the color without *hue,* appearing at the extreme end of the scale of *grays;* the color that is the opposite and the *complement* of *black,* being the result of the admixture of all *light-waves.* It is highly *luminous,* but devoid of *chroma,* and possesses strong powers of reflection (see *cool colors* and *warm colors*). Also, any *pigment* or other coloring matter employed to produce this visual effect. The term is loosely applied to silvery metals and colorless liquids.

WHITE EARTH—In *painting,* the name applied to any of the natural substances occurring in *white* or near-white (e.g., *chalk* and *alumina*). Used as one of the ingredients in the mixing of a *ground;* as a *glazing* agent; as an agent in *gesso* work, etc. See also *zaccab.*

WHITE LEAD—By far the most popular *white pigment* in the history of the *painting art.* It was one of the first artificially prepared pigments, and *techniques* for its preparation were described by Theophrastus, Pliny, and *Vitruvius;* numerous *medieval* recipes for its manufacture are recorded. Though generally *stable,* it is darkened if in a lean *tempera* or aqueous *film* when exposed to hydrogen sulphide in the air, even in low concentration. This accounts for much of the blackening of the white *touches* used on *Renaissance* drawings and probably explains why Far Eastern painters never adopted this pigment for general use. Occurring in the form of a white *amorphous* powder, it is used also in *ceramic glazes* and as a substitute for *red lead* in protective coatings; known also as *flake white.* See *titanium white* and *ch'ien fên.*

WHITING—A form of *calcium carbonate* occurring as a white, *amorphous* powder, commonly termed *chalk.* Used in the *arts* as a covering for painting *grounds,* and in the preparation of grounds *for gilding;* used also as a substitute for *feldspar* in the making of *ceramic glazes.* Often termed *Paris white,* it is of organic formation consisting of egg shells, oyster shells, coral, *pearls,* and the like. It has very little *opacity* in any *painting medium,* and is rarely found on the artist's *palette* except as an adulterant or as base for the making of *lake colors.* It was used in combination with *glue size* for Spanish and Italian *tempera* painting grounds, sometimes with the addition of *plaster of Paris.* Traces of iron often bring it to cream color. Known also as *marble dust, Spanish white* ,and *English white.*

WILLOW LINE—In Chinese *painting,* a *brush* stroke technique resulting in small bodies having thick centers and sharply-pointed ends. Known natively as *liu yeh miao* (q.v.).

WIND BANDS—In Chinese *art,* the two vertical strips affixed to the top of a *scroll painting.* Formerly, they hung free, as in Japanese mountings of today, and it is said that they were intended to flap and frighten off flies and other insects. Modern *wind bands* of China are decorative strips pasted down flat; known natively as *fêng tai.*

WINGED BULL—Assyrian *symbol* of force and domination, of frequent occurrence in ancient architectural *sculpture,* in which pairs of winged human-headed bulls and lions of *colossal* size usually guarded the portals of *palaces.*

WIPING—In *etching,* a technique employed in preparing an *intaglio plate* for printing. The etching *ink* is spread on the entire plate and is then wiped from the surface, leaving the ink in the lines only. Accomplished by *wiping* the warm plate with a *tarlatan* cloth to produce a *rag-*

wiped print, or finishing the *wiping* of the plate with the palm of the hand to produce a *hand-wiped print.*

WIRE LINE TECHNIQUE—In Chinese *painting,* a *brush* stroke technique creating the effect of iron wire. There is consistent evenness in thickness throughout the length of each line, with sharp angles at regular intervals, giving an effect of stiffness. Executed in *vertical brush* style, with heavy *ink* application allowing for long lines, the result often has the appearance of a series of chisel cuts, esp. when the angles are closely spaced.

WOOD—A substance of numerous uses in the *arts,* deriving from the *fibrous* structures of trees and similar large plants. It is the material of many fine pieces of *sculpture;* serves as handles and tools for *designers* and *craftsmen;* as *supports* for *paintings;* blocks for *printing, woodcuts,* and *wood-blocks;* as the basis for *architecture* from time immemorial; as the chief *medium* in *furniture* making, etc. Characteriz-ed by dimensional change corresponding to change in climate and moisture presence, causing drying, cracking, and warping. The use of *wood* in the arts continues through the ages on an ever-growing scale. See each type of *wood* (with uses, structure, etc.) in its proper alpha-betical location. See also *grain, texture, figure, annual ring,* and *dendrochonology.*

WOOD-BLOCK—A *die* that has been cut from *wood.* From the block, impressions are made on *paper* or on *fabric.* Compare with *woodcut* (q.v.); see also *baren.*

WOOD-BLOCK PRINT—An impression on *paper* or *fabric* from a *wook-block.* In the Orient the flat of the block (rather than an edge) is used as the surface to be incised with the desired *design.* In Western *woodcuts,* the edge often bears the *carving.* See *baren.*

WOOD CARVING—A variety of *sculpture* found to have been pursued from very early times. While unknown in Babylonia, Assyria and Persia, it was common in Egypt from the days of the earliest dynasties. In 11th century Scandinavia, the *wood* was covered with *canvas* and then *stuccoed* or painted. Earliest *Romanesque* pieces were *colossal* wooden crucifixes. The *art* was the most important aspect of German sculpture in the 15th and 16th cents., and stonework was influenced by its exquisite *altarpieces* and *triptychs.* Spain, France and Italy contributed to the world treasury of *wood carvings,* featuring *choir stalls, screens,* and other religious objects. See *Maori carving.*

WOODCUT—A wooden block upon which a picture, *design,* lettering, etc., has been *engraved, carved,* or otherwise incised (usually with a hand tool) for reproduction. The technique of carving a block of wood in such manner that all of the wood is cut away to a slight depth except the lines forming the design. The term is also applied to *print* or impression made from the *woodcut.* The actual carving is frequently executed with a *skew chisel* (q.v.); see also *wood-block.*

WOOD ENGRAVING—(1) The *art* of cutting designs in *relief* upon a polished block of *wood.* (2) Any *print* made from such a *carved* block. Differs from the *woodcut* (q.v.) in that the actual carving (not the untouched remainder) is the design for reproduction.

WOODEN PANEL—In the *art* of the *Middle Ages,* the *support* usually used for *paintings,* upon which the *ground* (q.v.) was placed for evenness of *texture.* Later replaced by *canvas,* which is still the principal *oil painting* support employed throughout the world.

WORLD OF ART—A Russian *art* movement of the early 20th century, growing out of *Blue Rose* (q.v.) and in protest against the *Wandereres;* better known as *Mir Iskusstva* (q.v.).

X

XANTHIAN SCULPTURES—Name given to a large, famous series of exquisitely executed pieces of *statuary* discovered during excavation operations at the site of *Xanthus,* ancient capital of Lycia which fell to Cyrus' army in 546 B.C., and again to Brutus in 42 B.C. The *sculptures,* chiefly *sepulchral,* include some of the world's rarest examples of detailed *relief* work in stone. The collection is now in the British Museum. Sometimes referred to as *Xanthic Sculptures.*

XANTHORHAMNINE—A fine *yellow* coloring matter, originally of secret origin, but discovered by the Greeks to have been made by Orientals from ripe Persian or Turkish berries, and from Avignon grains.

XANTHORRHEA GUM—A natural *resinous* product derived from the Australian XANTHORRHEA tree, used widely in the *sizing* of *paper* and manufacture of various *waxes.* Used also as a *surface film* or coating applied to *paintings* and *statuary.*

XYLENES—Name of a wide group of *coaltar* derivatives somewhat resembling *benezene,* from which valuable *dyes* and *pigments* are produced. Chemically $C_6H_4(CH_3)_2$, they are known also as *xylos.* Less volatile than other diluents, they are also favored as *thinners* in *lacquer.*

XYLOGRAPHY—The *art* of rendering *engravings* or *carvings* in *wood,* or of reproducing *prints* from such cuts; also, a technique of decorative *painting* on wood. A selected *design* is drawn on wood and then incised into it. The remaining smooth surfaces are then rolled under controlled pressure with prepared *pigments.* The *color* penetrates the wood leaving no outside film, and after polishing or applying *enamel,* the piece of wood has become a *xylograph,* the *pattern* of which cannot be destroyed by washing, scrubbing, sandpapering, etc. The art was highly developed as early as the 15th century.

Y

YABYOM—The principle in Tibetan *art* dictating that no single object or element is complete within itself, and that each requires presentation or union with its opposite in order to be considered a complete unit or entity. Thus, most of the *works of art* of Tibet, esp. in *painting* and *sculpture,* represent at the same time male and female figures, light and darkness, good and evil, etc. This belief is somewhat tangential to the Western theory of duality, asserting that all things are understandable only in terms of their opposites; e.g., light could not be defined if darkness did not exist; cold would have no meaning if heat did not exist, etc.

YACHTING STYLE—In France, the name applied to the *Art Nouveau* style, popular between 1890 and 1905. See *Art Nouveau.*

YAKSHA—In the *art* and *mythology* of India, the divine guard of all treasures below the earth's surface. Frequently represented in *paintings* and *sculpture* as a stalwart, armed defender.

YAKSI—The *sculpture* of India from 200 to 25 B.C., revealing a direct sense of the full beauty of the human form, conceived not as an articulate biological organism, but as the totality of many individually beautiful and mechanistically joined parts.

YAMATO—(Literally, *pictures* of old Japan) A school of *painting* in native style, reaching its peak in the 12th century, centered largely in the vicinity of Kyoto. Rustic and domestic scenes were the principal subjects.

YANG—In Chinese *abstract art,* the male element in the universe, source of life, light and heat. It was *represented* by a circular diagram bisected by a wavy line, one half *red* (the *yang*) and the other half *black,* representing *yin,* the female element, to which was ascribed darkness, cold and death. This *symbolism* emerged with the HAN DYNASTY (206 B.C.-204 A.D.).

YANG CHÜ—In Chinese *art,* the narrow strips of *brocade* or special *silk* affixed to the top and bottom of a *painting* and immediately adjacent to it within the four borders, or *ssŭ hsiang* (q.v.). In *restoration* or remounting, these may be trimmed and the picture itself left untouched. Very fine old brocade is most frequently used for this purpose, even when the painting is new; however, the original brocade may be kept through several mountings.

YANG HUNG—In Chinese *painting,* a variety of *red* coloring matter imported as a dry *pigment* in cake or stick form; rubbed down with water to render it brushable. The *color* approximates *cerise.*

YANG WÊN—In Chinese *art,* the *color* arrangement of an artist's *seal* or *yin chang* whereby the characters of the *intaglio*-engraved seal will print *white* against a *vermilion* background. Known also as *pai wên.*

YELLOW—One of the *primary colors* (q.v.); having a bright, clear golden *hue;* having the *color* of that part of the *spectrum* falling between *orange,* and *green;* the color of the lemon. Technically, a response to *wave-lengths* of about 585 *millimicrons.* United with *blue,* it yields green; with *red,* it produces orange. See *orpiment.*

YELLOW EARTH—In *painting,* the term applied to a certain variety of *ochre* (q.v.) used as a *pigment.* Belonging to the class of *iron pigments* (q.v.), it is known also as *yellow ochre.*

YELLOW LAKE—A series of *lake colors* of vegetable origin, better known as *quercitron lake* (q.v.).

YELLOW OCHRE—In *painting,* one of the *iron pigments* better known as *yellow earth* (q.v.). Belongs to the group known as *yellow pigments.*

YELLOW PIGMENTS—In *oil paintings,* the general term applied to a wide range of *yellows* and near-yellows. The classification embraces *yellow ochre, raw sienna,* the *cadmium pigments, aureolin, cobalt* yellow, *lemon yellow,* and *Naples yellow.* While all are considered *stable,* the cadmiums and aureolin have a tendency to injure some other colors when mixed with them or applied over or under them on the *canvas.*

YEN CHIH—In Chinese *painting,* the *rouge* pigment, ranging in shade from eglantine to peach blossom. It is prepared from the botanical MIRABILIS JALAPA (yen chih hua), a vine with red flowers and leaves, from which the color is extracted and mixed with flour employed as a *glue;* now available in prepared form. Used widely in bird and flower work.

YIN—In Chinese *abstract art* of the HAN DYNASTY (206 B.C.-204 A.D.), the symbolic female element in the universe, *represented* by darkness, cold and death. The *symbol* was a circle, divided in diameter by a wavy line, one half *black* (the *yin*) and the other half *red,* representing *yang,* the male element, to which was attributed light, heat, and the source of life.

YIN CHANG—In Chinese *art,* the mark or *seal* of the *artist* added to the signature or *colophon* at one corner of the *painting.* Every Oriental artist has a number of different seals, and no *picture* is considered complete without the appended impression. Some works are signed with seals alone, the most common forms of which bear both the given name and surname, or the pseudonym by which the painter is known. The Chinese seal has a *decorative* function and is placed appropriately with respect to the subject of the work. Although there are professional seal cutters, most artists cut their own. This allows the general style of the painter to be carried through to the final detail. See also *k'uan* and *in.*

YIN CHU—In Chinese *painting,* a fine *vermillion pigment* somewhat deeper than *chu sha* (q.v.), falling between Mephisto red and Goya red. Used chiefly in *seal* pigment work. See *yin chang.*

YING HSIANG—In Chinese *painting,* a ceremonial *portrait,* usually painted posthumously with respect to the subject. It may be executed with the actual corpse as the *model,* or from a previous portrait, *photograph,* or verbal description given by a close relative; the last is known as *chui ying.* It is interesting to note that photographs are replacing *ying hsiang* in the death portraiture of modern China; by 1951 the practice of painting in this connection was fast becoming obsolete.

YIN WEN—In Chinese *art,* the *color* arrangement of an artist's *seal* or *yin chang.* In this group, the characters of the seal in *relief* are dipped into *vermilion,* executing a red impression with a white background. A variety of red *pigment* used solely for this purpose is known as *yin sê.*

YOKO—A large, horizontal Japanese *woodblock print,* approximating ten inches in height by fifteen inches in width.

YÜAN CHIN—In Chinese *painting,* literally 'far and near' as applied to depth and *perspective.* The term is generally used when referring to mountain scenes, but since mountains are a regular part of almost all Chinese *landscapes,* the term embraces landscape in general by extension.

YÜAN T'I—In Chinese *art,* a form of academic *painting* characterized by extreme precision with respect to forms, rules, and customs. Even when apparently loose in *hsieh i* (q.v.) style, it adheres closely to accepted *tradition* without individual invention. Toward the end of the CH'ING DYNASTY it was called *kuan p'ai* (official school).

YUNG HSIU—In Chinese *art,* a technique employing the use of *charcoal* in the making of the preliminary *sketch* before undertaking the actual *painting.* The charcoal of older times was prepared by charring or burning willow twigs; now it is purchased. Some artists use the burnt end of a tight paper wad; others use wet incense of deep color. In either case, the *medium* is selected because it is easily erased with a hair or feather *brush.* Some artist first use a very light *ink,* thereafter covering it with a heavy ink. Compare with *line doubling* (q.v.).

YÜ PAN HSÜAN—In Chinese *art,* literally *jade tablet paper.* It is a variety of stiff, very white, fairly thick paper, used as a *ground* in *calligraphy* and *painting.* See *chih.*

Z

ZACCAB–A type of *white earth* mixed with lime; used by the natives of Yucatan for *plaster, stucco,* and the like, in both *architecture* and *sculpture.*

ZAFFER BLUE–In *painting,* same as *cobalt blue* (q.v.).

ZAFFRE–A term in *painting;* see *smalt.*

ZAFFRE–In the making of *stained glass* (q.v.), a prized ingredient imparting a clear, deep *blue,* made from an oxide of *cobalt.*

ZAFIRO–General term in Spanish *art* applied to (1) *ultramarine;* (2) *sapphire;* (3) *lapis lazuli.*

ZAKOPANE–An *art* center situated on the northern slopes of the Tatra Mountains of Poland, famous for its superb *wood carvings.* Many of Europe's greatest *sculptors* drew *inspiration* from this *cultural* point.

ZINC BLOOM–See *zinc oxide.*

ZINC GREEN–In *painting,* a fine *pigment* of brilliant *green,* composed of the oxides of *zinc* and *cobalt.*

ZINC OLEATE–A white granular powder, greasy to the touch. It is a valuable ingredient in artists' *paints* as a *drier.*

ZINC OXIDE–A white pulverulent substance (ZnO) made by burning *zinc* in air. It is used chiefly as a *pigment* in *painting,* serving successfully as a substitute for *white lead.* Known also a *flowers* of *zinc, nihil album, philosopher's wool,* and *zinc bloom.*

ZINC PIGMENTS–Chief among these is *zinc white (zincweiss),* first used as a pigment in 1782 and available as an artists' *color* in 1834. Originally intended for *water-color* work only, it quickly proved its *value* when employed with *oil.* .It is somewhat weaker in *hiding power* than *lead,* which preceded it on the *palette* by many centuries. *Zinc yellow* is a bright, clear lemon *hue* which made its appearance in the mid-19th century. See *titanium white.*

ZINCWEISS—In *painting,* a brilliant white *pigment,* used esp. in *water-color* work; possesses both *stability* and *hiding power.* First used in France in the mid-19th century, its fine properties render it suitable also in *tempera* and *fresco* work. Often spelled *zinkweiss;* see *zinc pigments.*

ZINC WHITE—A term in *painting;* see *zincweiss* and *zinc pigments.*

ZINC YELLOW—See *zinc pigments.*

ZINNABER GREEN—In *painting,* a term generally descriptive of the deep brownish or olive shade of green, made by mixing yellow of the *chrome* group with *Prussian blue.*

ZO—In Japanese *sculpture,* any carved image of a deity.

ZOANON—In *sculpture,* a term applied generally to any *carved image* or *statue;* better known as *xoanon* (q.v.).

ZOCCOLA—In *sculpture* and *architecture,* an extended step, pedestal or *socle* (q.v.) situated under the *base* of a *column;* used chiefly as a support for a *statue.*

ZOLA—A substance having a vast number of uses in the *arts.* It is a *white,* solid material, crystalline or *amorphous* in structure, used (1) as an ingredient in *glues* and *printing inks;* (2) as a *plasticizer* for *casein* and *shellac;* (3) as a preservative for *leather* and *wood;* (4) as a fireproofing agent for *textiles;* (5) as a bonding agent in *cement* and *concrete*; (6) as an ingredient in the making of fine *glass,* and (7) as a hardening agent for *plaster of Paris.* It is a natural sodium borate or borax, chemically $Na_2B_4O_7IOH_2O$.

ACKNOWLEDGMENTS

In a work of this kind the author becomes indebted to many persons, both living and dead. This book has been made possible only through the cooperation of numerous authorities in the fields covered. The author expresses his genuine gratitude to the following societies, teachers, artists, publishers, authors and editors for their generous courtesies, assistance and efforts extended:

American Council of Learned Societies; C. Anastasoff, Journalist; B. W. Anderson, Director, *Precious Stone Laboratory,* London, Diamond, Pearl and Precious Stone Section, Lecturer in Gemmology, and Author of Gem Testing (publishehd by Emerson Books, Inc., New York, 1948); Archaeological Institute of America; Richard F. Bach, *Metropolitan Museum of Art,* New York; Betty Beatty, London (classical architecture); Thomas J. Bigham, Jr., Fellow and Tutor of the *General Theological Seminary* of the Episcopal Church, New York; Charles L. Black, Jr., *Columbia University;* Ben Zion Bokser, Jewish Theological Seminary (ecclesiastical arts); Paul E. Boucher, *Colorado College,* Author of Fundamentals of Photography (copyright 1940, 1947 by D. Van Nostrand Co., Inc., New York); Charles S. Braden, Jr., Chairman of Department of History and Literature of Religions, *Northwestern University;* Luka Brajinovic, Journalist, Rome; Quirinus Breen, *University of Oregon;* Lyman J. Briggs, Director, *National Bureau of Standards;* Nicholas Britsky, *University of Illinois;* Edgar Hall Broadhead, Organist and Instructor in Music, *Duke University*; Gertrude G. Bunzel, *Carnegie Institute of Technology*; Joseph H. Bunzel, *Fisk University*; Bureau of American Ethnology, *Smithsonian Institution;* Van H. Cartmell, Author, The Amateur Theatre Handbook (published by Blue Ribbon Books, 1945, copyright 1936 by Van H. Cartmell); Shirley Jackson Case, Dean *Florida School of Religion;* Century Dictionary and Cyclopedia (coypright by The Century Co., 1889, 1895); Barrett H. Clark (literature and drama); Joseph B. Code, Director, *Inter-American Institute,* Kansas City, Missouri; Samuel S. Cohon, Professor of Theology, *Hebrew Union College,* Cincinnati; Simon Conrad, *Capuchin College;* Kenneth H. Cousland, Professor of Church History, *Victory University,* Toronto; Gerald R. Cragg, Professor of Systematic Theology and Lecturer in Christian Ethics, *United Theological College,* Montreal; Clarence Tucker Craig, Professor of Ecclesiastical Language and Literature, *Oberlin College;* George W. Creswell, Chief of Publications Distribution Section, United States Department of the Interior, *Bureau of Mines*; Tom Peete Cross, Professor of Comparative Literature, *University of Chicago*; Edward A. Cykler, *University of Oregon*; L. Harold De Wolf, Professor of Philosophy, *Boston University*; Charles M. Diserens, *University of Cincinnati*; Francis Domanski, *Poslaniec Serca Jezusa*; E. I. Du Pont de Nemours and Company (substitute and synthetic art materials); Walter Dushnyck, Editorial Staff, America; Eastman Kodak Company, Rochester, New York (materials in photography); Burton Scott Easton, Professor of Literature Interpretation, *General Theological Seminary* of the Episcopal Church, New York; Albert H. Fay, Author, A Glossary of the Mining and Mineral Industry (published by U. S. Government Department of the Interior, *Bureau of Mines*); Vergilius Ferm, Compton Professor and Chairman of the Department of Philosophy, *College of Wooster,* Wooster, Ohio; Louis Finkelstein, Professor of Theology, *Jewish Theological Seminary* of New York; James Ford, Director, *Better Homes in America*; Robert Worth Frank, Professor of Philosophy of Religion and Ethics, *Presbyterian Theological Seminary,* Chicago; Samuel Maclean Gilmour, Professor of New Testament Literature and Exegesis, *Queen's Theological College,* Kingston, Ontario; John Gloag, London (classical architecture); Nelson Glueck, Professor of Biblical Archaeology, *Hebrew Union College,* Cincinnati; Edgar J. Goodspeed, Professor Emeritus of Biblical and Patristic Greek, *University of Chicago;* Mrs. Priwa B. Gross (Slavonic arts and crafts); Edward Rochie Hardy, Jr., Instructor, Department of Hebrew and Ecclesiastical History, *General Theological Seminary* of the Episcopal Church, New York; Philip Lawrence Harriman, *Bucknell University* (psychology in the arts); Robert B. Harshe, Director, *Art Institute of Chicago;* Charles Hartshorne, Department of Philosophy, *University of Chicago;* A. Eustace Haydon, Chairman, Department of Comparative Religion, *University of Chicago;* David Hecht, *Bowdoin College;* material from Hepner's EFFECTIVE ADVERTISING (by permission of the publisher, McGraw-Hill Book Company, New York); Eugene F. Hickson (paints and painting, United States specifications); Edwin J. Hipkiss, Curator of Decorative Arts, *Museum of Fine Arts,* Boston; Robert M. Holbrow, Editor, BOOKSELLER'S HANDBOOK, London; Howard Hollis, *Cleveland Museum of Art;* Daniel Clarence Holton, recently Professor in Theology, Aoyama Gakuin, Tokyo, and Dean of Theology Department, Kanto Gakuin, Yokohama; W. L. Hubbard and G. W. Andrews, Editors, AMERICAN HISTORY AND ENCYCLOPEDIA OF MUSIC (publisher, Irving Squire); Bernard C. Jakway, Educational Director, *National Home Furnishings Program,* Chicago; Janet, teacher of ballet and tap dancing, Springfield, Illinois (author, DICTIONARY OF DANCE TERMS, 1926); Hjalmar W. Johnson, Professor of Philosophy, *Augustana Theological Seminary,* Rock Island, Illinois; Paul E. Johnson, Professor of Psychology and History of Religion, *Boston University;* S. C. J. Jones, K. S. W. Easton and H. L. Yelland, London and Sydney (terms in literature); T. Almar Kamtonen, Professor of Systematic Theology, *Wittenberg College;* Elmer C. Kiessling, Professor of English, *Northwestern College,* Watertown, Wisconsin; Herman Kieval, Rabbi, *Beth Judah Synagogue,* Ventnor, New Jersey; Mrs. Ethyn W. Kirby, formerly ass't professor of History, *Wells College;* Janko Lavrin, *University College* and British Broadcasting Company; Lester Loeb (terms in photography); Benjamin March, late of the *Museum of Anthropology* of the *University of Michigan* (technical terms in Chinese painting); H. J. L. J. Massé, Author, CHATS ON OLD PEWTER (material quoted by permission of the publisher, A. A. Wyn, Inc., New York, 1949); Thomas T. McAvoy, Archivist, *University of Notre Dame;* John Thomas McNeill, formerly Professor of European Christianity, *University of Chicago;* Ronald F. Michaelis, Hon. Librarian, *Society of Pewter Collectors;* C. Powell Minnegerode, Director, *Corcoran Gallery of Art,* Washington, D. C.: Julian Morgenstern, President, *Hebrew Union College,* Cincinnati; Paul G. Morrison, Curator, Rare Book Room, *University of Chicago Libraries;* Ernest R. Mowrer, Professor of Sociology, *Northwestern University;* Harriet R. Mowrer, Lecturer in Sociology, *Northwestern University;* Hugo Munsterberg, Department of Literaure and Fine Arts, *Michigan State College;* National Bureau of Standards, *United States Department of Commerce,* Lyman J. Briggs, Director; National Committee on Wood Utilization, *United States Department of Commerce,* Office of Domestic Commerce (FURNITURE, ITS SELECTION AND USES); *National Geographic Society; National Knitted Outerwear Association* (technical terms in dyeing, knitting, textile arts); Maxim Newmark, New York; Eva May Newnan, Head of Department of Greek, *College of Wooster,* Wooster, Ohio; Robert Hastings Nichols, *Columbia University;* Percy V. Norwood, Professor of Ecclesiastical History and Liturgics, *Seabury-Western Theological Seminary,* Evanston, Illinois; Nicholas M. Oboukoff, *Oklahoma A. & M. College;* Daniel C. O'Grady, Professor of Philosophy, *University of Notre Dame;* Fred L. Parrish, Professor and Head of the Department of History and Government, *Kansas State College;* Frederick T. Persons, Librarian, *Congregational Library,* Boston; Robert H. Pfeiffer, Curator of the *Semitic Museum,* Harvard University, and Editor of JOURNAL OF BIBLICAL LITERATURE; E. T. Pickard, Chief of Textile Division, Bureau of Foreign and Domestic Commerce, *United States Department of Commerce;* Arthur Francis Pimbley, Author, PIMBLEY'S DICTIONARY OF HERALDRY; W. Norman Pittenger, *General Theological Seminary* of the Episcopal Church, New York; Michael Reu, late Dean of the Graduate School, *Wartburg Seminary,* Dubuque, Iowa; Grace W. Ripley, *Rhode Island School of Design;* Helene Riveles, New York (art schools and movements); Joseph S. Roucek, *University of Bridgeport* (Slavonic arts); *Royal Academy of Dancing* (European folk-dances); Andrew K. Rule, Professor of Church History and Apologetics, *Louisville Presbyterian Seminary,* Louisville, Kentucky: Morris D. Schoengold, New York (substitute and synthetic materials in the arts); Brice Schratz, *Capuchin College,* Washington, D. C.; Ernest Findlay Scott, Emeritus Professor of New Testament Criticism, *Union Theological Seminary,* New York; R. B. Y. Scott, Professor of Old Testament Literature and Exegesis, *United Theological College,* Montreal; Anne Seesholtz, Fellow in Theology, Marburg, Germany; Mary S. Sims, New York; Alfred A. Skerpan, *Kent State University; Smithsonian Institution,* Bureau of American Ethnology, M. W. Stirling, Chief; G. W. Stubbings, London (church music); Rudolph Sturm, Chief of the Department of Cultural Relations to the United States, Ministry of Information,

Czechoslovakia; Samuel L. Terrien, Instructor in Hebrew and the Old Testament, *Union Theological Seminary,* New York; Pavao Tijan, Editor, Rome; William R. Tilley, Technical Reports Section, *United States Department of Commerce*; F. H. Titmuss, London (WORLD TIMBERS AND THEIR USES, courtesy the Technical Press, Ltd., Surrey, England); Arthur B. Trelstad, *Bowling Green University;* Central Committee on Research, Design and Construction, and Subdivision on Definitions, *United States Department of Commerce*; Bureau of Mines of the *United States Department of the Interior;* Cyril Vollert, Dean of *St. Mary's College,* Kansas; Percy H. Walker (federal specifications—paints, surfaces and coatings); Leo R. Ward, Department of Philosophy, *University of Notre Dame*; Dora Ware, London (classical architecture); F. R. Webber, Editor, LUTHERAN CHURCH ART, New York; C. W. Weiant, Author, AN INTRODUCTION TO THE CERAMICS OF TRES ZAPOTES, VERACRUZ, MEXICO; Rev. F. B. Westbrook, London (ecclesiastical music); William G. Whitford, *University of Chicago*; Russell I. Whyte, Office of Domestic Commerce, *United States Department of Commerce* (FURNITURE, ITS SELECTION AND USES); Allen P. Wikgren, *University of Chicago*; Rolland Emerson Wolfe, *Crane Theological School, Tufts College*; G. Ernest Wright, Editor, THE BIBLICAL ARCHAEOLOGIST; Adel Wybrant, New York (ceramics); Adam Zoltowski (Slavonic arts). The author is anxious to extend due credit to the contributors to the ENCYCLOPEDIA OF THE ARTS, edited by Dagobert D. Runes and H. D. Schrickel, published by Philosophical Library in 1946. The author is mindful of the debt he owes to these distinguished scholars of whose writings he made considerable use and to whom grateful acknowledgment is hereby offered. The author desires especially to mention in this connection the articles and definitive interpretations of Walter Abell, *Michigan State College*; Phyllis Ackerman, New York; T. W. Adorno, New York; Walter R. Agard, *University of Wisconsin*; Vincent Aita, *Hunter College*; George Amberg, *Museum of Modern Art*; Van Meter Ames, *University of Cincinnati*; Rudolf Arnheim, *Guggenheim Foundation*, New York, and Trustee, *American Society for Aesthetics*; Joseph Aronson, New York; Victoria K. Ball, *Western Reserve University*; Iris Barry, *Museum of Modern Art*; Kenneth F. Bates, *Cleveland School of Art*; Marion Bauer, New York; Philip C. Beam, *Bowdoin Museum of Fine Arts*; Otto Benesch, *Fogg Museum of Art,* Harvard University; Arthur V. Berger, New York; Richard Bernheimer, *Bryn Mawr College*; Edward S. Bordin, *University of Minnesota*; B. A. Botkin, *Library of Congress*; Achille P. Bragers, New York; Theron I. Cain, *Massachusetts School of Art*; Schuyler Van R. Cammann, Washington, D. C.; Wing-tsit Chan, *University of Hawaii*; James Chillman, Jr., *Museum of Fine Arts,* Houston; Ralph W. Church, *Cornell University;* Kenneth J. Conant, *Harvard University,* and Vice-President, *Archaeological Institute of America*; Ananda K. Coomaraswamy, *Museum of Fine Art,* Boston; Arthur P. Davis, *Virginia Union University;* James Grote van Derpool, *University of Illinois*; Ernst F. Detterer, *Newberry Library,* Chicago; Frederick Dorian, *Carnegie Institute of Technology*; Mildred Eakes, *Cincinnati Conservatory of Music*; Henry Purmort Eames, *Scripps College,* California; L. C. Everard, *American Association of Museums*; Donald N. Ferguson, *University of Minnesota*; Theodore Finney, *University of Pittsburgh*; Raymond A. Fisher, *Carnegie Institute of Technology*; Finley Foster, *Western Reserve University*; Milton S. Fox, *Cleveland Museum of Art*; Thomas E. French, *Ohio State University;* Helen Gardner, *Art Institute of Chicago*; Mrs. Katharine E. Gilbert, Chairman, Department of Aesthetics, Art and Music, *Duke University*; D. W. Gotshalk, *University of Illinois*; Jennie Grainger, *University of Wisconsin*; Merry Cartwright Gray, Los Angeles; Balcomb Greene, *Carnegie Institute of Technology*; Hermann Gundersheimer, *Temple University;* Homer E. Sterling, *Carnegie Institute of Technology*; Robert A. Hall, Jr., *Brown University*; W. C. Handy, Composer, New York; George M. A. Hauffman, *Fogg Museum of Art,* Harvard University; Glen Haydon, *University of North Carolina*; Margaret N. H'Doubler, *University of Wisconsin*; Theodore Allen Heinrich, Berkeley, Calif.; J. Vincent Higginson, New York; Lawrence Hill, *Washington University,* St. Louis; Eugene Clay Holmes, *Howard University*; Max Horkeimer, *New School for Social Research,* New York; Walter R. Hovey, *University of Pittsburgh;* Charles W. Hughes, *Hunter College*; Helmut Hungerland, Associate Editor, JOURNAL OF AESTHETICS; Bernice Jamieson, *Rhode Island School of Design*; Iredell Jenkins, *Tulane University*; Gyorgy Kepes, *School of Design,* Chicago; W. A. Kerr; Lincoln Kirsten, Director, *New York City Ballet;* H. Felix Kraus, *Museum of Non-Objective Art,* New York; Richard Krautheimer, *Vassar College*; Ernst Krenek, *Hamline University*; Kalman Kubinyi, Lakewood, Ohio; Helmut Kuhn, *Erlangen University;* Yasuo Kuniyoshi, New York; G. B. Ladner, *Pontifical Institute of Mediaeval Studies,* Canada; Clark D. Lamberton, *Western Reserve University;* Betty Lark-Horovitz, *Purdue University;* Helmut E. Lehmann-Haupt, *Columbia University*; Nathan Lerner, *School of Design,* Chicago; Leopold Levis, *Cleveland Museum of Art;* Irene Lewisohn, *Museum of Costume Art,* New York; Marie Lien, *University of Minnesota*; Lester D. Longman, *State University of Iowa*; Jermayne Macagy, San Francisco; Clara Macgowan, *Northwestern University*; J. Arthur MacLean, *Toledo Mu-*

seum of Art; Norman Macleod, *Briarcliff Junior College*; Henri Marceau, *Philadelphia Museum of Art*; Margaret Fairbanks Marcus, *Cleveland Museum of Art*; John F. Matthews, New York; Richard Mayer, New York; John McAndrew, *Instituto Nacional de Anthropologia,* México, D. F.; Amy Woller McClelland, *University of So. California*; Norman C. Meier, *State University of Iowa*; J. Marshall Miller, *Columbia University*; Myra Miller, New York; L. Moholy-Nagy, late of the *School of Design,* Chicago; Grace L. McCann Morley, *San Francisco Museum of Art*; Valentine Muller, *Bryn Mawr College*; Thomas Munro, Director, *Cleveland Museum of Art*; E. Neale-Silva, *University of Wisconsin*; Virginia Nepodal, *Cleveland School of Art*; Eugen Newhaus, *University of California*; Alfred Neumeyer, *Mills College*; Richard J. Neutra, Los Angeles; Anna Wetherill Olmsted, *Syracuse Museum of Fine Arts*; Otto Ortmann, Baltimore; Stephen C. Pepper, *University of California*; Norman Pietan, New York; Irena Piotrowska, New York; R. F. Piper, *Syracuse University;* James A. Porter, *Howard University*; Lotte Pulvermacher-Egers, New York; Carroll C. Pratt, *Princeton University*; Herman Reichenbach, New York; Maurice Ries, Office of the Coordinator of Inter-American Affairs; Benjamin Rowland, Jr.; William S. Rusk, *Wells College*; Alois J. Schardt, Los Angeles; Ernst Scheyer, *Wayne University*; Laurence Schmeckebier, *Cleveland Institute of Art,* Director, *College Art Ass'n of America;* Carl L. Schmitz, New York; Max Schoen, *Carnegie Institute of Technology*; Viktor Schreckengost, Cleveland; Eric Schroeder, *Fogg Museum of Art,* Harvard University; Carl E. Seashore, *State University of Iowa*; Lucy T. Shoe, *Mount Holyoke College*; Robert C. Smith, *Library of Congress*; Wolfgang Stechow, *Oberlin College*; Oliver M. Stone, *Case School of Applied Science*; Carter B. Storr, Ottawa, Canada; George L. Stout, *Fogg Museum of Art,* Harvard University; William A. Strong, Cleveland; Carl Thurston, Pasadena, Calif.; Ramsay Traquair, Guysborough, Nova Scotia; John R. Tuttle, *Elmira College*; George C. Vaillant, *University of Pennsylvania Museum*; Harry M. Warfel, *University of Maryland*; Polaire Weissman, *Museum of Costume Art,* New York; R. D. Welch, *Princeton University*; Ralph L. Wickiser, *Louisiana State University*; Charmion Wiegand, New York; Thomas Wilfred, West Nyack, New York; Ralph B. Winn, *College of the City of New York*; Leon L. Winslow, Public Schools, Baltimore; S. Macdonald Wright, *University of So. California*; Robert W. Young; Sidney Zinc, New York; Paul Zucker, *Cooper Union Art School,* and Trustee, *American Society for Aesthetics.* The author is also desirous of acknowledging his great indebtedness to Dr. Joseph T. Shipley, editor of DICTIONARY OF WORLD LITERATURE (quoted extensively), and to his collaborators therein, especially: Kenneth Morgan Abbott, *Ohio State University;* Richard Armour, *Wells College;* Paul F. Baum, *Duke University*; Monroe C. Beardsley, *Yale University*; Theodore Bedrick, *University of Illinois,* Isadora Bennett (Reed); Adolph B. Benson, *Yale University*; C. D. Brenner, *University of California* (Berkeley); Wayne Burns, *Miami University;* Gilbert Chinard, *Princeton University*; Barrett H. Clark; Lloyd W. Daly, *University of Oklahoma;* Nathan Dane II, *Oberlin College*; Otto Alvin Dieter, *University of Illinois*; John Olin Eidson, *University of Georgia*; Frances H. Ellis, *Indiana University*; M. B. Emeneau, *University of California* (Berkeley); M. Blakemore Evans, *Ohio State University*; M. Bryllion Fagin, *Johns Hopkins University*; Leslie Fiedler, *Montana State University*; Chauncey E. Finch, *St. Louis University*; Allen H. Gilbert, *Duke University*; G. Giovannini, *Catholic University of America*; Robert A. Hall, Jr., *Brown University;* Marion Harman, *University of Illinois*; Howard Graham Harvey, *University of Rochester*; Helmut A. Hatzfeld, *Catholic University of America*; George R. Havens, *Ohio State University*; S. I. Hayakawa, *Illinois Institute of Technology;* H. G. Henderson, *Columbia University*; Ernest Herman Hespelt, *New York University;* John Hicks, *Miama University*; Urban Tigner Holmes, Jr., *University of North Carolina*; Charles C. Hower, *North Central College*; Charles W. Jones, *Cornell University*; Frank W. Jones, *Yale University*; William Robert Jones, *Ohio State University*; L. Clark Keating, *George Washington University*; Robert E. Kingery, *New York Public Library*; Manuel Komroff, Author; Samuel Noah Kramer, *University of Pennsylvania*; James Craig La Drière, *Catholic University of America,* and Trustee, *American Society for Aesthetics*; La Meri (Russell Meriwether Hughes-Carreras); Richard Lattimore, *Bryn Mawr College*; L. R. Lind, *University of Kansas*; Angeline Helen Lograsso, *Bryn Mawr College*; Clarence A. Manning, *Columbia University*; Berthe M. Marti, *Bryn Mawr College*; Oleg Maslenikov, *University of California* (Berkeley); William H. McCae, S. J., *Rockhurst College*; Paul McPharlin, First Honorary President, *Puppeteers of America*; Hubert J. Meessen, *University of Minnesota*; Henry C. Montgomery, *Miami University*; Nancy Moore, *Butler University*; Roberta Morgan; Bruce A. Morrissette, *Washington University*; William J. Mulloy, *University of California* (Los Angeles); Norman E. Nelson, *University of Michigan*; Allardyce Nicoll, *Yale University*; William Abbott Oldfather, *University of Illinois*; Henry Ten Eyck Perry, *University of Buffalo*; Daniel A. Reed; Helmut Rehder, *University of Wisconsin*; Walter A. Reichart, *University of Michigan*; Edouard Roditi; Harris Livingston Russell, *University of Il-*

linois; J. L. Salvan, *Wayne University*; Mehmed A. Simsar; Horatio Smith, *Columbia University*; Grundy Steiner, *University of Saskatchewan*; S. Byron Straw, *University of California* (Los Angeles); Frank Sullivan, *St. Louis University;* E. Bradlee Watson, *Dartmouth College*; Robert H. West, *University of Georgia*; Robert C. Whitford, *Long Island University*. Particular thanks are extended to Dr. Dagobert D. Runes, Dr. Joseph T. Shipley and Dr. Kurt F. Leidecker, without whose assistance this project would not have been possible.

The author is fully aware that in the preparation of a volume of this type, extending over many years of research and study, and duly considering his own shortcomings, some important concepts or terms may have escaped his attention. This was a major consideration in his reluctance to present the manuscript for final publication. However, the old adage by Samuel Johnson prevailed: *Dictionaries are like watches; the worst is better than none, and the best cannot be expected to go quite true.* The author earnestly trusts that the serious reader will not hesitate to communicate to him suggestions on improvement as well as enlargement for later editions.

The author makes no claim to originality in either the structure or the scope of his definitions; rather, he concentrated on general acceptability and simplicity of existing or available terminology. In no instance did he intend to present a novel interpretation; instead, he confined himself to the inclusion of a usable one. The acknowledgments listed above can only in small part indicate the measure of indebtedness of the author to the many men and women whose works were most graciously offered to him for consultation and use.